The Vehement Jesus

Studies in Peace and Scripture: Institute of Mennonite Studies

Vol. 1
The Gospel of Peace: A Scriptural Message for Today's World
by Ulrich Mauser; published by Westminster John Knox (1992)
ISBN-13 978–0664253493 paperback

Vol. 2
The Meaning of Peace: Biblical Studies
edited by Perry B. Yoder and Willard M. Swartley; 1st ed. published by Westminster John Knox (1992) ISBN-13 978–0664253127 paperback
2nd ed. with expanded bibliography published by IMS (2001)
ISBN-13 978–0936273303 paperback

Vol. 3
The Love of Enemy and Nonretaliation in the New Testament
edited by Willard M. Swartley; published by Westminster John Knox (1992)
ISBN-13 978–0664253547 paperback

Vol. 4
Violence Renounced: René Girard, Biblical Studies and Peacemaking
edited by Willard M. Swartley; published by Pandora Press U. S. and Herald Press (2000)
ISBN-13 978–0966502152 paperback

Vol. 5
Beyond Retribution: A New Testament Vision for Justice, Crime and Punishment
by Christopher D. Marshall; published by Eerdmans (2001)
ISBN-13 978–0802847973 paperback

Vol. 6
Crowned with Glory and Honor: Human Rights in the Biblical Tradition
by Christopher D. Marshall; published by Pandora Press U.S., Herald Press, and Lime Grove House, Auckland, NZ (2002)
ISBN-13 978–1931038041 paperback

Vol. 7
Beautiful upon the Mountains: Biblical Essays on Mission, Peace, and the Reign of God
edited by Mary H. Schertz and Ivan Friesen; published by IMS and Herald Press (2003)
ISBN-13 978–0936273358 paperback
Reprint by Wipf & Stock (2008)
ISBN-13 978–1556356544 paperback

Vol. 8
The Sound of Sheer Silence and the Killing State: The Death Penalty and the Bible
by Millard Lind; published by Cascadia Publishing House and Herald Press (2004)
ISBN-13 978–1931038232 paperback

Vol. 9
Covenant of Peace: The Missing Peace in New Testament Theology and Ethics
by Willard M. Swartley; published by Eerdmans (2006)
ISBN-13 978–0802829375 paperback

Vol. 10
Atonement, Justice, and Peace: The Message of the Cross and the Mission of the Church
by Darrin W. Snyder Belousek; published by Eerdmans (2011)
ISBN-13 978–0802866424 paperback

Vol. 11
A Peaceable Hope: Contesting Violent Eschatology in New Testament Narratives
by David J. Neville; published by Baker Academic (2013)
ISBN-13 978–0801048517 paperback;
ISBN 9781441240156 e-book

Vol. 12
Struggles for Shalom: Peace and Violence across the Testaments
edited by Laura L. Brenneman and Brad D. Schantz; published by Pickwick Publications (2014)
ISBN-13 978-1-62032-622-0

Vol. 13
Rooted and Grounded: Essays on Land and Christian Discipleship
edited by Ryan D. Harker and Janeen Bertsche Johnson; published by Pickwick Publications (2016)
ISBN-13 978-1-4982-3554-9

Vol. 14
The Irony of Power: The Politics of God within Matthew's Narrative
by Dorothy Jean Weaver; published by Pickwick Publications (2017)
ISBN-13 978-1-62564-886-0

The Vehement Jesus

Grappling with Troubling Gospel Texts

David J. Neville

CASCADE *Books* • Eugene, Oregon

THE VEHEMENT JESUS
Grappling with Troubling Gospel Texts

Copyright © 2017 David J. Neville. All rights reserved. Except for brief quotations in critical publications or reviews, no part of this book may be reproduced in any manner without prior written permission from the publisher. Write: Permissions, Wipf and Stock Publishers, 199 W. 8th Ave., Suite 3, Eugene, OR 97401.

Cascade Books
An Imprint of Wipf and Stock Publishers
199 W. 8th Ave., Suite 3
Eugene, OR 97401

www.wipfandstock.com

PAPERBACK ISBN: 978-1-62032-480-6
HARDCOVER ISBN: 978-1-4982-8750-0
EBOOK ISBN: 978-1-5326-4272-2

Cataloguing-in-Publication data:

Name: Neville, David J.

Title: The vehement Jesus : grappling with troubling Gospel texts / David J. Neville.

Description: Eugene, OR: Cascade Books, 2017 | Includes bibliographical references and index.

Identifiers: ISBN 978-1-62032-480-6 (paperback) | ISBN 978-1-4982-8750-0 (hardcover) | ISBN 978-1-5326-4272-2 (ebook)

Subjects: LCSH: Bible, New Testament—Criticism, Narrative. | Violence in the Bible. | Violence—Biblical Teaching. | Title.

Classification: BS2361.3.N466 2017 (print) | BS2361 (ebook)

Manufactured in the U.S.A.   NOVEMBER 6, 2017

For
Thorwald Lorenzen
and
Philip Matthews,
friends characterized by moral excellence and practical wisdom

Turn from evil and do good; seek peace and pursue it.
(Psalm 34:14)

Be disciples of Aaron, loving peace and pursuing peace.
Rabbi Hillel *(m. Avot* 1:12)

Peacemakers are blessed because they will be called God's children.
Jesus of Nazareth (Matthew 5:9)

Contents

Studies in Peace and Scripture Series Preface xi

Preface and Acknowledgments xv

Introduction 1

1. Crossing Swords, I: Not Peace but rather a Sword? 17
   (Matthew 10:34-36)
2. Perturbing Parables: An Unforgiving Slave and a Throne Claimant 39
3. The Judgment of Jerusalem 57
   (Luke 13:31-35; 19:41-44; 21:20-24; 23:26-31)
4. Crossing Swords, II: A Time for Swords? 93
   (Luke 22:35-38)
5. Turbulence in the Temple 113
   (Matt 21:12-17; Mark 11:11-25; Luke 19:45-46; John 2:13-22)
6. The Parable of the Vineyard Tenants 135
   (Matt 21:33-43; Mark 12:1-12; Luke 20:9-18)
7. Provocation at Passover 153
   (John 2:13-22)
8. The Rhetoric of Rage 183
   (Matthew 23)
9. Teleological Terror 219

Concluding Remarks 255

Bibliography 259

Author Index 277

Index of Ancient Sources 281

Studies in Peace and Scripture
Series Preface

Visions of peace abound in the Bible, whose pages are also filled with the language of violence. In this respect, the Bible is thoroughly at home in the modern world, whether as a literary classic or as a unique sacred text. This is, perhaps, a part of the Bible's realism: bridging the distance between its world and our own is a history filled with visions of peace accompanying the reality of violence and war. That alone would justify study of peace and war in the Bible. However, for those communities in which the Bible is sacred Scripture, the matter is more urgent. For them, it is crucial to understand what the Bible says about peace—and about war. These issues have often divided Christians, and the way Christians have understood them has had terrible consequences for Jews and, indeed, for the world. A series of scholarly investigations cannot hope to resolve these issues, but it can hope, as this one does, to aid our understanding of them.

Over the past century a substantial body of literature has grown up around the topic of the Bible and war. Numerous studies have been devoted to historical questions about ancient Israel's conception and conduct of war and about the position of the early church on participation in the Roman Empire and its military. It is not surprising that many of these studies have been motivated by theological and ethical concerns, which may themselves be attributed to the Bible's own seemingly disjunctive preoccupation with peace and, at the same time, with war. If not within the Bible itself, then at least from Aqiba and Tertullian, the question has been raised whether—and if so, then on what basis—those who worship God may legitimately participate in war. With the Reformation, the churches divided on this question. The division was unequal, with the majority of Christendom agreeing that, however regrettable war may be, Christians have biblical warrant for participating in it. A minority countered that, however necessary war may appear, Christians have a biblical mandate to avoid it. Modern historical studies have served to bolster one side of this division or the other.

Meanwhile, it has become clear that a narrow focus on participation in war is not the only way, and likely not the best way, to approach the Bible on the topic of peace. War and peace are not simply two sides of the same coin; each is broader than its contrast with the other. Since the twentieth century and refinement of weapons and modes of mass destruction, the violence of war has been an increasingly urgent concern. Peace, on the other hand, is not just the absence of war, but the well-being of all people. In spite of this agreement, the number of studies devoted to the Bible and peace is still quite small, especially in English. Consequently, answers to the most basic questions remain to be settled. Among these questions is that of what the Bible means in speaking of *shalom* or *eirēnē*, the Hebrew and the Greek terms usually translated into English as "peace." By the same token, what the Bible has to say about peace is not limited to its use of these two terms. Questions remain about the relation of peace to considerations of justice, integrity, and—in the broadest sense—salvation. And of course there still remains the question of the relation between peace and war. In fact, what the Bible says about peace is often framed in the language of war. The Bible very often uses martial imagery to portray God's own action, whether it be in creation, in judgment against or in defense of Israel, or in the cross and resurrection of Jesus Christ—actions aimed at achieving peace.

This close association of peace and war presents serious problems for the contemporary appropriation of the Bible. Are human freedom, justice, and liberation—and the liberation of creation—furthered or hindered by the martial, frequently royal, and pervasively masculine terms in which the Bible speaks of peace? These questions cannot be answered by the rigorous and critical exegesis of the biblical texts alone; they demand serious moral and theological reflection of the kind done in this volume.

This book both carries on and works behind the scenes of its companion volume, Neville's *A Peaceable Hope* (2013)—also in this series—to develop a hermeneutic of *shalom* and to show the inherently peaceful mission and message of Jesus. Neville looks squarely at the vehement portrayals of Jesus most troublesome to his premise in *A Peaceable Hope* that Jesus' message was peaceful, from the "not peace, but a sword" passages to the parable of the Throne Claimant to the scenes of clearing the Temple. *The Vehement Jesus* is an important read for those of us who take seriously Jesus' ministry and Gospel study. We hope with the author that wrestling with these texts will make you more, not less, attached to them.

Studies in Peace and Scripture is sponsored by the Institute of Mennonite Studies, the research agency of the Anabaptist Mennonite Biblical

Seminary. The seminary and the tradition it represents have a particular interest in peace and, even more so, an abiding interest in the Bible. We hope that this ecumenical series will contribute to a deeper understanding of both.

Laura L. Brenneman, New Testament Editor
Ben C. Ollenburger, Old Testament Editor

Preface and Acknowledgments

THIS IS NOT THE book I mapped out as a planned sequel to *A Peaceable Hope*, but it has been no less challenging than that postponed (and now perchance precluded) project. Long have I considered conducting a study of select passages in the Gospels that challenge the notion that the mission and message of Jesus were inherently peaceful. When the editorial director of Cascade Books responded positively to my proposal to write a book on how one might interpret these perplexing passages in peace perspective, I welcomed the opportunity to test what was largely taken for granted in my earlier book, *A Peaceable Hope*. First at Baker Publishing and then again at Wipf and Stock, Rodney Clapp has taken a risk on two manuscript proposals from me—both with a focus on peace at a time when, in publishing terms, peace does not pay (even though, as Thomas Aquinas discerned, peace is the end to which all the virtues are means). I am therefore doubly grateful to Rodney Clapp for his broad vision and gracious support.

Work on this book began during a period of study leave in the second half of 2012, which was supported by a grant from Charles Sturt University's Centre for Public and Contextual Theology. I am grateful to Professor Tom Frame, then director of St Mark's National Theological Centre, and also to the Council of St Mark's for releasing me from teaching and administrative responsibilities during that time.

For assistance in tracking down seemingly inaccessible reference materials, I here express my appreciation to staff members of St Mark's Anglican National Memorial Library: the library manager, Susan Phillips, and also Sylvia Young and Thyme Hansson, each of whom has responded to requests for help as if they were no trouble at all.

I never expected this to be an easy book to write, but for various reasons it has been even more difficult to complete than I had anticipated. Making time to read, reflect, and write alongside other pressing (and pressuring) responsibilities has been a constant challenge, but the interpretive complexity associated with texts explored in this study has proved even more formidable. For this reason, I here acknowledge the invaluable contribution to scholarship of every interpreter cited herein—as well as many others. As readers will detect, my writing reflects my indebtedness to conversation partners from whom I have learned and in dialogue with whom I have figured out what I (currently) think. Such is life, in my view.

While working on this book, I have been encouraged by several people who have either expressed interest in its progress or responded graciously to draft sections. When it was little more than a list of possible chapter titles, Laura Brenneman expressed interest in including the completed monograph in the Studies in Peace and Scripture series, and at the penultimate draft stage she reaffirmed her willingness to include the book in the sterling series she co-edits. John Kloppenborg, Tom Yoder Neufeld, and T. J. Lang made time to read chapters in which I engage with their interpretive labors, and each responded in a spirit of generous collegiality. Darrin Snyder Belousek's probing questions of my earlier discussion of Jerusalem's judgment in Luke's Gospel encouraged me to persist in my (perhaps misguided) quest to make sense of a theological and moral discrepancy at the heart of Luke's Gospel, and at an inopportune time Keith Dyer made time to look over a complete draft of the book. For what I have learned from these and other students of the Gospels, I count myself blessed.

From mid-September to mid-October in 2016, Richard Middleton was visiting Professor to the School of Theology at Charles Sturt University, spending two weeks at St Barnabas College in Adelaide and two weeks at St Mark's in Canberra. During his time in Canberra, we were neighbors, which made possible several conversations about shared interests, including biblical eschatology. I here acknowledge my appreciation to Richard Middleton for that fruitful fortnight, during which he expressed interest in and encouragement for my interpretive labors.

Among my teaching and research colleagues in Charles Sturt University's School of Theology and Centre for Public and Contextual Theology, I am grateful to the following people for encouraging conversations, occasional queries about progress on the "cranky Jesus" project, or simple (but indispensable) collegial camaraderie: John Painter, Matthew Anstey, Russell Warnken, Jeanette Mathews, Jeff Aernie, Jione Havea, Anthony Rees, Tim Harris, Chris Armitage, Heather Thomson, Jane Foulcher, Andrew Cameron, Peter Pocock, Michael Gladwin, Bernard Doherty, Ian Coutts, Geoff Broughton, Ockert Meyer, Stephen Pickard, Scott Cowdell, Wayne Hudson, Gerard Moore, Ben Myers, William Emilsen, Clive Pearson, Bruce Stevens, Cathy Thomson, and Rhonda White.

My life continues to be enriched by the love and daily companionship of my wife, Sonia, with whom I have discussed many of the interpretive challenges addressed in this book—and much else besides. I am also privileged to know Thorwald Lorenzen and Philip Matthews, candid critics but also faithful friends to whom I dedicate this book.

Three chapters of this book incorporate material from earlier publications, albeit revised, reconfigured, and/or recontextualized in each case. In chapter 2, my discussion of the parable of the Throne Claimant draws from a section of my essay, "Parable as Paradigm for Public Theology: Relating Theological Vision to Social Life," in *The Bible, Justice and Public Theology*, edited by David J. Neville, 153–57 (Sheffield: Sheffield Phoenix Press, 2014). Used with permission.

Chapters 3 and 9 recast several subsections and paragraphs from David J. Neville, *A Peaceable Hope: Contesting Violent Eschatology in New Testament Narratives*. Baker Academic, a division of Baker Publishing Group, 2013. Used by permission. Portions of chapter 3 have also been previously published in David J. Neville, "Calamity and the Biblical God—Borderline or Line of Belonging? Intratextual Tension in Luke 13," in *Bible, Borders, Belonging(s): Engaging Readings from Oceania*, edited by Jione Havea, David J. Neville, and Elaine M. Wainwright, 39–55 (Semeia Studies 75; Atlanta: SBL Press, 2014). Used and modified here with permission. The final section of chapter 9 also draws from my article, "Toward a Hermeneutic of Shalom: Reading Texts of Teleological Terror in Peace Perspective," which appeared in *Word & World* 34.4 (Fall 2014) 339–48, for which *Word & World* retains the copyright. The material is used here with permission.

Unless otherwise indicated, translations of New Testament texts are my own.

David J. Neville
St Mark's National Theological Centre
Canberra, November 2016

Introduction

FEW PERCEPTIVE PEOPLE ARE likely to dispute that violence constitutes a pressing moral concern. From the domestic to the global sphere, violence in various guises invades virtually every aspect of life: domestic violence and sexual abuse; random killings; turf wars; armed tribal and civil conflicts; ideologically motivated terrorism; warfare. Confoundedly, violence rooted in religion seems impossible to eradicate. For people of faith, therefore, violence is a crucial moral issue, but it also has profound theological and interpretive dimensions.[1] As increasing numbers of scholars seem to recognize, scriptural texts that sanction violence, especially with reference to divine prerogative, raise critical theological, moral, and interpretive concerns.[2]

In this book I invite readers to look over my shoulder as I investigate and interpret some Gospel texts that challenge the conviction that Jesus was a peaceful person. Our principal sources for understanding Jesus, the four biblical Gospels, convey the general impression that both his mission and his message were intentionally and indeed profoundly peaceful. In his transmitted teaching, Jesus advocated nonretaliation as a corollary of the moral commitment to love God, neighbors, and even adversaries,[3] and he

---

1. I write from a Christian perspective, so in this book I focus on the biblical Gospels, but theological and interpretive challenges relating to violence must also be faced in other religious traditions. For a fair-minded historical treatment of the interpretive imperative with respect to violent scriptures within the Abrahamic tradition, see Jenkins, *Laying Down the Sword*, passim.

2. See de Villiers, "Hermeneutical Perspectives on Violence," 252: "There are increasing signs that the study of violence is moving towards the centre of attention in biblical studies, theology and religion." I am not (yet) a Girardian, but among Girard's insights for which I am grateful is his discernment that the Bible, especially in the Gospels, features the unmasking and subversion of violence as a central existential and moral concern, not a peripheral dimension of the human condition. See, e.g., Girard, *I See Satan*, esp. 103–153.

3. I appreciate that this is an interpretive inference, reflecting a concern for moral

modeled a manner of life that makes for peace. Even when his own life was under threat, he embraced the nonretaliatory stance that he had earlier endorsed and repudiated violence enacted on his behalf.

Within these same Gospels, however, one also encounters texts that seem to undermine the profoundly peaceable posture of Jesus. For example, Matthew's Gospel records a saying of Jesus in which he apparently expresses the purpose of his mission as the very antithesis of peace: "Do not suppose that I have come to sow peace upon the earth; I have not come to sow peace but rather a sword" (10:34). Within this same Gospel one also encounters the most sustained vitriol on the part of Jesus against scribes and Pharisees (23:13–36), and Matthew persistently presents Jesus as a teacher of intimidating parables, several of which envisage God or God's agent(s) meting out divine vengeance on the unrighteous by and by. In certain respects, Luke's narrative portrait of Jesus matches Matthew's, albeit muted with respect to the vehement content and character of Jesus' teaching. Even so, in an enigmatic episode within Luke's passion narrative, Jesus is recalled as encouraging those of his disciples without swords to purchase one (22:35–38). In addition, more clearly than any of his canonical counterparts, Luke interprets the destruction of Jerusalem as divine judgment for failing to embrace Jesus as Israel's Messiah. Beyond such passages in Matthew and Luke, moreover, all four biblical Gospels tell the story of Jesus' disruptive conduct in the temple, which is often assumed to have involved a certain level of violence. Taken together, these texts portray Jesus as occasionally vehement or, as some argue, capable of and indeed prone to violence.

Within the literature on Jesus and the Gospels, there is a trajectory of scholarship that finds in favor of a revolutionary or violent Jesus. For some, Jesus himself was closer to a first-century Israelite zealot than a peaceful ambassador of God's heavenly reign, a historical reality largely (but not completely) concealed by the Gospel writers.[4] For others, Gospel texts in tension with a peaceful portrait of Jesus simply attest to the full—and hence flawed—humanity of Jesus.[5] By contrast with this scholarly trajectory, I

---

coherence that is difficult to attribute directly to Jesus, as articulated by Meier, *Marginal Jew*, 4:655: "In sum, the historical Jesus never directly connects his individual halakic pronouncements to some basic or organizing principle of love." Even so, the pattern of Jesus' appeal to biblical resources for his two distinctive love commands (Deut 6:4–5; 11:1; Lev 19:18, 33–34) evinces both theological-moral discernment and interpretive creativity on his part. See Neville, "Love of Enemies," forthcoming.

4. See, e.g., Brandon, *Jesus and the Zealots*; Bammel, "Revolution Theory," 11–68; Aslan, *Zealot*. For recent studies that also lean in this direction, see Bermejo-Rubio, "(Why) Was Jesus the Galilean Crucified Alone?," 127–54; Bermejo-Rubio, "Jesus and the Anti-Roman Resistance," 1–105; Martin, "Jesus in Jerusalem," 3–24.

5. See Pattison, "Shadow Side of Jesus," 54–67; Avalos, *Bad Jesus*, passim. See also

adopt what might be described as a more dialectical stance. The basic argument of this book is that various Gospel portrayals of the vehement Jesus are compatible with—perhaps even indispensable to—the composite canonical configuration of Jesus as a person of peace. For those whose understanding of peace entails principled passivity or rigid nonresistance, such a stance may seem nonsensical. But if one accepts that genuine peace is grounded in justice, particularly distributive and restorative justice, a corollary of such a standpoint is that passionate commitment to justice may well express itself in ways that are either confrontational or disruptive so as to challenge powerful and entrenched interests—albeit without violence. As both herald and harbinger of God's fair reign, Jesus' mission and message of peace (Acts 10:36) was inherently challenging to the status quo, so it is unsurprising that certain textual attestations reflect a vehement Jesus.

Although the clarification of terms can be rather tedious, a working definition of *violence* is probably necessary for a book in which the peaceable but occasionally vehement Jesus is defended against accusations of violence. *Violence* is an inherently loaded term, reflecting particular vantage points and vested interests; there is no neutral or context-free definition to which everyone might grant his or her assent.[6] One's conception of violence is also influenced by how one relates violence to other key concepts such as peace and power. If peace is perceived as but the absence of overt violence, for example, such a perception implicitly validates violence by making it determinative for comprehending peace, and one's conception of violence is likely to be restricted to obvious physical violence, without regard to forms of violence such as psychological violation or structural violence perpetuated by entrenched social inequalities. If no moral differentiation is made between violence and power, moreover, that likely leads to confusing peace with passivity.

A further qualification is that purpose or intention has a bearing on whether something done is deemed to be violent.[7] A surgeon's scalpel can cause as much injury as an attacker's knife; used in accordance with its intended purpose, however, a scalpel is not considered an instrument of violence. Rather, the injury it inflicts is for the well-being of the person temporarily harmed and is contextualized within a program of treatment and care to facilitate recovery to health and wholeness.

Berger, "Der 'brutale' Jesus," 119–27; Aichele, "Jesus' Violence," 72–91.

6. See Hauerwas and Berkman, "Violence." See also Kloppenborg, "Representation of Violence," 323, for whom "violence is always socially constructed."

7. Intention is crucial for the moral principle of double effect, but that is not my present point.

Important for my own understanding of violence are three notions brought into focus by Robert McAfee Brown in *Religion and Violence*: first, the "violation of personhood," which today we might be inclined to expand yet further to include violations against the integrity and biodiversity of our non-human world; second, structural or systemic violence; and third, the root cause of structural violence and violations of various other kinds—injustice.[8] Violence includes but is not limited to overt aggression that is lethal or causes lasting physical damage; it also extends to non-physical means of violating another's sense of integrity or well-being.[9] Moreover, unjust social arrangements that perpetuate poverty and social disadvantage are also inherently violent. Only by expanding one's understanding of violence to include concepts such as these is it possible to do justice to the various ways in which people around our world experience violence and testify to its life-diminishing effects. Arguably, only such an expanded conception of violence also does justice to a coherent theological vision in light of determinative biblical traditions. For, as Laura Brenneman affirms, "in theological terms, structural violence is everything that works against God's intended shalom for the world."[10]

As I discern the light of Jesus' moral vision refracted through the canonical Gospels, peace rather than violence is what emerges as the primary relational reality, both between God and people and also between people and peoples. Violence is a by-product of ruptured relations and hence a secondary or quasi reality, analogous to host-harming parasites or cancer cells. As a result, peace must be vigilantly and persistently pursued (Psalm 34:14) by means that match and thereby further the goal of *shalom*. As John Macquarrie avers, "Peace cannot be the rest that leaves things just as they are

---

8. Brown, *Religion and Violence*, 1–13. Especially important for Brown is the social analysis of the "spiral of violence" provided by Camara, *Spiral of Violence*, 25–40. Camara's three-stage analysis of the way in which systemic injustice breeds further violence is adapted by Horsley, *Jesus and the Spiral of Violence*, 20–28. For a response to Horsley that seeks to bring greater clarity to first-century sociocultural dynamics of conflict and violence, see Malina, *Social Gospel of Jesus*, 37–69. See also Yoder Neufeld, *Killing Enmity*, 2, who credits Johan Galtung with coining the expressions, "structural" and "cultural violence."

9. In this respect, I follow in the footsteps of Reid, "Violent Endings," 238; Carter, "Constructions of Violence," 85–92; de Villiers, "Hermeneutical Perspectives on Violence," 254–61; and van Henten, "Religion, Bible and Violence," 5–8. Van Henten also provides a valuable overview of various theoretical approaches to the relation between religion and violence.

10. Brenneman, "Peace and Violence," 3. (To expand one's working definition of violence in ways suggested by Brown and others may match global realities more closely, but it also makes more difficult the task of defending Jesus—or Gospel depictions of Jesus—against the charge of violence. See Yoder Neufeld, *Killing Enmity*, 4.)

but must remove everything that stands in the way of that full flourishing of human life that constitutes *shalom*. Peace . . . must eliminate injustice, but it will seek to do so by non-violent means."[11] Peace is thus a primary, substantive social good rather than a secondary or subsidiary social *desideratum*; genuine peace is a positive presence rather than the absence of whatever might be regarded as its opposite.[12]

Although the semantic range of dictionary definitions of *vehemence* includes *violence*, I use *vehemence* and its adjectival form to mean passionate intensity that may find expression in forceful actions or confrontational utterances but stops short of causing injury, death, or lasting damage. By analogy with the moral distinction between force and violence,[13] I perceive a similar distinction between vehemence and violence. In extremis, both force and vehemence are violent; but toward the other end of the continuum— and circumscribed by moral constraints—both force and vehemence may serve positive social ends without resulting in injury, death, or lasting damage. At what point either force or vehemence becomes violent in particular situations may be difficult to discern, requiring close attention to contextual factors and careful adjudication of conflicting perspectives and interests. In social environments characterized by complex interpersonal dynamics, however, moral judgment must take account of such complexities.

Within the competitive sociocultural context of the first-century Mediterranean world, Jesus was apparently capable not only of rising to the challenge of defending his dignity but also of castigating contemporaries with withering effect. Such rhetorical ferocity may well have been injurious to the social standing of those reproached, but it was neither lethal nor physically harmful. We have learned that abusive language can be psychologically damaging, however, and is all too often the precursor to physical violence. Although we are unable to unlearn what we now know about the close relation between verbal vehemence and various forms of violence, we need to exercise care about judging people from the past on the basis of anachronistic moral standards. Even so, it is nevertheless important to identify (as well as to lament) the long-standing legacy of violence both bequeathed and perpetuated by wounding words attributed to Jesus.

---

11. Macquarrie, "Peace," 637. See also Macquarrie, *Concept of Peace*, passim.

12. For clarifying reflections on peace as a positive presence or fullness rather than a negative absence, see Brenneman, "Peace and Violence," 1–4. Also helpful for comprehending peace in the biblical tradition is Swartley, "Peace and Violence," 141–54, distilling key points of his magnum opus, *Covenant of Peace*. In their respective discussions, both Brenneman and Swartley also offer important hermeneutical guidelines.

13. See, e.g., Carlson, "Religion and Violence," 14–18.

6   The Vehement Jesus

One way of dealing with Gospel depictions of the vehement Jesus is to distance such "recollections" from Jesus of Nazareth, the historical figure whose interrupted but unvanquishable life inspired the various—and varied—Gospel portraits of his mission and message. Perhaps the most common means of distancing disconcerting depictions of Jesus from the historical figure of Jesus himself is to forget, overlook, or repress such features within the Gospels.[14] Within the discipline of biblical studies, however, this task of distancing is generally conducted under the guise of the scholarly quest for the historical Jesus. At least since the landmark work of Albert Schweitzer, who traced from Reimarus to (and indeed beyond) Wrede the quest to reclaim the Jesus of history by means of a critical approach to the Gospels,[15] scholars have been alert to the likelihood of finding a Jesus amenable to their own tastes—a palatable Jesus—no matter how carefully formulated their criteria might be or how rigorously they might be applied. Even so, one still encounters scholarly appeal to the historical Jesus to arbitrate on this or that troubling text in the Gospel tradition. For example, in *How to Read the Bible and Still Be a Christian*, John Dominic Crossan argues winsomely that the historical Jesus is the ultimate norm or normative criterion for the biblical depiction of Jesus the Christ and hence for the Christian conception of God.[16] Crossan is among the most erudite scholars of the historical Jesus. Furthermore, his reconstruction of Jesus as a historical figure is appealing no less than challenging. But in the process of arguing that the historical Jesus is the discriminating norm for dealing with divine violence in the Bible, he overreaches on what may be inferred about Jesus of Nazareth as a historical figure.

Crossan contends that the problematic twofold portrayal of God and his Messiah as *both* nonviolent *and* violent is resolved intrabiblically. In other words, within the composite Christian Bible is to be found the solution to the problem of divine violence in that same Bible. At two points in his argument, however, one senses slippage. "Since," according to Crossan, "the Christian Bible proclaims that Jesus of Nazareth is the Messianic Son of God, he cannot be but one more beat in that rhythm of

---

14. On both the necessity and risk of "selective amnesia" with respect to troubling biblical texts, see Jenkins, *Laying Down the Sword*, 13–20.

15. Schweitzer, *Quest of the Historical Jesus*, published in 1906 and again, significantly revised, in 1913.

16. Crossan, *How to Read the Bible*, 34–36, 171, 185, 235–46. (For a similar—and similarly appealing—argument that the nonviolence of the historical Jesus is demonstrable enough to serve as a criterion for adjudicating against conflicting Gospel traditions, see Joseph, *Nonviolent Messiah, passim*.)

assertion-and-subversion."[17] If the biblical depiction of God is ambivalent with respect to violence, however, it is an inherent possibility, even probability, that the "Messianic Son of God" would be portrayed in both peaceful and violent terms. If this is the first step in an argument, it fails to convince, but perhaps at this point Crossan is simply priming his reader for an inference to follow.

Crossan's interpretive guideline, which he claims to have found within the Bible, is as follows: "The norm and criterion of the Christian Bible is the biblical Christ but the norm and criterion of the biblical Christ is the historical Jesus."[18] Not every Christian accepts the biblical Christ as the Bible's normative center, but the key question concerns the role of the historical Jesus as the "norm and criterion" for the biblical Christ (or biblical portraits of Jesus). For Crossan, it is not only the advent of the historical figure of Jesus that is determinative for Christians; beyond that historical datum is the precise nature of Jesus' response to the fundamental feature of his sociocultural matrix—Roman imperial rule and its attendant imperial theology. "Whether the historical Jesus was or was not Christ, the Messianic Son of God is not the present debate—that is a matter of faith," according to Crossan. "Instead, the debate is whether the historical Jesus, whether accepted or rejected as Christ and Messianic Son of God, was or was not invoking nonviolent or violent resistance against Rome—that is a matter of history."[19]

What becomes evident from reflecting on Crossan's line of argumentation is that not only the historical figure of Jesus per se but also a particular *historical judgment* about Jesus of Nazareth make him the normative criterion for evaluating biblical portraits of Jesus. To comprehend Crossan's reasoning, one must appreciate that he interprets the historical figure of Jesus within the matrix of Roman imperial rule and that he construes the mission of Jesus as nonviolent resistance to Roman rule. One datum in particular is crucial for Crossan's construction of Jesus' mission as nonviolent resistance to Roman rule: Jesus himself was crucified, but his followers were not also rounded up by the Romans and similarly executed.[20] On the basis of this

17. Crossan, *How to Read the Bible*, 240. The "rhythm of assertion-and-subversion" alludes to a repeated pattern discerned by Crossan within the biblical tradition in which "God's radical divine vision of justice and liberation is regularly muted or turned back into the normalcy of civilization's injustice and oppression" (238).

18. Ibid., 240.

19. Ibid., 240–41.

20. Ibid., 161, 167–68. See also Crossan, "Divine Violence in the Christian Bible," 232, where he gives credit for this insight to Fredriksen, *Jesus of Nazareth*, 9, 11, 240–41, 243, 253, 255, 257. Cf. Crossan, *Power of Parable*, 127–31, where this consideration is but one of four in support of viewing Jesus' mission and message as nonviolent resistance to Roman hegemony. For a contrary viewpoint, see Bermejo-Rubio, "(Why) Was

(contested) historical judgment, Crossan avers not only that the historical Jesus is the norm for reading the Bible nonviolently but also that the Bible itself gestures toward this intrinsic interpretive criterion.[21]

As much as I have learned from Crossan and as much as I would like his interpretive criterion to be sound, I am able to affirm only the first half of his thesis. There are good theological reasons to affirm that "the norm and criterion of the Christian Bible is the biblical Christ," but that affirmation is naturally contested by those without a faith commitment to Jesus as the mediator of divine presence and life-saving power. As for the second half of Crossan's hermeneutical dictum, "the norm and criterion of the biblical Christ is the historical Jesus," one is inclined to ask: whose historical Jesus, and on the basis of which presuppositions and historical judgments? The Gospels attest to the historical figure of Jesus, so in that general sense Crossan is correct to say that the biblical Christ—or biblical depictions of Jesus as the Christ—points to the historical Jesus. Beyond that shared but also varied witness to Jesus of Nazareth on the part of the Gospel writers, however, one is unable to reach back to an unmediated Jesus for the purpose of adjudicating between conflicting textual interpretations of Jesus.

At various points throughout this book, I would have liked to appeal more often and more confidently to the historical Jesus with a view to distancing Jesus from this or that troubling Gospel text. Although I accept that not everything attributed to Jesus by the Gospel writers derives directly from the historical personage to whom they attest, and although I am willing to exercise cautious judgment on whether or not certain texts are likely to be "authentic" or "true to Jesus," there are nevertheless reasons why I am unable to follow Crossan by appealing to the historical Jesus as the normative criterion for appraising the biblical Christ—or, more precisely, biblical portrayals of Jesus as (Israel's awaited) Messiah and Son of God. First, over two centuries of scholarly squabble have failed to settle the vexed question of the earliest and/or most trustworthy sources for apprehending Jesus as

---

Jesus the Galilean Crucified Alone?"

21. That this is a matter of interpretive discernment is perhaps conceded at the end of the chapter on the biblical Christ. See Crossan, *How to Read the Bible*, 185: "At this point, I can almost rest the case I lay out in *How to Read the Bible and Still Be a Christian*: accept and follow the *assertion* of the nonviolent historical Jesus as the image and revelation of a nonviolent God; understand and reject the *subversion* that changes him across two stages, first [in the Gospels] into rhetorical and then [in Revelation] into physical violence. In other words, I already have the solution to the challenge of *How to Read the Bible and Still Be a Christian*—for those who have eyes to see—within the Christian Bible itself: if the biblical Christ is the norm, criterion, and discriminant of the Christian Bible, then the historical Jesus is the norm, criterion, and discriminant of the biblical Christ."

a historical figure. The two-document hypothesis, which privileges Mark's Gospel and a putative sayings source, "Q," remains the regnant source theory, but there is a significant body of opinion against "Q," and some scholars consider certain noncanonical sources such as the Gospel of Thomas to be no less important for recovering Jesus than Mark or "Q." For me, things are even more problematic insofar as I consider it probable that the Gospels according to Matthew, Mark, and Luke are indirectly, rather than directly, related by virtue of their common dependence on an earlier, non-extant narrative source—a source-critical inference that places yet one more (hypothetical) source between Jesus and our extant sources for comprehending him.[22]

Furthermore, over two centuries of questing for the historical Jesus have failed to resolve the question of the means by which scholarship is able to search out Jesus and thereby construct a consensus-compelling portrait of him. The widely employed and ever-more refined "criteria of authenticity" have produced interesting and indeed compelling portraits of Jesus, but no single compelling picture. As a result, confidence in such criteria, or at least their capacity as means to achieve their intended end, has waned.[23]

Beyond the contested questions of sources and criteria for determining authenticity, the historical enterprise itself raises significant philosophical concerns. Neither historiography nor the practice of historical investigation is any less hermeneutical than any other discipline of enquiry, quite apart from linguistic factors inherent in historical research that provoke reflection on the intangible relation between language (oral and written) and reality. I am not a social constructivist, but there are undoubtedly constructive no less than reconstructive dimensions to the practices of historical enquiry and history writing.[24]

---

22. See Neville, "Phantom Returns," in critical dialogue with Burkett, *Rethinking the Gospel Sources*, 1–59. On the hypothesis that Matthew, Mark, and Luke are indirectly related as a result of common dependence on a shared narrative source, Mark may still be the earliest of the Synoptic Gospels. Even if that is the case, however, Mark's relative priority is somewhat less demonstrable and also less significant for the study of early Christian origins.

23. See, e.g., the 2012 essay collection edited by Keith and Le Donne, *Jesus, Criteria, and the Demise of Authenticity*. For a cautionary rejoinder, see Hägerland, "Future of Criteria," 43–65.

24. Regarding historiographical matters relating to the study of Jesus and the Gospels, including the roles of memory and reception, see the varied but occasionally overlapping perspectives in: Meyer, *Aims of Jesus*, 13–110; Meyer, *Reality and Illusion*, esp. 87–113; Crossan, *Historical Jesus*, xxvii–xxxiv; Crossan, *Birth of Christianity*, 47–89; Wright, *New Testament*, 29–144; Keck, *Who Is Jesus?*, esp. 1–21; Reiser, "Eschatology," 216–26; Theissen and Winter, *Quest for the Plausible Jesus*, esp. 226–59; Dunn, *Jesus Remembered*, 9–136; Denton Jr., *Historiography and Hermeneutics*; Selby, *Comical*

Even if consensus with respect to historiography, sources, and criteria could be reached, that would not resolve the question of whether a scholarly construct of the historical Jesus should either replace or serve as the means to arbitrate on the canonical Jesus, by which I mean the fourfold depiction(s) of Jesus in the biblical Gospels. This is because there is no recourse to the Jesus of history unmediated by some perspective or other. "The days of questing after the historical Jesus, free from the interpretations and memories of those who considered themselves his followers, are behind us," as Rafael Rodríguez remarks in response to Dale Allison's *Constructing Jesus*. "For better or for worse, the only access to the historical Jesus available to contemporary historians runs right through the perceptions, interpretations and representations of him in our ancient sources."[25] Or, as distilled in Francis Watson's second of "Seven Theses on Jesus and the Canonical Gospel," "Jesus is known only through the mediation of his own reception. There is no access to the singular, uninterpreted reality of a 'historical Jesus' behind the reception process."[26] As a result, this study generally grapples with troubling Gospel texts by interpretive means other than by seeking to reach back behind such texts to *the* historical Jesus.

For Christian interpreters down through the centuries, the canonical Jesus has been normative for morality and ethics; furthermore, for more discerning Christian interpreters down through the centuries, the normative status of the canonical Jesus for morality and ethics has been affirmed, albeit in tandem with an interpretive guideline of some kind. By analogy with the early church's rule of faith and Augustine's interpretive rule of love, I interpret the variously interpreted Jesus of the canonical Gospels in accordance with the interpretive rule of peace—a hermeneutic of *shalom*.[27] Lest it seem viciously circular to interpret Gospel texts that apparently implicate Jesus in violence by means of a hermeneutic of *shalom*, this is but the application and adaptation of an interpretive rule described by Charles

---

Doctrine, esp. 165–219; McKnight, *Jesus and His Death*, 3–46; Allison, *Constructing Jesus*, 1–30; Le Donne, *Historiographical Jesus*, 1–91; Wedderburn, *Jesus and the Historians*, 1–273; Schnelle, *Theology of the New Testament*, 25–59; Watson, "Quest for the Real Jesus"; Watson, *Gospel Writing*, esp. 1–113 and 409–619; Eve, *Behind the Gospels*, esp. 86–134; Keith, "Social Memory Theory," parts 1 and 2; Keith, "Narratives of the Gospels."

25. Rodríguez, "Jesus as his Friends Remembered Him," 244.

26. Watson, *Gospel Writing*, 606. In this book's prologue, Watson avers: "The uninterpreted Jesus is a chimera, a mythical entity that supposedly existed in and for itself prior to its becoming something else for others" (6).

27. For a guide to formulations of the rule of faith in the early church and its various functions, including its role in relation to biblical interpretation, see Ferguson, *Rule of Faith*.

Cosgrove as "the rule of moral-theological adjudication."[28] More obviously than Crossan's normative interpretive criterion, moreover, *shalom* is an interpretive norm discernible as intrinsic to Scripture as a whole and to the Gospels in particular, especially insofar as it coheres with and fleshes out various forms of the love command. In practice, such an approach serves as something of an interpretive feedback loop: first, a compelling theological-moral interpretive norm is discerned from within the Gospel tradition as a whole; second, individual Gospel traditions are then interpreted in light of that critical norm; and third, how well such traditions are understood by means of this interpretive double movement and thereby contribute to the overall portrait of Jesus is then factored into the continuing appraisal of the interpretive approach itself.

Integrally related to my interpretive stance in this book is the awareness that the very task of interpretation, especially biblical interpretation, is a moral no less than meaning-making activity. In an illuminating study of *Jews and Anti-Judaism in the New Testament*, Terence Donaldson contends, clearly and cogently, that "there is an ethical element in the process of interpretation; interpreters need to take responsibility for the decisions they make."[29] Indeed, interpretation is a moral process in more ways than one. On one hand, responsible interpreters should respect the otherness of any given text, resisting the temptation to colonize it within their own ideological frame of reference. Although I have chosen to read texts that apparently implicate Jesus in violence from a peace-oriented perspective, such an interpretive stance does not authorize the violation of texts to mean what I would like them to mean. On the other hand, as Donaldson points out, "interpretations about texts can have—indeed, have had—consequences in the real world, which means that interpreters have a responsibility to consider the ends to which their interpretations might be put."[30] Historically speaking, Gospel texts addressed in this book have often found themselves caught up in the justification of various forms of violence—from the persecution of Jews and the slaughter of colonized peoples to preemptive, no less than defensive, warfare. In view of that history of interpretive effects and in light of the biblical hope of messianic *shalom* as the ultimate goal of history, this book is an exercise in respectful reading but also, as and when necessary, resistant reading of biblical texts whose inherent meaning or history of effects is or has been violent. As David Rhoads observes near the end of his

28. Cosgrove, *Appealing to Scripture*, 2–4, 154–80. (My own preference, in view of the Bible's inherent theological-moral nexus, is to speak of theological-moral interpretive adjudication.)

29. Donaldson, *Jews and Anti-Judaism*, 156.

30. Ibid.

essay, "The Ethics of Reading Mark as Narrative," "The ethics of reading involves being responsible for the rhetorical effects of the text itself and of our interpretations of it, so that we can counter its potentially harmful effects."[31]

Readers familiar with *A Peaceable Hope* may be interested in the relation between that earlier book and this one. In chronological terms, *The Vehement Jesus* is a sequel to *A Peaceable Hope* and at points revisits concerns explored in the earlier book. Conceptually, however, it is more of a "prequel" insofar as it reexamines a conviction largely taken for granted in the earlier book, namely, the profound peacefulness of Jesus' mission and message as these are displayed in the canonical Gospels. Indeed, in *A Peaceable Hope*, the peaceful character of Jesus' historic mission and message, as depicted in the Gospels, serves as the key criterion for evaluating expressions of violent eschatology in those same Gospels, as well as in Acts and Revelation. If the Gospel writers did not present Jesus as a peaceful person, however, the argument of that book collapses. For people who take their moral bearings from Jesus, as he is presented in the canonical Gospels, much is at stake.

A sense of how much is at stake in whether or not the biblical Gospels portray Jesus as profoundly peaceful—not simply inclined to peace—may be illustrated with reference to two contrasting positions on the moral legacy of the Gospel portrait(s) of Jesus. The first of these concerns the question of whether or not the Jesus of the Gospels should be normative for ethical guidance and moral conduct. Throughout the church's history, the teaching and example of Jesus in the Gospels have been regarded as morally binding for would-be Christian disciples, even though moral theologians down through the centuries have found ways to evade some of his more rigorous moral instructions, especially with respect to violence and wealth. In a pluralist, post-Christian world, however, the moral legacy of Jesus is inevitably under scrutiny. A striking example of such critique from a biblical scholar is *The Bad Jesus* by Hector Avalos. Writing from an explicitly atheistic standpoint, Avalos contests the Christian conviction that Jesus was wholly good and argues that Gospel depictions of Jesus that are inimical to secular humanist values preclude granting normative status to Jesus. As a result, according to Avalos, "this study [*The Bad Jesus*] aims to show that there is no reason to regard anything Jesus taught or did as authoritative for modern ethics."[32] The stance of Avalos is vastly different from that articu-

---

31. Rhoads, "Ethics of Reading Mark," 218. See also Selby, *Comical Doctrine*, 239–48, where the author concludes her epistemological appraisal of New Testament hermeneutics by exploring its implications for "an ethics of reading appropriate to the gospel."

32. Avalos, *Bad Jesus*, 13. For a much briefer discussion of some of the same problem texts as discussed by Avalos, albeit from a faith-oriented standpoint, see Strauss, *Jesus Behaving Badly*, also published in 2015.

lated by David Clough, whose "modest proposal" is that "the teaching and example of Jesus Christ in relation to violence is relevant to all Christian debates about the legitimacy of violence."[33]

Second, even among Christian ethicists for whom the Gospels in the New Testament provide normative moral guidance, questions remain regarding what moral inferences may legitimately be made on the basis of the Gospel accounts of Jesus' mission and message. Especially with respect to violence committed to protect the welfare of others, there is deep discord. For example, in a chapter on "Violence in Defense of Justice" within *The Moral Vision of the New Testament*, Richard Hays presents a methodologically nuanced argument in favor of adopting the "norm of nonviolent love of enemies" articulated in Matt 5:38–48 as supported by the New Testament as a whole and hence as determinative for the church as a "community of peace."[34] By contrast, in debate with Hays, Nigel Biggar contends that a non-pacifist stance such as the just-war tradition provides a more coherent explanation for New Testament texts pertaining to the moral value and validity of violence, including most especially the absence of any Gospel text that explicitly criticizes soldiers for being soldiers.[35] Although instructive at various levels, the debate between Hays and Biggar serves to showcase the inherent significance of disagreement over the interpretation of canonical Gospel testimony to the character and conduct of Jesus.

Given the sporadic nature of the textual data discussed in the chapters that follow, discerning how best to structure the argument proved problematic. Although disputed,[36] the relative rarity and dispersed distribution of texts that envisage a vehement Jesus make it possible to argue that they do not negate the predominantly peaceable presentation of Jesus' historic mission and message in the Gospels. Indeed, in various ways, the fourfold Gospel canon is determinative for interpreting the vehement Jesus as an inherently peaceful person. For example, the parallel to Matt 10:34 in Luke 12:51

---

33. Clough, "On the Relevance of Jesus Christ," 200. Since, like me, Clough affirms the theological conviction concerning the "revelation of God in Jesus Christ," his "modest proposal" regarding the relevance of Jesus for Christian reflection on the morality of violence bears directly on whether or not the teaching and example of Jesus, as attested in the biblical Gospels, are normative for Christian ethics.

34. Hays, *Moral Vision*, 317–46. The case argued by Hays is supported by Swartley, *Covenant of Peace*, passim.

35. See, in chronological sequence, Biggar, "Specify and Distinguish!," 164–84; Hays, "Narrate and Embody," 185–98; Biggar, "New Testament and Violence," 73–80; Hays, "Thorny Task of Reconciliation," 81–86; Biggar, "Against Christian Pacifism," 34–59. For another Augustinian response to Hays regarding the legitimacy of violence in certain circumstances, see Verhey, "Neither Devils nor Angels," 599–625.

36. See, e.g., Bermejo-Rubio, "Jesus and the Anti-Roman Resistance," 1–105.

provides both the impetus and interpretive guidance for understanding an apparently violent text in nonviolent, albeit not tame, terms.[37] Nevertheless, only after the body of the book had been drafted in six chapters did its present shape emerge—and only after radical reorganization.

My grappling with troubling Gospel texts now begins, naturally enough, with a chapter devoted to the counterintuitive content of Matt 10:34, "Do not suppose that I have come to sow peace upon the earth; I have not come to sow peace but rather a sword." The book proper thus opens by considering a contentious expression of the vehement Jesus within the Gospel that not only opens the New Testament but also bears most responsibility within the fourfold Gospel canon for inculcating a vision of the vehement Jesus. That opening chapter is followed by a discussion of two perplexing parables, the parable of the Unforgiving Slave in Matt 18:23-35 and the parable of the Throne Claimant in Luke 19:11-28. So, from a troubling text toward the end of Matthew's second of five discourses, attention first turns to a parable that concludes Matthew's fourth discourse of Jesus before refocusing on a parable near the culmination of Luke's distinctive central section (9:51-19:46). The parable of the Unforgiving Slave offers insight into Matthew's own retributive mind-set, reflected also in various other parables found only in his Gospel, whereas the parable of the Throne Claimant diverts the discussion to perturbing features of Luke's Gospel. As a result, chapter 2 plays a transitional role, shifting the spotlight from Matthew to Luke's Gospel for the following two chapters. Chapter 3 probes four passages in Luke's Gospel that envisage the destruction of Jerusalem as divine judgment for rejecting Jesus as Israel's messiah, whereas chapter 4 scrutinizes the uniquely Lukan Passover-related passage in which Jesus is recalled as encouraging his disciples to purchase swords.

In any discussion of Jesus and violence, his disruptive actions within the temple often take center stage. Chapters 5-7 home in on this incident common to all four Gospels along with the parable of the Tenants in the Vineyard, which in terms of narrative logic closely follows the temple incident in all three Synoptic Gospels. Focusing on canonical configurations of the temple incident, chapter 5 argues that none of the Gospel writers presents Jesus' conduct in the temple as violent, even if it may fairly be characterized as forceful and provocative. More troubling is what his actions and words may—and have been taken to—symbolize at an ideological level, especially when understood in relation to Matthew and Mark's respective accounts of the cursing by Jesus of a fig tree. In chapter 5, then, not only is considerable

---

37. Other ways in which the fourfold Gospel canon provides resources for interpreting the vehement Jesus as inherently peaceful are displayed in this book and in *A Peaceable Hope*.

attention given to Mark's intercalation of Jesus' temple actions by his cursing of a fig tree but an alternative to the most widely held interpretation of this sandwich story is also ventured. Since, in the synoptic tradition, Jesus' parable of the Vineyard Tenants seems related, in narrative terms, to his temple actions, chapter 6 explores whether this parable takes for granted divine retaliatory violence in response to human recalcitrance. Chapter 7 then refocuses on the distinctively Johannine version of the temple incident, which contains narrative details that have contributed significantly to the reception of this event as a violent outburst on the part of Jesus.

In chapter 8 the spotlight returns to Matthew's Gospel, focusing on Jesus' diatribe against scribes and Pharisees in Matthew 23. Set by Matthew within his Jerusalem section and also in close connection with his fifth and final discourse, this collection of honor-wounding denunciations reinforces one's sense that this most influential of Gospels was written within a social environment characterized by deep-seated religious antagonism. The discussion of Jesus' rhetorical hostility in Matthew 23 leads fairly naturally into a reconsideration of Jesus' eschatological expectations found in Matthew and Luke's Gospels, especially as these relate to anticipations of ultimate divine vengeance. Chapter 9 thus revisits the central theme of *A Peaceable Hope*, reiterating some of its central contentions, reconsidering an especially enigmatic passage (Luke 17:22–37), and proffering some concluding interpretive inferences.

In terms of Gospel texts considered, there is not a strictly linear progression from beginning to end of the discussion that composes the argument of this book. Even so, there is a progression of sorts. The opening chapter on a discordant Matthean text with a Lukan parallel is a defensible point of departure, and the closing chapter on teleological terror is an apt endpoint. In between, texts associated with Jerusalem as either the content or context of Jesus' message and mission predominate. Moreover, whereas the central section focused on the temple incident pays attention to texts from Mark and John, these chapters are enclosed within sections focused on texts from Matthew and Luke.

None of the Gospel texts explored in this book gives up its secrets easily. Each resists straightforward exegesis and proves almost intractable in terms of its interpretive horizons. Even so, my experience has been that patient persistence with such texts has been rewarded—if not with complete clarity or certainty, then at least with something of a blessing from wrestling without yielding or relinquishing too readily.

1

Crossing Swords, I

Not Peace but rather a Sword?

(MATTHEW 10:34–36)

IN VIEW OF THE mission of Jesus taken as a whole—including his teaching on nonretaliation and his nonretaliatory response to violence directed against himself—two of his sayings featuring swords apparently undermine his commitment to peace as integral to his proclamation of the reign of God. The first of these is the saying found in Matt 10:34 and Luke 12:51, in which Jesus apparently repudiates peace as the purpose of his mission: not peace but rather a sword! The second is Jesus' instruction to his disciples, found only in Luke's passion narrative, to purchase swords (Luke 22:35–38). Both of these texts are enigmatic no less than contrary to the general tenor of Jesus' mission and message. Taken either at face value or symbolically, they have been pressed into the service of dubious contentions.[1] Although

---

1. The text of Matt 10:34 appears on the frontispiece to Brandon, *Jesus and the Zealots*, and also Aslan, *Zealot*. For Brandon, both Matt 10:34 and Luke 22:35–38 comprise evidence that Jesus and his disciples sympathized with both the objectives and means of Zealotism (201–6). Regarding Luke 22:35–38, see also Brown, *Death of the Messiah*, 1:270n7: "This text has been (mis)-used as a general declaration of the right of Christians to bear arms; as support for the right of the medieval papacy to exercise both material and spiritual power (two swords); and as a proof that Jesus encouraged armed revolution!" For the way in which the two swords of Luke 22:38 came to be understood as representing temporal and spiritual power, with competing claims to both by kings and popes, see Bovon, *Luke 3*, 184–88.

both sayings presume violence to be in some sense inevitable, it takes things too far to rope them into the service of condoning violence as compatible with the reign of God heralded by Jesus.

The purpose of this chapter is to examine the first of these sword sayings of Jesus with care, in the hope of understanding it better and thereby ascertaining whether or not it endorses violence in some sense or in certain contexts. The uniquely Lukan episode in which Jesus advises his disciples to arm themselves with swords is discussed in chapter 4.

There are three versions of Jesus' adamant assertion that he came not to sow peace but rather strife: Matt 10:34–36; Luke 12:51–52; and saying 16 in the Gospel of Thomas. However they may be related, these three texts share enough in common to be regarded as variations on a theme. Their respective literary contexts differ widely, however, making it impossible to discern the saying's original life-setting and hence its original sense. Since our ignorance in this respect is not critical to determining the moral implications of this saying, especially in relation to violence validated in Jesus' name, this chapter explores the meaning of this saying in its most stark canonical form (Matt 10:34) and hence in its Matthean context. Luke's use of the term "division" at 12:51 probably interprets the "sword" of his source, whatever that may have been. The Thomasine version is probably secondary to, and possibly dependent on, both synoptic versions of the saying. Without any obvious thematic connection to the sayings that come before and after it, saying 16 in the Gospel of Thomas reads:

> Jesus said, "Perhaps people think that I have come to bring peace upon the world. They do not know that I have come to bring divisions on the earth—fire, sword, war. For there will be five in a house, and three will be against two, and two against three; father against son, and son against father. And they will stand as solitary."[2]

As with the versions of this saying in Matt 10:34–36 and Luke 12:51–53, the version in *Gos. Thom.* 16 both pivots on the antithesis between peace and its opposite and also relates this antithesis to familial discord. The contrast between expectation (that Jesus' purpose was to promote peace) and its overturning in Jesus' apparent statement of purpose more closely resembles Matt 10:34, as does the specific reference to the sword. But the reference to fire seems to reflect familiarity with the saying's immediate context in Luke 12:49–50. The final phrase is more than likely a Thomasine addition (cf. *Gos. Thom.* 49 and 75).

2. Gathercole, *Gospel of Thomas*, 275. For another translation, see Goodacre, *Thomas and the Gospels*, 183.

FORCEFUL EXPRESSION WITHIN AN APOCALYPTIC MATRIX

To make sense of Jesus' "not peace but rather a sword" saying, it is helpful to examine the saying's rhetorical dynamic and also illuminating to identify its historical ideological matrix. Greater familiarity with both this saying's rhetorical dynamic and its ideological context contributes to a reconfigured understanding of its probable meaning.

In a study of forceful and imaginative sayings of Jesus, Robert Tannehill devotes considerable attention to this saying, focusing particularly on the way in which literary form and expression contribute to its dynamic force.[3] Tannehill first draws attention to the fact that the central saying itself is marked by its antithetical expression, which enhances its rhetorical force considerably: *not* peace *but rather* a sword! Although it would have been possible to express this apparent statement of purpose without reference to peace, to refer to peace—and indeed to do so before its antithesis—evokes the expectation for eschatological *shalom* associated with the messianic era before (apparently) dashing it. As Tannehill observes, "The word 'sword' is more forceful because of contrast with its opposite, part of its meaning is clarified by this antithetical setting, and the reader is immediately involved in what is being said because of the sharp rejection of his [or her] hopes for peace."[4]

If the reference to peace evokes the hope of the human heart for eschatological *shalom*, the use of the word "sword" is metonymic imagery. In other words, here "sword" is not only a vivid image associated with warfare, used in this instance to represent such conflict generally, but it is also used metaphorically of familial conflict. The contrast is not between peace and war but between peace and an image of warfare used metaphorically. In the Matthean form of this saying, this is clear from the epexegetical nature of the saying in Matt 10:35. In other words, both the explanatory γάρ (*gar*, for) of Matt 10:35 and the way in which its opening words parallel the apparent expression of purpose in 10:34 indicate that the second saying explicates the first such that "sword" signifies severance between people—family dissension—not killing. In its Lukan form, the saying makes explanation redundant by simply substituting the word "division" (διαμερισμός, *diamerismos*) for "sword" (Luke 12:51), a noun reinforced by the use of two cognate verbs in what follows. "The two words ['peace' and 'sword'] do not stand on the

---

3. Tannehill, *Sword of His Mouth*, 140–47.
4. Ibid., 141.

same level," according to Tannehill.⁵ Here "peace" is primary and associated with eschatological hope, whereas the word "sword" is not only secondary and disruptive of human flourishing but also metonymic and metaphorical. Although Jesus here seems to relate the purpose of his coming to a "sword" rather than to *shalom*, the saying itself nevertheless reinforces the primacy of peace and the comparative pettiness of "sword," which merely serves a rhetorical function.

The family severances listed in Matt 10:35–36 to illustrate what Jesus means by his "sword" saying derive from Micah 7:6. For Tannehill, "This reference to Scripture may call to mind a broader prophetic-apocalyptic motif of the breaking of family relationships in the final tribulation . . . stirring the fears and hopes associated with this motif."⁶ This suggestion on Tannehill's part is more than a possibility, however. In all likelihood, the *apocalyptic eschatological expectation of messianic woes* provides the ideological matrix within which to make best sense of this enigmatic saying.⁷

Although the saying in its Matthean and Lukan forms makes the same basic point, Matthew's parallel expressions of family discord seem to envisage the most grievous instances of breakdown within a Jewish household: son against father, daughter against mother, and daughter-in-law against mother-in-law, since married women generally joined the households of their husbands. Such family discord is not simply disconcerting; it is, rather, an expression of flagrant disregard for the fifth commandment to honor father and mother (Exod 20:12; Deut 5:16). Matthew echoes Micah 7:6 most precisely, not only by listing the same three family relationships in the same order but also by including the same startling conclusion: one's enemies comprise those who share one's home (10:36).

Luke's elaboration of family discord is different but no less effective. Whereas Matthew concludes with a summary statement, Luke begins with a description of how a household of five will henceforth be divided, three against two and two against three. Perhaps, as Tannehill suggests, the five referred to in Luke 12:52 correspond to the family members mentioned in 12:53, thereby maximizing the level of family tension to include divisions not only between individual family members but also between coalitions

---

5. Ibid.
6. Ibid., 142.
7. To this decisive point I return at various points in what follows. In the italicized phrase, both eschatological expectation associated with messianic agency and an overarching apocalyptic vision of reality are important. Eschatological hope and apocalyptic vision are not synonymous, but in the Gospels and elsewhere eschatology is apocalyptic in the sense that it presupposes divine initiative and agency.

within the family as a whole.⁸ Perhaps the reference to three versus two and two versus three signals generational breakdown (son, daughter, and daughter-in-law against father and mother). In any case, Luke reinforces the impact of interfamilial conflict by reiterating each instance of family conflict in reverse form, for example, father against son and son against father.

Yet one further aspect of Luke's presentation of this saying is distinctive. Unlike Matthew's version of Jesus' sword saying, Luke prefaces his "not peace but rather division" saying with apparently related sayings in which Jesus seems to associate the purpose of his mission with catastrophe and foreboding. Immediately preceding Jesus' question, "Do you suppose that I have come to bring peace to the earth?" (12:51), Luke has Jesus utter two other stark sayings: "I came to cast fire upon the earth, and how I wish it were already alight. I have a drowning by which to be drowned, and how distressed I am until that occurs" (12:49–50).⁹

Both the juxtaposition of Luke 12:51 alongside 12:49–50 and the shared verbal pattern of 12:49 and 12:51 imply that these sayings belong to the same literary unit and therefore should be understood in light of each other.¹⁰ In its Lukan setting, the question regarding peace as the (apparent) purpose of Jesus' mission is contrasted not only with division in what follows (12:51a–53) but also with the "fire" and "drowning" that precede it. In other words, the possibility that the purpose of Jesus' mission was to bring peace to the earth is crushed between two jaws of a vice identified as fire and division. Tannehill also surmises that the association of the "fire" and "baptism" sayings with Jesus' "not peace but rather division" saying implies that Luke 12:49–50 should probably be interpreted in terms of suffering, tribulation, and eschatological judgment.¹¹ In short, the passage as a whole associates Jesus' mission with eschatological strife, not peace.

As part of his discussion of Matt 10:34–36 and Luke 12:49–53, Tannehill addresses the forceful effect created by this cluster of sayings being presented in purposive terms.¹² The peaceable Jesus who blesses peacemakers and teaches nonretaliation seemingly disavows peace as the purpose of his mission and claims instead to have come for the express purpose of bringing a sword of strife. Tannehill asserts that this is clearly not intended to serve as a summary of Jesus' mission in its entirety, but it is doubtful whether

---

8. Tannehill, *Sword of His Mouth*, 146.

9. In Luke 12:50a, Jesus uses the language of immersion, but since this almost certainly implies his death, the image of drowning seems fitting. See Mark 10:38–39, which has no contextual parallel in Luke.

10. Tannehill, *Sword of His Mouth*, 145.

11. Ibid., 145–46.

12. Ibid., 143–44.

one can be quite so confident about this. He is on surer ground when he observes that the burden of this text is that the kind of family divisions it forecasts "are inherent in Jesus' mission and therefore a fate which we cannot avoid if we follow him."[13] Moreover, the tension caused by these forceful sayings provokes reflection on primary values, especially concerning fundamental family relationships, with a view to their reordering in light of Jesus' mission. In other words, Jesus' sword saying is less a statement of intention than a description of certain inevitabilities for those who associate with him and his mission. Perhaps Tannehill would not go so far as this, but there is good reason to suppose that the apparent expression of intent in Jesus' sword saying has more to do with inevitability than with express purpose.

For this interpretive possibility to make sense, one must come to grips with the apocalyptic eschatological mind-set presupposed by this and other comparable sayings. Ben Meyer, Dale Allison, and Brant Pitre (among others) have argued persuasively that Jesus' sword saying is best understood within the context of the Jewish expectation that messianic woes must inevitably precede the long-awaited messianic *shalom*.[14] With reference to a range of Jewish texts preceding, contemporaneous with, and somewhat later than the first century of the Common Era, Meyer, Allison, and Pitre demonstrate that this saying resonates with a Jewish interpretive tradition that perceived the familial discord of Micah 7:6 as emblematic of eschatological tribulation. For Allison and Pitre, an important dimension of their respective arguments is to show that a version of the sword saying was, in all probability, uttered by the historical Jesus, who shared the expectation of a time of tribulation with other eschatologically oriented Israelites. The reasons put forward in favor of regarding the sword saying as authentic to Jesus are persuasive, not least because this saying clashes with the general early Christian impression that associated Jesus' mission with peace.

Understood within the conceptual matrix of Jewish expectation of tribulation as an inevitable precursor to the messianic era, Jesus' sword saying may be taken to mean something other than the express purpose of bringing violent conflict. The apocalyptic mind-set of Jesus and the Gospel writers is decisive in this connection. Within an apocalyptic vision of reality, the world and its peoples are the handiwork of a good Creator but

13. Ibid., 143.

14. See Meyer, *Aims of Jesus*, 202–219; Allison, *End of the Ages*, 5–25; Allison, "Q 12:51–53 and Mark 9:11–13," 289–310; Allison, *Intertextual Jesus*, 132–34; Allison, "Eschatology of Jesus," 286–89; Pitre, *Jesus, the Tribulation*, 198–216. For a study that relates the various New Testament writings to the messianic woes provoked by the mission of Jesus, albeit by means of three different expressions of eschatology (realized, consistent, and inaugurated), see Pate and Kennard, *Deliverance Now and Not Yet*.

nevertheless under the sway of evil forces. Only God or an agent of God is able to rescue the world and its people from captivity to the forces of evil. Such a vision of reality holds out hope for God's ultimate reclamation of the created order but in the meantime explains the dark dimensions of human existence in terms of a dualistic but also predetermined struggle between good and evil. In light of the basic conviction that God the Creator will ultimately vanquish all opposition, dualistic elements of Jewish apocalyptic are relativized by the belief that God has predetermined events to a significant extent, permitting opposing forces only so much time to wreak havoc in God's world. Thus, Jewish apocalyptic retains—and indeed sustains—hope in God's ultimate deliverance while also accounting for present distress.

On this understanding of the way things are, human alienation from God is deep-seated and therefore well nigh impossible to overcome. People are unable to extricate themselves from their captivity to oppressive forces, thereby requiring a divine or divinely sent liberator. Their plight is so radical, however, that most are unable to recognize liberation for what it is. Inexplicably, God's agent of redemption does not meet with open arms. This paradoxical state of affairs is well illustrated in the prologue to the Fourth Gospel: although the Light of the world was coming into a world whose very being is contingent on his agency, the world fails to recognize him and his own people largely fail to welcome him; indeed, only those born of God are able to receive him (John 1:3–5, 9–13; cf. 3:19–21). This passage is in many respects the most illuminating commentary on Jesus' enigmatic sword saying.

Perceived within the ideological matrix of Jewish apocalyptic eschatology, the saying, "I came not to sow peace but rather a sword," may be understood to mean that Jesus' messianic mission provokes the time of tribulation that must inevitably precede God's promised peace. In apocalyptic terms, eschatological *shalom* comes only after intense tribulation, but this necessary postponement of promised peace expresses the self-aware conviction that human recalcitrance is intractable, not that God or God's agent(s) of liberation expressly will for the world and its people to be overwhelmed by conflict. Since, according to this vision of reality, eschatological *shalom* can only be reached through distress caused by inevitable resistance to God's life-saving agency, Jesus' sword saying more likely intimates the inexorability of strife as a repercussion of his mission than an expression of purpose to cause or even provoke conflict. Although Pitre dismisses the view that this saying of Jesus relates more to the effect than to the purpose of Jesus' mission,[15] yet another Gospel text attests to the contemporary conception

15. Pitre, *Jesus, the Tribulation*, 208. For Pitre, Jesus' sword saying should be understood to mean that Jesus expressly sought to "unleash" end-time tribulation as

that an inevitable outcome may be construed in terms of the divine will or purpose. In Mark 4:11–12 Jesus informs those around him that although the mystery of divine reign has been given to them, to those on the outside all things occur by means of parables so that "seeing, they might see but not perceive, and hearing, they might hear but not comprehend, lest they should happen to turn and be forgiven." Here Mark presents Jesus as appealing to Isa 6:9–10 as prophetic precedent for the incomprehensible reality (from an insider perspective) that many, if not most, people responded inadequately to Jesus and his message, as illustrated by the preceding parable of the Seed Sower. Commenting on the perplexing reason given in Mark 4:11–12 for Jesus speaking in parables, Morna Hooker remarks: "Jewish thought tended to blur the distinction between purpose and result, for if God was sovereign, then, of course, what happened must be his will, however strange this appeared."[16] Such a conceptual tendency is that much more comprehensible within an apocalyptic frame of reference.

In many respects, context determines meaning. Although there is good reason to consider Jesus' sword saying as authentic, it is impossible to place this saying in a precise context within Jesus' historical mission. All that seems possible is to contextualize this saying within the matrix of Jewish apocalyptic eschatological expectation regarding tribulation as precursory to the messianic age. The sword saying of Jesus has left its mark on subsequent history through its incorporation into the Gospels of Matthew and Luke, so it would be worthwhile to investigate both literary contexts within which this saying is found to ascertain what light the respective narrative frameworks might shed on it. Since Luke's version of Jesus' sword saying is most likely an (apposite) interpretation, however, only Matthew's narrative contextualization of this saying is examined here.

---

precursory to eschatological restoration. For a similar view, see Beasley-Murray, *Jesus and the Kingdom of God*, 328: "Jesus sees it as part of his mission to create the apocalyptic conditions described by Micah." On this view, the sword saying does not envisage Jesus as embracing a mission of sword-slaying, but it does seem to understand him as intentionally precipitating conflict as means to an end, indeed, means that do not conform to the end of *shalom*.

16. Hooker, "Mark's Parables of the Kingdom," 92. For a different perspective on Mark 4:11–12 within its narrative context, see Hatina, *In Search of a Context*, 184–238. To my mind, many of Hatina's observations on Mark 4 point in the direction of an apocalyptic orientation that helps to make sense of his argument "that the obduracy expressed by means of the quotation [in Mark 4:12] is not the result of some divine *fiat* of double predestination, but the result of the outsiders' already willful rejection of Jesus' word" (185). Despite Hatina's defense of a "telic" interpretation of Mark 4:11–12, his emphasis on human responsibility for provoking divine judgment is not far removed from an interpretation featuring effect rather than purpose.

JESUS' SWORD SAYING IN MATTHEAN CONTEXT

Jesus' sword saying in Matt 10:34 falls within a coherently structured literary block. Matthew's narrative structure is a long-standing interpretive puzzle, but there is broad agreement that the second discourse in Matthew 10 is situated within an artistically structured narrative block that begins with 4:23 and ends at 11:1. Three summaries introduce and conclude three major sections within this larger block, as follows:

4:23–5:2 Narrative summary introducing first of five discourses

5:2–8:1 Sermon on the Mount (authoritative words of Jesus)

8:2–9:35 Jesus' authoritative deeds (matching his words)

9:35–10:5a Narrative summary introducing second discourse

10:5b–42 Commissioning of Jesus' disciples

11:1 Narrative summary (echoing 4:23; 7:28; 9:35)

The narrative summary at Matt 9:35 echoes 4:23 and serves as a transition between Matthew's two-paneled depiction of Jesus as Messiah of word and deed (5:2–9:34) and the point at which he presents Jesus as incorporating his chosen Twelve into his own mission (9:36–10:42).[17] The summary at Matt 11:1 echoes not only both earlier summaries at 4:23 and 9:35 but also the formulaic conclusion to the Sermon on the Mount at 7:28 (cf. 13:53; 19:1; 26:1). Beyond this point, Matthew's narrative structure becomes less transparent, but to this point there is a clear (and instructive) narrative progression.

Jesus' sword saying occurs within the final major section (9:35–11:1) of this artistically arranged narrative block (4:23–11:1), in which Jesus' disciples are commissioned by Jesus to participate in his own mission. This is evident from comparing Matt 10:1, 7–8 with the summaries of 4:23, 9:35, and 11:1. The twelve disciples are not instructed to teach, perhaps to reinforce the authoritative status of Jesus as teacher,[18] but otherwise they are

---

17. For different but complementary reflections on ways in which literary and thematic features of this section of Matthew's Gospel depict Jesus as God's messianic agent of peace, see Mauser, *Gospel of Peace*, 56–61.

18. For Matthew, Jesus is the uniquely authoritative teacher reminiscent of Moses. This is evident not only from the prominence within the Gospel of Jesus' five major discourse sections but also from the priority given to Jesus' teaching in the summaries of Matt 4:23; 9:35; 11:1. See also Matt 5:1–2; 7:28–29; 23:8–10. Not until the final commission of 28:19–20 are the disciples instructed to teach, the content of which is the teaching of Jesus to the disciples. The image at the conclusion of Jesus' third and central discourse of the teaching scribe trained in the reign of the heavens (13:52) applies first and foremost to Jesus, but one suspects that the evangelist conceived of his own role

commissioned to do what Jesus does. It is also noteworthy that the second discourse in Matthew 10 shares a number of significant structural, formal, and thematic features with the first discourse in chapters 5–7. First, not only does Matt 9:35 echo 4:23 but it also begins a transitional passage (9:35–10:4) that is reminiscent of 4:23–5:2 in that both begin by focusing more broadly on Jesus in relation to crowds and then narrow the focus to Jesus and his disciples.[19] Second, the discourse proper is arranged in triadic fashion, with three formal "Amen" sayings concluding each subsection (10:15, 23, 42).[20] Triadic arrangement also features prominently in both the Sermon on the Mount and the miracle section that follows.[21] Third, Jesus' sword saying in Matt 10:34 is similar in both form and style to a series of seven "I have/have not come" declarations in the Gospel as a whole, all but one of which appear in the narrative block beginning at Matt 4:23 and ending at 11:1. And fourth, there are significant thematic connections between Matthew's first and second discourses. In various ways, all such features bear on the interpretation of Jesus' sword saying in Matthean perspective.

As indicated above, the commissioning discourse proper comprises three subsections, with each subsection concluded by a formal "Amen" saying (10:15, 23, 42). The first subsection focuses on specific instructions of various kinds: whom to go to, what to say and do, how to negotiate hospitality, and how to respond to an inhospitable response. The "Amen" saying of Matt 10:15 sounds an eschatological note by pronouncing a warning on inhospitable towns. This first subsection not only reinforces ways in which the Twelve emulate key aspects of Jesus' own mission activities (10:7–8; cf. 10:1) but also sounds the peace theme in relation to negotiating hospitality: "Upon entering the house(hold), greet it, and if the house is indeed worthy [cf. 10:11] let your peace come upon it, but if unworthy let your peace return to you" (10:12–13). It is easy to read this instruction as expressing little more than a standard Semitic greeting, but to do so is to miss the strong eschatological connotations of the Hebrew *shalom*. In this context, "peace" is not simply something expressed in accordance with social convention but something that can be granted or conveyed. In all likelihood, this peace is

---

in similar terms. On Matthew's parallels between Jesus and Moses, see Allison, *New Moses*, passim.

19. Davies and Allison, *Gospel according to Saint Matthew*, 2:143.

20. See Weaver, *Matthew's Missionary Discourse*, 74. Cf. Davies and Allison, *Gospel according to Saint Matthew*, 2:160–62, where the final third of this discourse is probably overanalyzed.

21. See Davies and Allison, *Gospel according to Saint Matthew*, 1:61–72, where one also finds their rationale for an alternative triadic arrangement of the commissioning discourse in Matt 10:5–42 than that proposed here.

intricately linked with the substance of the message given to the Twelve to proclaim, "The reign of the heavens has drawn near" (10:7), which echoes precisely the proclamation of both John the Immerser and Jesus (3:2; 4:17). Eschatological peace comes with God's heavenly reign and its effects (10:8). As Davies and Allison surmise, "For Matthew and his tradition the apostolic greeting of peace was probably a sign of the inbreaking of the kingdom, a symbol of God's eschatological work of establishing reconciliation and šālôm. . . ."[22] In short, the peace of Matt 10:13 is no less weighty in an eschatological sense than the "day of judgment" of 10:15. This is critical in view of what may be described as the *participatory correspondence* of the commission given by Jesus to the Twelve relative to his own mission. By this I mean what Dorothy Jean Weaver discerns about the mission to which the Twelve are commissioned by Jesus—that it is "not merely parallel to, but rather an integral part of, the ministry of Jesus himself."[23] In other words, if eschatological peace is integral to the mission of the disciples, it is so only insofar as it is integral to the mission of Jesus because their commission is but a corresponding participation in his mission.

The pervasive theme of the second subsection of Jesus' commissioning discourse is signaled by its opening image: Jesus informs the Twelve that he sends them out as sheep among wolves (10:16). There are occasional notes of encouragement (10:19-20, 22b), but by and large this subsection details the various kinds of trouble in store for anyone sent out by Jesus to participate in his mission, whether the original Twelve or subsequent "sent ones" (see 10:18). Especially noteworthy is the description in Matt 10:21 of family betrayal, a theme with which the sword saying in the final subsection of this discourse resonates.

Curiously, with the exception of the opening and closing verses of this second subsection, its subject matter largely parallels the trials presaged in Jesus' eschatological discourse in Mark 13:9-13 and (less closely) Luke 21:12-19. This together with explicit eschatological references in Matt 10:22-23 lead Davies and Allison to infer that, in Matthean perspective, both the pre- and post-Easter missions belong to the "eschatological affliction, the period of trial and tribulation which heralds the coming of God's new world."[24] This is a plausible inference, but it is noteworthy that

---

22. Ibid., 2:176.

23. Weaver, *Matthew's Missionary Discourse*, 73. Weaver reinforces this observation by speaking of a "fundamental parallelism" between the mission of Jesus and that to which he commissions his disciples (82).

24. Davies and Allison, *Gospel according to Saint Matthew*, 2:182. On the same page, they write: "Indeed, one can argue that Mt 10 is not about mission as such but about mission as tribulation."

in this subsection Jesus nowhere advises disciples that he sends them out for the express purpose of experiencing affliction. His words warn of the *inevitability* of betrayal and persecution, but they do not indicate that his commissioning of disciples to participate in his mission is either for the purpose of experiencing affliction or to provoke tribulation. Put differently, well aware that "the eschatological peace in which wolf and sheep will live together in harmony (Isa 11:6; 65:25) is not yet a reality,"[25] Jesus does not send out his sheep to provide food for wolves or even to provoke vicious wolves to prey on them. Rather, Jesus knowingly sends out his disciples into an environment already inhabited by predatory wolves, but he sends them out as vulnerable sheep or guileless doves, presumably because wolf-like aggression is incongruent with the character of his own and (thus also) his disciples' mission. Hence the need for serpent-like shrewdness or practical wisdom to deal with inevitable harassment.[26]

The third and final subsection of Jesus' commissioning discourse is the longest of the three, in part because it reprises aspects of the earlier two subsections. It begins and ends by restating the corresponding nature of the relation between Jesus the teacher and his disciples. Like Jesus, like disciple, according to Matthew (10:24–25, 40). A series of sayings in Matt 10:26–31 offers encouragement not to fear the inevitable consequences of the disciple's association with this particular teacher, in part because God is to be feared more and in part because, whatever may befall a disciple, God knows and cares. In turn, these exhortations lead into a cluster of sayings relating to loyal identification with Jesus. Building on Weaver's perception that the focal themes of this discourse shift from mission to persecution to relationships, Stephen Barton summarizes the third subsection of the discourse as follows: "The main point of the section is to show that persecution arises out of the disciple's relationship to Jesus and through him to the Father, that this relationship provides grounds for fearless endurance and witness, and will, in the end, bring sure reward."[27]

Within the context of this discourse, the parallel sayings on the reciprocal consequences of acknowledging or denying Jesus in Matt 10:32–33 apparently reinforce the preceding commands not to fear (10:26–31). At first glance, this seems to be the syntactic implication of the causal conjunction

---

25. Luz, *Matthew 8-20*, 87.

26. On the varied and evocative faunal imagery of Matt 10:16, see Davies and Allison, *Gospel according to Saint Matthew*, 2:180–81; Luz, *Matthew 8-20*, 87–88.

27. Barton, *Discipleship and Family Ties*, 165. Cf. Weaver, *Matthew's Missionary Discourse*, 104: "But rather than focusing either on ministry (as in 10.5b–15) or on persecution (as in 10.16–23), 10.24–42 combines these two emphases within a discussion focusing on relationships."

οὖν (*oun*, therefore/then) in Matt 10:32. On closer inspection, however, the repetition of the phrase μὴ οὖν φοβηθῆτε/φοβεῖσθε (*mē oun phobēthēte/phobeisthe*; therefore, do not fear/be afraid) in Matt 10:26 and 31 serves to enclose the three exhortations not to fear. This might well signal that the οὖν of Matt 10:32 is resumptive, beginning again, so to speak, from the axiom enunciated in 10:25 that if the master of the house can be slandered, his household slaves can expect worse. If the substance of Matt 10:26–31 were to be excised, 10:32–33 would still follow naturally from 10:24–25. Furthermore, elsewhere in the synoptic tradition, Jesus' saying on the reciprocal consequences of acknowledging or denying him is clustered together with sayings on carrying one's cross and preserving one's life by losing it (see Matt 16:24–28; Mark 8:34–9:1; Luke 9:23–27).[28] As a result, to take Matt 10:32–39 as a coherent literary unit within the third subsection of the commissioning discourse has much to commend it.

Taken alone, the sword saying in Matt 10:34 seems to suggest that the purpose of Jesus' mission as a whole is violent rather than peaceful. Understood within its immediate literary context, however, various features militate against such an interpretation. First, what precedes Jesus' sword saying, both immediately and in the earlier subsections of the discourse, makes clear that its interpretive context is that of inevitable tribulation as a result of associating with Jesus and participating in his mission. Only the prospect of trial and trouble that might lead to the weakening of resolve on the part of disciples explains the need for the promise of reciprocal acknowledgment for those who acknowledge Jesus before others and the warning of reciprocal denial for those who deny Jesus before others (10:32–33).

Second, the opening words of Matt 10:35, ἦλθον γὰρ (*ēlthon gar*, for I came), indicate that this saying about familial strife is epexegetical. Matthew 10:35–36 *explains* or *clarifies* the meaning of the vivid saying of 10:34. Moreover, the recognition that this explanatory saying closely echoes Micah 7:6 reinforces the supposition that it presupposes the prospect of eschatological tribulation ahead of the messianic era. In this connection, the uniquely Matthean phrase in 10:36 not only confirms the allusion to Micah 7:6 but also recalls the opening, and hence governing, lines of the third subsection of the discourse in which disciples are cast as members of Jesus' household. As Barton observes, "The redactional aim implicit here is to reinforce the idea that discipleship involves membership of the household of Jesus and is

---

28. Matthew 16:27, although contextually parallel to Mark 8:38 and Luke 9:26, does not reiterate Jesus' warning about the reciprocal consequences of acknowledging or denying him.

likely to bring division between the disciple and the members of his natural kin-group household."[29]

Third, the sayings constructed in threefold parallelism in Matthew 10:37–38 spell out the implications for disciples of Jesus' "mission statement" articulated in 10:34–36.[30] Taken together, these three parallel sayings indicate that the required relativizing of family loyalties as a result of a disciple's primary loyalty to Jesus is one way of accepting one's cross as a consequence of following Jesus. Jesus' reference to accepting one's cross, the first such reference to "cross" in Matthew's Gospel, is especially important in this context.[31] As Weaver observes, the image of a cross in Matt 10:38 is no less violent than the image of a sword in 10:34; in the case of the cross, however, this is something disciples of Jesus must accept for themselves, not inflict on others.[32] Furthermore, reference to taking up one's cross as the cost of loyalty to Jesus evokes the culmination of Jesus' own life on a cross. Accepting one's cross is to identify not only with Jesus himself but also the manner of life that resulted in his execution on a cross and the means of his mission that precluded inflicting violence on others even when his own life was under threat. For Weaver, "The obvious implication of this statement [in Matt 10:38] is that Jesus himself already faces the death-dealing violence described here in terms of the 'cross.' Accordingly, if the disciple is to 'follow' Jesus, he must face that same violence."[33] This is insightful and important, but Weaver seems not to consider that the reference to "cross" in this literary unit might bear on the meaning of Jesus' sword saying. To my mind, this cross saying within the same literary unit as the sword saying serves to remind readers or hearers that whatever Jesus' sword saying might mean, it neither overrides the character of the life and mission that ended on a cross nor invites participation in Jesus' mission in a way that puts the sword before the cross.

Fourth, the final saying within this literary unit reinforces the cross saying rather than the sword saying. Earlier I suggested that the immediate literary context for Jesus' sword saying begins at Matt 10:32. In support of this suggestion, it is possible to see Matt 10:39 as enclosing this unit with

29. Barton, *Discipleship and Family Ties*, 168. The term οἰκιακός (*oikiakos*, household member), as Barton notes, appears within the NT only in Matt 10:25, 36, which makes more likely the inference that 10:36 recalls 10:25.

30. See Weaver, *Matthew's Missionary Discourse*, 114.

31. For another discussion of Matt 10:34 that emphasizes the importance of its proximity to the saying regarding discipleship in terms of cross-bearing (10:38), see Wells, "Didn't Jesus Say He Came Not to Bring Peace, but a Sword?," 157–60.

32. Weaver, *Matthew's Missionary Discourse*, 114–15.

33. Ibid., 115.

10:32–33 in chiastic fashion, with 10:39a mirroring 10:33 and 10:39b mirroring 10:32. To illustrate the point by means of paraphrase, one who finds his life by denying Jesus will lose it by being disowned by Jesus before his heavenly father (10:39a; cf. 10:33), and one who loses her life for Jesus' sake, by virtue of acknowledging Jesus before others and suffering the consequences, will find it by being acknowledged by Jesus before her heavenly father (10:39b; cf. 10:32). In any case, this paradoxical climactic saying reinforces the cross saying that immediately precedes it in two ways: first, it associates the acceptance of one's cross out of loyalty to Jesus as not only a path in life but also the means to life; and second, its paradoxical content resonates with the life-altering insight that accepting one's cross out of loyalty to Jesus is integral to life in its fullness in a way that wielding a sword could never come close to accomplishing or even approximating.

In short, when Jesus' sword saying is examined closely within its immediate literary context, its apparent vehemence is muted. It clearly does not signal that the purpose of Jesus' mission was to wield the sword rather than to proclaim peace or to conduct his mission peacefully. The "sword" he purportedly brings is symbolic, and the sword saying as a whole, taken in context, is no less paradoxical than the saying about finding life through losing it. The "sword" Jesus brings is neither the principal purpose nor the inclusive intent of his mission but rather its inevitable, albeit incongruous, after- or (perhaps better) counter-effect. This is not a novel interpretation,[34] but it is contested by Weaver, who writes: "By linking this warning [of the severing of family ties in Matt 10:34–36] to the threefold formula 'I have come,' Jesus indicates to his disciples that the situation which he here depicts is not simply the unfortunate, if inevitable, result of their ministry. Rather, the situation of sharp separation within the family and enmity within the household reflects one function of Jesus' ministry, something which he 'has come' specifically in order to bring about. If the disciples experience the violent severing of familial ties, this is because Jesus himself has brought the 'sword' which effects that action."[35]

With due respect for Weaver's interpretive skills, I nevertheless consider her reading of Matt 10:34–36 to be too wooden. The sword saying of Jesus in Matt 10:34 is a pointed distillation of one dimension of what Barton discerns to be the primary point of the third and final subsection of the commissioning discourse—that "persecution arises out of the disciple's

---

34. See Luz, *Matthew 8–20*, 110 (citing Luther and Calvin), but cf. Wells, "Didn't Jesus Say . . . ?," 162–66.

35. Weaver, *Matthew's Missionary Discourse*, 114.

relationship to Jesus."[36] The disciple's association with Jesus inevitably brings with it the kind of negative responses experienced by Jesus himself. Moreover, loyalty of the kind demanded by Jesus puts strain on all other loyalties. Although this dynamic is perfectly understandable in sociohistorical, sociocultural, or socioreligious terms, it is even more comprehensible when perceived in apocalyptic perspective. Interpreted within an apocalyptic frame of reference, familial conflict based on religious loyalty is an expression of conflict at a metaphysical level in which the forces of darkness hold sway over God's world and resist divine initiatives to restore God's will and purpose in the world. In apocalyptic perspective, divine initiatives are intrinsically beneficial for the world, reflective of God's providential goodness and care. Nevertheless, because of hostility to God on the part of forces opposed to God, both spiritual and human, divine initiatives for human well-being inevitably provoke conflict at various levels, including within families.

In F. W. Beare's commentary on Matthew's Gospel, he writes of Jesus' sword saying in Matt 10:34: "The 'sword' is used metaphorically. It is the instrument that divides families. The *effects* produced by the preaching are given as the *purpose* for which Christ came. This is in accord with a Semitic manner of speaking, and indeed thinking, about God. 'Does evil befall a city unless the Lord has done it?' (Amos 3:6). Whatever comes to pass is seen as the fulfilment of the divine purpose. The ultimate effect of the coming of Christ is reconciliation to God and enduring peace; but the immediate effect of the preaching of peace is often strife."[37] Beare's basic insight is correct, in my view, but it is further strengthened by perceiving in Jesus' sword saying not merely a Semitic expression regarding the fulfillment of God's will in the world but a Semitic expression cast in apocalyptic terms. Perceived in apocalyptic perspective, as Jesus' mission as a whole undoubtedly was by Matthew, Jesus' sword saying expresses not simply certain divisive effects of Jesus' mission but also, and at an even more basic level, the incongruent inevitability of hostility in response to divine initiative. From within an apocalyptic worldview, a hostile response to divine initiative is inevitable because of a mind-set shaped by relative dualism,[38] but such hostility is also

---

36. Barton, *Discipleship and Family Ties*, 165. (Barton's summary is cited in full above.)

37. Beare, *Gospel according to Matthew*, 249 (emphasis original). On Luke 12:51, see Gaston, *No Stone on Another*, 339: "Here as often in Semitic thought result is expressed in terms of intention."

38. By "relative dualism" I mean a dualistic worldview qualified by the monotheistic conviction that the God of Israel is the creator of everything. Cosmological dualism, which aids in explaining the presence of evil, is contextualized within an overarching belief or hope that evil is not God's metaphysical equal.

incongruous in view of divine sovereignty and providence. Interpreted in this light, Jesus' sword saying does not express the purpose of his mission but rather its divisive consequences.

If such an interpretive conclusion may be drawn from the immediate context of Jesus' sword saying, is there anything from its broader contexts to corroborate such a view? In view of the coherent narrative framework provided by Matthew for the beginning of Jesus' public mission, the whole of Matt 4:23–11:1 is important for a contextual narrative analysis of Jesus' sword saying. It is clear from the arrangement of this narrative block that Matt 4:23–9:35 provides a summary profile of Jesus' mission, with 9:35–11:1 concerned with the incorporation of Jesus' disciples into his mission. That observation alone leads to the inference that the focus of Jesus' sword saying relates more to the disciples than to his own mission, despite the "I have/ have not come" formulation. Added to this, the description of Jesus' mission up to the point of Jesus' sword saying provides compelling grounds for reading against the grain of its face value. There is an undoubted rigor to Jesus' teaching in the Sermon on the Mount, but nothing in this compilation of his teaching suggests that the purpose of his mission is to wreak violence or even to provoke it. To the contrary, Jesus' teaching in the Sermon on the Mount, especially in his beatitudes and so-called "antitheses," propound a recipe for peace. Similarly, the summary description of Jesus' deeds in Matthew 8–9 envisages Jesus routing demons, provoking consternation, and challenging religious preconceptions, but the overriding impression is of one who acts to bring healing and wholeness to people afflicted in body and mind. At the narrative point at which disciples are commissioned to participate in Jesus' mission in corresponding fashion, Matthew makes clear that this is a consequence of Jesus' compassion for harassed and helpless crowds (9:36). And what the disciples are commissioned to do is precisely an extension of Jesus' own compassionate mission: proclaiming the impending nearness of God's heavenly reign and liberating people from oppressive forces, whether demons or disease or both. In short, the larger literary framework within which Jesus' sword saying must make sense articulates a mission that is both peace-oriented and peaceable in its conduct.

This broad-brush appraisal is reinforced by a more fine-grained analysis of Matthew's use of peace terminology. As Weaver points out, the vocabulary of peace is used sparingly in Matthew's Gospel: the noun "peace" appears twice in Matt 10:13 and twice in 10:34, and the noun "peacemaker" or "peace practitioner" occurs only at 5:9.[39] For Weaver, not only the paucity of peace references but also their overall ambivalence requires

---

39. Weaver, "As sheep in the midst of wolves," 123.

contextualizing within the broader "portrait of peace" sketched across the Gospel as a whole. To that end, her study of mission and peace in Matthew's Gospel shows how Matthew's depiction of the respective missions of the biblical prophets, John the Baptist, Jesus, Jesus' original disciples, and the later disciples of Jesus are conducted peacefully. Briefly stated, Weaver shows that Matthew's Gospel in its entirety presents those sent by God as acting peaceably and for peace. In and of itself, this is an important observation, but it is further reinforced by the narrative plotting of both the vocabulary of peace and Jesus' various "I have/have not come . . ." sayings.

All of Matthew's explicit references to peace occur between 4:23 and 11:1, with all four occurrences of the noun ἡ εἰρήνη (*hē eirēnē*) appearing in the commissioning discourse. Matthew's first reference to peace occurs within Jesus' beatitudes, when Jesus blesses peacemakers who will be known as children (literally, "sons") of God. Here, within Jesus' vision of life in harmony with God's heavenly reign, practitioners of peace are acknowledged, by virtue of their peacemaking, to belong to God's family because in this particular respect they are like God. Peacemakers, along with the meek, the merciful, the pure in heart, and those who crave justice, are attuned to the reign of God. The blessing pronounced on peacemakers is the seventh beatitude and is directly followed by the blessing on those who are persecuted for their righteousness or justice. In compositional terms, it is noteworthy that the first and eighth beatitudes enclose Jesus' blessings as a whole by virtue of the promise that God's heavenly reign belongs to those blessed (5:3, 10).[40] Apparently as an afterthought, Matthew adds a ninth blessing, which reinforces the substance of the eighth beatitude. Not only is the blessing on peacemakers followed by a blessing on those who are persecuted for doing what is right in God's sight but the perturbing reality of persecution for living in accordance with the priorities of divine reign is also emphasized by the addition of a ninth beatitude that mars the compositional *inclusio* created by the first and eighth beatitudes. No doubt there is more than one reason for this, but one reason for the emphasis on the reality of persecution in the eighth and ninth beatitudes is the inevitable, yet incongruous, experience of affliction for loyalty to Jesus and his vision of life. Peacemaking and justice provoke hostility and conflict but not because that is their purpose; peacemaking and justice provoke hostility and conflict because the wider world is out of step with God's will and way.

Keeping in mind the narrative design and integrity of Matt 4:23–11:1, it is critical that Jesus' blessing on peacemakers occurs where it does—in the

---

40. See also Mauser, *Gospel of Peace*, 36–37, who remarks on the verbal and thematic resonances between the seventh and eighth beatitudes in Matt 5:9–10 and Jesus' consonant command to love enemies in 5:44–45a.

opening lines of Jesus' first discourse. By virtue of their narrative placement, the beatitudes establish the character of Jesus' public teaching. If God's heavenly reign has drawn near enough to exert pressure on the present (4:17), the beatitudes compose its spiritual and moral charter. Thus, when Jesus commissions his disciples to convey their peace or to let it return to them, depending on how they are received (10:13), such peace is freighted not only by eschatological associations but also by the vision of life characterized by the beatitudes. In tandem with the other beatitudes, the blessing on peacemakers governs the description of Jesus' mission in Matt 4:23–9:35. And since the remainder of this narrative block envisages the disciples being commissioned by Jesus to share in his mission (9:35–11:1), the blessing on peacemakers also governs the description of how Jesus' mission is to be continued and extended by his disciples. The mission of the disciples is envisaged as a mission of peace practitioners because they are participating in a peacemaking mission.

When readers or hearers come to Jesus' sword saying, in which the vocabulary of peace occurs twice more for the final time in Matthew's Gospel, it grates because at the literal level it contradicts everything that comes before it. This alongside its narrative placement near the end of this coherent narrative block invites an interpretation of the saying against the grain of its literal meaning. As I have argued already, such an interpretation is provided immediately thereafter in Matt 10:35–36, in which it becomes clear that the "sword" of which Jesus speaks is the inevitable, if incongruous, hostility and accompanying familial divisions provoked by his mission. The theological and social dynamics reflected in Matt 10:34–36 may be understood to "flesh out" the placement of the blessing on peacemakers immediately preceding the two concluding blessings on those who are persecuted because of justice or for the sake of Jesus (5:9–11).

Such considerations are further supported by the precise way in which Jesus' sword saying is formulated in Matt 10:34. At four points in Matthew's Gospel, Jesus makes explicit asseverations about his mission (5:17; 9:13; 10:34–35; 20:28). In total, however, there are seven statements in which Jesus affirms or denies that he has come to do something.[41] The first six of these seven statements are expressed in the first person and are clustered

41. For earlier influential discussions of such "I have (not) come" sayings in the synoptic tradition, see Bultmann, *History of the Synoptic Tradition*, 150–66, and Arens, *ΗΛΘΟΝ-Sayings in the Synoptic Tradition*. More recently, see Gathercole, *Preexistent Son*, 81–189, for whom such sayings, especially those clustered in Matt 10:34–36 and Luke 12:49–51, constitute the clearest basis in the Synoptic Gospels for affirming the presence of a preexistent (angelomorphic) Christology. For an intratextual, audience-oriented discussion of these sayings in Matthew's Gospel, see Carter, "Jesus' 'I have come' Statements."

within the narrative block beginning at Matt 4:23 and ending at 11:1. The seventh occurs much later in the narrative and is expressed with reference to the Son of humanity (20:28). In Matt 5:17 Jesus declares, "Do not suppose that I have come to destroy the law or the prophets; I have not come to destroy but rather to fulfill [them]." In Matt 9:13 he says, as the clinching words of his response to the Pharisees' question about his reason for eating with toll-collectors and sinners, "For I have not come to call righteous but rather sinful people." Then in Matt 10:34 Jesus asserts, "Do not suppose that I have come to sow peace upon the earth; I have not come to sow peace but rather a sword." This is followed immediately by a sixth such statement: "For I have come to set a person against his father and a daughter against her mother and a daughter-in-law against her mother-in-law."

As with the vocabulary of peace in Matthew's Gospel, the first such statements occur near the beginning of Jesus' first discourse and the last such statements expressed in the first person occur near the end of Jesus' second discourse. Remarkably, the formulation of the paired statements in Matt 10:34 parallels 5:17 exactly: "Do not suppose that I have come to . . . ; I have not come to . . . but rather to . . . ." This is instructive. In the case of Matt 5:17, it is clear that what Jesus means by fulfilling, rather than destroying, the Torah and the prophets is elaborated in what follows, including the so-called antitheses of 5:21–48, a number of which are peace-oriented. In light of the formal parallelism between the sayings of Matt 5:17 and 10:34, one expects that what Jesus means by sowing a sword, rather than peace, upon the earth will be elaborated in what follows. This expectation is confirmed by the immediately succeeding "I have come" saying in Matt 10:35, whose function is to explain or clarify the saying that precedes it. In other words, the pattern of Matthew's "I have/have not come" sayings supports what has already been argued about the meaning of Jesus' sword saying on other grounds.[42]

---

42. For Gathercole, *Preexistent Son*, 113–76, the various "I have come" sayings in Matt 10:34–36 and Luke 12:49–51 most obviously refer to divine judgment as the purpose of Jesus' coming, but his exegesis is focused on whether these sayings imply a coming from heaven and hence preexistence. Since such "I have come" sayings are most closely and amply paralleled by various announcements on the part of heavenly angels—beginning with references from the book of Daniel and including some from apocalyptic texts roughly contemporaneous with the Gospels—one wonders why the apocalyptic frame of reference for making sense of such analogies does not feature more explicitly in Gathercole's exegesis of these sayings.

CONCLUDING COMMENTS

Close attention to various aspects of Jesus' sword saying within its narrative context leads to the following conclusions. First, this saying has nothing to do with wielding a literal sword. Jesus' statement about sowing a sword implies inevitable family discord arising from discordant attitudes toward Jesus. The version of the saying in Luke 12:51, which features the language of "division" rather than "sword," is closely equivalent in meaning.

Second, Jesus' sword saying makes best sense within a Jewish apocalyptic frame of reference, in which a time of tribulation was expected to precede the messianic age characterized by *shalom*. Although consistent with the conviction that a literal sword is not in view, the idea that the intended purpose of Jesus' mission was to ignite the tinderbox of tribulation so as to hasten the messianic era is not much less disturbing than the idea that Jesus' express purpose was to usher in God's heavenly reign by violent means. Within an apocalyptic worldview, however, Jesus' sword saying is less an expression of purpose than of the inevitability (and incongruity) of hostile resistance to divine initiatives for the world's good. To reiterate, this is perhaps nowhere better expressed than in the prologue to the Fourth Gospel, in which the Light of life comes into the world but is not received by those whose very existence derives from that generative source (John 1:3-5, 9-11). Or, to recall remarks by T. W. Manson on Matt 10:34-36 and Luke 12:49-53,

> The manifestation of the Kingdom means warfare to the bitter end against evil; and evil is so firmly entrenched in human life and human relations that much suffering and heartbreak are inevitable before it can be cast out. Those who think that the Messiah will come and transform the world by a wave of the magic wand are sadly mistaken. The coming of Jesus brings tension: it brings to sharpest issue the struggle between the Kingdom of God and the forces of evil. It compels men to take sides; and members of the same family may be in opposite camps.[43]

Third, both the immediate literary context of Jesus' sword saying within Matthew's commissioning discourse and its broader context within the larger narrative block beginning with 4:23 and ending at 11:1 encourage an interpretation of this saying in line with the general tenor of Jesus' mission and message. Such contextual considerations are further supported by Matthew's use of peace terminology and also by his formulation and narrative placement of Jesus' "I have/have not come" sayings.

---

43. Manson, *Sayings of Jesus*, 120-21.

Finally, regarding this particular sword saying, Allison conjectures that Jesus himself may have deliberately set one passage of Scripture (Micah 7:6) against others ("prophetic promises of peace") so as to provoke reflection on discordant eschatological expectations with a view to discerning a "deeper concord."[44] Whether Matthew discerned such a "deeper concord" is open to dispute, especially in light of the tension between Jesus' pronouncement of blessing on peacemakers in Matt 5:9 and his affirmation in Matt 10:34 that he came not to sow peace but rather a sword. "The conflict between these two sayings reaches deep," as expressed by Ulrich Mauser. "It signals the tension between opposite ends of one and the same thing, the kingship of God, and this tension must not be quickly and cheaply released, otherwise the subject itself becomes very seriously distorted."[45] Provided one reads Matthew's Gospel as an expression of apocalyptic hope, it is possible to read both 5:9 and 10:34 as integral, indeed, complementary dimensions of Jesus' mission as the Messiah of peace.

---

44. Allison, "Q 12:51–53 and Mark 9:11–13," 303.

45. Mauser, *Gospel of Peace*, 36. Cf. Davies and Allison, *Gospel according to Saint Matthew*, 2:217n22, who consider that Matthew provides no indication of how he harmonized the sayings he recorded at 5:9 and 10:34—they discern a possible answer in Matt 10:12–15, which they take to imply that "the disciple, though a peacemaker, does not purchase peace at any price."

2

Perturbing Parables

An Unforgiving Slave and a Throne Claimant

SCHOLARSHIP ON THE PARABLES of Jesus is vast, and several of his individual parables have been afforded book-length treatments. In line with the central concern of this book, however, only three parables that seemingly envisage God, the reign of God, or Jesus as implicated in violence are addressed: the parable of the Vineyard Tenants, found in the same relative context in all three Synoptic Gospels (Matt 21:33–43; Mark 12:1–12; Luke 20:9–18); the parable of the Unforgiving Slave in Matt 18:23–35; and the parable of the Throne Claimant in Luke 19:11–28. The parable of the Vineyard Tenants is considered in chapter 6, following discussion of the temple incident in chapter 5. Together, this second chapter and chapter 6 serve as dual spotlights focused on a select number of Gospel parables in which violence is apparently indispensable and hence integral, thereby raising the question of whether violence is inextricably associated with God or divine sovereignty.

Certain parables in the Synoptic Gospels seem to anticipate divine retributive violence at the end of the age (eschatological vengeance). Some of these feature in chapter 9. This chapter, by contrast, focuses on two parables in which the eschatological element, if present, is neither essential nor decisive, although that is a somewhat controversial judgment, especially in the case of the parable of the Throne Claimant. Whether or not a parable relates to the *eschaton* or divine judgment at the end of the age is relatively unimportant in this context, however. The chief concern is whether any of Jesus' parables projects a picture of God as resorting to violence, either ultimately or more proximately.

In the scholarly study of the parables, one preoccupation has been to ascertain whether and, if so, how much of any given parable is "authentic," that is, attributable to the historical Jesus.[1] As important as such a concern is, not only for comprehending Jesus as a historical figure but also for interpreting the parables in sociocultural contexts vastly different from their original settings, discussion of the parables in this book concentrates on their respective canonical renderings. The primary reason for this is that, from the perspective of New Testament theology and ethics, it is the canonical record of Jesus' parables that has shaped Christian morality and moral vision, not putative earlier versions of his parables.

TEACHING FORGIVENESS BY THREATENING TORTURE?

The Parable of the Unforgiving Slave (Matt 18:23–35)

This parable is found only in Matthew's Gospel, although another much briefer parable featuring the theme of forgiveness in relation to disproportionate debts appears in Luke 7:41–43. The parable of the Unforgiving Slave is placed at the end of the fourth of Matthew's five discourses, which begins with Jesus' disciples asking him to identify the greatest or most honored person in God's heavenly reign (18:1). In response, Jesus utters the solemn saying that entry into God's heavenly reign is contingent on becoming like children and that within the kingdom of the heavens humility counts for true greatness. The discourse continues by featuring two main themes: preventing "falling away" (18:5–10) and restoring to community any who stray (18:12–35). Throughout, the discourse is directed toward disciples and is concerned with interpersonal conduct and relations within the community of faith. Moreover, it begins with the question of status within the kingdom of the heavens (referred to three separate times in Matt 18:1–4) and ends with a parable of God's heavenly reign to reinforce Jesus' instruction to forgive without keeping a record of wrongs (18:21–35).

In many respects, this parable serves its hortatory purpose well. The parable begins by clearly and indeed emphatically signaling that its purpose is to reinforce Jesus' endorsement of forgiveness without limits: "For this reason [διὰ τοῦτο, *dia touto*], the kingdom of the heavens is comparable to

---

1. See, e.g., Meier, *Marginal Jew*, 5:230–376, for whom only four parables attributed to Jesus in the Gospels meet his criteria of authenticity (see 12–17): Mustard Seed, Tenants in the Vineyard, Talents/Minas, and Invited Guests (or "Great Supper"). In versions of three of these four parables, violence is a prominent feature.

a human king."[2] This king's compassionate magnanimity and mercy is on display when he both releases his exorbitantly indebted slave and forgives his unrepayable debt (18:27). Moreover, his question toward the end of the parable is both morally compelling and theologically coherent within a biblical framework: "Was it not necessary for you also to have shown mercy to your fellow slave, as I myself showed mercy to you?" (18:33). Here, as elsewhere in the biblical tradition, the presumption shines through that human conduct should be patterned on divine character traits.[3] In what follows this question, however, what is affirmed of the king and, by extension, Jesus' heavenly father is both theologically and morally confounding.

At the end of this parable, the king,[4] angered by the discrepancy between his own magnanimity and his slave's mercilessness, puts the unforgiving slave at the (non)mercy of tormentors until he pays the whole of his unrepayable debt. The noun here translated as "tormentor" and often as "torturer," ὁ βασανιστής (*ho basanistēs*), occurs only here in the entire New Testament, although the cognate noun, ὁ βασανισμός (*ho basanismos*, torment or torture), appears six times in the book of Revelation. It is conceivable that Matt 18:34 refers to jailers rather than to tormentors, but both the context and the plural form of the noun suggest that more than incarceration is envisaged. How the king is entitled to do this after both releasing the slave and forgiving his debt, or how payment in full is conceivable if the slave is in the hands of tormentors are questions external to the parable's more finely focused field of vision. But only the moral torpidity that comes with overfamiliarity can desensitize readers to this parable's jarring conclusion. Even if some form of behavior modification was called for to bring the "evil slave" (18:32) to his moral senses, surely measures other than torture and more in keeping with the king's initial compassion could have been employed.[5]

---

2. Although Matt 18:23 relates the succeeding parable most immediately to Jesus' saying on forgiveness in 18:22, the placement of the parable as the culmination of the discourse makes it reasonable to read it as reinforcing the teaching of the discourse as a whole, especially the second part concerned with restoring to community any who stray.

3. See Luz, *Matthew 8-20*, 474, who considers that Matt 18:32-33 "reveals the thinking that underlies the entire parable. The slave should have imitated the king in granting mercy. Theologically the *imitatio Dei* stands in the background here (cf. 5:48; Luke 6:36)."

4. After being identified in royal terms in Matt 18:23, the king is thereafter referred to as the slave's lord or master.

5. Here I demur from the otherwise illuminating discussion of this parable by Reiser, *Jesus and Judgment*, 276: "for the sake of justice he [the king] can do nothing else but withdraw his act of forgiveness and hand this blockhead over to the torturers." Note within this assertion implicit restrictions on the notions of justice and sovereignty.

After all, it should not escape notice that the king's ultimate determination effectively mimics, while also intensifying, the merciless slave's cruel (as well as ineffectual) treatment of a fellow slave. This is precisely the opposite of the social norm for magnanimous rulers or the biblical norm for God. This is a parable, of course, so not every detail should be squeezed for potential meaning. One should not push this parable's logic too far, according to Christopher Marshall: "The reaction of the king is intended to underline the eschatological seriousness of the demand placed upon the messianic community to practice forgiveness, as well as to clarify that forgiveness is not a matter of cheap grace or eternal leniency."[6]

With respect to the parable itself, Marshall's point is fair and well made. Even allowing for the interpretive guideline of end stress in relation to parables, one need not take this parable to mean that forgiveness within God's heavenly reign is enforced by means of torment. As Snodgrass points out, "For most parables what comes at the end is the clinching indicator of intent."[7] Accordingly, even though the king's revised and severely punitive action occurs at the end and must therefore feature prominently in one's appraisal of the parable, that recognition need not lead one to say that those who do not forgive as they have been forgiven will ultimately be handed over to tormentors. Expressed in more prosaic terms, this parable might be said to warn against undermining divine compassion and forgiveness by failing to pass on to others what has been vouchsafed to us. Or, in words that Jesus taught people to pray, "Forgive us . . . inasmuch as we also have forgiven . . ." (Matt 6:12; cf. Luke 11:4).[8]

As attractive as such a reading of this parable might seem, it comes aground on Jesus' concluding interpretive application in Matt 18:35. There he affirms that his heavenly father will *likewise do* to those within the community of faith who do not sincerely forgive others within it. In short, in God's heavenly reign, failure to forgive leads inevitably to unremitting torment. One might be inclined to cite this concluding application as but another example of Jesus' use of hyperbole to provoke circumspection, except that Matthew's Gospel is peppered with parables that not only end

---

6. Marshall, *Beyond Retribution*, 77. Cf. Reiser, *Jesus and Judgment*, 280: "Because we ourselves have received God's grace, we can and should give up judging; we should forgive and be generous. Otherwise, we have received grace in vain."

7. Snodgrass, *Stories with Intent*, 30. Snodgrass's interpretation of the parable of the Unforgiving Slave supports Marshall's reading. Cf. Carter, *Matthew and the Margins*, 370–75; Carter, "Resisting and Imitating Empire," 262–68.

8. Cf. Travis, *Christ and the Judgement*, 223. Commenting on Matt 18:34, Travis opines: "In theological terms, this suggests that, when people refuse or abuse God's forgiveness, they turn their backs on the only way their sins can be removed, so that at the final judgement they will be faced by irrevocable condemnation."

violently but also picture God (or God's agents) as a violent avenger(s).[9] In other words, both the ending to the parable of the Unforgiving Slave and its application at the culmination of Jesus' fourth discourse in the Gospel are of a piece with a prominent dimension of Matthew's theology—divine judgment as severe and unremitting retribution. This contrasts markedly, however, with the image of God that, according to Jesus in Matt 5:43–48, authorizes indiscriminate regard for others, including enemies, and is also reflected in the earlier part of the parable of the Unforgiving Slave (18:27).

Matthew's stark contrast between the God of indiscriminate love and the God of retributive vengeance puts readers in an interpretive bind. The reception history of Matthew's Gospel reveals that to hold competing images of God in dialectical tension is impossible at the institutional level when ecclesial authority, power, and interests are at stake. Good minds in touch with sensitive viscera might be capable of combining for good seemingly incompatible God-images,[10] but that is not what the church triumphant has made of Matthew's contrasting conceptions of God. Divine judgment is not antithetical to divine goodness, but to affirm this depends on what is understood by divine judgment. If divine judgment entails enforcement of what is good by means of torture or punishment for evil that is solely retributive and/or incessant, such judgment can hardly be said to cohere with goodness.

Recognizing that Jesus' parable of the Unforgiving Slave culminates on a disquieting theological note, Thomas Yoder Neufeld devotes a chapter to this parable in his *Killing Enmity: Violence and the New Testament*.[11] Nearly half of his chapter is devoted to surveying the parable's story line, to exploring the nature and function of parables, and to contextualizing the parable within the fourth of Matthew's five discourses, which Yoder Neufeld describes as "a 'sermon' on relationships within the community."[12] The perplexing problem this parable presents, as Yoder Neufeld sums up succinctly, is that "the threat of torture serves as a motivation for forgiveness. What is perhaps most striking is that this tale is placed in immediate proximity with Jesus' summons to boundless grace."[13]

Regarding the nature of Jesus' parables and their role or function, Yoder Neufeld correctly observes that although many of Jesus' parables relating

---

9. See Reid, "Violent Endings in Matthew's Parables"; Reid, "Which God Is With Us?"

10. See, e.g., Luz, *Matthew 8–20*, 468–77; Snodgrass, "Key Questions," 181–84; and Black, "Shouting at the Legally Deaf," 311–22.

11. Yoder Neufeld, *Killing Enmity*, chap. 3, entitled "Forgive, or else!"

12. Ibid., 40–45.

13. Ibid., 37.

to divine reign trade on common conceptions of authoritarian rule, such connotations are often, if not invariably, subverted in Jesus' teaching. He also points out that many of Jesus' parables are replete with violent language and imagery, the question being whether the purpose of such imagery is to draw critical attention to daily realities of violent injustice or to provoke "parabolic judgment" by "sifting" those who are open to divine reign from those who are not.[14] Regarding Jesus' parable of the Unforgiving Slave, these are pertinent considerations. To adapt questions that Yoder Neufeld raises in relation to another of Matthew's disconcerting parables, is the dominant voice of this parable really that of Jesus or does Matthew retell the parable with a twist whose violence is fundamentally incongruous with the magnanimous mercy of Jesus?

Within the fourth discourse of Jesus in Matthew's Gospel, the prospect of divine violence features well before the culminating parable of the Unforgiving Slave. After identifying with a little child (18:5), Jesus continues by warning against causing "little ones" to fall from faith. For anyone within the community who trips up a "little one," the implicit threat seems to be a fate worse than drowning in the chaotic waters of the sea (18:6–8). Then Jesus warns against falling from faith because of temptation to sin. Echoing his hyperbolic warnings from the Sermon on the Mount (5:29–30), Jesus recommends self-mutilation as a means of avoiding the "eternal fire" of Gehenna (18:8–9).[15] "The rage of Jesus, indeed God's, is violent in the extreme," Yoder Neufeld writes, "but ironically a measure of the gravity of violence, most especially against 'little ones.'"[16] The threat of divine violence in this section of the discourse can thus be seen to serve a twofold function: as an index of the gravity of sin that undermines faith, especially for the vulnerable within the community of faith; and as a warning of future judgment for those who pay no consideration to the well-being of the vulnerable or who persist in sin that undermines faith. The prospect of divine violence at the conclusion of the discourse is of a piece with this earlier section, except that its purpose seems more singular—recurring retribution.

Within its present literary context, the parable of the Unforgiving Slave is clearly intended to reinforce the importance of forgiveness. Even the king's initial forgiveness of debt is a once-only occurrence, however, which is emphatically reversed once he learns that the forgiven slave fails to

---

14. Ibid., 38–40.

15. That Jesus' Gehenna sayings relating to sins of the eye, hand, or foot have sexual sins in view is well argued by Allison, *Jesus of Nazareth*, 178–82. On sexual matters, Jesus seems to have been uncompromising, but this is not to say that such vivid sayings were intended to be taken literally.

16. Yoder Neufeld, *Killing Enmity*, 42.

emulate his own forgiveness. One could probably accept that the forgiveness of an unpayable debt reinforces the command to forgive without keeping count, except that the king reverses his earlier forgiveness, reimposes the entire debt, and reverts to a form of retribution both more cruel than his initial punitive solution (18:25) and even less likely to result in retrieving the debt. And all this, as Yoder Neufeld points out, is explicitly said to be analogous to the reign of heaven (18:23) and also to the way in which God repays refusal to forgive (18:35).[17]

For reasons such as these, interpreters have adopted various measures to draw the sting from the tail of this parable. Some dispute whether this parable goes back to Jesus and attribute it instead to Matthew, perhaps as an elaboration of a dominical parable (cf. Luke 7:41–42). Others accept that the parable itself derives from Jesus but that Matthew is responsible for its present context and purpose, as well as for its concluding elaboration.[18] The evangelists evidently adapted and recontextualized sayings of Jesus, so it is reasonable to suppose that in this case there might well be some discrepancy between the parable in the form in which Jesus taught it, if authentic, and Matthew's adaptation of it. Without the final analogy in Matt 18:35, for example, this parable can be heard as a forceful brain-teaser regarding the moral incompatibility between either presuming or relying on divine forgiveness and at the same time withholding forgiveness to others. On such a reading, the conclusion to the parable, at which point the king hands the unforgiving slave over to tormentors until his unpayable debt is paid, underscores the gravity of failing to emulate divine mercy, with the incongruousness of the king's actions preventing an equating of divine judgment with torture. Once one allows that a parable Jesus told was different from how it is (re)told in one or more of the Gospels, however, it is almost anyone's guess as to how and to how much the original differs from its later adaptations. This question is especially fraught for parables found in only one of the Gospels.

Yoder Neufeld expresses the legitimate concern about absolving Jesus of projecting a violent God-image in this parable by attributing it instead to Matthew. Parables are not straightforward lessons, and their point is not superficially transparent. It is therefore possible for the parable of the

---

17. Ibid., 45–46.

18. Some who differentiate between parables as Jesus taught them and their adaptation by the evangelists discern more mundane concerns on the part of Jesus. Jesus was apparently less interested in God and divine reign than in drawing attention to inequalities of various kinds. As burdened about justice as Jesus (and his contemporaries) may have been, this was not, in my view, at the expense of theological and/or religious concerns.

Unforgiving Slave, replete as it is with incongruous features and disturbing details, to reinforce instruction against whose grain it apparently cuts. To drive home this point, Yoder Neufeld proposes various ways in which this parable can be seen to reinforce Jesus' teaching on forgiveness.[19] First, evident absurdities within the parable itself, such as handing the unforgiving slave over to tormenters until he pays his (unpayable) debt, effectively deconstruct the king's cruelty, in part by echoing the absurdity of Jesus' instruction about the number of times one should be prepared to forgive. Second, this parable may serve to illustrate *dimensions of forgiveness*, for example, that forgiveness is an expression of "sovereign freedom at work," which may and indeed should be emulated,[20] or that there is a close but not predictable correlation between forgiveness and repentance. Third, to focus solely on the issue of violence might well lead one to overlook the point that the slave's fundamental fault was to act contrary to his master's magnanimous mercy. And related to this, the parable presses home the point that forgiveness divinely granted occurs within what Yoder Neufeld describes as "the framework of divine accountability and reckoning."[21] One who reckons on the forgiveness offered by God is then accountable to God's own reckoning as to whether one's life and relationships have been shaped by divine grace and mercy.

Yoder Neufeld recognizes that this final point—or at least the precise way in which this parable drives home this point—is what perplexes certain readers today. "It is the violence associated with the consequences of not forgiving that constitutes the *skandalon* of this passage," he writes.[22] For this reason, he reviews three ways of avoiding what seems integral to the meaning of this parable: that God judges whether and how people "extend" divine forgiveness in their social relations. The first of these is to deny that this parable is concerned with God, divine forgiveness, and divine judgment; rather, its purpose is to expose unjust and violent dimensions of the world within which disciples must exercise discernment about acting in conformity with divine rule. A second approach is to reinterpret *divine* judgment in terms of the inescapable consequences of sinful human decisions. And a third resolution is Willard Swartley's suggestion that, since the Bible rarely refers to divine violence against humanity but generally identifies human vi-

---

19. Yoder Neufeld, *Killing Enmity*, 48–54. For similarly sagacious remarks, see Black, "Shouting at the Legally Deaf," 315, 317–20.

20. Yoder Neufeld considers that the master/slaves analogy transposes into the (heavenly) father/sons analogy in Matt 18:35, but this stretches things too far, in my view.

21. Yoder Neufeld, *Killing Enmity*, 52.

22. Ibid.

olence as the reason for divine judgment, to apply the language of "violence" to God is to commit a "category fallacy." Yoder Neufeld's critical response to such proposals is respectful, nuanced, and persuasive.[23] The parable of the Unforgiving Slave bespeaks divine judgment no less than divine mercy, albeit within certain limits. He writes: "Let me propose that this parable has a limited function. We should allow it to lay bare a brutal world but also to lend weight and urgency to the injunction to forgive. We should not take it to set out a theory of judgement, or even to serve by itself as an adequate analogy of judgement. The 'story world' of this parable should not be allowed to undermine the fundamental conviction pervading the writings of the evangelists that the divine judge is just, loving, merciful and always, from a 'debtor's' perspective, surprisingly so."[24]

There is little to gainsay in Yoder Neufeld's illuminating discussion of the parable of the Unforgiving Slave. On two points, however, more might be—or might have been—said. First, although I am in fundamental agreement with all that Yoder Neufeld affirms about divine judgment in response to what he perceives to be the "scandal" of this parable, at no point does he address head on whether the character of divine judgment is analogous to torture. Rather, his interpretive procedure is to accept that this parable points to an understanding of the judging God as both merciful and severe but also to draw attention to *other biblical resources* that display divine mercy tempering divine judgment.[25] As insightful as Yoder Neufeld's remarks are in this regard, surely the theological conclusion to be drawn from this "tempering" is that divine judgment cannot be conceived as torment for the purpose of retribution alone.

Furthermore, in relation to the "scandal" of this parable, Yoder Neufeld might have extended his deliberations on ways in which certain biblical traditions envisage divine mercy as tempering divine judgment by discussing more restorative or transformative constructions of divine judgment.[26] Although the parable of the Unforgiving Slave ultimately construes divine judgment as purely punitive no less than cruel, there are other conceptions

---

23. Ibid., 52–54.

24. Ibid., 54. In his very next sentence, Yoder Neufeld correctly remarks that this parable does not, by itself, set out a fully fledged theory of forgiveness. That divine judgment inevitably *surprises* is reinforced by Black, "Shouting at the Legally Deaf," 320–22.

25. Yoder Neufeld, *Killing Enmity*, 54.

26. Readers familiar with the concluding pages of Yoder Neufeld's treatment of the parable of the Unforgiving Slave might consider my criticism uncharitable at this point. Since chapter 3 of *Killing Enmity* focuses on the relation between divine judgment and violence, however, more attention to non-retributive or restorative conceptions of divine judgment within biblical traditions would have enriched this discussion.

of judgment in the biblical tradition. And in view of the retributive mindset displayed throughout much of Matthew's Gospel, especially in contrast to his canonical counterparts, there is good reason to attribute to Matthew the strictly retributive and indeed vengeful analogy to divine judgment at the conclusion to the parable. Yoder Neufeld is loath to pit Matthew against Jesus, but one senses that he does so without explicitly saying so. By and large, his discussion of the parable of the Unforgiving Slave focuses on the parable prior to its concluding analogy in Matt 18:35. (This might explain why his discussion of divine judgment does not consider non-retributive constructions.) Moreover, leading up to his various considerations for reading this parable as "Jesus' teaching on forgiveness," he writes: "Even if we grant that *Matthew* has placed this parable into this 'sermon', and that *he may well have (over)stressed the lesson in verse 35*."[27] Here Yoder Neufeld reveals that, if pressed, he cannot attribute to Jesus an understanding of divine judgment analogous to cruel and senseless torture. At this point, in my view, his interpretive instincts are correctly attuned, and it would have been fruitful for him to have been more explicit about this and what interpretive judgments must follow.

Although the parable of the Unforgiving Slave is apparently intended to reinforce the command of Jesus regarding merciful and limitless forgiveness, its concluding analogy in its present form threatens to undermine the instruction it is intended to reinforce. For this reason, I suggest that it should be read counter to its intended purpose, by which I mean that, instead of reading the parable of the Unforgiving Slave to reinforce the command of Jesus to forgive, the parable should itself be read in light of Jesus' command, thereby retaining the close relation between the parable and Jesus' instruction on uncalculating forgiveness but also destabilizing its concluding analogy attributed to Jesus. At the crucial point, according to the interpretive rule of end stress, the parable backfires and may therefore be deconstructed by the command it purportedly reinforces, provided any such deconstruction retains while also reconfiguring the indispensable notion of divine judgment.

---

27. Yoder Neufeld, *Killing Enmity*, 49; emphasis added. For the view that Matt 18:35 is the evangelist's elaboration of a dominical parable, see Luz, *Matthew 8–20*, 475–76. "The fundamental question," according to Luz, "is whether one can still experience the judging 'Father' of Matt 18:35 as the same Father who through Christ forgives human guilt in unending love."

CHALLENGING CONVENTION ABOUT GOD'S SOVEREIGN REIGN?

The Parable of the Throne Claimant (Luke 19:11-28)

The parable found in Luke 19:11-28 is known by various names, among them the parable of the (Ten) Minas or Pounds, the parable of the Nobleman-King or King-Judge, the parable of the Throne Claimant, or, more simply, Luke's Kingship Parable. The most apposite of these is probably the parable of the Throne Claimant because this descriptor captures the concept that a man of means by birth craves yet more power and recompenses those who oppose his self-aggrandizing aspirations with royal ruthlessness.

Within Luke's account of Jesus' mission and message, this parable occurs at a critical narrative juncture—near the culmination of Jesus' journey to Jerusalem (9:51-19:46). As is well known, Luke's central section comprising Jesus' journey to Jerusalem is both distinctive and crucial to his shaping of the Jesus story. In Luke 9:51 Jesus fixes his face for Jerusalem, and in 19:45 he enters the temple precincts within Jerusalem. The close proximity of Jesus to Jerusalem is apparently decisive for the Lukan perspective on the parable of the Throne Claimant.[28] In Luke 19:11 the rationale provided for this parable is that Jesus was near Jerusalem and it seemed to his audience that the reign of God was about to appear forthwith (παραχρῆμα, *parachrēma*). Immediately following the parable, moreover, Luke narrates that on saying these things Jesus journeyed ahead, going up to Jerusalem (19:28). Then follows Jesus' non-triumphal approach to Jerusalem (19:29-40),[29] his lament over Jerusalem (19:41-44), and his "occupation" of the temple to teach people in Jerusalem (19:45-48). The parable of the Throne Claimant thus concludes Jesus' instruction within the section of Luke's Gospel most evidently devoted to the teaching of Jesus on various vital themes, for example, discipleship, prayer, wealth, and divine mercy. As such, this parable is something of a capstone to the teaching of Jesus en route to Jerusalem. Yet its content perplexes and perturbs.

Various features of this parable invite comment, including the parable's relation to its alleged Matthean parallel (Matt 25:14-30),[30] its apparent

---

28. On the immediate literary context of this parable, see Dowling, *Taking Away the Pound*, 75-77.

29. See Kinman, "Parousia, Jesus' 'A-Triumphal' Entry," 279-94, who argues that in Lukan perspective Jesus does not enter Jerusalem in triumph. On this point he is persuasive, but his further interpretive inference that Jesus' prophecy of Jerusalem's destruction was provoked by his failure to receive a celebratory welcome to the city is unconvincing.

30. See, e.g., Meier, *Marginal Jew*, 5:278-310, 346-62. For Meier, a dually attested and hence probably authentic parable of Slaves Entrusted with Money stands behind

allusion to the attempt by Archelaus to secure for himself his father's title as king,[31] its redaction to serve Luke's purposes, and its significance for Luke's (and perhaps even Jesus' own) eschatology.[32] Here the focus is to explore certain perturbing features of the parable that have long been understood to reflect on Jesus and/or his understanding of God.

The parable of the Throne Claimant is commonly understood as an eschatological parable, cautioning against imminent eschatological expectations (at least before the time of Luke's own composition) while also warning against either inaction or non-industrious action during the time granted by the apparent delay of the *parousia*.[33] Such an interpretation is perhaps inevitable if this parable is understood to be a variation on Matthew's parable of the Talents.[34] Taken alone and read in narrative context, however, various features of Luke's parable of the Throne Claimant resist not only the standard eschatological interpretation but also the alternative eschatological interpretations proffered by Luke Timothy Johnson and N. T. Wright, in which this parable is construed to signal imminent eschatological resolution, either when Jesus enters Jerusalem as king (Johnson) or when God's reign in Jesus is shown to have been established by the destruction of Jerusalem (Wright).[35]

Two key features of the parable of the Throne Claimant prove problematic for any eschatological interpretation. First, the explicit rationale for

---

Matt 25:14-30 and Luke 19:11-27. In his view, the throne claimant subplot is likely a Lukan addition that does not alter the basic meaning of the parable.

31. See Josephus, *Jewish War*, 2.1-38, 80-111; Josephus, *Jewish Antiquities*, 17.208-249, 299-323. For contrasting ways of emphasizing the evident allusion to Archelaus in this parable, see Schultz, "Jesus as Archelaus," and Van Eck, "Social Memory and Identity," the latter of which discusses the rather different Josephan texts and Luke's parable of the Throne Claimant from the perspective of a social-scientific model of social memory.

32. For surveys of scholarship on this parable, see Dowling, *Taking Away the Pound*, 46-59; Van Eck, "Do not question my honour," 4-6.

33. See Bock, *Luke 9:51-24:53*, 1525: "Often called the 'Parable of the Pounds,' a more precise title might be the 'Parable of Stewardship and Judgment upon the Return.'" In defense of this traditional interpretation, see also Carroll, *Response to the End of History*, 97-103. Cf., however, Carroll, *Luke*, 377-82, in which his earlier interpretation is modified by suggesting that the throne claimant's conduct is incongruent with the operation of God's reign but rather intimates what lies ahead for Jesus in Jerusalem and, a generation later, for Jerusalem itself.

34. See Snodgrass, *Stories with Intent*, 519-43. On balance, Snodgrass considers these two parables to be unrelated, but he discusses them together among a group of parables concerned with "future eschatology."

35. See Johnson, "Lukan Kingship Parable," and also his *Gospel of Luke*, 288-95; Wright, *Jesus and the Victory of God*, 631-39.

the parable in Luke 19:11 resists any interpretation along the lines of imminent resolution. Jesus tells this parable to counter his audience's supposition that, since he was nearing Jerusalem, the reign of God must be near and about to appear. As for the view that this parable expresses Luke's revised eschatological schema that the return of Jesus is purposefully delayed and was not envisaged by Jesus to occur hard on the heels of his departure, the parable is unconcerned with the duration of the throne claimant's time away.[36] Indeed, in terms of the parable's story line, the throne claimant returns as king in no time.

Since the parable focuses on the industriousness of slaves during their master's absence, it is possible to argue that this emphasis supports the traditional eschatological reading. The (extended) time between ascension and return makes provision for ever-expanding witness to Jesus. A second fundamental feature of the parable also grates against this reading, however. Any eschatological interpretation of the parable of the Throne Claimant must envisage the royal aspirant who secures his kingship as analogous to Jesus as (returning) Lord or, less commonly, to God as judge. Yet everything one learns about the throne claimant and his actions contravene Jesus' instructions for living in accordance with divine reign.[37]

In the first instance, the throne claimant pursues power and position, in stark contrast to Jesus' teaching on what constitutes genuine greatness (see Luke 9:46–48; 22:24–26). If the parable has an eschatological dimension, therefore, perhaps it comprises Jesus' warning against eschatological expectations associated with conventional royal rule, that is, expectations equating divine reign with imperial or at least "lording over" modes of ruling. It can hardly be gainsaid that this parable mirrors what is constitutive of conventional kingdoms and fiefdoms, which might well have been what Jesus' audience had in mind, in Lukan perspective, if nearness to Jerusalem prompted its supposition that the arrival of God's kingdom must be near.

---

36. By contrast, Matt 25:19 draws attention to the master's extended absence in the parable of the Talents, which reinforces the note of delay in the two preceding eschatological parables (24:48; 25:5). Of course, the story logic of the parable of the Throne Claimant requires that sufficient time must elapse for his ten slaves to be able to make money with their respective minas, but that detail is not explicitly foregrounded.

37. In what follows I restrict my attention to the discrepancy between the behavior of the throne claimant and the theological-moral vision of Jesus as Luke presents it. Others go further by "rehabilitating" the third slave. Indeed, Dowling's survey of scholarship on this parable groups interpretations according to whether the third slave is castigated or commended. See Dowling, *Taking Away the Pound*, 46–59. For considerations that lead interpreters to read against the grain of this parable such that it implicitly honors the third slave, see the reading scenario in Malina and Rohrbaugh, *Social-Science Commentary on the Synoptic Gospels*, 384–86; Pilch, *Cultural Handbook*, 233–38; and Van Eck, "Do not question my honour."

Moreover, the parable makes it abundantly clear that the throne claimant is preoccupied with wealth. He hands out ten minas to ten slaves with the explicit instruction to multiply his money (19:13), a detail missing from the parable of the Talents.[38] Then, immediately upon his return from securing his regal title, he assembles the slaves to whom he had entrusted money to ascertain how much more had been made by trade. This is in stark contrast to Jesus' instruction on the dangers of wealth, a prominent theme in Luke's central section (see 12:13–34; 16:1–15, 19–31; 18:18–30; 19:1–10). Indeed, Luke explicitly links the parable of the Throne Claimant to the preceding episode (19:11), in which the wealthy toll collector, Zacchaeus, divests himself of ill-gotten gain and is commended by Jesus with the words, "Today salvation has happened in this house . . ." (19:9).

Beyond his evident lust for wealth, the throne claimant instills fear by reinforcing his reputation for unjust gain. He is known as one who takes out what he does not put in and reaps what he does not sow. Indeed, Luke ensures that this detail is first uttered by the fearful slave and subsequently reiterated by his master without disagreement or qualification, except perhaps to reinforce his own severity.[39] In the manner of one accustomed to lord it over others, he takes pride in his capacity to get what he wants, irrespective of the means. And finally, the manner in which the throne claimant deals with those who opposed his quest to rule—by ordering their execution in his presence—is at complete odds with Jesus' instruction on loving enemies (Luke 6:27–36; 10:25–37).[40]

As with other parables, particular details within Jesus' parable of the Throne Claimant are not to be understood literally or allegorically but rather analogically.[41] Even so, it is worth reflecting on whether Luke could have conceived of Jesus returning in the manner of the triumphant throne

---

38. See Yoder Neufeld, *Recovering Jesus*, 175, for whom this Lukan detail provokes the comment that the parable "looks like a severe lesson in capitalism."

39. In Matt 25:26 the master reiterates the third slave's remarks about his reputation for reaping where he does not sow but not the negative character assessment (callous or "sclerotic") of his slave. In Luke 19:22 the successful throne claimant "owns" not only his reputation for taking what he has not stored and reaping what he has not sown but also the negative character assessment (severe or "austere") of his slave. In short, Luke lingers longer on the unsavory character of the slave's master, perhaps to preclude a favorable comparison with Jesus. In and of itself, however, this negative parabolic characterization does not preclude the Throne Claimant from representing either Jesus or God.

40. Jeremias, *Parables of Jesus*, 58–60, could not countenance Jesus comparing himself with such a "rapacious," "brutal oriental despot" and therefore placed responsibility for this comparison with Luke.

41. See Snodgrass, *Stories with Intent*, 1–31, 540–41.

claimant and thereby overturning central dimensions of his own moral instruction: the dangers of amassing both power and wealth, concern for underprivileged people (justice), and peaceable love of enemies. Certain eschatological texts might be forwarded as comparable in their content to the parable of the Throne Claimant, most notably the comparisons between the future day or days of the Son of humanity and the past days of Noah and Lot (Luke 17:22–37), but most Lukan eschatological texts bespeak a peaceable hope.[42] As a result, there are reasons to dispute the traditional interpretation according to which the returning throne claimant is aligned with the returning Jesus.

Put differently, various levels of incongruity between Jesus' moral teaching, as recorded by Luke, and the characterization of the throne claimant destabilize interpretations of this parable in which the figure of the throne claimant reflects analogically on Jesus. As Merrill Kitchen observes, "The character of Jesus Christ is portrayed consistently in Luke's Gospel as 'the centre of the story of salvation' and is therefore the hermeneutical key for interpreting all symbolic or metaphorical literary material within the Gospel of Luke. . . . If he is a consistent character, his speech will affirm his imputed ethics. It is Jesus who tells the parable of the pounds, so the reader must assume that the ethic depicted in the parable is intentional and careful, directly reflecting the ethical intention of the Lukan Jesus."[43] In other words, the characterization of the throne claimant in Jesus' parable is so evidently incongruous with Jesus' own moral instruction that it provokes a reappraisal of the traditional interpretation of the parable.

As David Seccombe points out in his study of "Incongruity in the Gospel Parables," however, incongruity, hyperbole, and the bizarre are characteristic of Jesus' teaching.[44] Commenting on the parable of the Throne Claimant, Seccombe finds a comparison between Archelaus and the reign of God consistent with the rest of the Jesus tradition. And within this overarching shock-inducing comparison, he considers the note of slaughter on which the parable ends to be apposite to Jesus' first-century context, both to spice up the story and to provoke the question: "What might the King Messiah do to those who oppose his kingdom?"[45]

---

42. See Neville, *A Peaceable Hope*, 89–173. (Luke 17:22–37 is reconsidered in chapter 9, below.)

43. Kitchen, "Rereading the Parable of the Pounds," 232. Further support for Kitchen's reading of this parable is provided by Dowling, *Taking Away the Pound*, 80–116.

44. Seccombe, "Incongruity in the Gospel Parables," 161–67. Cf. Luz, *Matthew 21–28*, 37, who notes that "improbabilities and excesses belong to the parables of Jesus."

45. Seccombe, "Incongruity in the Gospel Parables," 170–71.

What, indeed?! Perhaps twenty-first-century Western squeamishness over brutal violence needs to be set aside in favor of hearing this parable with first-century ears. Perhaps in the absence of the various social, democratic, and legal institutions we now take for granted in certain parts of our world, we must simply accept that divine justice or judgment is sometimes synonymous with arbitrary retribution that is beyond moral appraisal. This seems to be the end effect of accepting an analogical association between the actions of the throne claimant and Jesus' comprehension of God's reign. As a result, even if it could be demonstrated that Jesus intended such an analogical association, the historical influence of such an association places interpreters today in the uneasy position of having to assess the theological and moral value of this legacy, features of which include: arbitrary power as intrinsic to divine reign; justice as retributive judgment (primarily or solely); and the moral validity of violent retaliation. Insofar as the parable of the Throne Claimant inculcates and reinforces such theological and moral "values," the interpretive imperative might well be to contest this parable of Jesus in the service of a more edifying theological vision.

Although the parable of the Throne Claimant is regularly understood to provide biblical warrant for the inscrutability of divine power and for construing divine judgment as retribution first and foremost, much about this parable militates against the conventional interpretation in which the throne claimant is aligned analogically with Jesus (or divine reign). Contextually construed within Luke's narrative framework, and hence in relation to fundamental features of his theological vision, this parable more likely destabilizes conventional convictions concerning the nature of divine reign, divine agency, and divine justice. In other words, seen in light of signal Lukan motifs such as divine visitation in Jesus, rescue and release, social reversal, compassionate justice, and the primacy of peace,[46] the parable of the Throne Claimant portrays features of imperial or imperially authorized rule that are frequently aligned with divinity but that are nevertheless undermined and indeed overturned by the reign of God displayed in the mission of Jesus.

Some readers might well wonder whether this interpretation of the parable of the Throne Claimant is but a case of "secularizing Jesus." In the opening chapter of *Resurrecting Jesus*, Dale Allison critiques a discernible trend to reinterpret certain Gospel texts in non-religious or non-theological terms.[47] Although much of Allison's critique addresses over-simplified

---

46. On these facets of Luke's theological vision, see Dowling, *Taking Away the Pound*, 97–110; Swartley, *Covenant of Peace*, 121–76; Marshall, *Compassionate Justice*, 1–282. See also Green, *Theology of the Gospel of Luke*, passim.

47. Allison, *Resurrecting Jesus*, 1–26.

categorizations of scholarly quests for the historical Jesus, his final section focuses on "the secularizing of Jesus" in various Gospel texts, most of them parables. Among the parables considered, Allison comments briefly on the parable of the "Hidden Talents" in both its Matthean and Lukan contexts, drawing attention to the viewpoint of William Herzog that, if this parable does go back to Jesus, it more likely extols the third slave for refusing to participate in systemic economic exploitation.[48] Yet his brief description of this parable elides features distinctive to Luke's version of the parable, which cannot be overlooked in its interpretation. Allison interprets Luke 19:12–27 in much the same way as the parable of the Talents in Matt 25:14–30,[49] but my disquiet about this traditional interpretation of the parable of the Throne Claimant arises from Luke's narrative plotting of this parable as well as from his own theological vision shaped by his understanding of Jesus and his mission, not from a concern to secularize Jesus. Although I consider this parable to sketch the antithesis of God's reign as Jesus conceived it, and hence not to be about Jesus and his final judgment of both the faithful and the faithless at his delayed return, this is not because I doubt Jesus (or Luke) was concerned about such matters. The interpretation of this parable is not a straightforward exercise, and there are good reasons to reconsider its meaning and significance in its Lukan context (both narrative and theological).

CONCLUDING COMMENTS

Vengeance features in both parables discussed in this chapter, but is such vengeance envisaged as divine retribution in each parable? Some would say that neither the original version of the parable of the Unforgiving Slave nor the original version of the parable of the Throne Claimant envisages the vengeful king as analogous to God. Such alternative readings helpfully destabilize traditional interpretations of these and other parables, especially in relation to biblical conceptions of divine agency or justice and also their reception in the history of interpretation. Indeed, regarding the parable of the Throne Claimant, I have come to the conclusion that the vengeful king is probably not analogous to God but rather to common (mis)conceptions of divine sovereignty, in which God's way in our world merely mimics the tyrannical rule of earthly kings. In its canonical contextualization, however, the parable of the Unforgiving Slave does seem to countenance the prospect of divine vengeance for human recalcitrance or faithlessness.

---

48. Allison, *Resurrecting Jesus*, 21; cf. Herzog, *Parables as Subversive Speech*, 150–68.
49. See also Allison, *Constructing Jesus*, 65–67.

In the parable of the Unforgiving Slave, the final anger-venting vengeance of the slave's master serves to warn of the potentially calamitous consequences of failing to emulate, within the community of faith, the master's initial compassion-inspired and calculus-free forgiveness. Moreover, the rhetorical question of Matt 18:33 is both theologically and morally compelling: within—and indeed beyond—the community of faith, we should display mercy toward others, as divine mercy has been displayed toward us. Restricting attention to the parable proper, its chilling culmination in Matt 18:34 may be regarded as reinforcing the theological-moral integrity of what is expressed in 18:33. Once the parable's application in Matt 18:35 is taken to heart, however, the parable does damage to the moral integrity of God—or, at least, one's idea of God. If this is how things really are in God's heavenly domain, can we in good conscience pray for God's will and way to be established here on earth? Like some other parables with violent endings in Matthew's Gospel, the violent ending of this parable more likely reflects Matthew's retributive-apocalyptic mind-set rather than Jesus' theological-moral vision. Since the concluding analogy of Matt 18:35 ultimately undermines the theological-moral values that the parable of the Unforgiving Slave was apparently intended to reinforce, it is probably best considered in light of Jesus' command to forgive rather than as a distillation of Jesus' instruction on divine justice.

The parable of the Throne Claimant composes a capstone to the teaching of Jesus during his journey to Jerusalem (9:51–19:46), a distinctive section of Luke's Gospel devoted to decisive dimensions of Jesus' theological and moral instruction for his disciples. As such, interpretations of this parable in which its theological and moral content jars with central features of Jesus' teaching are profoundly perturbing—even if considered to be more compelling overall than the interpretation to which I have been drawn. Since everything one learns about the throne claimant contravenes Jesus' teaching on central implications of living and acting in conformity to the reign of God, as Luke presents such teaching, one is entitled to question whether the parable, as Luke contextualizes it, presents the throne claimant as analogous to Jesus or his vision of divine sovereignty. Crucially, the parable is not presented as a parable of God's reign, unlike some other Lukan parables (13:18–21); rather, it is presented as proffered in response to the inference that, because Jesus was approaching Jerusalem, the reign of God was imminent. For these reasons, I consider this parable to display features of conventional royal rule. In Luke's Gospel the parable of the Throne Claimant is told to warn against associating such features with Jesus' messianic mission and hence the rule of God.

3

The Judgment of Jerusalem

(LUKE 13:31–35; 19:41–44; 21:20–24; 23:26–31)

IN THIS CHAPTER I return to an interpretive conundrum that remained unresolved in Part 2 of *A Peaceable Hope*, namely, that Luke's understanding of Jerusalem's destruction as divine judgment for rejecting Jesus as God's Messiah militates against his own Christology of peace.[1] For narrative, historical, and theological reasons, Jerusalem as the site of the temple is significant for Luke. Nevertheless, within Luke–Acts there is a discernible ambivalence about the salvation-historical role of Jerusalem and its temple that makes this evangelist's attitude toward the city rather difficult to discern. On one hand, it seems, Jerusalem is integral to God's saving plan and purpose; on the other, however, Jerusalem is destined for destruction due to its failure to receive Jesus as God's appointed and anointed one. Especially in light of Luke's peaceable Christology, his evident emphasis on Jerusalem's destruction as divine judgment is perplexing and perturbing.

During the first century of the Common Era, Jerusalem was on the map, so to speak. Following Pompey's conquest of the city in 63 BCE, Jerusalem had come to hold geopolitical significance for the Roman Empire.[2] For first-century Israelites, however, Jerusalem had inestimable historical and cultic-cultural significance: first, it was the historic seat of the Davidic monarchy; and second, as the site of both the original and reconstructed

---

1. See Neville, *A Peaceable Hope*, 89–173, esp. 111–17.

2. On the relationship between Rome and Jerusalem over centuries, see Goodman, *Rome and Jerusalem*.

temples, Jerusalem was undoubtedly the cultic center of the Jewish world and indeed considered by some to be the very navel of the earth.[3] For many Israelites, the temple in Jerusalem was God's earthly dwelling place, the locus of divine presence and protection. As a result of Herod's large-scale building program within Jerusalem, especially his extensive expansion and elaborate refurbishment of the temple, the city with its temple became a source of wonderment and sociocultural prestige.[4] Diaspora as well as Judean Jews paid the annual temple tax and whenever possible journeyed to Jerusalem for the major festivals of Passover, Pentecost, and Tabernacles.

Despite the significance of Jerusalem for first-century Israelites, it would seem that each of the four biblical Gospel writers regarded the destruction of Jerusalem and the temple as indicative of divine judgment. To varying degrees, the manner in which the actions of Jesus in the temple are narrated by each evangelist might well symbolize divine judgment.[5] Similarly, the parable of the Vineyard Tenants, recorded by the first three evangelists in the immediate aftermath of Jesus' disruptive actions within the temple precincts, hints at divine judgment against the Jewish leadership, albeit without explicitly connecting this with Jerusalem's destruction (Matt 21:41; Mark 12:9; Luke 20:16). The description of the tearing of the temple curtain at the time of Jesus' death (Matt 27:51; Mark 15:38; Luke 23:45) may also symbolize divine judgment on the temple and its religious role. Within the parable of the Wedding Banquet in Matt 22:1–14, there is a seemingly gratuitous reference to burning a city. In retaliation against invitees to his son's wedding banquet who first spurn his invitations and then ignore, insult, or kill his slaves, a king sends armed troops, destroys the murderers, and burns their city (Matt 22:7). This incongruous or at least unnecessary detail, together with the placement of this parable immediately after the parable of the Vineyard Tenants, leads many to infer that it alludes to divine retaliation against Jerusalem,[6] especially in view of Jerusalem's identification in Matt 5:35 as "the city of the great king." The invective in Matt 23:29–36 (cf. Luke 11:47–51) more obviously associates the destruction of Jerusalem with divine judgment, especially in view of the following oracle against Jerusalem (23:37–39; cf. Luke 13:34–35). Then there is the notorious text in

---

3. On various attitudes toward Jerusalem in post-biblical Jewish thought, see Parsons, *Luke: Storyteller*, 91–93.

4. For descriptions of both the city of Jerusalem and its renovated temple that exude a sense of cultural pride, see Josephus, *Jewish War*, 5.136–247; Josephus, *Jewish Antiquities*, 15.317–19, 380–425. See also Matt 5:34–35; Mark 13:1; Luke 21:5; John 2:20. On the temple as an "emotional repository," see Barton, "Why Do Things Move People?"

5. See the discussion of this narrated episode in chapters 5 and 7, below.

6. See, e.g., Kloppenborg, *Tenants in the Vineyard*, 198–99.

Matthew's passion narrative in which the people as a whole call out, "His blood upon us and upon our children" (Matt 27:25), which is often taken to be yet another allusion to the destruction of Jerusalem as divine judgment for the innocent blood of Jesus. As disconcerting as any of these texts may be, however, none so explicitly equates Jerusalem's destruction with divine judgment for rejecting the prophetic-messianic mission of Jesus as does a series of related Lukan texts examined in this chapter.

Jesus could well have been prescient about Jerusalem's impending disaster, even if this was as much a matter of prophetic insight as of predictive foresight. There is a significant difference, however, between perceiving that Jerusalem was bound for disaster and attributing that disaster to divine recompense. In other words, it is one thing to affirm that Jesus regarded Jerusalem's destruction to be ineluctable, quite another to hold that he perceived the city's inescapable demise to be the result of divine vengeance for failing to respond positively to his own mission and message. Too many affirmations of Jerusalem's destruction as divine judgment ignore the affronting atrocities perpetrated by Roman (as well as Jewish) forces against largely innocent people—atrocities too glibly attributed to God's will and, in some sense, agency.[7] Yet that is the character of divine judgment if Jerusalem's destruction is interpreted as such.

For the Gospel writers, there was biblical precedent for attributing Jerusalem's destruction to divine judgment. Within the prophetic tradition, the destruction of Jerusalem by the Babylonians in 587 BCE was interpreted as divine judgment (see 2 Kings 21–25; Jer 12:7–13; 13:20–27; 25:1–14; Ezek 14:12–15:8; also Lamentations 2). When Jerusalem experienced a similar fate at the hands of the Romans in 70 CE, it was understandable and perhaps inevitable that the more recent calamity would be understood in light of the earlier one. Furthermore, most, if not all, of the New Testament writers reflected upon Jerusalem's destruction from within a Jewish mind-set shaped by the biblical tradition. In time, acceptance of Jesus as Messiah distanced people from Jewish faith and practice, but the earliest Christians were Jews whose faith in Jesus as Messiah may have brought them into conflict with fellow-Jews but could not detach them from their Jewish frame of reference. In the case of the Gospel writers, then, one supposes that to speak of Jerusalem's destruction as divine judgment was to affirm God's judgment on people and institutions separate *but nevertheless inseparable* from themselves and their respective audiences. In other words, to interpret

---

7. For a harrowing account of Roman treatment of Jerusalem's inhabitants once the city walls had been breached, see Josephus, *Jewish War*, 6.220–442. For texts that give voice to the sense of abject desolation caused by the Roman razing of Jerusalem, see *4 Ezra* 10:21–23 and *2 Baruch* 10:5–19; 35:1–5.

Jerusalem's destruction as divine judgment was perhaps as much a result of *self*-examination as of claiming divine favor for oneself and one's group at the expense of obliterated opponents. But was this the case for Luke?

JERUSALEM IN LUKE-ACTS

As the site of Jesus' crucifixion, understood as the inevitable outcome of his life's work, the ancient city of Jerusalem is integral to the narrative accounts of all four biblical Gospel writers. In the Gospel according to John, Jesus moves back and forth between Galilee and Jerusalem at various times. By contrast, Luke shares with Matthew and Mark a different conception of the unfolding of Jesus' public activity. The broad shape of Jesus' mission is threefold: first, a period of proclaiming the presence and applying the pressure of divine reign (or kingdom of God); second, preparation for activity in Jerusalem by means of a series of "passion predictions" and movement toward Jerusalem; and third, a few days of provocation and proclamation in Jerusalem itself before his arrest and eventual execution by crucifixion. For Luke, however, Jerusalem's significance is enhanced by several variations to this pattern.

First, Luke's Gospel both begins and ends within the temple in Jerusalem. Luke's narrative proper begins with an angelic appearance to the priest Zechariah while he is on incense duty within the sanctuary of the temple (1:5–23).[8] Later, within Luke's distinctive birth and infancy narrative, Jesus is born in Bethlehem but is shortly thereafter taken to the temple in Jerusalem for presentation to the God of Israel in accordance with the Torah, which Luke describes as the "Law of Moses" and the "Law of the Lord" (2:22–39). Within this temple section near the beginning of Luke's Gospel, Simeon's hope of seeing the coming "Messiah (Anointed) of the Lord" to bring about the "consolation of Israel" is realized,[9] and the prophet Anna, said to be a permanent resident of the temple, speaks of the child Jesus to all who are awaiting the "liberation of Jerusalem." As if to foreshadow the adult Jesus' teaching presence within the temple later in his Gospel (19:45–21:38),

---

8. Appointed by the custom of casting lots, Zechariah's responsibility was to enter the "holy place" in front of the curtain of the "holy of holies" (only ever entered once a year by the high priest on the Day of Atonement) to clear burnt incense from the altar of incense and to light fresh incense. (Both the setting of this opening episode and Luke's parallel temple sections near the beginning and end of his Gospel suggest that the torn temple curtain of Luke 23:44–45 refers to the curtain separating the "holy of holies" from the "holy place.")

9. The realization of Simeon's hope foreshadows Peter's declaration regarding Jesus' identity in Luke 9:20: "the Messiah (Anointed) of God."

Luke concludes his birth and infancy overture with a unique story about the twelve-year-old Jesus making his presence felt in the temple during a Passover visit to Jerusalem (2:41–52).[10]

If the beginning to Luke's Gospel is distinctive, so also is its end. The post-resurrection encounter with Jesus en route to Emmaus occurs not far from Jerusalem (24:13–35), and Luke indicates that two further appearances of the risen Lord occur in or near Jerusalem (24:33, 36). Jesus instructs the Eleven and those with them to remain in Jerusalem until they receive from him the promised Holy Spirit, whose empowerment will animate the proclamation of repentance and forgiveness of sins among all the nations, "originating from Jerusalem" (24:47–49). In the coda to the Gospel, Jesus takes his leave from the company of disciples near Bethany, just outside Jerusalem,[11] after which the disciples joyfully return to Jerusalem, praising God in the temple, precisely where Luke's story begins.

As in Matt 4:1–11, Luke 4:1–13 describes Jesus responding to three specific tests put to him by the devil. The tests are the same, but in Luke's account the final two tests are reversed so that the devil's provocation to test divine providence by leaping from a high point of the temple in Jerusalem forms a climax. It is not the visionary experience in which the devil shows Jesus all the kingdoms of the civilized world that forms the culmination of this sequence of tests but rather the test contextualized on the temple in Jerusalem, which was understood to be the locus of divine presence and hence the center of the known world.[12] In striking fashion, Luke concludes this series of tests by noting that the devil removed himself from Jesus "for a time" or perhaps "until an appointed time" (4:13). Since Luke probably envisaged the third testing of Jesus to parallel—and thereby foreshadow—Jesus' eventual time of testing in Jerusalem, when he is arrested, suffers, and dies, it seems reasonable to interpret Luke 4:13 to mean that the devil maintained a certain distance from Jesus until his suffering and death in Jerusalem. Between Jesus' baptism and the beginning of his Galilean ministry, according to Luke, his testing by the devil prefigures his destined course and goal.

10. In Luke 2:49 Jesus responds to his mother's somewhat reproachful question by saying, "Why search for me? Were you unaware that it was necessary for me to be among those of my father?" Jesus' response contains the first occurrence in Luke's Gospel of the impersonal δεῖ (*dei*, it is necessary). Used specifically in relation to Jesus' life and purpose, this term appears in Luke's Gospel as often as in the other three canonical Gospels combined. See also Luke 4:43; 9:22; 13:33; 17:25; 19:5; 22:37; 24:7, 26, 44.

11. The geographical movement in Luke 24:50–53 first reverses and then replicates Jesus' threefold "drawing near" to Jerusalem via Bethphage and Bethany in 19:28–46.

12. See Lanier, "Luke's Distinctive Use of the Temple," 437–39, referring to Ezek 38:12; 1 Enoch 26:1; Jub 8:19.

Like Matthew and Mark, Luke records Jesus as journeying from Galilee to Jerusalem to meet his inevitable end. In Luke's Gospel, however, Jesus' journey to Jerusalem features much more prominently than in either Matthew or Mark's Gospel, taking up the substance of some ten chapters (9:51–19:46) and serving as the setting for much of Jesus' teaching on discipleship, prayer, money, mercy, and the like. (Much of Jesus' teaching in Luke's central section is distinctive to Luke.) Luke also gives Jesus' journey to Jerusalem an explicitly theological interpretation. During Jesus' transfiguration, shortly before the beginning of his journey to Jerusalem, Moses and Elijah discuss with Jesus his forthcoming "exodus," which he was about to fulfill or bring to completion in Jerusalem (9:30–31). Here Luke clearly associates what lies ahead for Jesus with the figure of Moses and his role in Israel's exodus from Egypt. Although some restrict Jesus' "exodus" to either his death, resurrection, or exaltation—or all three together—there is good reason to interpret this particular "exodus" as Jesus' journey as a whole, from Galilee to Jerusalem and thence to God by means of his ascension to heaven. The journey Jesus is bound to traverse culminates in his "taking up" to God, which means that Jesus' journey to Jerusalem is an inescapable and integral dimension of his journey to God. For this reason, according to Luke 9:51, when the days of his "taking up" are close to realization, Jesus fixes his face on Jerusalem, which remains his goal until arriving at the city, even though Luke does not belabor his progress toward Jerusalem.[13]

The book of Acts picks up from the end of Luke's Gospel, with the disciples in and around Jerusalem. There are several points of contact between the conclusion to Luke's Gospel and the beginning of Acts, none more pronounced than Jesus' instruction to his apostles to remain in Jerusalem until their receipt of the promised gift of the Holy Spirit to empower witness for Jesus to the ends of the earth, expanding out from Jerusalem (Acts 1:4–8). The first seven chapters narrate the church's beginnings at Pentecost, together with both the progress and the persecution of the church in

---

13. With Matera, "Jesus' Journey to Jerusalem (Luke 9:51–19:46)," I consider Luke 19:45–46 to be the culmination of Luke's central section, even if also transitional. Jesus' travelogue en route to Jerusalem is traceable via Luke *9:51–53*, 56–57; 10:1, 38; *13:22, 31–33*; *17:11*; *18:31*, 35; *19:1*, 11, *28–45* (italicized references explicitly identify Jerusalem as the destination). Within this travelogue, Luke 13:22 provides the narrative rationale for Luke's structuring of his central section as a journey to Jerusalem. The journey motif serves Luke's purpose of presenting Jesus' teaching in an apt and hence memorable way. The exemplary but counterintuitive way of Jesus is taught to disciples on the way to Jerusalem. The journey of Jesus toward God provides the pattern for discipleship in the way of Jesus, perhaps providing the precedent for designating the early Christian movement as "the Way (of the Lord)" (Acts 9:2; 18:25–26; 19:9, 23; 22:4; 24:14, 22; cf. 2:28; 16:17).

Jerusalem. Only at Acts 8:1 does Luke's history of Christian origins move beyond Jerusalem, although Luke makes clear that Jerusalem remains the mother church (8:14–17; 11:1–18; 15:1–33; 21:17–26). Toward the end of Acts, Paul journeys to Jerusalem and runs afoul of Jewish authorities there (19:21; 20:16—23:31), thereby paralleling Jesus' journey to Jerusalem in Luke's Gospel.

Jerusalem is clearly central to Luke's narrative and salvation-historical concerns. Not only must Jesus journey to Jerusalem, teach and die in Jerusalem, and ascend to heaven from just outside Jerusalem, but the infant church must also be gifted with the Spirit in Jerusalem, establish itself in the face of fierce hostility within Jerusalem, and expand outwards from Jerusalem. "Like the neck of an hourglass," as James Edwards observes, "Jerusalem is the point *to which* the narrative focus of the Third Gospel irrevocably flows, and *from which* the mission of the early church extends in its sequel in the Book of Acts."[14] In light of the favored status of Jerusalem as the salvation-historical setting for so much of Luke's two-part narrative, however, it is surprising, indeed, disconcerting that Jerusalem's devastating demise should be emphasized more by Luke than by any of his biblical counterparts. For it is not simply that Jerusalem is accorded favored status within the time frame of Luke–Acts. Its imminent destruction, construed as divine judgment, also features more prominently within Luke's Gospel than in any other canonical Gospel. As Charles Scobie remarks, "The emphasis on Jerusalem is typical of Luke; the city holds a central, if somewhat ambiguous place in his theology."[15]

The principal basis for describing Jerusalem as an ambiguous or ambivalent feature within Luke's symbolic world is a series of four passages in which Jerusalem's destruction is either intimated or predicted and seemingly interpreted as divine judgment for failure to embrace Jesus and his message. Such passages comprise a discordant note in Luke's otherwise melodious theology. The four passages are these: Luke 13:31–35; 19:41–44; 21:20–24; and 23:26–31.[16] Two of these passages, Luke 19:41–44 and 23:26–31, are unique, and all four contain distinctive features. Taken together, they

---

14. Edwards, *Gospel according to Luke*, 411.

15. Scobie, "A Canonical Approach to Interpreting Luke," 332. On the ambivalent role of Jerusalem within Luke–Acts, see also Parsons, "Place of Jerusalem"; Parsons, *Luke: Storyteller*, 84–95.

16. Preceding these passages is Luke 11:45–52, which is similar in tone and content but is not directed against Jerusalem. For more detailed discussion of these "omens," see Tiede, *Prophecy and History*, 65–96; Chance, *Jerusalem*, 115–27; Walker, *Jesus and the Holy City*, 69–80. Three of these passages are often described as "laments," despite their variances from constituent features of the biblical lament genre. See Campbell, "NT Scholars' Use of OT Lament Terminology."

present an interpretation of Jerusalem's destruction as divine recompense for rejecting the prophetic-messianic presence of Jesus.

DIVINE LEAVE-TAKING: LUKE 13:31-35

Luke 13:31-35 occurs midway through Luke's central section in which Jesus makes his way toward Jerusalem. Indeed, some place this passage at or near the precise midpoint of a literary chiasm that composes Luke's central section in its entirety.[17] However that may be, the important point in narrative terms is that twice in brief compass within Luke 13 the reader or hearer of Luke's Gospel is explicitly reminded for the first time since 9:51-53 that Jesus is bound for Jerusalem. Luke 13:22 reads: "And he [Jesus] travelled through towns and villages, teaching and effecting his journey to Jerusalem." There follows a passage in which, in response to a question about whether only a few will be saved, Jesus addresses the theme of eschatological salvation and reversal. Then this:

> At that hour certain Pharisees approached, saying to him [Jesus], "Be gone and journey on from here because Herod intends to kill you." And he said to them, "Leave and tell that fox, 'See, I cast out demons and enact healings today and tomorrow, and on the third day I am finished.' Nevertheless, it is necessary for me to journey on today and tomorrow and the next day because it is impossible for a prophet to perish outside Jerusalem. Jerusalem, Jerusalem, which kills the prophets and stones those sent to her, how often I wished to gather together your children as a bird her brood under her wings, and you wished it not. See, your house is left to you.[18] I tell you, you will by no means see me until the occasion comes when you say, 'Blessed is the one coming in the name of the Lord'" (13:31-35).

---

17. See Bailey, *Poet & Peasant and Through Peasant Eyes*, 79-85; Talbert, *Reading Luke*, 111-13. According to Bovon, *Luke 2*, 320, the place of this passage within the structure of Luke's journey section is one of two "principal questions for commentators." The other concerns relations between the Pharisees and Jesus.

18. Many translate the opening sentence of Luke 13:35 as follows: "Your house is abandoned." See, e.g., Fitzmyer, *Luke (X-XXIV)*, 1033; Green, *Gospel of Luke*, 539; Bovon, *Luke 2*, 329-30; Culy, Parsons, and Stigall, *Luke*, 470, 473; Carroll, *Luke*, 292-93. My translation envisages divine Presence departing its symbolic locus on earth, as in Ezekiel 8-11, and thereby leaving the elect people of God bereft of divine protection. In this respect, my translation approximates that of Edwards, *Gospel according to Luke*, 407: "Look, your house is left to you desolate" (cf. Matt 23:38). I am less confident about Edwards's exegetical inference, 408: "'Is left' is a 'divine passive,' a reference to God without using his name, meaning 'God will destroy this place.'"

These two texts recall that Jesus is en route to Jerusalem, and the second, Luke 13:31–35, is fascinating for several reasons. First, although it is possible to envisage the approach of Pharisees to Jesus in positive terms, the effect of their warning is to inject a sense of foreboding into Luke's narrative at this point. Following the reference to Pilate in Luke 13:1, the reference in 13:31 to Herod Antipas, Rome's vicegerent in Galilee and Perea, foregrounds the sociopolitical context of Roman rule, which is displayed as neither benign nor beneficent. Even before the particulars of Jesus' response to these Pharisees, Luke 13:31 creates a sense of the ominous, which is progressively heightened in what follows.[19]

Second, the response of Jesus makes plain that his work is progressing in accordance with divine necessity and therefore cannot be interrupted or thwarted, even by those invested with the authority of imperial rule. Even so, Jesus clearly envisages that his divinely mandated movement to Jerusalem leads to inevitable confrontation with human authorities. This might well be hinted at in Jesus' words about being "finished" on the third day, although it is possible to read this as referring to the completion of his work. The ineluctable confrontation is nevertheless made explicit in Jesus' asseveration that it is impossible for a prophet to perish outside Jerusalem, even though plenty had.[20] In Luke's salvation-historical schema, it is theologically incongruous for the prophet who fulfills what it means to be a prophet to meet his destined end anywhere but in Jerusalem. Or, as Joel Green observes, "The additional note about the impossibility of a prophet's being killed outside of Jerusalem . . . constitutes an innovation that can be explained only in light of the role Jerusalem plays in the narrative as a whole."[21]

---

19. On the structure and theological significance of Luke 13 in its entirety, see Shirock, "Growth of the Kingdom." Even if Shirock's chiastic analysis of this portion of Luke's central section is not quite as tidy as he makes out, his observations on theological emphases within Luke 13 are nevertheless illuminating.

20. On this hyperbolic utterance, see Fitzmyer, *Luke (X–XXIV)*, 1032: "Behind this statement lies a traditional belief about the fate of prophetic figures in the city of Jerusalem." Biblical texts that probably informed this tradition include: 1 Kings 19:1–18 (the threat against Elijah); Jer 2:30b (Jeremiah to Jerusalem: "Your own sword devoured your prophets like a ravening lion"); Jer 26:20–24 (Uriah); Jeremiah 38 (the plot against Jeremiah in Jerusalem); 2 Chron 24:17–22 (Zechariah, son of Jehoiada, who in later tradition morphs into the son of Berechiah [Zech 1:1; Matt 23:35]); and 2 Kings 21:16; 24:4, which was later applied to the slaughter of prophets in Jerusalem (see Josephus, *Jewish Antiquities*, 10.3–38). If, as conjectured by some, the pseudepigraphical *Lives of the Prophets* may be dated to the lifetime of Jesus of Nazareth, its preoccupation with where prophets died and how, as well as with where they were finally laid to rest, may reflect first-century Israelite views that the likely fate of a prophet was to die violently, especially at the hands of powerful people whom they challenged.

21. Green, *Gospel of Luke*, 537.

Third, Luke 13:33 casts the words and actions of Jesus in a prophetic light.[22] Not only is this consistent with Luke's conception of Jesus' mission in prophetic-messianic terms but it also provides the appropriate sociocultural and religious context for interpreting his words of judgment addressed to Jerusalem in Luke 13:34–35. Jerusalem is addressed in personal terms by a prophetic figure whose protective care for its inhabitants fails to be understood as such by its "gatekeepers," who are resistant to change. The prophetic warning of Luke 13:34–35 evokes a tradition of tension between prophetic figures speaking for God and people of power whose interests make them suspicious of divine oracles. Within Luke's unfolding narrative, moreover, this cautionary prophecy on the part of Jesus foreshadows explicit expressions of judgment yet to be uttered. As John Carroll writes, "What this passage hints, Jesus will later state explicitly: the city that repudiates God's visitation, forsaken (by God), will with its children meet destruction (19:43–44; 21:20–24; 23:28–31)."[23]

When this passage is perceived in prophetic perspective, it is noteworthy that the intimation of judgment announced at the beginning of Luke 13:35 alludes to oracles of Jeremiah, one of Israel's prophets most closely associated with the destruction of Jerusalem at the hands of the Babylonians in the early sixth century BCE. Jeremiah 12:7 begins a divine dirge for Jerusalem (12:7–13), the Lord's house and heritage abandoned to her enemies. Here the Lord's "house" is Jerusalem, perhaps by virtue of its intrinsic association with the temple of the Lord, also called the Lord's "house" (see Jer 7:1–15; 26:1–24). Although Jer 12:7 might well be evoked by the opening words of Luke 13:35, "See, your house is left to you," it is more often held that these words allude to Jer 22:5, in which the Lord utters an oath that "this house shall become a desolation" (NRSV). Here, however, "this house" may well refer to the Davidic dynasty,[24] even though Jer 22:1–4 seems to envisage Jerusalem as the "house of the king of Judah." Within the prophetic book of Jeremiah, the word "house" evokes various interlocking associations—the temple, the throne of David, and, as the locus of both temple and

---

22. See Shirock, "Growth of the Kingdom," 25–29, who holds that Luke 13 in its entirety evokes a prophetic tone and prophetic motifs. On the centrality of the "rejected prophet" motif to Luke's apologetic or legitimating concerns, see McWhirter, *Rejected Prophets*, 57–74. For McWhirter, Luke's principal precedents for depicting Jesus as yet another of God's rejected prophets are Moses and Jeremiah, but especially Jeremiah. See also Hays, "Persecuted Prophet and Judgment on Jerusalem," who argues that Luke was heavily influenced by Jeremiah, especially its related motifs of the persecuted prophet and divine judgment of Jerusalem.

23. Carroll, *Luke*, 295.

24. Jeremiah 22:10–30 comprises a series of oracles against wayward descendants of Josiah.

throne, the city of Jerusalem. For Luke, an association of the word "house" with the Davidic dynasty is unlikely, but one need not choose between the other two associations, since in both Babylonian and Roman times the fates of both Jerusalem and the temple at its cultic, sociocultural, and political heart were inextricably interrelated.[25]

Various features of Jer 22:5 bear on the interpretation of Luke 13:35. The oracle of judgment in Jer 22:5 occurs within a literary section, 21:1–24:10, explicitly contextualized during the ten-year period between the two Babylonian deportations of 597 and 587/86 BCE after Zedekiah had been installed as regent in place of King Jeconiah (or Jehoiachin). In short, the literary context of Luke's allusion to Jer 22:5 evokes the historical context of the lead-up to the destruction of Solomon's temple and Jerusalem by the forces of King Nebuchadrezzar of Babylon. This section of Jeremiah makes for somber reading. Through Jeremiah, the God of Israel takes responsibility for turning the weapons of Israel against Jerusalem. Moreover, Jer 22:8–9, which echoes Deut 29:22–28, provides the rationale for Jerusalem's humiliating destruction—because Israel abandoned the covenant with the Lord their God and worshiped other gods.[26] Within this context, Jer 21:10, which concludes the opening frame of this literary block, is incendiary: "For I have set my face against this city for evil and not for good—declares the LORD. It shall be delivered into the hands of the king of Babylon, who will destroy it by fire" (JPS).[27]

Although the larger literary context of Jer 22:5, alluded to in Luke 13:35, is Jeremiah 21–24, its immediate literary context warns against injustice, oppression, and violence:

> Thus says the Lord: Act with justice and righteousness, and deliver from the hand of the oppressor anyone who has been robbed. And do no wrong or violence to the alien, the orphan, and the widow, or shed innocent blood in this place. For if you

---

25. For the view that Luke 13:35 refers to the temple, see Lanier, "Luke's Distinctive View of the Temple," 436–37, although he recognizes the possibility of a broader reference to include Jerusalem.

26. How best to explain ideological similarities between Jeremiah and the Deuteronomistic corpus is contested. For a brief overview of alternative explanations, see Carroll, "Surplus Meaning," 201–202. For Finsterbusch, the books of Deuteronomy and Jeremiah are comparable in narrative terms. See Finsterbusch, "Violence against Judah and Jerusalem," 81–82.

27. In view of Luke's allusion to this section of Jeremiah midway through his own central section, one wonders whether the beginning of his central section, in which Jesus fixes his face for Jerusalem (9:51), alludes to Jer 21:10. Despite some strong verbal similarities, however, Jer 21:10 LXX much more explicitly signals divine displeasure against Jerusalem.

> will indeed obey this word, then through the gates of this house shall enter kings who sit on the throne of David, riding in chariots and on horses, they, and their servants, and their people. But if you will not heed these words, I swear by myself, says the Lord, that this house shall become a desolation (Jer 22:3–5, NRSV).

In short, Jer 22:5 concludes a conditional oracle of judgment uttered against the king on the Davidic throne: if the Davidic line reigns with justice, it will be preserved; but if its reign is characterized by injustice, oppression, and violence, the house of David will be desolate. These marks of covenant loyalty recall Deut 16:1–20; 24:10–22 (also Jer 7:1–7). Justice, peace, and regard for the poor and powerless also feature prominently in Luke's Gospel. In Lukan perspective, the prophet Jesus recalls the prophet Jeremiah.

At least once within the larger literary unit of Jeremiah 21–24, Jerusalem is seemingly addressed in personal terms (22:20–23; cf. sections of Jeremiah 2–3). The personal address of Jer 21:13–14 seems also to be directed against Jerusalem. Similarly, in Luke 13:34 Jesus addresses Jerusalem in personal terms, offering protection but cognizant of Jerusalem's hostility to prophets. Although the imagery is different, the sentiment expressed in Luke 13:34 matches that of Jer 2:30, "Your own sword devoured your prophets like a ravening lion" (NRSV). The whole of Jeremiah 2 may not be addressed to Jerusalem per se (see 2:4), but the introductory words of Jeremiah's prophetic oracles identify Jerusalem as the primary audience for his message as a whole (2:1–2).

Yet one further significant feature of the broader literary context of Jer 22:5, alluded to by Jesus' intimation of judgment in Luke 13:34, is that an oracle of restoration is incorporated within it (23:1–8). A remnant of the Lord's dispersed flock will be returned to its fold; a king who rules justly will be raised up in a day of salvation; and the Lord of the exodus will henceforth be known as the Lord of the restoration from exile.[28]

To read Luke 13:35a, "See, your house is left to you," as an allusion to Jer 22:5 is a key to unlocking a series of fruitful associations between Luke 13:31–35 and Jeremiah 21–24. Jesus speaks to Jerusalem as the prophet Jeremiah once spoke to Jerusalem. As Jeremiah spoke of the house of the LORD being abandoned to its enemies, so Jesus warns that "your house is left to you."[29] Moreover, as Jeremiah envisaged the prospect of restoration beyond

---

28. For some Jeremiah scholars, this brief oracle of restoration near the end of the first half of the book prefigures a prominent motif in the second half of the book (Jer 26–52).

29. It cannot be coincidental that forms of the multivocal verb ἀφίημι (*aphiēmi*) occur not only in Luke 13:35 in relation to "your house" but also in 19:44 and 21:6 in relation to the stones of both Jerusalem and the temple.

judgment, so Jesus concludes his prophecy of judgment with a conditional prophecy of restoration.[30] Reflecting on the conclusion to this enigmatic passage, Bovon remarks: "At a primary level, the text states a tautology: you will not see me when I will be absent. At a secondary level, the text pronounces a judgment: God hides his face until the coming of the Messiah. At a tertiary level, it expresses a tremendous hope: the one who dies has a future in front of him; the one who disappears does not disappear forever."[31]

Midway through his journey to Jerusalem, then, Jesus warns of divine judgment against Jerusalem but also leaves open the possibility that he will be received in the words of Psalm 118:26, a text that envisages celebratory thanksgiving *within the temple* (118:19-29). As Jesus nears Jerusalem, this blessing is indeed uttered—not by Jerusalem or its inhabitants, however, but by disciples (19:37-38). Although reminiscent of Jesus' contingent prophecy in Luke 13:35, the praise of the disciples in 19:38 probably does not fulfill that prophecy by realizing its fundamental condition—recognition of Jesus as one coming (as king; cf. Jer 23:5-6!) in the name of the Lord—although it may well prefigure a deeper hope: recognition of the messiahship of Jesus on the part of Israel as a whole.[32] Immediately thereafter, Jesus utters a second pronouncement of judgment on Jerusalem and reclaims the temple as a house of prayer, yet again with reference to words of his prophetic predecessor, Jeremiah (7:11).

The oracle of judgment in Luke 13:34-35 is paralleled closely in wording by Matt 23:37-39, but not in context. Whereas this oracle occurs midway through Luke's central section in which Jesus is bound for Jerusalem, Matthew locates it after Jesus' stinging invective against scribes and Pharisees within Jerusalem itself, well after his entry into Jerusalem disturbs the entire city (Matt 21:10-11).[33] In its Lukan setting, this oracle of woe serves the narrative purpose of raising the question whether Jerusalem might respond differently to this particular prophet, even as it intimates that divine judgment is inevitable. Luke 19:41-44 reinforces the ineluctability of divine judgment for Jerusalem and offers the reason why.

---

30. See Allison, "Matt. 23:39 = Luke 13:35b as a Conditional Prophecy."

31. Bovon, *Luke 2*, 332.

32. Scholarly opinion is divided on whether the joyful praise of disciples in Luke 19:37-38 fulfills the conditional prophecy of 13:35b. With Carroll, I consider that 19:37-38 prefigures *eschatological* fulfillment. See Carroll, *Luke*, 295.

33. Matthew 23:37-39 is considered briefly in chapter 8, below.

70   The Vehement Jesus

DIVINE VISITATION: LUKE 19:41–44

At the culmination of Jesus' journey to Jerusalem, as Jesus draws ever closer to the city, he weeps over it and utters an indictment against it. There is profound pathos in this scene, reflective of abyssal anguish on Jesus' part, but the pathos fails to ameliorate the stridency of the words pronounced by Jesus on Jerusalem and its inhabitants.

> And as he [Jesus] drew near, on seeing the city he wailed over it, saying: "If only you had perceived on this day the things that lead to peace. . . . Now, however, it [such perception] has been concealed from your eyes because days will come upon you and your enemies will construct barricades opposing you and will surround you and will squeeze you from all directions, and they will raze you and your children within you and will not leave stone upon stone within you—the reason being that you have not perceived the time of your visitation."

In terms of narrative sequence, Luke is in relative agreement with both Matthew and Mark at this point—and indeed has been since Luke 18:15. Describing Jesus' movement from Jericho to Jerusalem (18:35–19:46), however, Luke's narrative is distinctive in various significant respects. He situates his own unique story of Zacchaeus in Jericho, concluding with the distinctive pronouncement, "For the Son of humanity came to seek and to save the lost" (19:1–10). Then follows Jesus' parable of the Throne Claimant who gave ten slaves ten minas with which to make more money while he went away to claim authority to rule (19:11–28).[34] The reason why Jesus tells this parable, according to Luke 19:11, is that he was near Jerusalem and it seemed to his (not precisely defined) audience that the reign of God was about to appear forthwith. On completing the parable, Jesus progresses toward Jerusalem, first by *drawing near* to Bethphage and Bethany beside the Mount of Olives (19:29), at which point he sends two disciples to fetch a colt on which to ride the rest of the road to Jerusalem. In Luke 19:37 he again *draws near* while descending from the Mount of Olives, at which point the crowd of disciples praises God loudly for all the works of power they have seen. In Lukan perspective, however, Jesus does not arrive to Jerusalem in triumph, for although he is acclaimed by a throng of disciples, his official reception is decidedly cool (19:39–40). It is at this point that Luke narrates Jesus' tearful judgment against Jerusalem, as he *draws near* enough to see the city. The "drawing near" of Luke 19:41 reads like an elaboration

---

34. This parable is discussed in chapter 2, above. For McWhirter, *Rejected Prophets*, 82, this parable illustrates the judgment oracles of Jesus.

of the "drawing near" of Jesus in 19:37. One even has the sense that Luke might have envisaged Jesus weeping for the city while his disciples shout out their words of praise. Because Luke 19:41–44 is uniquely Lukan, it is commonly treated as a self-contained pericope. But the author's compositional technique of having Jesus draw ever nearer to Jerusalem before entering the temple (19:28, 37, 41, 45) suggests that he considered Luke 19:28–46 as a single literary unit. Having uttered his oracle of judgment against the city of Jerusalem, Jesus enters the temple, reclaiming the "den of bandits" as a house of prayer and setting for teaching. Although Luke 19:41–44 is here in focus, it cannot be understood in isolation from its immediate literary context.

Positioned precisely at the narrative juncture when Jesus arrives at his divinely purposed goal ever since Luke 9:31 and 51, Luke 19:41–44 is crucial at various levels. At the level of narrative progression, it recounts Jesus arriving to Jerusalem without official welcome, even though, in Luke's understanding, Jesus deserves the kind of welcome reserved for royalty.[35] His disciples are exultant, but some Pharisees, who appear here for the final time in Luke's Gospel, instruct Jesus to reprimand them. The reply of Jesus in Luke 19:40 sounds rhetorical and even hyperbolic, but in light of later references to stones it has an ominous ring to it. At a historical level, Luke 19:43–44 evidently relates to Jerusalem's destruction in 70 CE, even if the wording of Jesus' prediction draws from biblical (e.g., Isa 29:3; Ezek 4:2; Hos 10:14) rather than contemporary sources and even if, as Tannehill notes, the affirmed causal connection is "a great oversimplification."[36] At an ideological level, Luke 19:44 offers a theological rationale for Jerusalem's destruction, which raises the issue of discerning divine action in history, especially in relation to calamitous events. And at an interpretive level, the passage as a whole provokes the question whether Luke's depiction of Jesus' oracle of judgment on Jerusalem coheres with his Christology of peace.

Related to the narrative placement of Luke 19:41–44, an important textual question bears on the interpretation of this passage. Responding to the instruction of some Pharisees to rebuke his boisterous disciples, Jesus replies assertively that the stones will cry out if or when these (disciples) are silent (19:39–40). The best attested text of Jesus' reply in the manuscript tradition combines ἐάν (*ean*), ordinarily translated as the conditional conjunction "if," with the future indicative form of the verb σιωπάω (*siōpaō*, will be(come) silent). Although ἐάν ordinarily governs the subjunctive mood,

---

35. See Kinman, "Parousia, Jesus' 'A-Triumphal' Entry," 284–89.
36. Tannehill, *Luke*, 285.

here it occurs with a future indicative.³⁷ Perhaps this grammatical irregularity hints at a disturbing historical prospect. Taken alone, the response of Jesus in Luke 19:40 seems to suggest that if the disciples were to be silent, surrounding stones would cry out instead. But if the stones of Luke 19:40 are understood to prefigure the dismantled stones of both Jerusalem (19:44) and the temple (21:5-6), then Jesus' reply can be understood to mean that when the disciples (eventually) become silent the seared and scattered stones of both Jerusalem and the temple will cry out in reminiscence of their witness to his arrival to Jerusalem as king. Such a reading resonates with Luke's apparent understanding of Jerusalem's destruction as divine judgment.³⁸

It is often claimed that Jesus' "forecast" of Jerusalem's destruction in Luke 19:43-44 is an *ex eventu* prediction, that is, a prophecy attributed to Jesus after and indeed in light of the event allegedly foreseen. Even if the wording of this particular oracle is influenced by the later siege and destruction of Jerusalem, as I think probable,³⁹ one should not necessarily infer that Jesus himself was blind to Jerusalem's imminent destruction. The important point here, however, is that Jerusalem was besieged and destroyed by Roman forces within a generation of Jesus' death. According to Luke, moreover, Jesus not only anticipated this event but also explained it theologically in advance.

In light of resonances between Jesus' earlier prophecy of Luke 13:34-35 and Jeremiah, it is noteworthy that the mournful prophecy of judgment in Luke 19:41-44 begins and ends with further allusions to Jeremiah. Jesus' tears for (literally, *upon*) Jerusalem in 19:41 recall the tears of Jeremiah for his decimated people (Jer 9:1; 13:17; 14:17).⁴⁰ The wailing of Jesus is thus not only an expression of grief but also a prophetic sign of impending disaster

---

37. For Lukan scholars puzzled by this, see Fitzmyer, *Luke (X-XXIV)*, 1251-52; Bock, *Luke 9:51—24:53*, 1566. Cf., however, Culy, Parsons, and Stigall, *Luke*, 610, who note Acts 8:31 as a parallel grammatical construction.

38. Some consider that Luke 19:40 alludes to Hab 2:11, within the second of five woes in Hab 2:6-20. Although the imagery of stones crying out is shared, Hab 2:9-11 may well be directed against Babylonian empire-building.

39. See Bovon, *Luke 3*, 18: "Luke, who doubtless is familiar with the siege of Jerusalem by Titus in 70, prefers the biblical language over historical reporting. Speaking of the future (as seen by Jesus), he dispenses with details and precise descriptions."

40. See Hays, "Persecuted Prophet and Judgment on Jerusalem," 468. In addition to the connection in Jeremiah between judgment on Jerusalem and weeping, Hays also draws attention to Lam 1:1, present in the LXX but absent from the Masoretic Text, in which Lamentations as a whole is presented as Jeremiah's lament over Jerusalem laid waste.

for Jerusalem.⁴¹ In other words, even before Jesus' prophecy of Jerusalem's demise, his prophetic tears already intimate imminent peril.

This prophecy of judgment ends by referring to "the time of your visitation," a clear allusion to Jer 6:15 LXX, in which "visitation" signifies divine punishment (also Jer 10:15).⁴² Within an early section of the book of Jeremiah in which the God of Israel turns against the people of Israel because of unfaithfulness (4:5–6:30), Jer 6:15 concludes the second of two brief oracles, the first of which anticipates divine punishment of Jerusalem by means of an enemy from the north (6:1–8) and the second of which envisages divine judgment against the remnant of Israel as comparable to a thoroughgoing gleaning of a vine (6:9–15). Insofar as Jeremiah provides the biblical backdrop to Luke's conception of divine visitation in 19:44, "your visitation" can only signify divine judgment of the kind experienced by Jerusalem at the hands of the Babylonians. As a result, if at this point one fixates on Luke's allusion to a biblical intertext without also paying attention to Luke's own development of the "visitation" motif, one's reading of Luke is likely to undercut his peace emphasis.

In between the two enclosing allusions to Jeremiah, Jesus' oracle of doom can be understood simply as prescience on his part. Had Jerusalem accepted Jesus and his mission as the path to peace, disaster could have been averted. The capacity to perceive that possibility is neutralized, however, by the impending pressure of what might be described as the folding forward of historical inevitability. Things are too far gone to change course. To make room for this reading, I have translated Luke 19:42b as the beginning of a sentence that lasts until the end of 19:44, with the ὅτι (*hoti*) of 19:43 understood in a causal sense. In Western logic, something still future cannot cause something in the present, but here the pattern of thought seems to be that the inevitability of a future outcome (Jerusalem's destruction) makes impossible either insight or action in the present with the potential to avert such an outcome. Understood this way, Jesus is simply pronouncing—and lamenting—inevitable disaster for Jerusalem because it cannot change.

An interpretation of this passage must nevertheless consider with care its final clause, "the reason being that you have not perceived the time of your visitation." Here a theological rationale is given for the horror that will inevitably befall Jerusalem. Indeed, without the evident concern to provide a theological rationale for Jerusalem's destruction, this clause is redundant because a reason has already been provided. Taken at face value, however, the first two words of this final clause, together with verbal and conceptual

---

41. See Fitzmyer, *Luke (X–XXIV)*, 1258.
42. See Hays, "Persecuted Prophet and Judgment on Jerusalem," 469.

echoes of the opening words of Luke 19:42, seem to require that this final clause be understood as interpreting Jerusalem's destruction as divine retribution for failing to accept Jesus and his mission.

The opening two words of the final clause in Luke 19:44, ἀνθ' ὧν (*anth hōn*), can be understood simply in terms of cause and effect, but the first word of 19:43, ὅτι, already suggests causality, even if not the kind to which we are accustomed. Even if the ὅτι of Luke 19:43 is taken to mark the beginning of a new sentence and understood to mean "for" or "yet," however, Luke's distinctive use of ἀνθ' ὧν elsewhere makes it difficult to read this phrase purely in terms of historical causality. The phrase occurs in Luke 1:20; 12:2–3; 19:44; and Acts 12:23. At Luke 1:20, it identifies Zechariah's less-than-wholehearted acceptance of the angel Gabriel's announcement as the reason for his being struck dumb until his baby is born. At Luke 12:2–3, it intimates that the eschatological response (by God) to human secrets is to expose them. Such exposure is integral to divine judgment. In Acts 12:23, it identifies Herod's failure to give glory to God as the reason for his divinely instigated death. In each of these occurrences, tit-for-tat divine punishment is inferred. In Luke 19:44, then, it seems inescapable that Luke attributes Jerusalem's destruction to divine judgment. Finally, even though Luke alone among the Gospel writers uses the phrase ἀνθ' ὧν, it is used regularly in the Septuagint. As Fitzmyer remarks, "The expression occurs frequently in the LXX. See Jer 5:14, 19; 7:13; 16:11, especially with retributive force."[43] In view of Luke's special affinity with Jeremiah in relation to the theme of Jerusalem's destruction, this is but one more indication that Luke envisages the dreadful destruction of Jerusalem as divine judgment for rejecting Jesus.

In three ways, the final clause of this oracle of woe against Jerusalem echoes its opening clause in Luke 19:42, which some consider an example of aposiopesis, the cutting short of verbal expression as if choked off by emotion.[44] First, ἔγνως (*egnōs*), here meaning to perceive or recognize,[45] occurs at the beginning of each clause. Second, each clause contains a temporal expression with the same referent; both "on this day" in 19:42 and "the time of your visitation" in 19:44 clearly refer to Jesus' arrival at Jerusalem, even if both expressions might also signify something more expansive such as the mission of Jesus in its entirety. And finally, even if not identical in meaning, the two phrases, "the things that lead to peace" (19:42) and "your visitation"

---

43. Fitzmyer, *Luke (X–XXIV)*, 958.

44. See, e.g., Bovon, *Luke 3*, 17, for whom aposiopesis is "a rhetorical construction used by Israel's prophets."

45. See ibid.: "It is a question not of the intellectual knowledge favored by the Greeks but of an existential comprehension such as that cherished by the Hebrews."

(19:44) contain closely associated themes and are integrally related within Luke's thinking.[46]

The use of the motif of divine visitation to characterize the identity and significance of Jesus is distinctively Lukan. If the Fourth Gospel is the Gospel of incarnation (John 1:14-18) and Matthew's Gospel is the Gospel of *Immanu-el* (with us is God), Luke's variation on this theme of divine presence in Jesus is the visitation of God in the prophetic-messianic mission of Jesus. Zechariah's praiseful prophecy in Luke 1:68-79 begins and ends with the theme of divine visitation for human salvation, and its concluding lines interrelate the themes of divine visitation and direction in the path of peace. In Luke 7:16, those who witness the restoration to life of a widow's son near Nain praise God by exclaiming, "A great prophet has been raised up among us," and—as an extension of this—"God has visited his people." The prophet Jesus and his mission of restoration signify divine presence—visitation. When this prophet intent on Israel's restoration and Jerusalem's liberation reaches Jerusalem, however, the city fails to perceive its time of visitation. In Israel's scriptures, divine visitation could be for salvation or judgment.[47] Until this point in Luke's Gospel, divine visitation in the prophetic mission of Jesus betokens *shalom* and salvation (cf. 19:10), but Luke 19:41-44 intimates that failure to discern the time of visitation brings in its wake the lowering visitation of judgment.

DAYS OF VENGEANCE: LUKE 21:20-24

The literary context of this passage is Luke's second temple section, prefigured in certain respects by those sections of Luke's infancy and birth narrative situated within the temple (1:5-23; 2:22-52), especially the story of the twelve-year-old Jesus "mixing it up" with teachers in the temple. After reclaiming the temple as a house of prayer in Luke 19:45-46, Jesus teaches daily in the temple until just before Passover (19:47-21:38). His predictions of the temple's destruction within the framework of what is often described as the synoptic apocalypse or eschatological discourse is similar in content, literary context, and structure to parallel passages in Matthew and Mark (Matt 24:1-36; Mark 13:1-37; Luke 21:5-36).[48] Whereas Matthew and Mark indicate that Jesus' spoke this discourse to disciples while seated on

---

46. So also Green, *Gospel of Luke*, 689-90.

47. See Fitzmyer, *Luke (I-IX)*, 382-83; Bock, *Luke 1:1-9:50*, 178-79; Green, *Gospel of Luke*, 689.

48. Regarding key features of Luke 21 that bear on my understanding of this eschatological discourse, see Neville, *A Peaceable Hope*, 136-42.

the Mount of Olives, however, Luke records no change of either venue or audience for this discourse. In Luke's version of events, therefore, the setting for this discourse in which Jesus predicts the demise of both the temple and the city of Jerusalem is the very temple itself, with his disciples the primary audience but in the hearing of "all the people" (20:45). Jerusalem's destruction is forecast in the hearing of any of its inhabitants who care to listen.

The discourse begins with a prediction of the temple's demolition. Days will come in which the fine stones of the temple will be dismantled, with stone not left upon stone that will not be destroyed (Luke 21:5–6). This recalls Jesus' earlier oracle of doom for Jerusalem, in which stone will not be left upon stone when the city is first choked and then razed (Luke 19:43–44). Later in the discourse, Jesus again turns his attention to the destruction of Jerusalem as a whole, echoing his earlier warning on reaching the city.

> When you see Jerusalem surrounded by army encampments, realize then that her desolation has drawn near. Then those in Judea should flee to the hills and those within her should get out and those in the crop-fields should not enter back into her because these are days of vengeance in fulfillment of all that is written. Alas for pregnant and nursing women in those days, for there will be great distress upon the earth and wrath for this people, and they will fall at the edge of a sword and will be taken captive into all the nations, and Jerusalem will be trampled by gentiles until the times of the gentiles will be fulfilled.

In Lukan perspective, Jesus seems to envisage that flight from Jerusalem would be possible even after army encampments encircle the city.[49] Here, however, the perspicacity of Jesus' prescience is less important than Luke's presentation of his interpretation of this impending event. Whereas righteous Simeon had perceived in Jesus the consolation of Israel and the prophet Anna had seen him as the fulfillment of hopes for the liberation of Jerusalem, God's Messiah now warns of Jerusalem's inevitable desolation.

As various phrases within Luke 21:20–24 reveal, there is more to this oracle of woe than mere foresight. Jesus not only sees what is coming but also adjudges that Jerusalem has it coming. Taken alone, the phrases, "days of vengeance (or punishment)" and "wrath for this people," might well be taken as rhetorical flourishes to emphasize both the inevitability and

---

49. One wonders about the wisdom, let alone realism, of the advice to escape from Jerusalem after its encirclement by army encampments. By contrast, Luke 23:26 illustrates Jesus' warning not to return to Jerusalem from surrounding fields used to grow produce. In the case of Simon of Cyrene, he is caught up in the turmoil surrounding Jesus' crucifixion; later, Jesus warns, people returning to the city from their labor in surrounding crop-fields will be caught up in the mayhem of Jerusalem's destruction.

the seriousness of Jerusalem's imminent demise. Read as echoes of Luke 19:41–44, however, these phrases tremor with intimations of divine judgment. Moreover, the note that these "days of vengeance" fulfill the scriptural record ("all that is written") reveals that Jerusalem's future (albeit imminent) destruction is in some sense scripted by the scriptural pattern of divine judgment for covenantal disloyalty. This scriptural pattern is traceable to the prophet Jeremiah, whose literary legacy clearly influenced Luke, but in this passage he alludes also to other scriptures to show that a broad biblical pattern of divine judgment for covenant unfaithfulness is once again about to play itself out.

It is possible to identify numerous biblical allusions within Luke 21:20–24,[50] but two are telling. The first of these phrases, "these are days of vengeance," is commonly regarded as alluding to Hos 9:7–9, in which punishment is pronounced for iniquity and hostility to God's prophet. Without discounting this particular allusion, the phrase might well also allude to Jer 51:6 [28:6 LXX].[51] Although Jer 51:6 occurs within a long oracle of judgment against Babylon, it shares various thematic associations with Luke 21:20–24. The second key phrase, "and Jerusalem will be trampled by gentiles," alludes to the LXX version of Zech 12:3, in which the more positive sense of the original Hebrew seems to have been inverted *against Jerusalem*. So, although Luke makes little use of the terminology of "wrath" (only in 3:7 and here in 21:23),[52] when interpreted in light of other associations within this context, it is difficult to understand "wrath for this people" as meaning anything other than devastating divine judgment. As Carroll reasons, "Is this *orgē* [wrath] Rome's, or God's, or (most likely) God's through the agency of Rome? Not only Jesus' earlier laments over Jerusalem's resistance to the divine purpose (13:34–35; 19:41–44) but also the eschatological discourse's intertextual engagement with prophetic texts that picture Jerusalem's (and the first temple's) demise as the working out of divine judgment on a recalcitrant city—both suggest that divine wrath is in evidence."[53] In

---

50. See Pao and Schnabel, "Luke," 376–77. On biblical echoes within Luke 21:20–24, see also Green, *Gospel of Luke*, 738–39: "Jesus draws the details for his portrait predominantly from the LXX, with the result that he produces a virtual collage of scriptural texts that draws the anticipated destruction of Jerusalem and the temple into an interpretive relationship with the fall of the city at the time of the Exile."

51. Pao and Schnabel, "Luke," 376.

52. See Bovon, *Luke 3*, 114; on the meaning of "wrath" in Luke 21:23, Bovon differentiates between "a reaction of one's mood" and "an expression of the judgment of God as sovereign judge," but such a distinction is perhaps too tidy when divine wrath is expressed through militaristic means.

53. Carroll, *Luke*, 418. (In a footnote to this inference, Carroll cites John Nolland's reference to the prophetic pattern provided by Jeremiah 25.)

short, according to Luke's understanding, Jerusalem's trampling by Gentiles is, in accordance with scriptural precedent, the mode of divine judgment.

BLESSED ARE THE BARREN: LUKE 23:26–31

At the point in the passion narrative when Jesus is led away for execution and Simon of Cyrene is co-opted to carry his cross, Luke is in relative agreement with the shared narrative sequence of Matthew and Mark. At this precise point, however, Luke inserts into his account an episode in which Jesus utters words of foreboding to women lamenting his fate.[54] Evoking some of the language and imagery of earlier texts, Jesus advises "daughters of Jerusalem" that their expression of grief should be for themselves and their children rather than for him:

> Following him [Jesus] was a large company of people and of women who hit themselves and wailed for him. Turning toward them, Jesus said, "Daughters of Jerusalem, do not wail over me but rather wail over yourselves and over your children because days are coming, see, during which they will say, 'Blessed are the barren and the wombs that have not generated life and breasts that have not nurtured.' Then they will begin to say to the mountains, 'Fall on us,' and to the hills, 'Cover us,' because if they do these things to a green tree, what will happen when it is dry?"

By means of various motifs, Luke associates this episode with earlier related texts. Jesus directs his words to "daughters of *Jerusalem*," forewarning them of disaster soon to befall them and their children. These children are reminiscent of Jerusalem's "children" in Luke 13:34 and 19:44 (perhaps also the unborn children alluded to in 21:23). The countercultural blessing on women who are barren—blessed only insofar as they will not have to witness the killing of their children—echoes the woe pronounced upon pregnant or breast-feeding women in Luke 21:23.[55] The wailing of women

---

54. Among the ways in which Luke's account of Jesus' crucifixion is distinctive, Luke frames his narration of the crucifixion with references to expressions of grief for Jesus by non-aligned crowds (23:27, 48). As Luke 23:28 makes plain, these crowds included residents of Jerusalem. These narrative embellishments enhance the pathos of Luke's account, but the mood is one of grim foreboding rather than a sense of distress that children of those now mourning for Jesus will in due course experience something comparable to his misfortune.

55. On the likely authenticity of this pair of "blessing" and woe to women, see Pitre, "Blessing the Barren." Cf Pitre, *Jesus, the Tribulation*, 316–17, 365–66, where he continues to maintain the authenticity of Luke 23:27–31 but retracts his earlier judgment that this passage composes textual evidence for the view that Jesus advocated

over Jesus recalls the wailing of Jesus over Jerusalem in Luke 19:41, an intratextual resonance made that much stronger by Jesus redirecting toward Jerusalem the women's wailing for him. The phrase at the beginning of Luke 23:29, "See, days are coming," echoes both 19:43 and 21:6, albeit now cast in the present tense (perhaps to intensify foreboding). Moreover, this expression is, as John Nolland points out, "Septuagintal language, notable in Jeremiah (7:32; 16:14; 38:31 [= 31:31 in MT]), where it evokes Jeremiah's certainty about the exile and restoration sequence awaiting Judah."[56] As in each previous prophecy of judgment on Jerusalem, this passage contains yet another clear allusion to a prophetic text. Luke 23:30 alludes to Hos 10:8, in which the same imagery articulates a craving for relief from punishment for covenant unfaithfulness.[57]

This passage, like others before it, undoubtedly anticipates the historical destruction of Jerusalem. Beyond the intertextual allusion to Hos 10:8, however, there would seem to be no unambiguous indication that Jerusalem's destruction is conceptualized in terms of divine judgment. That said, the imagery drawn from Hos 10:8, seeking a quick end from terror, is explained by the ominous proverbial saying of Luke 23:31. Whatever the meaning of this saying, which is ambiguous, it seems to relate what will eventually befall Jerusalem with what is in process of occurring to Jesus. The reversal Jesus calls for with respect to wailing (not for himself but for inhabitants of Jerusalem) would seem to be paralleled by that which is now done to Jesus being turned against many more, which in context can only mean the inhabitants of Jerusalem. Framed in the form of a (rhetorical?) question, the proverbial ending to this exchange infers a greater calamity from a lesser one. The passage as a whole has Jerusalem's destruction in view, and the proverbial question seems to associate that event with Jesus' death.[58]

If this is correct, how does Luke envisage that Jerusalem's destruction relates to Jesus' death? In the exegetical tradition, the following "decodings" of Jesus' proverbial utterance in Luke 23:31 have been offered.[59] First, if hu-

---

childlessness for women.

56. Nolland, *Luke 18:35–24:53*, 1137. Cf. Brown, *Death of the Messiah*, 922-23: "With slight variations the LXX uses 'coming are days' in the present tense in a number of prophecies of joy and of woe: Jer 7:32; 16:14; Amos 2:4; Mal 3:19 (4:1)." Jeremiah 7:32 is a prophecy of woe, but 16:14 forms part of a prophecy of restoration and 31:31 begins the well-known prophecy of hope for a new covenant with Israel and Judah.

57. See also Rev 6:12-17, in which the same imagery occurs within the context of eschatological judgment.

58. Cf. Bovon, *Luke 3*, 302-3, who considers that the implicit connection between the death of Jesus and the destruction of Jerusalem is apparent as early as Jesus addresses the mourning women.

59. See Fitzmyer, *Luke (X–XXIV)*, 1498-99; Brown, *Death of the Messiah*, 926-27;

manity generally behaves in this way before the measure of its wickedness is full, how much worse will things be when wickedness overflows? Second, if the Romans treat me in this way, how much more will they mistreat Jerusalem? Third, if Jews (or representatives of the Jews) treat me in this way, how much more severely will they be treated (by God) in return? Fourth, if I have been permitted (by God) to undergo what I am experiencing, how much more can Jerusalem expect divine judgment. And fifth, it is impossible to decipher this proverbial utterance more precisely than to say that it intimates something worse to come than that which is now occurring.

Each but the first of these interpretive options is defensible. Perhaps the third and fourth interpretations compete for the most scholarly support. On reflection, however, it is possible to combine the second and third interpretations so that the subject of the first part of the saying, the protasis, incorporates all those involved in hostility toward Jesus (both non-Jews and Jewish leaders), while the implied subject of the second part of the saying, the apodosis, is God (a divine passive) enacting future, albeit imminent, judgment by means of overwhelming Roman force. If this is granted, there is not a great deal to differentiate between the second, third, and fourth interpretations.

If this proverbial saying is seen in isolation, the fifth indefinite interpretation seems most plausible to me. Taken alone, the saying simply infers that something more calamitous will happen than what is now happening. If the tree (or wood) represents Jesus, as seems likely, what is done to Jesus while he is alive (green) pales by comparison with what is likely to be done after he d(r)ies.[60] The contrast is strictly between the severity of action done by indeterminate others before and after Jesus' death, which, with consummate artistry, Luke narrates next (23:33–49).

In its current literary context, however, this enigmatic proverbial saying cannot finally be interpreted in isolation (even though I think it helpful to begin by considering it on its own). Not only does it conclude a series of sayings that, taken together, compose an oracle of doom for Jerusalem but it also culminates the series of four Lukan passages in which Jerusalem's inevitable destruction is conceptualized as divine judgment. In both its immediate and its broader context, therefore, Luke 23:31 is perhaps best

---

Bock, *Luke 9:51—24:53*, 1847–48; Bovon, *Luke 3*, 305.

60. This seems to be the view of Tannehill, *Luke*, 339–40: "Apparently, the time of Jesus' crucifixion is compared with green (or moist) wood and the time of Jerusalem's destruction with dry wood. Green wood makes poor firewood; it will burn much better when it has had time to dry. Already Jesus is suffering violence, but when the prophesied time of 'great distress' (21:23) comes (i.e., when the wood is dry), the destructive fire will burn fiercely and consume many."

understood to mean that if Jesus can be so harshly treated by his opponents (Jewish and non-Jewish) that it leads to his death, a much worse fate awaits Jerusalem because it was complicit in—not merely the site of—his death.

JERUSALEM'S JUDGMENT: LUKE'S TEXTS IN REVIEW

Having examined Luke 13:31–35; 19:41–44; 21:20–24; and 23:26–31 in narrative sequence, the inescapable conclusion is that they compose a series of interrelated texts. Among the various verbal and thematic interconnections between these textual siblings, the following are especially unifying. First and foremost, Jerusalem is explicitly referred to either in each passage itself or in its immediate literary context, and in the first two passages Jerusalem is addressed in personal terms. Second, each passage contains both lament (13:34; 19:41–42; 21:23; 23:27–29) and destruction motifs (13:31, 33, 34–35; 19:43–44; 21:6, 20, 24; 23:30–31). Third, there is a strong presence throughout of both maternal imagery (13:34; 21:23; 23:28–29; also 19:44, with Jerusalem pictured as the mother of her inhabitants) and terminology for children (13:34; 19:44; 23:28; also implied in 21:23). Fourth, the series is punctuated by impending temporal notices (13:32–33; 19:42, 43, 44; 21:6, 23, 24; 23:29). Less persistent but no less striking is the vocabulary of stones and stoning (13:34; 19:40, 44; cf. 21:5–6), together with ἀφίημι (*aphiēmi*) terminology (13:35; 19:44; cf. 21:6 and the imagery of flight in 21:21).

Within Luke's narrative progression, these textual siblings do not simply resonate with each other, whether by foreshadowing or echoing. This they most certainly do, but in narrative terms these four passages develop an accumulating effect as, one after another, they instill an ever-increasing sense of foreboding. Their narrative placement reinforces this sense of menacing development. Luke 13:31–35 and 19:41–44 occur at the midpoint and culmination, respectively, of Jesus' journey to Jerusalem, a distinctive structural feature of the Gospel. The third text, Luke 21:5–6, 20–24, occurs within Luke's temple section and is contextualized in such a way that Jesus' forewarning of the destruction of both the temple and Jerusalem occurs within the temple itself. The fourth and final text, Luke 23:26–31, takes up the bulk of the passage immediately preceding Luke's crucifixion account, thereby adding to the sense of significance of Jesus' death—the point at which the green tree dies and begins to dry.

The interpretive significance of the interconnectedness of these passages and their cumulative effect is that they not only contribute to the dramatic impact of Luke's unfolding narrative but also interanimate each other. In other words, not only does each passage contribute an added dimension to a larger whole but each may also be read in light of that larger whole to which it contributes. As a result, inasmuch as each of these passages taken singly intimates an understanding of Jerusalem's destruction as divine judgment, that intimation is both confirmed and reinforced by all four taken together. In Lukan perspective, one cannot but conclude, Jerusalem's destruction by overwhelming Roman force is also divine judgment for rejecting Jesus' prophetic-messianic presence and mission.[61]

INTERPRETING LUKE ON JERUSALEM'S JUDGMENT

If the foregoing analysis of four interrelated Lukan passages commends itself, Luke's interpretation of Jerusalem's destruction as divine judgment for rejecting the prophetic-messianic mission of Jesus raises various problems, even if not always perceived as such by exegetes and interpreters. The first relates to the reception history of this view of Jerusalem's destruction and its role in fostering anti-Jewish sentiment down through the centuries. A second is the knock-on effect of such a perception for conceptualizing eschatological judgment. A third difficulty is the almost intolerable tension that Luke's theological conception of Jerusalem's destruction creates for his Christology and hence theology as a whole. And a fourth problem concerns the implications of Luke's theological interpretation of Jerusalem's destruction for conceptualizing divine action, a theological issue too intricate and intractable to be addressed here.[62] In what follows, after sketching the parameters of the first two problems, I appeal to Luke's Christology of peace to unsettle careless appeal to his interpretation of Jerusalem's destruction in terms of divine retribution.

First, present-day biblical interpreters can hardly be unaware of the damaging reception history of Luke's theological conception of Jerusalem's destruction, a reception history that stretches back to the early centuries of the Christian church.[63] For example, Origen, the illustrious third-century

---

61. Cf. Longenecker, "Rome's Victory and God's Honour," 96–99, who contends that Luke's defense of divine honor in the wake of Jerusalem's destruction features divine abandonment of the temple *but not divine judgment by means of Roman might* (a "theodicy of conscription"). I would like to follow Longenecker in what he denies as well as in what he affirms, but that is difficult in light of the four textual siblings discussed in this chapter, especially when considered in relation to their biblical intertexts.

62. For preliminary remarks on this difficulty in relation to Luke 13, albeit in light of its textual siblings, see Neville, "Calamity and the Biblical God," 51–54.

63. Among NT writers, Luke is not alone in this respect, but I restrict my focus to his theological conception of Jerusalem's destruction because interpretive grappling with Luke's rationale for the razing of Jerusalem by Roman forces is not necessarily

biblical theologian, clearly expressed the view in his *Contra Celsum* (1.47; 2.13; 4.22, 73) that Jerusalem's destruction was justly deserved divine recompense for Jewish complicity in the crucifixion of Jesus. So, too, did Eusebius of Caesarea in his influential *Ecclesiastical History* (3.5–7). In *Josephus and the New Testament*, Steve Mason correctly castigates both Origen and Eusebius for distorting Josephus on the reason for the fall of Jerusalem to the Romans.[64] Josephus never so much as hints that the Roman razing of Jerusalem was divine payback for Jewish mistreatment of Jesus or his brother, James, but both Origen and Eusebius manipulate his account of the Judean revolt in support of their own theological rationale for Jerusalem's destruction. Their reason for doing so might well be traceable to Luke, however; in both *Contra Celsum* 2.13 and *Ecclesiastical History* 3.7, first Origen and then Eusebius cite at least one of the Lukan passages examined in this chapter.

Remarkably, in a study of "Anti-Judaism and the Gospel of Luke," Daryl Schmidt makes but passing reference to this series of Lukan texts (13:31–35; 19:41–44; 21:20–24; 23:26–31) to reinforce his argument that Luke presents Jesus as standing in the long line of prophets rejected by Israel.[65] Writing in response to Schmidt, Allan McNicol opines that precisely these Lukan texts, which together articulate an interpretation of Jerusalem's destruction as divine retribution for rejecting Jesus as Israel's messiah, come closest to expressing an incipient anti-Judaism. Regarding such texts, together with others in Acts that place responsibility for the death of Jesus at the feet of Jews (2:22–23, 36; 3:12–13; 4:10; 5:30; 10:39; 13:27–28), McNicol writes: "A wedge appears to have been driven into the text at this point that led later generations of real readers, acclimatized in a culture of anti-Judaism, to use these texts in a destructive way."[66] Origen, Eusebius, and others in their wake confirm McNicol's characterization of the damaging reception history of Luke's theological interpretation of Jerusalem's destruction.

The second problem associated with Luke's interpretation of Jerusalem's destruction as "days of (divine) vengeance" relates to the connection sometimes drawn between divine judgment as instanced in the Roman razing of Jerusalem and eschatological judgment. Scholarly opinion that the destruction of Jerusalem is not only integral to Lukan eschatology but also prototypical of eschatological judgment takes two forms.[67] The first of these is that Luke 21 has nothing in view beyond the destruction of Jerusalem.

---

applicable more broadly.

64. Mason, *Josephus and the New Testament*, 9–19.
65. Schmidt, "Anti-Judaism and the Gospel of Luke," 82–88.
66. McNicol, "Response to Daryl D. Schmidt," 116–17.
67. I discuss both forms of this interpretive position in *A Peaceable Hope*, 136–43.

The anticipated arrival of the Son of humanity (21:25–28) is but theological commentary on the trampling of Jerusalem by Roman soldiers: the mission of Jesus is vindicated by Jerusalem's destruction. On this viewpoint, the return of Jesus as promised in Acts 1:11 is different from the prophesied coming of the Son of humanity but implicitly no less devastating. The second form of this interpretive position is that the prophesied coming of the Son of humanity equates to the expected return of Jesus but that there is nevertheless a correlation between this as-yet-future event and the historical destruction of Jerusalem. On this viewpoint, Jerusalem's "days of vengeance" comprise a precursor to eschatological judgment: the historical destruction of Jerusalem is a paradigmatic preview of divine judgment at the end.

Having outlined two difficulties associated with Luke's interpretation of Jerusalem's destruction as divine judgment, I turn to the task of appraising this evangelist's understanding of Jerusalem's judgment in light of his prophetic-messianic Christology. There is general agreement that Luke presents Jesus in prophetic terms, but that prophetic profile is often overemphasized to the extent that it overshadows and thereby undervalues more exalted dimensions of Luke's Christology. By characterizing this evangelist's Christology as "prophetic-messianic," I affirm both prophetic and more exalted aspects of his understanding of the identity and significance of Jesus, for example, Jesus as God's Messiah (2:11, 26; 9:20), as God's Son (1:32, 35; 3:22; 9:35; 10:21–22), and as divine "visitation" (7:16; 19:44).[68]

Earlier I acknowledged that in light of Israel's prophetic tradition, in which Jerusalem's destruction in the sixth century BCE was interpreted as divine judgment, it was natural, perhaps even inevitable, from within Israelite tradition to interpret Jerusalem's destruction in 70 CE along similar lines. Such a view is commonplace. For example, in *An Introduction to the Gospels and Acts*, Charles Puskas and David Crump write that "if Luke's depiction of Jesus as Israel's final prophet reflects an authentic reminiscence of the historical Jesus, then condemning the city in which he is finally rejected and crucified, using language borrowed from his prophetic predecessors, is precisely what one would expect him to do."[69] Puskas and Crump's book is a valuable introductory text, but in this instance it also illustrates how readily biblical scholars ignore interpretive pressure points. What Puskas

---

68. For fuller discussion of Luke's "divine identity" Christology, see Hays, *Reading Backwards*, 55–74; Hays, *Echoes of Scripture*, 221–64.

69. Puskas and Crump, *An Introduction*, 146–47. For a similar view, see McWhirter, *Rejected Prophets*, 76: "For Luke, the Jesus who utters woes, parables, and judgment oracles against Jerusalem is a prophet like Hosea, Zephaniah, Zechariah, Isaiah, Jeremiah, and Ezekiel. In their day, God sent Gentile armies against his people. Now, after the first coming of the Messiah, God will send them again, for many of the same reasons."

and Crump aver is well and good, *provided Jesus added nothing new to the profile of a prophet*. All too often, Jesus is interpreted in biblical categories without taking into account ways in which his mission and message stretch and indeed reshape such categories. Insofar as Jesus is understood by Luke to fulfill Scripture, he also reconfigures biblical expectations, thereby placing the onus on responsible interpreters to reappraise biblical precedents and categories for understanding Jesus even as they appeal to them.

Israel's prophetic heritage provides the necessary matrix for understanding how and why Luke interpreted Jerusalem's destruction as divine retribution, but it also provides interpretive resources for reading Luke in more hopeful terms. Prophecies of divine judgment were sometimes conditional, so perhaps Luke considered that those prophecies of judgment against Jerusalem that he attributes to Jesus were only fulfilled historically because they did not provoke change. Furthermore, beyond destruction interpreted as judgment, certain prophets dared to hope for forgiveness and restoration. Hosea was one such prophet, Jeremiah another. Noting that the various Lukan pronouncements of divine judgment on Jerusalem allude to Hosea 9–10, Christopher Marshall comments: "Yet just as Hosea's threats are followed by the counternote of mercy . . . so Jesus' warnings of judgment are not necessarily the last word on the matter but are meant to provoke Israel to repentance."[70]

In a similar vein, Bruce Fisk interprets Luke 13:31–35 and 19:41–44 as similar in kind to Jeremiah's provisional prophecies of judgment against Jerusalem followed by promises of restoration.[71] Three points within his larger argument pertain here. First, he follows Dale Allison by interpreting Luke 13:35b as a contingent prophecy,[72] thereby making room for the prospect of hope for Jerusalem beyond calamity, especially if Luke 13:34–35 and 19:41–44 are read in light of each other. Second, he notes that the mournful indictment against Jerusalem in Luke 19:41–44 is restricted to the immediate future, again leaving open the prospect of restoration beyond devastation. And third, he draws attention to frequent offers of forgiveness within Luke–Acts subsequent to Jesus' prophecy of woe against Jerusalem.[73]

---

70. Marshall, *Beyond Retribution*, 165.

71. Fisk, "See My Tears," 147–78.

72. See Allison, "Matt 23:39 = Luke 13:35b as a Conditional Prophecy," 75–84.

73. Responding via personal communication to my earlier discussion of Jerusalem's judgment in Luke's Gospel (*A Peaceable Hope*, 111–17), Darrin Snyder Belousek makes a similar observation in support of the view that, for Luke, God's judgment of Jerusalem is not solely retributive but rather tempered by mercy. For his own study of holistic salvation in Luke's Gospel, see Snyder Belousek, *Good News*. Also relevant in bigger-picture terms is Snyder Belousek, *Atonement, Justice, and Peace*, in which the

Together, these considerations lead Fisk to suggest that, for Luke, the judgment visited on Jerusalem may not be God's final word for Jerusalem.

Fisk follows in the footsteps of those who interpret Jerusalem's judgment within Luke–Acts in "tragic" terms, that is, as a lamentable feature of the narrative in which biblical hopes for the redemption of Israel (expressed at various points, but especially in Luke 1–2) fail to find fulfillment.[74] Such an interpretive perspective holds out hope for Jerusalem beyond historical calamity construed biblically as divine judgment and checks against charges of Lukan "anti-Judaism." In this connection, moreover, the mournful mode of Jesus' prophecy of judgment for Jerusalem is hermeneutically significant. Discussing Tannehill's thesis that Luke narrates the story of Israel in tragic terms, Terence Donaldson writes:

> because of Israel's failure to recognize Jesus or to repent at the preaching of the apostles, Jerusalem has been destroyed and left desolate (Luke 13.33–35; 19.41–44; 21.20–24; 23.27–31). But while Luke is constrained to tell of the destruction of Jerusalem rather than of its redemption, and of the desolation of Israel rather than of its consolation, he takes no pleasure in this turn of events. It is an occasion for weeping, not for gloating: Jesus weeps over the prospect of Jerusalem's destruction (only in Luke; see 19:41) and he later urges the "daughters of Jerusalem" to weep over the coming calamity (23.27–31).[75]

Even if seen solely in terms of prophetic precedent, the mournful manner of Jesus' prophecies against Jerusalem expresses a deep-seated conviction that divine judgment is enacted grudgingly, indeed, distressfully. Judgment may be a divine prerogative, but it is in some sense an alien or extrinsic divine disposition. Perhaps the mournful mode of Jesus' prophecies against Jerusalem even signals reticence to attribute human destruction directly to the divine will. Influenced by an interpretation of divine judgment in the Hebrew Bible that envisages the created order as constructed so that certain human actions bring about inevitable negative consequences, Brendan Byrne interprets Luke 19:41–44 as follows: "The destruction is not so much a divine punishment as a consequence of the fateful choice that

---

biblical resources for the Christian doctrine of atonement are interpreted in line with a restorative rather than (strictly) retributive notion of divine justice.

74. See especially Tannehill, "Israel in Luke–Acts," reprinted with related essays in Tannehill, *Shape of Luke's Story*, 105–124. (In Lukan terms, the destruction of Jerusalem is also tragic because it is the inevitable consequence of unwillingness on the part of Jerusalem's leadership to embrace what might have averted that impending disaster.)

75. Donaldson, *Jews and Anti-Judaism*, 70, echoing Tannehill, "Israel in Luke–Acts," 75.

Jerusalem makes."[76] It is doubtful whether the biblical conception of divine judgment can be reduced to an autonomous act-consequence construct, however, especially in the Deuteronomistic tradition, which seems to have had a determinative effect on both Jeremiah and Luke.[77] Indeed, in the case of Luke's understanding of divine judgment, one wonders whether his conceptual framework was shaped more by Deuteronomistic ideology than by his own Christological convictions.[78] So although Tannehill, Fisk, and others detect a glimmer of hope for Jerusalem beyond divinely ordained devastation, their acceptance of Luke's interpretation of Jerusalem's destruction as divine judgment is nevertheless at odds with Luke's Christology of peace. Even though the theological tension generated by Luke's attribution of both "visitation" in Jesus and Jerusalem's destruction to divine action is probably irresolvable, to probe this pressure point is perhaps the most promising way forward.

Of the four biblical Gospel writers, Luke is most evidently the evangelist of peace. This is because peace is central to Luke's theological and moral vision, as Willard Swartley has argued for decades, most recently in his *Covenant of Peace*.[79] First, the vocabulary of peace is much more prominent in Luke's Gospel than in any of the other canonical Gospels. As Swartley points out, the Greek term for peace, ἡ εἰρήνη (*hē eirēnē*), occurs fourteen times in Luke's Gospel, with only one parallel occurrence in Mark 5:34 and one parallel occurrence in Matt 10:34.[80] This is a larger number

76. Byrne, *Hospitality of God*, 156. On the "act-consequence" interpretation of divine judgment in the Hebrew Bible, see Koch, "Is There a Doctrine of Retribution?" and Via, *Divine Justice*, 14–22. Although possibly anachronistic in relation to the ancient Israelite mind-set, it seems necessary to differentiate between expressions of the "act-consequence" construct that emphasize divine agency (in some sense) and those that dilute divine involvement in retribution, as in the citation from Byrne.

77. On mediated divine agency in relation to expressions of divine retribution in Jeremiah, see Fretheim, "Violence and the God of the Old Testament," 116–24.

78. For texts illustrative of the Deuteronomistic mind-set, including the historical pattern of Israel's violent rejection of God's prophets, see Kloppenborg, *Tenants in the Vineyard*, 220–21. In this connection, see also part 1 of Turner, *Israel's Last Prophet*, in which the motif of the rejection of the prophets is traced as an expression of Deuteronomistic theology. For my current interpretive purpose, I emphasize the tension between Deuteronomistic and Lukan theology, but there are also positive continuities between Deuteronomistic and Lukan theology and ethics. See, e.g., McConville, "Retribution in Deuteronomy," who argues that divine justice in Deuteronomy is conceived as tempered by compassion. On compassion as determinative for Luke's conception of justice, see Marshall, *Compassionate Justice*, 13–245.

79. Swartley, *Covenant of Peace*, 121–76.

80. Ibid., 122. See Luke 1:79; 2:14, 29; 7:50; 8:48 (cf. Mark 5:34); 10:5–6 (three occurrences); 11:21; 12:51 (cf. Matt 10:34); 14:32; 19:38, 42; 24:36. The peace greeting in Luke 24:36 is textually uncertain, however, and the references in 11:21 and 14:32 lack

than the total occurrences of ἡ εἰρήνη and its cognates in the three other biblical Gospels combined.[81] Luke's considerably more frequent use of the vocabulary of peace signals the theological and ethical significance he attached to this theme, but it is not simply numerical frequency that counts. With rare exceptions, Luke's peace references carry significant theological and/or moral weight.

Equally important is Swartley's observation that the majority of Luke's distinctive peace references occur at structurally significant junctures in his Gospel.[82] Three references to peace appear in Luke's infancy narratives (1:79; 2:14, 29), and the risen Jesus' greeting of peace comes near the end of the Gospel (24:36), thereby enclosing the narrative as a whole. Something similar is achieved in Luke's central section. Near the beginning of Jesus' journey to Jerusalem, there is a cluster of three references to peace (10:5–6), and the peace theme is sounded twice more when Jesus reaches Jerusalem (19:38, 42). Thus, both the Gospel as a whole and Luke's most distinctive section within it are bracketed by references to peace.

The comparatively large number of references to peace in Luke's Gospel, the theological and/or moral significance of most such references, and their strategic narrative plotting combine to compel the conclusion that peace is central to Luke's understanding of the identity and significance of Jesus. Furthermore, although the book of Acts fails to foreground peace as much as Luke's Gospel,[83] Acts 10:36 reinforces the close thematic connection between Christology and peace by summing up, in a crucial speech by Peter, the mission of Jesus in its entirety as God's peace proclamation to Israel.

Beyond Luke's explicit references to peace and their narrative role, Swartley identifies three other Lukan features that complement and thereby reinforce his emphasis on peace. First, although Luke records no blessing on peacemakers (cf. Matt 5:9) or dominical command to practice peace (cf. Mark 9:50), Swartley shows how both the content and arrangement of Jesus' teaching in Luke 6:27–36, the central section of Luke's parallel to Matthew's Sermon on the Mount, accentuate (peacemaking and peace-promoting) love of enemies.[84] Second, Swartley documents how Luke's sociopolitical

---

the theological depth of the other references.

81. See Matt 5:9; 10:13 (twice), 34 (twice); Mark 5:34; 9:50; John 14:27 (twice); 16:33; 20:19, 21, 26.

82. Swartley, *Covenant of Peace*, 129–30.

83. There are seven references to peace in Acts (7:26; 9:31; 10:36; 12:20; 15:33; 16:36; 24:2), half as many as in Luke's Gospel, and only Acts 10:36 carries the theological and moral weight of most peace references in the Gospel.

84. Swartley, *Covenant of Peace*, 130–31. (Such an observation takes on added

stance is critically countercultural in relation to deep-set Roman values but nevertheless congruent with a peaceful moral vision. Significant dimensions of this peaceful moral vision include: concern for those ordinarily disregarded by people with power, rank, and status such as the poor, the infirm, and the disreputable; a critique of wealth and the wealthy; condemnation of injustice and oppression matched by a call for social relations to be based on humble service; and repudiation of violence.[85] And third, complementing Luke's focus on peace, Swartley draws attention to the prominence within Luke's Gospel of the theme of righteousness or justice.[86] In Lukan perspective, Jesus both proclaims and embodies peace with justice, whether peace as the fruit of justice or justice as the mode of peace.

Integral to Luke's Christology is his use of the motif of (divine) "visitation" to characterize the mission of Jesus in its totality.[87] Drawing upon biblical (especially Septuagintal) and post-biblical traditions of divine visitation for the purpose of either rescue or retribution, Luke applied this motif to the peaceable and restorative mission of Jesus. A close association between "visitation" and *shalom* is especially evident in the two visitation references that enclose Zechariah's prophecy of praise (1:67–79) and also in the uniquely Lukan account of the restoration to life of a widow's only son near Nain (7:11–17). Even the "visitation" reference in Luke 19:44 is closely associated with peace (19:42), although Luke evidently envisages that God's peaceful and peace-oriented presence in Jesus will give way to retribution because divine visitation in the mission of Jesus was not discerned by Jerusalem.

Since divine visitation in the biblical tradition is associated with both rescue and retribution, scholars routinely affirm that both associations are present in Luke's Gospel—albeit usually without pausing to ponder the theological implications. The question provoked by Luke 19:44 is whether divine visitation in Jesus and the retribution predicted for failing to discern divine visitation in Jesus equally and compatibly convey the character of the creator—and hence judge—of all the earth.

---

significance if, as Dale Allison argues, much of Luke 6:27–42 plausibly goes back to Jesus in something like its present form. See Allison, *Constructing Jesus*, 305–81.)

85. Swartley, *Covenant of Peace*, 133–34.

86. Ibid., 140–44.

87. For my earlier discussion of the significance of the "visitation" motif for Luke's theological and moral vision, see Neville, *A Peaceable Hope*, 107–11. More recently, see also Hays, *Reading Backwards*, 66–69; Lanier, "Luke's Distinctive Use of the Temple."

CONCLUDING COMMENTS

Within a Gospel narrative that features peace in its most pregnant Christological sense—peaceable and restorative divine visitation in Jesus—it is theologically and morally incongruent that Luke should interpret Jerusalem's destruction by Roman forces as divine judgment. That on this matter his viewpoint resonates somewhat with that of certain Jewish contemporaries, Josephus and the authors of *4 Ezra* and *2 Baruch*,[88] reveals that he was, unavoidably, a person of his age. Such affinities in outlook may also bespeak a perspective on Jerusalem's destruction from within the framework of first-century Israelite faith, deeply indebted to the prophetic tradition and resonant with Deuteronomistic patterns of thought. Whether Luke was Jewish himself—perhaps a proselyte to Judaism or so-called "God-fearer" before accepting Jesus as the Jewish Messiah—or (as is commonly supposed) a non-Jewish Christian has a bearing on whether one considers that he reflected on Jerusalem's destruction as divine judgment on *us* or *them*? If Luke was Jewish,[89] his theological interpretation of Jerusalem's destruction may be regarded as the result of communal *self*-examination, which makes room to limit such an interpretation to his own situation and audience. If he was non-Jewish, however, the damaging reception history of his theological interpretation of Jerusalem's destruction is but the inevitable unfolding of a biblical dictum.

Even allowing for Luke's biblical heritage and social location, his Christology of peace seems not to have nuanced his interpretation of Jerusalem's destruction, even though he was capable of seeing certain other things differently from his contemporaries as a result of reflecting on the mission and message of Jesus. Among the canonical Gospel writers, to state things starkly, Luke's Christology is the most explicitly peaceable, but his theological interpretation of Jerusalem's destruction is the most obviously

---

88. According to Josephus, Jerusalem's downfall in 70 CE coincided with the precise day of its capitulation to the Babylonians centuries earlier. See Josephus, *Jewish War*, 6.249–70. A major theme of his account of the Judean revolt is that Jerusalem's destruction was less a consequence of Roman might than of divine displeasure inflamed by intra-Jewish factional violence. See Mason, *Josephus and the New Testament*, 64–99. For translations of *4 Ezra* and *2 Baruch*, both of which discern (but also wrestle with the notion of) divine chastisement in Jerusalem's destruction, see Stone and Henze, *4 Ezra and 2 Baruch*. On these and related Jewish responses to the destruction of Jerusalem, see Jones, *Jewish Reactions to the Destruction of Jerusalem in A.D. 70*. See also Esler, "God's Honour and Rome's Triumph," and Longenecker, "Rome's Victory and God's Honour."

89. See McWhirter, *Rejected Prophets*, 123–24. Appealing to the work of Jacob Jervell, David Tiede, and Donald Juel, McWhirter calls for scholars to reconsider whether Luke might have been Jewish.

retributive. As a result, one wonders whether Luke perceived and internalized all the follows—or should follow—from his own Christology of peace.

From an interpretive perspective, it is difficult to integrate both Luke's Christology of peace and his interpretation of Jerusalem's destruction as divine judgment into a coherent theological-moral outlook. Even if one allows Luke the latitude to hold both together in tension, an interpretive choice now seems inevitable if one is to avoid a schizoid theological perspective. And insofar as Luke correctly perceived *in Jesus* divine visitation for human restoration, his Christology of peace relativizes his theological interpretation of Jerusalem's devastation as divine retribution.

Jesus himself may well have perceived with prophetic foresight that Jerusalem was bound for destruction, but his prophecies are likely to have been symbolic and intuitive, like those of his prophetic predecessors.[90] Even if one grants to Jesus greater prescience than his prophetic predecessors, one decisive clause in what Luke attributes to Jesus reveals that, however faithfully he may have been concerned to transmit the substance of Jesus' message, he unavoidably gave it his own coloring. The final clause in Luke 19:41–44 bears the imprint of Luke's "divine visitation" Christology and is therefore likely to represent his own interpretation of Jerusalem's destruction rather than that of Jesus.[91] Here, in short, Luke's Christology undermines his redundant theological rationale for Jerusalem's destruction: "the reason being that you have not perceived the time of your *visitation*" (19:44b). Not only does Luke's theological interpretation of Jerusalem's destruction reveal a profound tension within his own Christology but its articulation in terms of "visitation" also identifies such an interpretation as an adaptation of Jesus' own position rather than as originating with Jesus.

---

90. See Meyer, *Aims of Jesus*, 246–47.

91. Cf. Gaston, *No Stone on Another*, 334–39, for whom the theme of peace and the motif of visitation derive from Proto-Luke (dated to circa 50 CE) and reflect the mid-century Palestinian church's ambivalent attitude toward Israel arising from the failure of its mission to Israel. Even if not original to Luke, however, the motif of divine visitation in Jesus is a distinctive feature of his Gospel.

4

Crossing Swords, II

A Time for Swords?

(LUKE 22:35–38)

IN THE SYNOPTIC TRADITION, the denouement of Jesus' mission begins with preparations for Passover on the part of Jesus and with preparations to truncate Jesus' mission on the part of Judas and the chief priests (Matt 26:1–16; Mark 14:1–11; Luke 22:1–6). From this point onward, the first three Gospel writers narrate the same basic story line, but Luke's account is clearly the most distinctive by virtue of unique additions and changes in the relative sequence of certain incidents. Even in his introduction to the passion narrative, Luke decides against including the story of Jesus' anointing by a woman in Bethany (Matt 26:6–13; Mark 14:3–9), no doubt because he had already included a similar episode much earlier in his Gospel (7:36–50). Between the plot to put an end to Jesus' mission and its realization with the arrest of Jesus, Luke describes Jesus' final Passover meal with his disciples, his prayer of distress on the Mount of Olives while his disciples sleep, and events associated with Jesus' betrayal by Judas (22:7–53). Among the distinctive features of Luke's description of these events, the following are especially significant: first, Luke's placement of Jesus' response to the dispute over rank and status among the disciples immediately after Jesus' forecast of betrayal following the meal (22:21–30); second, Jesus' words to Simon in Luke 22:31–32, which provoke Simon Peter's declaration of loyalty and

Jesus' subsequent prediction of his denial; third, Jesus' instruction to his disciples to purchase swords (22:35–38); fourth, a relatively abbreviated account of Jesus' prayer to forego, if possible, his "cup" (22:39–46); and fifth, the related details that, at the point of Jesus' betrayal, those with him ask about using their swords and Jesus heals the wound of one whom one of his disciples strikes with a sword (22:49, 51). In view of such differences, one may surmise that Luke abbreviated Jesus' prayer of anguish, even if one accepts the textual integrity of 22:43–44, to make room for his attention to the role of swords leading up to Jesus' arrest.

SETTING THE SCENE

For those who find Luke 22:35–38 either inscrutable or disturbing (or both), perhaps the easiest way to deal with Jesus' instruction to his disciples to purchase swords is to deny that Jesus ever said any such thing. This is the judgment of the majority of fellows of the Jesus Seminar:

> The Fellows were virtually unanimous in putting this complex [of sayings in Luke 22:35–38] in the gray or black category, for the following reasons: (1) the sayings appear to have been assembled to suit the symposium context and to anticipate the impending arrest; (2) Luke has apparently composed the narrative in which the sayings are embedded, since this segment has no parallel; (3) the allusion to Isa 53:12 and the Lukan formula, often repeated, "what is written about me must come true," suggests that the imagination of the early community is at work, stimulated by the scriptures. Further, there is nothing in the words attributed to Jesus that cuts against the social grain, that would surprise or shock his friends, or that reflects exaggeration, humor, or paradox. In sum, nothing in this passage commends itself as authentically from Jesus, except, perhaps, the human element: Jesus suffering bitter disappointment.[1]

For John Dominic Crossan, once a leading fellow of the Jesus Seminar, the instruction to purchase swords in Luke 22:36 is to be taken literally rather than metaphorically or ironically but does not derive from Jesus himself. Rather than a recollected saying of Jesus, it represents an adjustment within the history of early Christianity to permit carrying swords for defensive purposes. In his 2001 essay, "Eschatology, Apocalypticism,

---

1. Funk, Hoover et al., *Five Gospels*, 390–91. (Sayings placed by Seminar fellows in the gray or black category indicate that such sayings are deemed to be inauthentic or at best doubtful.)

and the Historical Jesus," Crossan develops the idea that, within the gospel tradition, the various sayings on staves and swords reflect a development from an original commitment to nonviolence (in response to potential or actual aggression) to an accommodation that made allowances for swords as defensive weapons.[2] Luke 22:35-38 represents the later accommodation rather than the earlier radical commitment.

Crossan's view on Gospel sources is integral to his reconstruction of the early Christian development from a posture of radical nonviolence to the acceptance of the defensive sword. He considers that a written form of Q—indeed, a Q Gospel, itself dependent on a common tradition of sayings of Jesus—preceded the composition of Mark's Gospel. Both earlier Gospels (Q and Mark) contained sayings of Jesus regarding the carrying of staves while involved in itinerant mission, but such sayings were not identical. Two later Gospel writers, Matthew and Luke, borrowed from both earlier Gospels (Q and Mark), albeit in somewhat different ways. Whereas Matthew conflated the slightly different sayings from Q and Mark in his commissioning discourse (10:9-10), Luke incorporated the relevant sayings from both earlier Gospels relatively discretely by recounting two separate commissionings (Luke 9:3, based on Mark 6:8, and Luke 10:4, based on Q). In Crossan's view, the earliest Gospel, Q, in all probability prohibited the carrying of staves along with other travel provisions, whereas Mark permitted both staves and sandals. In turn, Matthew and Luke redacted their respective sources in such a way that both upheld Q's prohibition of staves against Mark's permission of the same. Since carrying staves was standard practice while travelling on foot in the ancient Mediterranean world, Crossan considers Mark's permission to carry staves on mission to be secondary to Q's prohibition. As he writes,

> The staff was the basic and ubiquitous defensive weapon against dogs and thieves and one would not have been expected to travel anywhere without it. Even if one were guaranteed food and lodging on the way, the staff was minimal defensive equipment. Recall, for example, what Josephus says about communal hospitality for Essene travelers: "Consequently, they carry nothing whatever with them on their journeys, except arms as protection against brigands" (*Jewish War* 2.125). I consider, therefore, that the change from prohibited staff in the Q Gospel to permitted staff in Mark is a change from absolutely no protection to

---

2. Crossan, "Eschatology, Apocalypticism," 107-9. Here Crossan builds on proposals found in parts VI and VII of his *Birth of Christianity*, 237-52.

normally basic protection, from absolute nonviolence to minimal defensive violence.³

In short, Mark's permission of staves is already a concession to social realities, an accommodation away from the radical nonviolence advocated in Q. Luke's permission of swords is a further step in the same direction. Although Crossan does not put it this way, he seems to suggest that, although Luke suppressed Mark's permission of staves in his commissioning accounts, his story of Jesus instructing his disciples to purchase swords is a contextual elaboration of Mark's acceptance of staves for the purpose of self-defense. In any case, Luke 22:36 is but one step further along a trajectory of which Mark 6:8 represents an earlier stage.

Jesus' instruction to purchase swords in Luke 22:36 is preceded by his reminder of earlier prohibitions in 22:35. This reminder echoes precisely the smaller list of prohibitions apparently given to the later and larger group of emissaries in Luke 10:4, not the slightly larger list given to the twelve apostles (9:1–6, 10a) with whom Jesus has just eaten his final Passover meal (22:14).⁴ This might be interpreted as confirmation of Crossan's historical reconstruction from an original prohibition of any defensive instruments to the acceptance of staves for defensive purposes to the acceptance of swords for the same reason. Luke initially suppressed the Markan acceptance of staves but then took things even further by having Jesus instruct his disciples to arm themselves with swords when circumstances called for necessary adjustments.

From the aftermath of Jesus' instruction to purchase swords in Luke 22:35–38, Crossan himself finds confirmation that deliberation on carrying swords for defensive purposes is a live question in the Gospel traditions. At Jesus' arrest, all four canonical evangelists record that Jesus was (ineffectually) defended with a sword, causing injury to the high priest's slave (Matt 26:51–54; Mark 14:47; Luke 22:49–51; John 18:10–11). Crossan does not read these texts as historical reminiscences but rather as evidence of deliberation over the validity of using the sword in self-defense. "I take only one relatively secure conclusion from those texts," he writes. "Behind them, there must be some sort of discussion about the defensive sword. To use or not to use? Ever or never?"⁵

---

3. Ibid., 108.

4. For Bovon, this is an intentional differentiation on Luke's part between the past mission of the disciples to Israel and their future universal mission. See Bovon, *Luke 3*, 182: "Luke is thinking that what awaits the Christian preachers is less the mission in Israel (of the Twelve, Luke 9) than the evangelization of the world (the Seventy, Luke 10)."

5. Crossan, "Eschatology, Apocalypticism," 109.

There is food for thought in Crossan's discussion of Gospel texts on staves and swords. Furthermore, his hypothetical reconstruction of developments relating to self-defense based on such texts is difficult to discount. Nevertheless, three considerations create misgivings. First, those who do not share Crossan's source-critical conclusions will likely find his ruminations on staves and swords more provocative than compelling. Second, although Crossan's hypothetical reconstruction does not implicate Jesus, it does implicate Luke (alongside Mark) in providing a rationale for violent self-defense. Yet Luke is the evangelist of peace, and there is nothing in his second book, Acts, to suggest that any Christian missionaries known to him carried swords. Admittedly, little may be inferred from silence, but silence on this matter in Acts is not what one would expect if, as Crossan avers, the question of whether or not to carry swords was a topical concern in Christian circles known to Luke and for whom his Gospel and Acts were written. And third, the available evidence from the church of the first three centuries indicates that Jesus' instruction to purchase swords in Luke 22:36 was not taken to heart.

Even if, on historical-critical grounds, one could be confident that Jesus never advised followers to arm themselves with swords, such confidence would not necessarily resolve the issue for New Testament theology and ethics. For the vast majority of post-apostolic disciples of Jesus, what the biblical evangelists attest about Jesus takes priority over any historical reconstruction based on critical judgments about the principal sources for knowledge regarding Jesus—the four canonical Gospels. This is a crucial matter for New Testament theology.[6] If I were certain that Jesus of Nazareth never instructed his disciples to arm themselves with swords (of whatever kind), that would feature prominently in my moral appraisal of violence. Because of Luke 22:36, however, I cannot be completely certain, and even if I were certain, that certainty would not be shared by everyone else willing to make a judgment on this matter.

The difficulty associated with deciding on whether or not Jesus' instruction to purchase swords is authentic may be illustrated with reference to the criterion of multiple attestation, an important criterion in historical

---

6. The role of historical-critical judgments in New Testament theology and ethics is a vexed question. Since I consider it impossible to reach back behind the Gospels and their putative sources to an "uninterpreted Jesus" (see Watson, *Gospel Writing*, 6, 606), in New Testament theology and ethics I privilege the canonical portraits of Jesus over reconstructions of the historical Jesus. That said, New Testament theology must take account of historical-critical research on Jesus within his sociocultural matrix. In short, the relation between New Testament theology and historical enquiry is both critical and dialectical.

Jesus scholarship.⁷ This criterion is premised on the plausible inference that a tradition is more likely to be authentic if it is attested or witnessed to in multiple independent, and hence corroborating, sources. Attestation in either a single source or in multiple sources derived from a single source instills less confidence regarding the historicity of a tradition than attestation in multiple independent sources. Although the collective judgment of Jesus Seminar fellows regarding the authenticity of Jesus' sayings in Luke 22:35–38 does not make much of their attestation in only one source, the point is made in the margin that there are "no parallels" to these sayings.⁸ From a historical-critical perspective, this is an important consideration. That said, however, single attestation is not a fail-safe criterion for determining that a saying or tradition is inauthentic. Although Jesus' instruction to purchase swords is found only in Luke's Gospel, such a circumstance does not preclude the possibility that in this instance Luke incorporated earlier tradition. If so, this does not necessarily imply that this particular saying is authentic, but in that case it is remarkable that Jesus' advice to purchase swords is attested by the Gospel writer who most emphasized the peaceful dimensions of Jesus' mission and message.⁹ As a result, it is perhaps significant in historical perspective that, from among traditions known to him, Luke should elect to include or even to introduce one in which Jesus instructed disciples to purchase swords, especially since he depicts Jesus as giving this advice as part of a deliberate revocation of earlier mission-related instructions (22:35; cf. 9:3; 10:4). In other words, from a historical-critical perspective, single attestation in this particular case is offset to some extent by the dissonance between this saying and Luke's thematic emphases. One might argue that since the other biblical evangelists were able to recount the story of Jesus' final night without reference to Jesus' advice to purchase swords, this was surely possible for Luke, especially since this was inimical to his theological and moral portrait of Jesus, unless he felt the burden of recording a tradition he believed to be authentic.

Although the question of whether or not Jesus ever sanctioned violence is profoundly—indeed, existentially—significant for me, I see no way of coming to a firm conclusion one way or the other regarding the historicity

---

7. Important as this criterion may be, it should not be applied in isolation or inflexibly. For a critique, see Goodacre, "Criticizing the Criterion of Multiple Attestation." Cf. Allison, "How to Marginalize," 3–30; Allison, *Constructing Jesus*, 1–30, where "recurrent attestation" of topics or motifs is commended over multiple attestation of sayings or events as a point of departure for questing after the historical Jesus.

8. Funk, Hoover et al., *Five Gospels*, 390.

9. See Swartley, *Covenant of Peace*, 121–51, and (building on Swartley) Neville, *A Peaceable Hope*, 91–117.

of Jesus' advice to purchase swords in Luke 22:36. To make things even more difficult, moreover, I do not share the confidence of those who consider that, in this instance, Jesus, or Luke's Jesus, was speaking either metaphorically or ironically.[10] That is not to say that the scene as described by Luke contains neither symbolism nor irony, only that Jesus' advice to purchase swords, in explicit contrast with earlier missional instructions, strikes me as neither symbolic nor ironic. Conscious of competing interpretations, I nevertheless offer my own narrative-contextual reading of this perplexing passage in quest of Luke's rationale for including this incident so as to ascertain what it contributes to his distinctive portrait of Jesus—as well as the moral repercussions that follow.

LUKE 22:35–38 IN CONTEXT

Luke's use of "sword" language provides a useful point of departure. Of the New Testament writers who refer to swords, Luke and John the prophet-seer are the only two to use two words for swords: ἡ μάχαιρα (*hē machaira*) and ἡ ῥομφαία (*hē rhomphaia*). Luke uses ἡ ῥομφαία once only in connection with Simeon's warning to Jesus' mother that, as a result of her child's destined role, a sword will pierce her soul (Luke 2:35). Here "sword" is manifestly symbolic, representing deep anguish.[11] When he employs the term ἡ μάχαιρα, however, it generally signifies the real thing: Luke 21:24; 22:36, 38, 49, 52; Acts 12:2; 16:27. In this list of references to ἡ μάχαιρα, Luke 22:36 is the only occurrence of this specific term routinely claimed to have either symbolic or ironic significance. The evidence of Luke's choice of vocabulary for swords does not permit firm conclusions, but the pattern of evidence is at least suggestive. Having used ἡ ῥομφαία symbolically early in his narrative, would not the use of that same term have commended itself to Luke had he intended Jesus' words in 22:36 to be understood symbolically,

---

10. For a helpful threefold categorization of interpretive approaches to Luke 22:35–38, see Schertz, "Swords and Prayer," 191–92, 198–203. Among those who emphasize the new situation implied by this passage, however, not all embrace a strictly metaphorical interpretation of Jesus' command to purchase swords. See, e.g., Kattathara, *Snag of the Sword*, who (if I understand him correctly) emphasizes the new circumstances about to be faced by the disciples without Jesus but who also considers Jesus' command to be both literal and symbolic—literal in view of the moral legitimacy of self-defense (grounded in natural law) and symbolic insofar as carrying swords (the means of self-defense) instills confidence and courage for mission in the absence of Jesus. Some of what Bovon says suggests he is open to a similar view.

11. All but one of John's uses of the term ἡ ῥομφαία are also clearly symbolic. See Rev 1:16; 2:12, 16; 6:8 (non-symbolic); 19:15, 21.

especially since his use of ἡ μάχαιρα in 21:24 signifies the sword of literal slaughter on a grand scale?

It is generally recognized that the uniquely Lukan episode in which Jesus advises his disciples to purchase swords is part of Luke's expansion of Jesus' words to his disciples at his Passover meal with them. To read Luke 22:35–38 in isolation from its literary context leads inevitably to misinterpretation, especially with respect to violence and its scriptural validation. Yet what is the larger literary context within which this passage should be read and understood? Scholars often note the connection between this episode and the slightly later account of Jesus' betrayal, in which swords are brandished both by Jesus' followers and by the arresting party (22:47–53). This is undoubtedly correct—and indeed decisive—but Luke clearly placed the substance of 22:35–38 within the context of Jesus' Passover meal. This indicates that the scene in which Jesus instructs his disciples to arm themselves with swords is to be interpreted within the broader context of the passage from Passover meal to Jesus' arrest (22:14–53).[12] Further support for this narrative contextualization of 22:35–38 is provided by the *inclusio* created by Luke's references to ἡ ὥρα (*hē hōra*) at both 22:14 and 22:53,[13] although one should not press for strict delimitations either before or after these references.

"And when the hour arrived, he reclined and the apostles with him." So begins Luke's account of Jesus' Passover meal with his disciples (22:14). The "hour" is at one level simply the hour when the Passover meal was to begin. In view of what follows, however, including the content of Jesus' conversation with his apostles, surely this "hour" has salvation-historical and eschatological connotations. Key interrelated motifs within this section bear this out: suffering; scriptural fulfillment; the reign of God; Jesus' prophetic prescience; testing; and satanic resurgence. When, immediately prior to his own arrest, Jesus later pronounces that "this is your *hour* and the authority of darkness" (22:53), one senses a shift in the balance of power within Luke's narrative. A decisive narrative transition has occurred, one in which the authority of darkness now holds sway.

12. For a different literary contextualization of Luke 22:35–38, see Schertz, "Swords and Prayer," 192–97. For Schertz, the chiastic arrangement of Luke 22:31–62 is Luke's own "reading guide." Although Schertz's analysis is enticing no less than illuminating, it seems to envisage something of a hiatus in Jesus' Passover table talk with his disciples, although she appreciates that the first two scenes in her chiastic arrangement relate to what precedes them no less than to what follows. Since Schertz regards Luke's style as largely episodic, with literary units inter-looping, perhaps our respective analyses are complementary.

13. See Brown, *Death of the Messiah*, 291–93, although Brown does not consider these references as having an enclosing function.

The "authority of darkness," which characterizes the hour of those marshaled against Jesus, is associated with the resurgence of Satan. During the Passover meal, Jesus refers to his betrayer's presence at the table (22:21–22). This causes consternation among the disciples (22:23), but Luke's reader knows that Judas has already colluded with the chief priests and temple officers to betray Jesus (22:3–6). According to Luke, this is because Satan entered into Judas, a note reminiscent of Luke's comment following Jesus' threefold testing in the wilderness that the devil departed from him until an appointed time (4:13). Although it is an exaggeration to describe the time of Jesus as a Satan-free period,[14] Luke clearly envisaged the devil as on the retreat during Jesus' mission but as resurgent at its culmination. In Lukan perspective, Satan's influence accounts for Jesus' betrayal by Judas, which comes to realization in 22:47–53; following the Passover meal, moreover, Jesus informs Simon that Satan has sought out all the disciples to sift them like wheat (22:31). In other words, the adversary of God has now resumed his assault on the Messiah of God, in part by testing his companions. When, at his arrest, Jesus identifies that *hour* with the "authority of darkness," this is undoubtedly a reference to satanic resurgence. Satan now seems to have the upper hand.

The textual connection between Luke 22:3, 21–22, 31, 53 and 4:13 reminds readers of Jesus' testing by the devil. It is worth recalling that the central temptation is the promise of all the kingdoms of the world, provided Jesus worships the devil (4:5–8). The resurgence of Satan may be understood to imply the renewal of the devil's temptations, especially in view of the "cup" that looms before Jesus and that Jesus asks to have revoked, if possible (22:42). Immediately prior to Jesus' reference to Satan's intentions with regard to his disciples, he identifies his disciples as those who have persisted with him in his trials (πειρασμοί, peirasmoi). These are what Jesus was subjected to by the devil in the wilderness (see 4:2, 13). Jesus has only just put a stop to an incongruous dispute among his disciples about which of them is regarded as greatest among them by reminding them, first, how kings of the nations exercise their reign, and second, that that is not their calling (22:24–27). If the context of Jesus' reference to his trials in Luke 22:28 is important, at least one significant dimension of his trials is the continued temptation to rule like the kings of the nations, the very nations promised to him by the devil.[15]

---

14. See Conzelmann, *Theology of St Luke*, 28; cf. Garrett, *Demise of the Devil*, 37–43.

15. It is perhaps not too far-fetched to suggest that the dispute among the disciples regarding their relative rank and status belongs to Satan's attempted sifting.

In certain respects, the dispute over status among the disciples in Luke 22:24 reprises an earlier occasion on which the disciples are described as prepossessed with precedence. Toward the end of Luke's Galilean section (4:14–9:50), there is a fascinating sequence of events following the mission of the twelve apostles in which: Jesus feeds multitudes in the wilderness; Peter identifies Jesus as the Messiah of God; Jesus warns of his suffering and death, advising all of the cost of following him; Jesus is transformed on a mountain and the following day expels a demon from a child the disciples could not assist; and Jesus explicitly instructs his disciples that he will be delivered into human hands, but the disciples are prevented from understanding what he means and are afraid to ask him about it. Immediately following this sequence of events (9:10–45), Luke narrates that the disciples were pondering which of them was greatest. Luke has already indicated that the meaning of Jesus' saying about his being delivered into human hands was hidden from them (9:45), and he introduces their ponderings regarding status in a telling manner: "But a question entered into their midst as to which among them might be the greatest" (9:46). Luke continues by saying that Jesus, "upon seeing the question of their hearts," places a child beside him to make the point that the littlest among them all is the greatest (9:47–48). In other words, at this point in the narrative, relative rank and status is on the minds of the disciples but not (yet) openly contested.

It is noteworthy that Luke's description of Satan's entrance into Judas (22:3) closely matches his earlier description of how the question of status arose among the disciples in 9:46. As Satan *entered into* Judas, a question regarding relative rank and status *entered into their midst* or *entered in among them*. At the Passover meal, when Jesus announces that the *hand of his betrayer* is with his own upon the shared table, one is reminded that Satan has entered into Judas (22:3). And when Jesus' announcement provokes the disciples to question which of them might be about to do such a thing, leading in turn to an explicit dispute over greatness, one is reminded of the earlier occasion, in which Jesus' warning about being *betrayed into human hands* falls on blocked ears and the disciples ponder which of them might be greatest (9:44–46). In short, the burning question of relative precedence among the disciples, largely hidden to this point, is now on the table, so to speak. This reflects the disciples' understanding of the reign of God's Messiah, which is why Jesus responds to their dispute over which of them is the greatest both by reminding them of the manner in which kings of the nations rule and by pointing out that in contrast to the standard pattern of ruling, he, the Messiah of God, is among them as one who serves (22:25–27).

What follows Jesus' affirmation that he is among the disciples as one serving (22:27c) is often understood to move in a different direction. Luke

22:28–30 might seem to mark a shift in tone from correction to praise and reward, but it is better understood as a continuation of Jesus' corrective instruction regarding the implications of his disciples' allegiance to him. The words, "You are those who have remained with me in my trials" (22:28), may sound commendatory, but in context they merely describe the reality that Jesus' disciples have persisted with him thus far. This is commendable at one level, but Luke has only just made clear that, despite remaining with Jesus, his disciples have yet to learn that not only is Jesus among them as one serving but also that their own sense of status should reflect divine reign revealed in Jesus. This is borne out in what Jesus continues to say by way of instruction and exhortation. Having clarified that his own mode of reigning stands in stark contrast with the lording-over kind of ruling that marks the kings of the nations, Jesus now passes on to his disciples a kingdom, perhaps conceived as a mode of ruling, as was conferred on him by his father, so as to be able to eat and drink at Jesus' table in Jesus' own kingdom (22:29–30a). Although not always read as reflective of what has only just occurred at the Passover meal, what Jesus confers upon his disciples is a mode of rule or greatness in conformity with his own mode of greatness—as one who serves. What his disciples can expect in the kingdom conferred upon Jesus is what they have just experienced at Passover, which is to serve as the pattern of their own "kingdom." In the present context, Jesus' promise that the disciples will sit on thrones judging (or, perhaps better, exercising authority) over the twelve tribes of Israel (22:30b) is contingent on their modeling of greatness on his manner of exercising authority.

Jesus' promise of future thrones for the disciples probably explains his warning about Satan's intent to sift them all as if they were wheat (22:31). Luke is regarded by many as gentle on the disciples. Relatively speaking, this is correct. Nevertheless, Luke does not present Jesus' inner circle of disciples in altogether flattering terms, especially in relation to learning from Jesus wherein true greatness lies. In view of what has just transpired after the Passover meal, Luke's reader has every reason to suppose that, as far as the disciples are concerned, the promise of thrones is likely to overshadow any instruction about not being like the kings of the nations but rather as ones who serve (22:26). The manner of Satan's sifting has already been revealed in Luke 4:1–13. Satan's sifting offers a way other than that of serving and suffering; indeed, Satan's sifting includes, even if it cannot simply be reduced to, the promise of conventional forms of greatness, lording it over subjects in the name of benefaction (22:25). Jesus foresees that Simon Peter will deny allegiance to himself and his way of suffering (22:15), but he looks beyond that denial to Peter's rehabilitation. Peter's predicted denial of Jesus is part and parcel of his (and his fellow disciples') incapacity to comprehend the means by which the Messiah of God embodies and enacts the reign of God—by serving and suffering. Nevertheless, Jesus still has a role for him when once he has recovered: to exercise greatness not by lording over but by strengthening his brothers. In Peter's case, Jesus not only foresees his weakness but also sees in that experience of weakness the wherewithal to lead his associates in a manner more in keeping with Jesus' own model of leadership.

To this point in Luke's narration of Jesus' Passover meal, Jesus' own testing has been referred to at various points (22:15, 21–22a, 28, 34), but the focus has been on his corrective instruction for his apostles, who are also facing a testing of their own. Their test has to do with whether or not they are able to live up to the demands of discipleship articulated by Jesus in Luke 9:23—self-renunciation (as opposed to status enhancement) and taking up one's cross continually in pursuit of Jesus and his way. At this "hour" of Satan's resurgence, however, Jesus' own time of trial intensifies. This is obvious enough in Luke's account of Jesus' prayer to have "this cup" removed from him (22:39–46), but perhaps the resurgence of Satan's testing of Jesus is to be seen already in Jesus' advice to his disciples to purchase swords.

From the beginning of the Passover meal to this point in Luke 22, there are no clear delimitations between pericopes. Nor does Luke 22:35 signal a clear break from what has gone before. In Lukan perspective, therefore, Jesus' instruction to his disciples to arm themselves with swords is but a continuation of his Passover teaching. It has already been observed that Jesus' question in Luke 22:35 evokes his earlier missional instructions in 10:4, which in turn are reminiscent of Jesus' slightly fuller but closely similar instructions in 9:3. Once again, therefore, Jesus' Passover teaching recalls the culmination of the Galilean section of Luke's narrative, in which Jesus is acknowledged to be both the Messiah of God by none other than Peter (9:20) and Son of God by none other than the divine voice (9:35), in which Jesus twice forecasts his betrayal (9:21–22, 44), and in which Jesus twice teaches on the counterintuitive nature of discipleship (9:23–26, 47–48). Luke 22 recounts Jesus' betrayal and arrest, thereby fulfilling within this narrative segment several occasions on which Jesus presages his ignoble end, the first two of which occur at 9:21–22 and 9:44. Luke actually depicts Jesus as forecasting his betrayal and suffering some six times: explicitly in 9:21–22, 44; 17:25; and 18:32–33; implicitly in 12:50 and 13:32–33. That this was the way things must go is central to Luke's Gospel, so in narrative terms it is significant that Luke 22 resonates so strongly with the bulk of Luke 9, which falls between two sets of missional instructions. Indeed, if the second set of missional instructions for the Seventy-two is a Lukan construction to prepare for a mission to the nations beyond Israel,[16] their

16. See Bovon, *Luke 2*, 26, in which one reads that Luke conceived of this second

apparent revocation by Jesus in Luke 22:36 creates what might best be described as narrative turbulence for readers or hearers. Precisely this narrative turbulence, reinforced by the apparent incongruity of Jesus' advice to purchase swords, is what leads many interpreters to read Jesus' words either metaphorically or ironically. There is, I think, a more excellent way.

A TWO-LEVEL READING OF LUKE 22:35–53

Both the narrative context (explored above) and the combined weight of certain details within Luke 22:35–38 (and beyond) lead me to propose that Luke narrates this and the succeeding episodes at two levels. Perhaps a better image for Luke's narrative technique at this point is that of stereoscopic projection. Two narrative depictions are brought together or superimposed to create the perception of a depth dimension that neither description alone facilitates. The first, taken alone, seems (to many) a superficial description of events, although this perhaps reflects an unwillingness to tune into Luke's theological-interpretive wavelength.

Immediately after giving the instruction to purchase swords, Jesus solemnly advises his disciples that a scriptural saying, "and with the lawless he was reckoned" (Isa 53:12), must be realized in (or perhaps by) himself. This is a direct, if brief, citation from the end of the fourth Servant Song in Isaiah 52:13–53:12, which anticipates the exaltation of an innocent servant of the Lord who suffers on behalf of many. Invested with Christological significance in accordance with Luke's conception of prophecy fulfilled, this citation may well look forward to what imminently awaits Jesus, but it also resonates with what has gone before. It recalls Jesus' earlier prediction to the Twelve that, in Jerusalem, "everything written through the prophets about the Son of humanity will be fulfilled" (18:31), thereby placing the forthcoming suffering (and vindication) of Jesus within the interpretive framework of prophecy fulfilled.[17] More immediately, moreover, it reinforces the words of Jesus at the beginning of the Passover meal (22:14–16), as well as his teaching at the table that he is among his disciples as one who serves (22:27).[18] The Christological significance of Jesus' solemn saying is further intensified

---

sending out as "a training exercise, a dress rehearsal." Cf. Garrett, *Demise of the Devil*, 47–49, who suggests that the mission of the Seventy(-two) prefigures the mission of the Spirit-empowered church, as displayed in Acts.

17. See Tuckett, *Luke*, 45. This interpretive framework has also been described as Luke's "scriptural apologetic" for the undeserved suffering and death of Jesus. See, e.g., Schmidt, "Luke's 'Innocent' Jesus."

18. See Carroll, *Luke*, 442.

by yet another self-referential statement: "For even that which concerns me has an end (in view)" (22:37b). Although somewhat ambiguous, this affirmation, when read in light of the larger saying of which it forms a part, reinforces the sense of scriptural fulfillment on the part of Jesus. The first part of Jesus' declaration in Luke 22:37 indicates that prophetic words must be fulfilled in or by him, the second that the prophecy itself is about to find its resolution or indeed is already in process of being fulfilled.

The reason for emphasizing this is that many interpreters are reluctant to relate Jesus' words about fulfilling prophecy to his instruction to purchase swords. According to Bovon, for example, "Verse 37 is very surprising, less because of its contents than because of its position. What is it doing here?"[19] An answer to Bovon's question should take into account Luke's conception of Jesus' mission as in some sense scripted by Scripture, unfolding in accordance with a divine plan and purpose discernible in prophetic writings. All too often, scholarly appraisals of Luke 22:37 as the rationale for Jesus' instruction to purchase swords are simply anachronistic assertions to the contrary.

In its immediate narrative context, then, Jesus' instruction to his disciples to purchase swords finds its rationale in the scriptural saying about the suffering servant being counted among lawless ones. The literary nexus between swords and their scriptural rationale could hardly be closer. Jesus' reference to prophetic fulfillment is tightly sandwiched between his instruction to purchase swords in Luke 22:36, which ends with the word "sword," and his disciples' response, "Lord, behold two swords here" (22:38a). Moreover, Luke 22:37 is introduced by the solemn phrase, "for I tell you," thereby explicitly linking the prophetic rationale to the preceding instruction to purchase swords.[20] Similarly solemn pronouncements also occur during the Passover meal itself (22:16, 18) and in Jesus' prediction that before morning Peter will deny knowing him (22:34).

Although I consider it safe to say that the formal fulfillment formula of Luke 22:37 provides the rationale for the rescinding of Jesus' earlier missional instructions in 22:36, it is not easy to explain how. Three interpretive options commend themselves, either alone or, more likely, together in progressive fashion: (1) immediately, as soon as the disciples disclose that they have two swords (22:38); (2) shortly, when Jesus is arrested and finds himself in the company of people wielding swords, followers no less than

---

19. Bovon, *Luke 3*, 183.

20. This point is also well made by Hays, *Luke's Wealth Ethics*, 95–96. (Within the larger context of a discussion of the three interrelated passages—Luke 9:1–6; 10:1–11; 22:35–38—Hays also offers a reason for the rescinding of Jesus' earlier missional instructions in 22:36. See Hays, *Luke's Wealth Ethics*, 88–100.)

temple police (22:47); and perhaps also (3) on the following day when Jesus is crucified between two malefactors (23:32-43), yet only in tandem with one or, more likely, both of the previous interpretive options.

In support of the first interpretive option is Jesus' response to his disciples' disclosure of the presence of two swords: "It is enough" (22:38). Often understood as an abrupt conversation stopper, on the assumption that Jesus' disciples are not on his wavelength, it makes better sense of Luke's composition to read the laconic reply of Jesus to signal that the presence of two swords suffices to fulfill the aforementioned prophecy.[21] Taken alone, however, it is difficult to comprehend how the mere presence of two swords in the possession of the disciples could be construed as fulfilling the prophetic snippet cited by Jesus, except perhaps in the collective imagination of Luke's intended audience by evoking the weapon most closely associated with revolutionary warfare. On this reading, in any case, Jesus' instruction to purchase swords is immediately made redundant by the apparently incongruous presence, within the company of his own disciples, of two swords. In narrative terms, however, there is no reason why this interpretive option should stand alone. As Luke's story unfolds, more pieces of the puzzle fall into place.

There is clearly a close connection between Luke 22:35-38, in which Jesus instructs his disciples to purchase swords only to learn that they have two already, and 22:47-53. Not only does the later passage conclude by echoing the beginning of the Passover scene (22:14), but it is replete with references to—and inferences regarding—swords. In Luke 22:49 those around Jesus ask, "Lord, should we strike by sword?" Without waiting for a reply (in narrative time), one of those around him strikes at the high priest's slave and severs his right ear (22:50), presumably with a sword. For Luke's audience, this is only explicable on the basis of the two swords disclosed in 22:35-38. Then, after healing the slave's ear, Jesus confronts the arresting party with these words: "As against a bandit (λῃστής, *lēstēs*) have you come out with swords and clubs?" (22:52b). Since it had been possible to take hold of Jesus while he had been with them daily in the temple (22:53), it is a reasonable inference that the manner of his arrest indicates that he is considered a lawless bandit—at least by the temple establishment.[22]

---

21. See Minear, "Note on Luke xxii 36," 130-31, followed by Hays, *Luke's Wealth Ethics*, 97-98. Although I also follow Minear here, I am not convinced by his explanation of the disciples' "lawlessness" as disobedience to Jesus' earlier command, which his retraction of earlier commands is designed to bring to light.

22. Cf. Lampe, "Two swords," 345, who sees the injury to *the* slave of the high priest as "lawless aggression" directed against the high priest himself via his representative. In both passages featuring swords (22:35-38, 47-53), according to Lampe, Luke

In connection with this second interpretive option, one must address the sense of yet another laconic utterance by Jesus in Luke 22:51. A little earlier, at 22:49, Luke does not record Jesus as responding to the question of those around him, "Lord, should we strike by sword?" Only after one of his own has wounded the high priest's slave does Jesus respond—and then cryptically—after which Jesus touches the slave's ear with healing effect. Although careful attention to what Luke records Jesus as saying at this point is important, so also is Luke's narrative progression.

In an illuminating study of Luke 22:51, David Matson argues for understanding Jesus' three-word utterance to mean that, in view of the divine plan for his life and mission, his disciples should permit his arrest to proceed.[23] The words of Jesus at this point are indeed a response to his disciples, but not a rebuke of one's recourse to a sword; rather, they compose a response to the disciples' question in Luke 22:49, by means of which Jesus advises them not to interfere with his arrest. On the apocalyptic matrix for comprehending Jesus' words and hence their translation, Matson's case is compelling. Jesus did not say, "No more of this (sword-striking)," but rather something closer to "Allow for this (to take its course)." Regarding some of Matson's inferences based on contextual grounds, however, I demur. Although he is correct to emphasize the broader context of the divine plan, he pays too little attention to Luke's narration at this point. To reiterate, before recording Jesus' response to the disciples' question, "Lord, should we strike by sword?" Luke recounts that one of them strikes out with a sword. Moreover, immediately after responding verbally to his disciples' question, Jesus heals the slave wounded by a sword. Both the narrative pause that makes space for one of the disciples to strike by sword and the *uniquely Lukan detail* that Jesus heals the slave wounded by this sword-strike suggest a concern on Luke's part to discount any possible misunderstanding that swords are capable of furthering the divine plan and purpose. Referring to this act of healing recorded solely by Luke, Matson remarks: "In a stunning act of divine reversal, Jesus heals the slave of the high priest (22:51b), allowing the arrest to proceed and God's plan to continue."[24] This act of healing is superfluous to Jesus' arrest, however.[25] In Luke's account, what Jesus says both before and after healing the wounded slave is what clears the way for his arrest. So although Matson

---

presents the disciples *en masse* as "lawless."

23. Matson, "Pacifist Jesus?"

24. Ibid., 167.

25. Indeed, in narrative terms, one could argue that by healing the wounded slave, Jesus was hindering his own arrest by demonstrating his benevolence.

may be right that this Lukan scene does not evoke the theme of enemy-love, as argued by many, it is hardly incompatible with that theme.

As for the third interpretive option for reading fulfillment of prophecy as the rationale for Jesus' instruction to his disciples to purchase swords—namely, his crucifixion between criminals—this episode on its own is probably too far removed from Jesus' saying in Luke 22:37. Moreover, it contains no references to swords. Together with the previous scenes featuring swords, however, Luke might well have expected his audience to make certain connections. Since Jesus was arrested in a manner befitting a bandit, the simple reality that Jesus was *crucified* might be understood by many of Luke's readers to signify that he was reckoned among the lawless (at least by the Romans). Or that Jesus was crucified *with malefactors* (κακοῦργοι, *kakourgoi*) might well be taken to mean that he was reckoned among the lawless.[26] Alternatively, that Jesus was interrogated, humiliated, tortured, and executed *by Romans* might have signaled that Jesus, having been found to be in the company of sword-bearers at his arrest, was reckoned (by Luke) among the lawless throughout his suffering and death at the hands of the Romans. After all, on the only other occasion that Luke uses the term ὁ ἄνομος (*ho anomos*, lawless one), it is in Peter's post-Pentecost speech when he accuses fellow Israelites of having Jesus killed *by means of the hands of the lawless*, signifying non-Jewish executioners (Acts 2:23).

On narrative contextual grounds, then, an interpretation that relates the scriptural fulfillment of Luke 22:37 to real (rather than symbolic) swords has much to commend it. In progressive fashion, and perhaps also in varied ways, Luke presents Jesus as ever more encompassed by the lawless. Such an interpretation is strengthened by reading Luke 22:35–38 at another, less obvious level, even though the impetus for such a second-level reading derives from the larger context within which this passage sits. In Luke 22:35–36 Jesus' revocation of earlier missional instructions begins with the seemingly innocuous phrase, ἀλλὰ νῦν (*alla nun*, but now . . .). Since the influential work of Hans Conzelmann,[27] many have invested this phrase with salvation-historical significance, indeed, as marking the beginning of the period of the church, which because of Jesus' absence implies vulnerability

---

26. It is noteworthy that Luke lingers over his crucifixion scene (23:32–49), in part to stress both the dignity and innocence of Jesus by contrast with those alongside whom he was executed. That Luke did not describe those crucified with Jesus as either "bandits" or "lawless ones" is not decisive; he would hardly have considered malefactors as law-abiding. Mark 15:28, almost certainly a scribal interpolation, attests to an understanding closer to Luke's time than ours that the crucifixion of Jesus alongside two bandits fulfilled the Scripture cited in Luke 22:37.

27. See Conzelmann, *Theology of St Luke*, 80–83.

to testing. Yet as Paul Minear demonstrates in response to Conzelmann, the "but now" of Luke 22:36 relates not to the salvation-historical period of the church but to what is about to unfold for Jesus in his passion.[28] One hesitates to interpret this phrase too narrowly or restrictively,[29] but its primary significance emerges in relation to its immediate context, even if its immediate import has further reaching ramifications.

Especially significant, in my view, is that the "but now" of Luke 22:36 falls between references to the "hour" of 22:14 and the "hour" associated with the authority of darkness in 22:53. This is the hour of Satan's resurgence and hence the intensification of trials, not only for the disciples but also—indeed especially—for Jesus. Satan's trialing of Jesus before his public mission (4:1–13) is *now* intensified, and Luke's dramatic account depicts Jesus as on the brink of capitulating to Satan's redoubled testing. Conzelmann was probably incorrect to interpret Jesus' reference to his trials in Luke 22:28 as referring to the present moment alone, "for nothing has yet happened."[30] At one level, perhaps the level of perception that obtained among Jesus' disciples, Jesus' public mission seems not to have been plagued by trials. Yet this saying points readers to another level of perception, namely, that throughout Jesus' mission he has been tested along the lines of his trials by the devil in the wilderness.[31] Now, however, the trials that persisted throughout Jesus' ministry intensify dramatically in the hour of Satan's resurgence. Thus, even if Conzelmann is incorrect in what he denies, he is correct in what he affirms: "Here the πειρασμός [*peirasmos*, trial] theme predominates (cf. xxii, 28, 40 [also 46]). . . . It is now that the πειρασμοί [*peirasmoi*, trials] hold sway."[32]

The passage following that in which Jesus instructs his disciples to purchase swords recounts his prayer to forego a "cup" (22:42). It begins and ends with Jesus imploring his disciples to pray so as not to enter into testing (22:40, 46). Between these exhortations, Jesus himself prays to have "this

---

28. Minear, "Note on Luke xxii 36," 128–34. (This is the primary and abiding insight of Minear's analysis.)

29. See, e.g., Lampe, "Two swords," 337, for whom Luke 22:36 marks the beginning of radically different circumstances for the disciples. In Lampe's view, the source for Luke 22:35–37 belongs among Jesus' symbolic warnings of future tribulation.

30. Conzelmann, *Theology of St Luke*, 80–81, 83.

31. This is another point on which I see things differently from Matson, "Pacifist Jesus?," 163–64. Luke 8:12 hints at the subversive activity of the devil during Jesus' public ministry, as do Jesus' various healings and exorcisms (see Luke 11:14–26; 13:16; Acts 10:38). Luke 10:17–20, which (*nota bene!*) concludes the mission of the Seventy(-two), is evidence that Luke understood Jesus' emissaries to be under his protection, not that Satan was inactive during Jesus' public mission. See Garrett, *Demise of the Devil*, 46–60.

32. Conzelmann, *Theology of St Luke*, 80.

cup" removed from him, if it be his father's will (22:41–42). If anything is to guide one's understanding of the content of Jesus' own prayer, it is surely what he urges his disciples to pray to avoid. In short, between his bracketing instructions to pray to avoid testing, Jesus himself probably prays to avoid the "cup of testing" he currently faces.[33]

In *The Politics of Jesus*, under the heading, "The Last Renunciation," John Howard Yoder proposes the following thought experiment: what might it have meant for Jesus had his prayer on the Mount of Olives been answered in the affirmative, especially in view of events that had provoked the temple authorities to conspire against him? For Yoder, "The only imaginable real option in terms of historical seriousness, and the only one with even a slim basis in the text, is the hypothesis that Jesus was drawn, at this very last moment of temptation, to think *once again* of the messianic violence with which he had been tempted since the beginning. Now is finally the time for holy war."[34]

Yoder proceeds to point out that at Jesus' arrest a sword is used in defense of Jesus, after which Matthew records words of Jesus that reveal the prospect of apocalyptic holy war to be the alternative to scriptural fulfillment in obedience to the divine will (Matt 26:51–54). Luke, by contrast, offers a proleptic interpretation of the sword used in defense of Jesus, by which Yoder means Jesus' earlier instruction to purchase swords so as to fulfill Scripture.[35] In other words, had Jesus' request to have his "cup" withdrawn been understood to have been granted, the most plausible alternative to what actually occurred would have been for Jesus to resist violently in the hope of provoking apocalyptic battle.

Yoder's discussion, albeit focused primarily on Luke's Gospel, ranges across all four Gospels. Yet he probably interprets Luke correctly at this point. As has been observed already, Luke's account of Jesus' prayer on the Mount of Olives is severely abbreviated, at least by contrast with its synoptic parallels (Matt 26:36–46; Mark 14:32–42). It is bracketed internally by Jesus' instructions to his disciples to pray so as to avoid testing, and it is bracketed externally by passages that raise the prospect of self-defense by means of swords. Indeed, only Luke recounts that those who had been instructed to

---

33. See Brown, *Death of the Messiah*, 157–62.

34. Yoder, *Politics of Jesus*, 46. (A personal note: Yoder was a gifted interpreter, and I have learned much from his biblical, historical, and moral theology. His failure to live up to some of his own insights on faithful Christian discipleship does not invalidate those insights, however much his interpersonal abuse of power belongs to an appraisal of his theological legacy. For an account of Yoder's sexual exploitation of women and of institutional failure to support victims of his manipulative sexual politics, see Waltner Goossen, "'Defanging the Beast.'")

35. Yoder, *Politics of Jesus*, 46–48.

buy swords ask whether they should strike by sword before one of them actually does so in Luke 22:49–50. From the perspective of narrative coherence, such observations suggest that Jesus' prayer on the Mount of Olives involves wrestling with the prospect of endorsing violent resistance on his behalf.

If such a reading of Jesus' Olivet prayer in Luke 22:40–46 has merit,[36] Jesus' preceding instruction that his disciples arm themselves with swords may be seen in the same light. Jesus, under renewed siege from Satan, wrestles with the prospect of achieving messianic ends by military means, reflected in his instruction to purchase swords. At one level, Luke's account foregrounds a scriptural rationale for Jesus' instruction to purchase swords, but at another level Luke hints at Jesus' own struggle with satanic swords—satanic because swords comprise the means by which authority is exercised in earthly kingdoms (cf. 4:5–7; 22:25). Here, I suggest, Luke's narrative technique reflects an apocalyptic mind-set, which envisages a double-dimensioned reality in which earthly struggle mirrors conflict between competing spiritual forces. In other words, the swords with which Jesus instructs his disciples to arm themselves are not symbolic swords, but Jesus' instruction itself reflects his own spiritual struggle, which is finally resolved through prayer. While his disciples sleep rather than pray, Jesus' resolve to accomplish the will of God through suffering is redoubled, and this renewed resolution is then made manifest in his resignation and repudiation of sword-striking before being arrested.

Whatever readers may make of my two-level reading of Luke 22:35–53 within the context of the Passover meal, it seems clear that Luke intended his audience to understand the two episodes featuring swords in relation to each other. More precisely, it seems clear that Luke intended for the cryptic earlier episode to be interpreted in light of the clearer later one, in which the way of swords is repudiated yet once more and indeed finally in favor of the way of the cross.

---

36. In "Swords and Prayer," Schertz adopts a similar interpretive line, following Yoder's *Politics of Jesus* as well as Trocmé, *Jesus and the Nonviolent Revolution*, and Kruger, "A Sword over His Head or in His Hand?" If Kruger is correct that Jesus' advice to buy swords in Luke 22:36 evokes the biblical image of God as divine warrior, a more nuanced treatment of how such a scriptural tradition finds expression in the Gospels would have been helpful. See, e.g., Swartley, *Israel's Scripture Traditions*, in which the Gospel writers are shown not only to have drawn upon such biblical motifs as the divine warrior *but also to have reconfigured them*. For Kruger, moreover, although Jesus decides against violence on the Mount of Olives, "at least for the time being" (602–3), divine violence nevertheless looms both proximately (against Jerusalem) and ultimately. For Schertz, perhaps influenced by Swartley, Jesus integrates rather than chooses between holy war and suffering servant traditions.

5

Turbulence in the Temple

(MATT 21:12–17; MARK 11:11–25;
LUKE 19:45–46; JOHN 2:13–22)

WHEN, IN HIS LANDMARK work on *Jesus and Judaism*, E. P. Sanders made the methodological decision to ground his quest for the historical Jesus in the most secure facts about him rather than in anything he purportedly said or taught, that decision led him to begin his investigation with Jesus' disruptive actions in the temple.[1] This book is not yet another attempt to reach back behind the Gospels to recover allegedly secure details about the historical figure of Jesus, but it is impossible to ignore the question of whether what is attributed to Jesus by this or that Gospel writer is grounded in what Jesus of Nazareth did or said. Since many agree with Sanders that Jesus did something both disruptive and provocative in the temple,[2] that is reason enough to investigate the Gospel accounts of this incident.

---

1. Sanders, *Jesus and Judaism*, 3–13, 61–76.
2. See, e.g., Funk et al., *Acts of Jesus*, 121–22, 231–32, 338–39, 373–74, and 567. A sufficient number of Jesus Seminar fellows agreed that Jesus did something provocative in the temple for its attestation in the synoptic tradition to rate a pink coding, meaning that the core information is probably reliable. For various reasons, by contrast, including the failure of Jesus' disruptive actions within the temple to cohere with his nonviolent conduct generally, David Seeley leans toward the conclusion that the temple incident is a Markan construct to serve his narrative and theological objective of insinuating that the temple's recent destruction could be interpreted both as God's judgment of the temple and God's vindication of Jesus and his mission. See Seeley, "Jesus' Temple Act," 263–83; Seeley, "Jesus' Temple Act Revisited," 55–63.

There are, however, two further reasons for devoting attention to Jesus' disruption in the temple. The first is that of the various features of Jesus' life and activity explored in this book, the temple incident is the only specific *action* of Jesus to have provoked the question of whether he conducted his mission wholly nonviolently.[3] Every other chapter in this book examines *utterances* of various kinds attributed to Jesus, even if some might be considered "speech-acts" because of their performative force. Moreover, not only is Jesus' provocation in the temple the only action of Jesus relevant to the theme of the vehement Jesus but it has also been integral to both scholarly and ecclesial discussions about the nature of Jesus' mission. As Thomas Yoder Neufeld says of Jesus' "prophetic demonstration" in the temple, "This episode has long been an important element in the debate regarding Jesus and violence."[4]

A second additional reason for focusing on Jesus' disruptive action in the temple is that this incident is the only aspect of Jesus' mission under consideration attested in all four canonical Gospels. In view of the distinctiveness of the Fourth Gospel, that is significant. This is not so much because of the principle of multiple attestation, which has played an important role in historical Jesus research, nor even because the Johannine version of this episode has so often been read as depicting Jesus using a whip on people. Beyond such considerations, the altogether different contextualization and configuration of this incident within the Fourth Gospel point toward a potential reappraisal of what is often inferred from the narrative setting of this incident in the Synoptic Gospels. By this I mean that it is perhaps possible to perceive the Johannine placement of the temple episode as something of a "protest" against correlating Jesus' disruption in the temple with Rome's literal destruction of the temple a generation later.

A full-scale study of Jesus' provocation in the temple would need to address the following issues: the incident's claim to historicity; the location of the incident within the temple precincts; the scale of the event; the significance of the event for Jesus himself, insofar as that is discernible; the meaning and significance of the event in the eyes of the Gospel writers, including what may be inferred from scriptural citations attributed to Jesus; the significance of the various narrative configurations of the temple incident in

---

3. Cursing and thereby killing a fig tree (Matt 21:18–22; Mark 11:12–14, 20–22) and "complicity" in the death of a herd of pigs (Matt 8:28–34; Mark 5:1–20; Luke 8:26–39) might be deemed intemperate actions on Jesus' part, but such events have not played a part in justifying force, aggression, or violence against people. Insofar as the cursing of a fig tree relates thematically to Jesus' provocation in the temple, however, it bears on one's appraisal of the temple incident and is therefore discussed in this chapter.

4. Yoder Neufeld, *Recovering Jesus*, 219.

the four canonical Gospels; and the "moral reception" of this episode in the church's history of interpretation.[5] In line with the principal purpose of this study, however, this chapter focuses on narrative configurations of the temple episode in the four canonical Gospels and what such configurations signal about the respective interpretations of the character of Jesus' conduct at this juncture of his mission.

Each of the four canonical Gospels recounts that Jesus did something disruptive in the temple at Jerusalem. The first three Gospels place this episode either immediately or shortly after his arrival to the city and only days before his arrest and execution (Matt 21:12-17; Mark 11:15-19; Luke 19:45-46). The Fourth Gospel, by contrast, places this incident near the beginning of Jesus' public activity (John 2:13-22), indeed, as only the second of his public actions, which follows the wine sign in Cana of Galilee (2:1-11). Related to this incident is a series of texts in which Jesus is either recalled as or accused of speaking of the temple's destruction. Near the beginning of the eschatological discourse recorded by Matthew, Mark, and Luke, Jesus predicts the demolition of the buildings that comprised the temple precincts such that no stone will be left upon another (Matt 24:1-2; Mark 13:1-2; Luke 21:5-6). During Jesus' hearing before the Sanhedrin, Matthew and Mark (but not Luke) note that testimony was given to the effect that Jesus either claimed to be able to destroy the sanctuary and rebuild it in three days (Matt 26:60-61) or actually threatened to destroy the sanctuary himself and after three days replace it with one not made by human hands (Mark 14:57-58). These two Gospel writers also recount that at Jesus' crucifixion people taunt Jesus by echoing this charge (Matt 27:39-40; Mark 15:29-30).[6] Whereas none of the canonical Gospels gives explicit credence to the accusation that Jesus threatened to tear down the temple himself, saying 71 in the Gospel of Thomas reads: "Jesus said, 'I will dest[roy

---

5. The scholarly scrutiny of Jesus' provocation in the temple might well be described as "legion," a term whose associations help to convey one's sense of being overwhelmed and even oppressed by the sheer quantum of secondary literature on this one episode in Jesus' public life. Helpful entries into both the scholarly literature and the various critical issues relating to this incident include: Evans, "Temple Action of Jesus" (2008); Snodgrass, "Temple Incident" (2009); Ådna, "Jesus and the Temple" (2011); and Ådna, "Temple Act" (2013).

6. Luke contains no contextual parallel to Matthew and Mark's notices that Jesus was heard to threaten to destroy the sanctuary, but in Acts 6:8-14 Stephen is brought before the Sanhedrin and falsely accused of saying that Jesus the Nazarene will tear down (future tense!) the temple ("the holy place"). One wonders whether the witness of Luke at this point hints at the possibility that the charge leveled against Jesus is deemed false because the threat against the temple was uttered on behalf of Jesus by Christian prophets after his death.

thi]s house, and no one will be able to [re]build it . . . ."[7] Based on a critical appraisal of relevant texts, Raymond Brown concludes that Jesus probably pronounced the imminent destruction and rebuilding of the temple sanctuary, albeit without precision on the timing or even on his own role in either destruction or rebuilding.[8] As a result, although the discussion that follows focuses on the temple incident itself, as contextualized by the respective Gospel writers, these other texts compose important strands in the textual web of evidence for comprehending that event, especially in relation to the study of Jesus as a historical figure.

THE TEMPLE INCIDENT IN MATTHEAN PERSPECTIVE

Even though the temple episode occurs at the same relative juncture in the narrative sequences of all three Synoptic Gospels, there are significant differences in how this incident is recounted—and hence interpreted—by Matthew, Mark, and Luke.[9] For Matthew, Jesus' temple action is part and parcel of his messianic entry into Jerusalem. Matthew 19:1–2 forms a transition from the fourth of Matthew's five discourse sections to the narrative section that brings Jesus to Jerusalem. At this point in Matthew's Gospel, Jesus leaves Galilee for Judea, followed by large crowds, whom Jesus heals. At Matt 20:17–19, Jesus is explicitly headed for Jerusalem and instructs his disciples of what that will mean for him. Upon leaving Jericho in Matt 20:29, Jesus is followed by a large crowd and restores the sight of two blind men, who call out to him as Son of David. In Matt 21:1 the narrator notes that, on reaching Bethphage at the Mount of Olives, Jesus and those following him draw near to Jerusalem. Here begins Matthew's account of Jesus' messianic entry into Jerusalem, fulfilling scriptural prophecy and acclaimed yet again as Son of David by crowds both in front of him and behind him. His entry into Jerusalem at Matt 21:10 provokes the city as a whole to raise the question of his identity, but there is more to Matthew's narration at this point. In describing Jesus' entry into Jerusalem, Matthew writes that the city as a whole was "shaken" (ἐσείσθη, *eseisthē*). This is the language of seismic disturbance. On four occasions Matthew uses the noun ὁ σεισμός (*ho seismos*)

---

7. See Gathercole, *Gospel of Thomas*, 477–80. Gathercole considers that "house" in this saying is a reference to the temple, that Jesus claims to be the agent of the temple's destruction, and that the saying envisages no future rebuilding of the temple.

8. Brown, *Death of the Messiah*, 1:427–60. Brown's view is shared by many.

9. In addition to commentaries on each of the Synoptic Gospels, see also Gurtner and Perrin, "Temple," 941–45, and Chanikuzhy, *Jesus, the Eschatological Temple*, 97–232.

to describe earthquakes (8:24; 24:7; 27:54; 28:2), and on three occasions he uses the cognate verb to describe the quaking of the earth or people (21:10; 27:51; 28:4). In Matt 27:50-54 and 28:2-4, both noun and verb clearly resonate with each other. By using this imagery when Jesus enters the city of Jerusalem, Matthew emphasizes the significance of Jesus' arrival to Jerusalem and also foreshadows the magnitude of what is about to unfold. On setting foot in Jerusalem, Jesus effectively causes the city to tremor. The crowd may identify Jesus as the prophet from Nazareth, but the episode as a whole underscores his arrival to Jerusalem as the messianic descendant of David (cf. Matt 1:1-17).

Of the first three evangelists, only Matthew explicitly signals that the manner in which Jesus arranged his entrance into Jerusalem—by riding donkeys rather than on foot—fulfilled messianic prophecy (Zech 9:9; Matt 21:4-5). The manner of Jesus' entrance into Jerusalem not only fulfills scripture but also underscores a distinctive dimension of Matthew's depiction of Jesus; for Matthew, Jesus is the messiah whose manner is meek (πραΰς, *praus*), reminiscent of Moses (Num 12:3). Although difficult to distil into a single English equivalent, the adjective πραΰς connotes meekness and gentleness. Among the biblical evangelists, only Matthew uses this terminology: in 5:5 Jesus pronounces a blessing on the meek because they will inherit the earth (cf. Psalm 37:11); in 11:29 Jesus identifies himself as meek and unassuming ("humble of heart"); and in 21:1-9 his entrance into Jerusalem conforms to his earlier self-description. Interpreting Matt 21:4-5, Ulrich Luz avers, "That Jesus rides on a donkey and on the colt of a donkey is to be understood as an expression of his kindness, peaceableness, and gentleness."[10] Insofar as Matthew conceived of Jesus' conduct in the temple as but part of his arrival to Jerusalem, the entirety of 21:1-17 is to be read under the rubric of the advent of Israel's meek messiah.

Like his synoptic counterparts, Matthew describes Jesus entering the temple precincts and casting people out, using a verb often (but not exclusively) associated with exorcising demons (ἐκβάλλειν, *ekballein*). The use of this verb implies a certain coerciveness, even forcefulness, but not lethal or even debilitating violence. Only Matthew, however, recounts that Jesus cast out *all* involved in selling or buying within the temple, as when his entrance into Jerusalem results in the quaking of *all* the city (21:10). The messianic Son of David does not deal in half-measures. And only Matthew narrates that after Jesus had cleared the temple precincts, blind and lame people come to him in the temple and are healed. For Matthew, economic

---

10. Luz, *Matthew 21-28*, 8. See also Boring, "Gospel of Matthew," 402-4, who points out that Matthew's explicit appeal to scriptural fulfillment enhances the emphasis on Jesus' messianic meekness.

activity within the temple precincts is replaced by messianic restoration. Moreover, as if to reinforce the messianic status of Jesus, children within the temple continue to shout out what the crowds had shouted when Jesus rode into Jerusalem: "Hosanna to the Son of David!" (21:9, 15).

In narrative terms, the temple incident in Matthew's Gospel is but one dimension of Jesus' messianic entry into Jerusalem, which is both prepared for and followed by acts of restorative healing (20:29–21:17). The messianic Son of David motif holds the section together.[11] Once in the temple, Jesus' expulsion of those engaged in economic transactions together with his overturning of tables and seats, explained with reference to scripture, is overshadowed by his healing activity and the joyful acclamation it occasions.[12] Indeed, in Matthew's version of events, what perturbs the temple hierarchy is not Jesus' clearing of the temple precincts but rather the wonders that he enacts and the noisy acclamation of children within the temple (21:15). Were Matthew's account of Jesus' prophetic provocation in the temple the only one on record, the general perception of this incident would be much different.

At the conclusion of the temple incident, Matthew records that Jesus went out of the city to spend the night at Bethany (21:17). Only on his return to the city does Matthew narrate the episode relating to the fig tree (21:18-22). In Matthew's version of events, the fig tree dies instantaneously, provoking the disciples to ask how it could die so suddenly.[13] Moreover, the episode featuring a fig tree is sandwiched between two entries into the temple, the first to evict and to heal—perhaps even to evict so as to make room for healing—and the second to teach (21:12-23).[14] Indeed, in nar-

---

11. See Mauser, *Gospel of Peace*, 50–53. Cf. Hagner, *Matthew 14-28*, 597, whose descriptive title for Matt 21:12–17 is "The Son of David in the Temple."

12. Cf. Hooker, *Signs of a Prophet*, 58, who detects in Matt 21:14 a contrast with the story of David in 2 Samuel 5. Provoked by the inhabitants of Jerusalem saying that he could be prevented from taking the city even by its blind and lame, so confident were they of the city's impregnability, David's success in taking the city led to the saying, "The blind and the lame shall not come into the house" (2 Sam 5:8b). In Matthew's version of Jesus' actions in the temple, the Son of David reverses the effects of King David's conquest.

13. For this and other features of Matthew's version of Jesus' cursing of the fig tree, understood to be the result of Matthew's redaction of Mark's account, see Telford, *Barren Temple*, 69–94.

14. Here the twofold depiction of Jesus as messiah of word and deed (Matthew 5–9) is replicated, only in reverse so as to lead into the fifth and final major discourse of the Gospel. The disruption of commerce necessary for sacrifices to be offered so as to make way for healing within the temple precincts is reminiscent of Jesus' earlier appeal to Hos 6:6 at Matt 9:13 and 12:7, found only in Matthew. See Hagner, *Matthew 14-28*, 601.

rative terms, Matthew's account of Jesus' teaching in the temple lasts until he leaves the temple at 24:1. Since Matthew brackets the fig tree incident between two—indeed, the only two—entries by Jesus into the temple, they would seem to be interrelated in meaning and significance.[15] Such an inference is supported by geographical and thematic links between the fig tree passage and its narrative context. First, "this mountain" in Matt 21:21 most naturally refers to the Mount of Olives, which is referred to explicitly on either side of Matthew's temple section (21:1; 24:3) and is in all likelihood the implied site of the fig tree incident.[16] And second, Jesus' teaching on prayer (21:21–22) relates thematically to his evacuation of sellers and buyers from the temple (21:12–13). It would seem that, in Matthew's narration of events, the cursing and immediate withering of the fig tree foreshadow Jesus' prophecy of the temple's imminent destruction in Matt 24:1–2, as Jesus departs from the temple.[17]

THE TEMPLE INCIDENT IN MARKAN PERSPECTIVE

Like Matthew, Mark also interrelates the fig tree episode and Jesus' temple action, albeit more obviously. Indeed, Mark employs a narrative technique now widely considered to be one of his compositional trademarks—intercalation or "sandwiched stories." At various points throughout his Gospel, Mark begins to narrate an event, interrupts that event to recount another episode, then completes the interrupted event. Scholars disagree on how often this compositional technique is employed by Mark,[18] but his narration of Jesus' disruption in the temple is one clear example of this trademark technique.

Within Mark's narrative structure, Jesus' entry into Jerusalem at Mark 11:1–11 opens a new major section concerned with Jesus in Jerusalem. The immediately preceding passage, concerned with the restoration

15. See Davies and Allison, *Gospel according to Saint Matthew*, 3:153–54.

16. Matthew 21:1 refers only to Bethphage at or near the Mount of Olives, whereas both Mark 11:1 and Luke 19:29 refer to Bethany and Bethphage as situated on the Mount of Olives. Although Matt 21:1 notes that Jesus arrived at Bethphage before staging his messianic entrance into Jerusalem, in 21:17 he spends the night in Bethany, from which he returns to the temple early in the morning.

17. Here I demur from Telford's view that, by means of redactional changes to Mark's account, Matthew tamed Mark's two-part fig-tree incident into a standard miracle story, "removed from the sphere of judgement and eschatology." See Telford, *Barren Temple*, 80. Cf. Chanikuzhy, *Jesus, the Eschatological Temple*, 145–49.

18. For one list of Mark's intercalations, see Black, *Mark*, 88. (Whether intercalation is a Markan or pre-Markan compositional technique is an important question but not one that needs resolution here.)

of Bartimaeus' sight, is the closing literary frame of Mark's central section (8:22—10:52). Although Mark recounts Jesus' entry into Jerusalem and the temple in much the same way as his synoptic counterparts, he postpones Jesus' provocation in the temple until the following day. According to Mark 11:11, Jesus enters into Jerusalem into the temple—a seemingly redundant but probably emphatic double movement into the center of Jewish religious and national life—and then . . . merely looks around at everything before leaving for Bethany with the Twelve. For John Dear, this description envisages Jesus as "casing the joint" before a nonviolent protest action.[19] Certainly Mark intimates that what is about to unfold is the result of calculated deliberation, not a vehement reflex response to what Jesus encounters in the temple. In any case, only Mark recounts Jesus' messianic arrival in Jerusalem and his provocation in the temple on consecutive days, not with the latter event as the immediate sequel to—and hence an extension of—the former. In so doing, he puts narrative distance between these two events, thereby making room to recontextualize Jesus' temple action.

Mark stages events at the beginning of his third major section in a three-day sequence.[20] Day 1 is the day of Jesus' messianic arrival to Jerusalem, at the end of which he enters the temple but merely looks around at everything. On the following day, Day 2, when Jesus and his entourage leave Bethany for Jerusalem, Mark narrates the episode involving a fig tree. Jesus is hungry, sees a fig tree from a distance, finds nothing but leaves on the tree, and addresses the tree in the hearing of his disciples. Mark 11:14 indicates that Jesus responds to the tree's absence of fruit by saying, "Nevermore may anyone eat fruit from you." Taken in isolation, this condemnation seems peevish, especially in view of the explanatory note at the end of Mark 11:13 that the reason Jesus found nothing but leaves on the tree is that it was not the season for figs.

Mark's narrative continues with Jesus and his disciples coming to Jerusalem a second time. On this occasion, when Jesus enters the temple precincts, he begins to drive out those selling and buying in the temple, he

---

19. Dear, "Didn't Jesus Overturn Tables?" 187. See also France, *Gospel of Mark*, 442. For an alternative reading, see Boring, *Mark*, 316: "Although the Markan Jesus has never been to the temple before, his 'looking around at everything' is not the curiosity of a Galilean tourist, but, as in 12:41–44, 13:1–2, his authoritative sizing up of the goings-on in the temple, marking it out for destruction."

20. See Telford, *Barren Temple*, 39–49; Smith, "Literary Structure," 112–17. Indeed, the final major section of Mark's Gospel, 11:1–16:8, is chronicled over eight consecutive days, albeit with the sixth day passed over in silence. See Boring, *Mark*, 312–13; Marcus, *Mark 8–16*, 768–69. This is one of two main reasons given for the focus on Mark in Borg and Crossan, *Last Week*, ix–x. In narrative terms, moreover, the events of the first three days are clearly interrelated.

overturns the tables of the coin-changers and the stools of the dove-sellers, and (unique to Mark's account) he disallows anyone from carrying anything through the temple complex.[21] Also unique to Mark is the added phrase in Jesus' scriptural citation: "Is it not written that my house will be designated a house of prayer *for* [or perhaps *among*] *all the nations*?" Like Luke but unlike Matthew, Mark then notes the antagonism of chief priests and scribes, who seek to destroy him but fear his popularity. Then when evening comes, they (presumably Jesus and his disciples) leave the city (11:18–19).

Early on Day 3 (implied), as they (Jesus and his disciples) journey back toward the city, they see the fig tree dried up from the roots (11:20). Whereas the fig tree dies instantaneously in Matthew's version of events, in Mark's the tree dies radically—from its roots. Peter is said to remember and says to Jesus, "Look, Rabbi, that fig tree you cursed has withered" (11:21).[22] Jesus makes of this an opportunity to teach about trusting God, wholehearted faith in prayer, and forgiveness. To illustrate wholehearted faith in prayer, Jesus says solemnly that if one were to say to "this mountain" to be taken away and cast into the sea, it will happen, provided that person's faith is undivided by doubt (11:23). It is often argued that "this mountain" is a reference to the temple mount. In light of Mark's enclosing of the temple incident within his story of the condemned fig tree, this is possible, but such an interpretation seems to suggest that Jesus may have encouraged prayer for the leveling of the temple mount.

Not only Mark's framing of Jesus' disruption in the temple by his cursing of a fig tree but also specific details within Mark's narration of events lead to the conclusion that the literary frame (fig tree story) is related in meaning to the enclosed episode (temple incident).[23] The first telltale narrative detail is that Mark envisages Jesus looking around at everything in the temple on the day that he arrives in Jerusalem (11:11). This builds suspense, but it also intimates that what occurs next does so purposefully rather than by happenstance. Second, *before* Jesus responds to the tree's fruitlessness, Mark takes pains to point out that the reason the tree had leaves but no figs on it is that it was not the season for figs (11:13–14). In narrative terms, this is an incongruous element, which provokes the reader or hearer to consider whether the story should be taken at face value.[24] A similar ef-

---

21. Precisely what Jesus is alleged to have prevented anyone from carrying through the temple is disputed.

22. The verb used by Peter to describe Jesus' having cursed the tree is the same verb used of those accursed in Jesus' scenario of final judgment and bound for eternal punishment in Matt 25:41.

23. For a compelling summary of textual resonances, see Black, *Mark*, 239–40.

24. See Byrne, *A Costly Freedom*, 178n12: "Mark's observation (11:13d) that 'it

fect is created by a third narrative detail, namely, the obscure manner in which Jesus responds to Peter's observation that the tree Jesus had cursed had withered. There is no obvious relation between Jesus' cursing of a tree and his instruction on wholehearted faith in prayer and forgiveness. The formal introduction to Mark 11:23, "Amen, I tell all of you . . . ," suggests that the conclusion to the story regarding the fig tree is more closely related to what comes before it than to what comes after it, yet the precise relation of 11:22-25 to 11:20-21 is difficult to discern.[25]

At least since William Telford's detailed discussion of Mark's intercalated account of the temple incident, the prevailing interpretation of Mark 11:11-25 is that the fig tree framing of the temple incident reinforces the symbolism of Jesus' actions in the temple.[26] In short, the fate of the fig tree foreshadows the fate of the temple, which is also symbolized by Jesus overturning tables and stools within the temple precincts. Both Jesus' overturning of tables and stools and also his cursing of a fig tree symbolize the temple's forthcoming destruction as divine judgment. So entrenched is this interpretation that it features in Rodney Decker's handbook on the Greek text of Mark's Gospel, within a series explicitly concerned to provide what the general editor describes as "a foundational analysis of the Greek text upon which interpretation may then be established."[27] In a relatively rare interpretive comment following his translation of Mark 11:12-19, Decker remarks: "This pericope is another example of Mark's 'sandwich stories' in which two events are described, with one sandwiched in the middle of the other. Here the cleansing of the temple (vv. 15-19) is enclosed in the account of the barren fig tree (vv. 12-14, 20-25). This sandwich uses the outer story to focus attention on and to explain the significance of the inner story:

---

was not the season for figs' does not . . . 'explain' Jesus' action so much as point to its 'prophetic' absurdity." See also Yarbro Collins, *Mark*, 525, for whom various features of Mark's story about the fig tree indicate it to be a "metaphorical narrative."

25. For a nuanced and illuminating interpretation, building on the work of Juel, *Messiah and Temple*, and Dowd, *Prayer, Power, and the Problem of Suffering*, see Boring, *Mark*, 316-25.

26. Telford, *Barren Temple* (1980). This interpretation features in most recent commentaries, as well as in studies from various interpretive standpoints, e.g., Stein, *Gospels and Tradition*, 121-33; Böttrich, "Jesus und der Feigenbaum," 328-59; Meier, *Marginal Jew*, 2:884-96; Brown, "Mark 11:1-12:12," 78-89; Yang, "Reading Mark 11:12-25," 89-95; Gray, *Temple in the Gospel of Mark*, 38-43; Wong, *Temple Incident*, 72, 111; Chanikuzhy, *Jesus, the Eschatological Temple*, 124-45; and Strauss, *Jesus Behaving Badly*, 62-69. For dissenting views, see Mann, *Mark*, 431-54; Gundry, *Mark*, 623-82, esp. 671-82; Berger, "Der 'brutale' Jesus," 123-24; Esler, "Incident of the Withered Fig Tree," 41-67; Wahlen, "Temple in Mark," 253-67; and Yarbro Collins, *Mark*, 523-26.

27. Culy, "Series Introduction," ix.

the barren fig tree is a picture of the temple, Jesus' cursing of the tree functions as his pronouncement of judgment on the temple."[28]

This reading of a puzzling passage has long served as my default interpretation.[29] On further reflection, however, it is not without its problems, and there is another way to interpret the close association between Jesus' disruption in the temple and his cursing of a fig tree. The principal difficulty for the prevailing interpretation is that the fig tree incident is not really required if what Jesus does and says within the temple inherently symbolize its imminent destruction.[30] Given other difficulties associated with the incident of the fig tree, which might well explain its absence from Luke's version of events at this narrative juncture, one wonders what is gained in narrative terms by the fig tree frame largely reinforcing the meaning of Jesus' symbolic actions in the temple.

I continue to consider that the Markan intercalation of the temple incident within his account of Jesus' cursing of a fig tree creates a powerful association between these events, but I am now less confident that both together prefigure the destruction of the temple.[31] The connection between

28. Decker, *Mark 9-16*, 86. See also Leander, *Discourses of Empire*, 265: "Sandwiched between a twofold story in which Jesus curses a fig tree for bearing no fruit (11:12-14, 20-22), the temple incident is often taken as communicating a not so subtle condemnation of the temple." This interpretation is sometimes softened somewhat by saying that these intercalated episodes symbolize divine judgment on Israel's religious leadership. See, e.g., Geddert, *Mark*, 259-77.

29. The view that the cursed fig tree foreshadows Jerusalem's impending judgment goes back to Ephrem the Syrian in the fourth century and Victor of Antioch in the fifth century, the latter known as the author of the earliest extant commentary on Mark's Gospel.

30. Cf. Esler, "Incident of the Withered Fig Tree," 49-52, for whom the primary problem for the interpretive proposal of Telford and others is that it conflicts with Mark's own apparent interpretation of the fig tree incident in 11:22-25. For an effective response to Esler, reaffirming the significance of intercalation at Mark 11:12-25, see Kirk, "Time for Figs," 509-527.

31. Indeed, I am now less confident that either event, as narrated by Mark, symbolizes the temple's destruction, envisaged by Jesus as divine judgment, especially when such an interpretation entails the replacement of the temple by the Christian community. It is possible to interpret the actions and words of Jesus within the temple as symbolizing the Messiah's reclamation of the temple, that is, as Jesus Messiah's prophetic or performative judgment on the temple, but without necessarily anticipating some more literal "judgment" such as destruction. As with the fig tree, Jesus' words effect what they express. Perhaps Jesus correctly perceived that Jerusalem was on a collision course with Rome, but such an intuition need not imply that he intended his temple actions and verbal denunciation to presage the Roman destruction of Jerusalem. Occurring shortly after the Messiah's entry into Jerusalem, Jesus' calculated actions and words in the temple reinforce that Israel's Messiah has arrived. The intercalated events of Mark 11:12-25 should not be interpreted in isolation from 11:1-11. For an overview of the

the temple incident and its fig tree frame is as close if Jesus' cursing of the fig tree relates to *his own imminent death* as if it relates to the temple's demise, yet without being redundant. Perhaps the association between the temple incident and its narrative frame is Mark's way of showing that Jesus presaged the inevitable outcome of his disruption in the temple. When Jesus condemns the tree and thereby brings about its death, might he not be prefiguring his own death as a consequence of his messianic provocation in the temple?

Textual support for such an alternative interpretation appears within Mark's own narrative and also within the wider Gospel tradition. First, the events recounted in Mark 11 follow hard upon this evangelist's central section, 8:22–10:52, whose narrative backbone features three three-part sequences: (1) Jesus teaches that the Son of humanity must suffer, die, and rise again (8:31; 9:30–31; 10:32–34); (2) one or more disciples react(s) in such a way as to reveal incomprehension of Jesus' messianic mission (8:32–33; 9:32–34; 10:35–41); and (3) Jesus provides corrective instruction on authentic discipleship (8:34–9:1; 9:35–50; 10:42–45). Within Mark's central section, in short, he presents Jesus as teaching about his forthcoming fate in redundant fashion, yet without any apparent deepening of comprehension on the part of his disciples. The third three-part sequence foregrounds Jerusalem as Jesus' intended destination, both in narrative description (10:32) and in words attributed to Jesus (10:33), and Jerusalem shortly becomes the primary setting for the remainder of Mark's narrative. On Jesus' arrival to Jerusalem, there is no indication provided by Mark that the disciples now understand what kind of Messiah they are following. Indeed, the manner of Jesus' arrival to Jerusalem is more likely to have reinforced the kind of assumptions that provoked Jesus' earlier correctional instruction.

Second, the account of Jesus' messianic entry into Jerusalem is, in Mark's Gospel, self-referential. Although Mark does not explicitly indicate that this event fulfills a messianic prophecy, as in Matt 21:4–5, he likely sees it as such. This seems clear from his unique addition to the crowd's acclamation, set out in chiastic fashion:

Hosanna!
Blessed is the one coming in the name of the Lord;
Blessed is the coming kingdom of our ancestor David.
Hosanna in the highest heavens! (Mark 11:9–10)

---

apocalyptic matrix for, and biblical backdrop to, interpreting Mark 11–12, see Shively, *Apocalyptic Imagination*, 190–96, albeit with the caveat that Mark's renovation—no less than retrieval—of apocalyptic and biblical motifs should bear on one's interpretation of his Gospel narrative.

For Mark, in other words, Jesus' entry into Jerusalem is staged as his messianic arrival, and it is recognized as such by people ahead of him and by those following him. It is a self-referential prophetic-messianic sign.[32] Since the dramatic episode that not only opens the third major section of Mark's Gospel but also immediately precedes the intercalated temple incident is presented as being self-referential, such narrative configuration encourages an interpretation of the two-part story of a fig tree's condemnation as also self-referential. By cursing a fig tree in the company of his disciples, Jesus yet again presages his own death, as so often in earlier parts of Mark's Gospel (2:20; 8:31; 9:9–13, 30–31; 10:33–34, 45).[33]

Third, each of Mark's three so-called "passion predictions" forecasts his death and, *after three days*, his rising again (8:31; 9:31; 10:33–34). Mark 15:1–16:8 narrates Jesus' crucifixion, burial, and resurrection over the course of three days, and it is a distinctive feature of the beginning of Mark's Jerusalem section that he features events on three separate days. If the condemnation of a fig tree by Jesus is understood as a self-referential action to symbolize his own impending death, an interpretive possibility strengthened by the verbal resonance between Mark 11:13 and 15:40,[34] the events over three days at the beginning of Mark's Jerusalem section mirror the final three days. The three days of Mark 11 progress from messianic

---

32. See Hooker, *Signs of a Prophet*, 43–44. For Hooker, all four evangelists rightly interpret Jesus' mode of entry into Jerusalem as a messianic claim on his part. Interpreters regularly express a similar opinion about what Jesus does and says within the temple in Mark 11:15–17, namely, that his scripturally authorized actions comprise a prophetic protest or symbolic judgment that reflects an exalted (prophetic-messianic) self-understanding.

33. Yet another possible association between the arrival of Jesus to Jerusalem and the two-part episode of the fig tree is Jesus' mastery over nature. In his instructions to two disciples dispatched to fetch a colt on which to ride into Jerusalem, Jesus specifically identifies the colt as one on which no one has yet sat (11:2). Then, when the colt is brought to Jesus, he sits on it (11:7). No comment is made about this, but colts that have never been ridden cannot be counted on to accept their first rider placidly. For an audience knowledgeable about equines, this hints at the mastery of Jesus over the natural order of things, as evidenced earlier in the Gospel (4:35–41; 6:35–52; 8:1–10) and yet again in the story of the cursed fig tree. For matching musings, see Gundry, *Mark*, 623–34, and Watson, *Fourfold Gospel*, 129–30. Cf., however, Hooker, *Signs of a Prophet*, 43: "The insistence of Mark and Luke that the animal had never been ridden before suggests that it was therefore fit to be ridden by a king or for some sacred purpose."

34. In Mark 11:13 Jesus sees a fig tree in leaf "from a distance" (ἀπὸ μακρόθεν, *apo makrothen*); in 15:40 women are said to have witnessed the crucifixion of Jesus "from a distance" (ἀπὸ μακρόθεν). Cursing the fig tree (11:14) might be understood to presage the divine curse of crucifixion (15:33–34; cf. Gal 3:13), and even the hunger of Jesus (11:12) might well prefigure his physical vulnerability at his crucifixion.

triumph to symbolic death, whereas the three days of Mark 15–16 progress from shameful death by crucifixion to messianic triumph via resurrection.

In this connection, it is remarkable that the first three days of Mark's Jerusalem section feature Bethany as the apparent home base for Jesus and the Twelve.[35] In light of the narrative pattern established by the three explicit references to Bethany in Mark 11:1, 11, and 12, the reader is naturally inclined to imagine Jesus and his disciples leaving Jerusalem for Bethany on the evening of their second day in Jerusalem (11:19) and returning to Jerusalem from Bethany on the morning of the third day (11:20, 27). Notably, Bethany features again at the beginning of Mark's passion narrative (14:1–11), thereby reinforcing the narrative pattern established at the beginning of the Jerusalem section. In the one event situated at Bethany, moreover, Jesus interprets a woman's anointing as preparation for his burial (14:8). This reinforces the interpretive case for understanding the earlier event in the vicinity of Bethany, the cursing and withering of a fig tree, as also prefiguring Jesus' own impending death.[36]

Fourth, in light of this larger literary context, certain details within the intercalated temple incident in Mark 11:12–25 are no less explicable on my alternative reading than on the prevailing interpretation. At 11:14, after recording the curse of Jesus addressed to a fig tree, one reads: "And his disciples heard." Then, immediately following the next recorded words of Jesus—his prophetic judgment against temple functionaries (11:17)—Mark notes that the chief priests and scribes *heard* and were deliberating about how they might destroy him (11:18a). Only in Mark's account of the temple incident do the chief priests and scribes consider how they might destroy Jesus precisely because of his prophetic denunciation within the temple precincts, and only in Mark does this occur after Jesus' words of condemnation addressed to a fig tree. Put differently, between the curse of a fig tree and Peter's recognition that Jesus had cursed it to death, Mark recounts that Jesus' prophetic challenge to current temple practices provoked religious authorities to seek to destroy *him*. Whereas the prevailing interpretation posits that the fig tree framing of the temple incident symbolizes the destruction of the temple, Mark's text explicitly foregrounds the threat to *Jesus*

---

35. See Gundry, *Mark*, 635: "His going out 'with the Twelve' to stay overnight in Bethany is a reminder of his prediction to them that in Jerusalem he will suffer and be killed (10:32–33). The mention of the Twelve has the purpose of recalling that prediction, the only [and indeed most recent] one of the passion predictions to name Jerusalem and be directed to 'the Twelve.'"

36. In this connection, see Brown, "Mark 11:1—12:12," 89, who points out that Mark 14:1 echoes 11:18 and 14:2 echoes 12:12.

himself.³⁷ This threat is reiterated in Jesus' parable of the Vineyard Tenants (12:1–12), which is narrated in the immediate aftermath of the intercalated temple incident. On my proposed interpretation, in much the same way as Jesus' parable of the Tenants in the Vineyard prefigures his own death, the two-part cursing of the fig tree is an "enacted parable" of Jesus in which he prefigures his own death as a consequence of his prophetic challenge to temple authorities.³⁸

Perhaps the teaching of Jesus in Mark 11:22–25 is not completely clarified by this alternative reading of Mark's intercalated temple incident. If Mark envisaged the two-part cursing of the fig tree along the lines I have suggested, however, Jesus' cryptic response to Peter's observation regarding the radically withered fig tree is nevertheless meaningful. In light of the prospect of Jesus' own death, his disciples must entrust themselves to God (11:22).³⁹ In the foreseeable absence of Jesus, moreover, wholehearted faith, prayer, and forgiveness must be the marks of his continuing community of disciples (11:23–25).

Fifth and finally, it so happens that yet another figurative fig tree features a little later in Mark's narrative. At Mark 13:28–29, within the context of his eschatological discourse, Jesus exhorts his disciples to learn a lesson from the fig tree: as they infer the onset of warm weather when they detect new leaves on the fig tree, so also they should discern the signs of the times when they witness certain things occurring. Little in Mark 13 is susceptible to straightforward interpretation, but if there is a relation between the fig trees of Mark 13:28 and 11:12–21, as some suggest,⁴⁰ the crucial point for my current purposes is that the fig tree of 13:28 serves as an analogy for eschatological salvation *associated with the future arrival of the Son of humanity*.⁴¹ If the figurative fig tree of Mark 13:28 symbolizes the salvific

---

37. For the view that the fig tree more likely symbolizes a person or group of people rather than an institution like the temple, see Wahlen, "Temple in Mark," 261–63, and Miquel, "Impatient Jesus," 148–49. For Wahlen, the withered fig tree represents the temple authorities; for Miquel, the chief priests and scribes.

38. In our ecologically sensitive times, cursing a fig tree to death seems indefensible, especially in the way Mark tells this tale. But if Mark envisaged this incident as an enacted parable prefiguring Jesus' own death, the radical withering of a fig tree participates in the pathos of Israel's crucified Messiah, who relinquishes his life for the benefit of many (see Mark 10:45).

39. One is reminded of John 14:1, early in the Johannine farewell discourse.

40. See, e.g., Telford, *Barren Temple*, 216–17, and Gray, *Temple in the Gospel of Mark*, 145–48.

41. For more detailed discussion of the analogy in Mark 13:28–29, see Neville, *A Peaceable Hope*, 64–73. Some argue for a more direct analogy with the nearness of the Son of humanity per se.

agency of the Son of humanity at his future arrival, perhaps the cursing to death of the earlier fig tree symbolizes the salvific agency of the Son of humanity by means of his death (cf. 10:45; 12:10–11).

The alternative interpretation of Mark's intercalated temple incident proposed above is supported by two further textual data from the wider Gospel tradition. First, in Luke's version of Jesus' arrival to Jerusalem, he dispenses with the episode concerned with a fig tree, even though he is likely to have been familiar with it in connection with the temple incident. Some consider that the parable of the fruitless fig tree in Luke 13:6–9 is his substitute for this episode. Be that as it may, it is remarkable that in Luke 23:31, immediately preceding his crucifixion, Jesus speaks proverbially about *his own death* using the imagery of a green tree that dries or *withers* (cf. Mark 11:20–21). The context of Luke 23:31 apparently interrelates the death of Jesus with the destruction of Jerusalem,[42] but that is a Lukan association and is not necessarily present in Mark 11:11–22. In any case, Luke 23:31 provides evidence from elsewhere within the Gospel tradition that Jesus was remembered to have signaled *his own death by reference to the withering of a living tree*. This adds credence to the interpretive suggestion that the cursing and radical withering of a fig tree in Mark 11:12–25 may be understood as an "enacted parable" prefiguring Jesus' own death as a consequence of his prophetic-messianic challenge to the temple authorities.

And second, the wider Gospel tradition reveals that Jesus' provocation in the temple could be conceived in close relation to Jesus' death and resurrection, as evidenced by the Johannine version of this event (see John 2:18–22). As Mark Matson observes, "The Synoptics link the Temple Incident with the rejection and death of Jesus temporally by placing the event at the beginning of the passion week. FG [The Fourth Gospel], however, links the two events at a deeper level by stating directly that Jesus' actions in the Temple somehow symbolize the destruction of his own body (2:21–22)."[43] If this association could be made by the fourth evangelist, so also could it be made by Mark in the form of an "enacted parable" of Jesus involving the cursing and withering of a fig tree.[44] In this connection, it is also noteworthy

---

42. This uniquely Lukan passage is discussed in chapter 3, above.

43. Matson, "Temple Incident," 148.

44. A possible weakness in my interpretive line is the traditional association between the fig tree and Israel, an association emphasized by Meier, *Marginal Jew*, 2:887. See also Black, *Mark*, 241: "Fig trees symbolize prosperity and peace (1 Kgs 4:25; 2 Kgs 18:31 = Isa 36:16; Joel 2:22; Mic 4:4; Hag 2:19; Zech 3:10); their loss or destruction is a conventional sign of prophetic judgment and national distress (Isa 28:3–4; Jer 8:13; Hos 2:12; Joel 1:7, 12; Amos 8:1–3; Mic 7:1)." Granted, but by virtue of Jesus' self-designation as "the Son of humanity," Mark presents Jesus Messiah as arrogating to himself the role of representative of suffering Israel assured of divine vindication (as in Daniel 7).

that what follows the Johannine version of Jesus' messianic arrival to Jerusalem is dominated by the moment, manner, and meaning of *his own death* (John 12:12–36).[45]

THE TEMPLE INCIDENT IN LUKAN PERSPECTIVE

For Luke, Jesus' entry into the temple marks the culmination of his journey to Jerusalem and hence the completion of Luke's lengthy central section (9:51–19:46).[46] As in Matthew's narration, Luke's account of Jesus' temple action is but part of a larger passage in which Jesus draws ever nearer to Jerusalem before finally entering into the temple (19:28–46). Curiously, although the movement of Jesus toward Jerusalem is a crucial feature of his narrative, Luke never explicitly records Jesus entering Jerusalem, as his synoptic counterparts do (cf. Matt 21:10; Mark 11:11, 15). Rather, in Luke's account, Jesus' entry into Jerusalem is marked by his entry into the temple.

Although both Matthew and Mark's accounts of Jesus' arrival in Jerusalem convey a sense of triumph, the same cannot be said of Luke's narration of this event. Indeed, Luke's version of this episode has been described by Brent Kinman as Jesus' "a-triumphal entry" into Jerusalem.[47] Even though Jesus approaches Jerusalem to the sound of messianic acclamation, such acclamation is voiced by the company *of disciples*, according to Luke 19:37–38, and their acclamation is met with disapproval on the part of certain Pharisees (19:39). Then follows the uniquely Lukan lamentation for Jerusalem (19:41–44), in which Jesus foresees Jerusalem's destruction and provides a theological rationale for it.[48] Having pronounced in advance Jerusalem's demise as impending divine judgment, Jesus enters the temple precincts and begins to drive out the vendors (19:45).

Luke's version of Jesus' temple action is the most understated of the four canonical accounts, taking up but twenty-five words, half of which compose the conflated scriptural rationale for Jesus' action drawn from Isa 56:7 and Jer 7:11. A prophetic action is clarified by means of pertinent sayings from the prophets. Jesus' action is confined to expelling from the

---

45. Even if my alternative reading of Mark's intercalated temple incident proves unconvincing, I proffer it in protest against interpretations that all too easily envisage the words and symbolic actions of Jesus as anticipating the divinely ordained destruction of the temple so as to be replaced by the Christian community. For another interpretation that contests readings of Mark 11 from the perspective of "Christian replacement theology," see Sabin, *Reopening the Word*, 73–84.

46. See Matera, "Jesus' Journey to Jerusalem (Luke 9:51–19:46)," 57–58.

47. Kinman, "Parousia, Jesus' 'A-Triumphal' Entry," 279–94.

48. Luke 19:41–44 is discussed in more detail in chapter 3, above.

temple precincts those who were selling, and his scriptural authorization is directed precisely to them (19:46). In Lukan perspective, it would seem that selling within the temple is incompatible with its primary role as a place of prayer.[49] No mention is made of what was sold in the temple, nor is Jesus said to have overturned tables or stools. As Luke relates the scene, Jesus ushers vendors from the temple in a relatively orderly fashion, explaining his action to those being evicted. His clearing action apparently makes room for an audience for his teaching, whereas his explicatory words begin the teaching that will take up his days within the temple until his arrest (see 19:47; 20:1; 21:37–38). As John Carroll observes, "Jesus occupies the temple as the location for his climactic public teaching."[50] Indeed, in light of the close proximity of Luke 19:47 and 20:1 to 19:46, it would not be farfetched to interpret the teaching of Jesus within the temple as his reclamation of the temple as a house of prayer, especially in light of Luke's understanding of divine visitation in the prophetic-messianic mission of Jesus (19:44).

Commentators routinely remark on Luke's removal of violent features from Mark's version of the temple incident. According to Jacob Chanikuzhy, for example, "In the Lucan narrative, the temple action is an appropriation of the temple free of violence."[51] Such scholars are correct that Luke's version of this episode is nonviolent, but it is a stretch to say that he removed violent features from any earlier account of this incident, whether or not that was Mark's. What imbues this scene with a sense of foreboding is not its concise content but rather its contentious context—its juxtaposition with the preceding pronouncement of Jerusalem's impending doom.

PREVIEW OF THE TEMPLE INCIDENT IN JOHANNINE PERSPECTIVE

What stands out most about the temple incident in the Fourth Gospel is its placement at the beginning of Jesus' public activity (2:13–22). In fact, if one accepts that John 1:19–51 is largely concerned with disciples gathering themselves to Jesus, Jesus' provocation in the temple is but the second

---

49. Illustrative of this Lukan emphasis is the opening line of Jesus' parable of the Pharisee and the Tax Agent: "Two people ascended into the temple *to pray*..." (18:10a).

50. Carroll, *Luke*, 388. See also Green, *Gospel of Luke*, 692: "The one act sets the stage for the other; or, better, in his prophetic critique of the temple, Jesus recovers the temple for its legitimate use—namely, revelatory teaching concerning the purpose of God even now coming to fruition."

51. Chanikuzhy, *Jesus, the Eschatological Temple*, 230. In concert with majority opinion, Chanikuzhy considers the Lukan version of the temple incident to be a redactional abridgment of Mark's account.

recorded event in Jesus' public life, following the wine sign of 2:1–11 as the first of his signs that revealed his glory.[52] Taken together, these two incidents, one situated in Galilee and the other in Jerusalem, set the tone for the Gospel as a whole.[53] The first celebrates life and the institution of marriage as the context for welcoming and nurturing new life, whereas the second strikes the note of discord that will lead to Jesus' death—and also new life of an altogether different order.

The vastly different contextualization of the temple incident in the Fourth Gospel has vexed scholars concerned with chronology and historicity. In view of the reality that the adult Jesus travels to Jerusalem but once in the synoptic portrayal of his public mission, thereby requiring the placement of Jesus' provocation in the temple at that particular point in his mission, one cannot help but wonder whether the Johannine contextualization of this episode might not match historical reality more closely than the synoptic context. After all, it would be passing strange for an able-bodied Galilean Israelite man to visit Jerusalem for Passover once only. Moreover, as Paula Fredriksen observes, "Nothing in John's chronology is intrinsically improbable."[54] In short, it is at least conceivable that Jesus' provocation in the temple did not occur in the final week of his life and was not the decisive event that precipitated his demise. In this connection, it is remarkable that although the Fourth Gospel probably reached its final form well after the destruction of the temple, the evangelist interprets this event in relation to Jesus' death and resurrection, not in relation to the temple's destruction.

Despite its completely different context within the Johannine narrative framework, the temple incident is recognizably the same as that recounted at the beginning of Jesus' final week in the synoptic tradition. There are nevertheless distinctive features in the Johannine version. There is no specific reference to Jesus' entry into the temple, even though that would be

---

52. Although Jesus' actions in the temple have all the hallmarks of a prophetic sign, this event is not characterized as a sign by the evangelist, even though John 2:23 could be taken to mean that this was one of the signs he did during the Passover festival in Jerusalem. Jesus is even asked for a sign to authorize his temple actions (2:18). Since these ultimately relate to Jesus' death and resurrection, perhaps one can say that this episode prefigures the last of his signs, which revealed his glory definitively.

53. For further observations on the narrative role of the temple incident in the Fourth Gospel, see Matson, "Temple Incident," 148–51. See also Ashton, *Understanding the Fourth Gospel*, 338: "in his version of the temple episode the [fourth] evangelist intervenes directly to suggest that the whole of Jesus' public career will be lived out under the shadow of the cross."

54. Fredriksen, "Historical Jesus," 251. Even so, there are grounds for thinking that the Johannine placement of the temple incident is for theological rather than historical reasons. See, e.g., Ashton, *Understanding the Fourth Gospel*, 136–40, 335–43.

the natural destination for a Jewish man travelling to Jerusalem at Passover. Rather, John notes what Jesus finds in the temple, his manner of driving animals out of the temple, his disruption to the business of coin-changers within the temple, and his command to the dove-sellers to remove their things from his Father's house (2:14–16). This is said to provoke the disciples to recall that it is written, "Zeal for your house will eat me up" (2:17), and Jewish authorities to request an authorizing sign (2:18). What Jesus says in response to this request for a sign is (mis)understood to refer to the temple or sanctuary, whereas his words, according to the evangelist, relate to "the sanctuary of his body" (2:21). Crucially, John 2:22 discloses that Jesus' provocation in the temple has been reconfigured in post-resurrection perspective. In other words, insofar as this incident is comprehended truly and fully in Johannine terms, Jesus' disruption to worship-related temple activities prefigures his own death and resurrection rather than the destruction of the temple.

CONCLUDING COMMENTS

In Christian reflection on the moral legitimacy of aggression, force, or violence, both Jesus' disruption to worship-related activities within the temple precincts and one ambivalent detail within the Johannine version of this incident have played important roles. Jesus' actions, as described by all four evangelists, are undoubtedly rather forceful and certainly provocative. Despite exaggerated assertions to the contrary, however, none of the canonical Gospel writers depicts Jesus as acting violently in the temple.

Of the first three evangelists, Luke describes the temple incident in the most economical and benign manner. Explaining his actions with reference to scripture, Jesus evicts vendors from the temple, thereby reclaiming it as a house of prayer and instruction. Like Luke, Matthew presents the temple incident as integral to Jesus' arrival to the city of Jerusalem, but unlike Luke, he emphasizes Jesus' arrival to the city of David as the messianic Son of David. Lest such an association conjure up the prospect of military might, however, Matthew's account depicts Jesus as Israel's meek messiah whose disruptive conduct in the temple is preparatory to, and indeed overshadowed by, his healing activity within the temple precincts.

More than either Matthew or Luke, Mark's account of the temple incident focuses on Jesus' disruption to worship-related activities within the temple precincts. Indeed, the uniquely Markan detail that Jesus prevented anyone from carrying anything through the temple complex (11:16) considerably magnifies the purported scale of the episode. This "magnification" is further reinforced by the Markan sandwiching of the temple incident between two scenes associated with Jesus' cursing of a forlorn fig tree. In the history of interpretation, this Markan intercalation is most often understood to reinforce the symbolic actions of Jesus within the temple. In other words, Jesus' cursing of the fig tree prefigures divine judgment of the temple (or, for some, temple authorities) by means of its destruction.

On this widespread interpretation, Jesus' disruptive conduct within the temple precincts may not be violent, but his actions are premised on the prospect of divine violence, which most exegetes regard as realized in the Roman razing and raping of Jerusalem. If that is how Mark perceived things, the temple incident is much more profoundly violent than if what Jesus is said to have done counts as violence. Since such an understanding grates against fundamental features of Mark's theological-moral vision, I have proposed that Jesus' cursing of a fig tree is a self-referential "enacted parable" that prefigures his own death as a consequence of his prophetic provocation in the temple.

In the Johannine version of events, there has been long-standing debate over whether Jesus used a whip on people as well as on cattle and sheep to drive them from the temple precincts. If he did strike people as well as livestock with his makeshift whip, so the argument goes, Jesus' own behavior motivated by righteous anger validates violence proportionate to the discerned need of any given situation. For this reason, the Johannine version of this episode is especially significant, not only in its own right but also in light of its reception history. As a result, a separate chapter is devoted to recent discussion of whether or not John 2:13–22 portrays Jesus as indulging in violence. Before turning to a more detailed discussion of Jesus' temple provocation in Johannine perspective, however, chapter 6 focuses on the parable of the Vineyard Tenants, which follows the temple incident in all three Synoptic Gospels and which is often considered to envisage—and thereby validate—the notion of divine retaliation provoked by human recalcitrance.

6

The Parable of the Vineyard Tenants

(MATT 21:33–43; MARK 12:1–12; LUKE 20:9–18)

FROM A THEOLOGICAL AND ethical perspective focused on violence in the Gospels, the parable of the Vineyard Tenants is significant for various reasons. First, in all three Synoptic Gospels this parable follows the temple incident fairly closely, leading many interpreters to read the parable in relation to Jesus' disruption within the temple. Second, some see this parable as a violent text in one way or another. And third, some consider this parable to illustrate New Testament texts that lean in the direction of Christian supersessionism over Judaism, an ideology whose history of effects is bloodstained by brutality in the name of Jesus.[1]

Within the synoptic tradition, the literary context of the parable of the Vineyard Tenants is crucial. In narrative terms, from the point of Jesus' entry into Jerusalem, this parable is the third or fourth passage shared between all three Synoptic Gospels in the same relative order, depending on whether one accepts the temple incident as occurring in the same basic sequence in all three Gospels and also on whether one treats the question regarding Jesus' authority as a separate literary unit. In any case, at the beginning of the Jerusalem section in all three Synoptics, there is a shared narrative progression from (a) the arrival of Jesus to Jerusalem to (b) the temple disturbance

---

[1]. Some consider that this applies principally to Matthew's version of the parable, especially because of Matt 21:43. See, e.g., Hays, *Moral Vision*, 423. Others see anti-Judaic supersessionism as inherent in the parable in all three canonical versions, albeit mitigated somewhat by Luke. See, e.g., Johnson, "Anti-Judaism and the New Testament," 1634–35.

to (c) the challenge to Jesus' authority and then to (d) Jesus' parable of the Vineyard Tenants. All three evangelists modify this narrative progression in various ways, whether by the insertion of additional material or by comparatively minor changes in sequence. At the precise narrative juncture at which Jesus relates the parable of the Vineyard Tenants, however, Matthew's contextualization of this parable is most distinctive by virtue of his inclusion of additional parables immediately before and after it.

Following Jesus' arrival to Jerusalem and his prophetic-messianic disruption within the temple, all three Synoptic Gospels recount, in the same relative sequence, that chief priests and other Jewish authorities approach Jesus in the temple to challenge his authority for doing "these things" (Matt 21:23–27; Mark 11:27–33; Luke 20:1–8). The "these things" to which they refer are not more clearly specified and could refer to any of Jesus' various activities, but they most naturally refer to the two most recent public events—Jesus' approach to Jerusalem and his temple action(s).[2] In typical challenge-and-riposte fashion, Jesus addresses the question put to him with a counter-question regarding the source of authority for John's baptizing activity. When his question is not answered, he retorts: "Nor do I tell you by what authority I do these things" (expressed identically in Matt 21:27b; Mark 11:33b; Luke 20:8).

Jesus himself may not have been concerned about disclosing the source of his authority, but the way in which the narrative progresses in all three Gospels suggests that the respective evangelists considered the question regarding Jesus' authority to warrant an answer. Whether or not the literary context of the parable of the Vineyard Tenants matches its original historical context, as argued by some,[3] this parable implicitly answers the question about the source of Jesus' authority to do "these things": he is the son of the vineyard owner sent with the owner's own status and authority. The clue that this is how all three evangelists construed this parable appears in the narrative detail that Jesus' interlocutors comprehended that this parable had been directed to them and/or concerned them (Matt 21:45; Mark 12:12b; Luke 20:19).[4]

As has already been observed, however, Matthew interposes a parable unique to his Gospel between the challenge to Jesus' authority and the

---

2. Cf. Meyer, *Aims of Jesus*, 168, who avers that the entry into Jerusalem, the temple incident, and the question regarding the source of Jesus' authority originally "constituted a single narrative unit and reflected a single continuous event."

3. See, e.g., Evans, *Mark 8:27–16:20*, 230; Snodgrass, *Stories with Intent*, 286–87, 296.

4. Matthew 21:45 refers to parables in the plural, presumably the parable of Two Sons as well as the parable of the Vineyard Tenants.

parable of the Vineyard Tenants. The parable of Two Sons in Matt 21:28–32 thereby becomes the first parable following Jesus' refusal to address the question regarding his authority. In and of itself, it does not address that question, but it does resonate with Jesus' counter-question regarding John's authority to baptize. Moreover, in view of Matthew's perception and description of clear and close continuity between the missions of John and Jesus,[5] the value Jesus attaches to John as one who came "in the way of righteousness" (21:32) reflects also on Jesus' own person and activities. If John's activity opened the door to the realm of God (21:31–32), the activity of his successor is also authorized by being conducted in the service of God's reign.

The parable of Two Sons is a parable of reversal.[6] The will of the father is enacted by the son who initially refuses to work in the vineyard but later reverses his decision. This son is compared by Jesus to toll collectors and sex workers, who believed John and therefore precede chief priests and other religious leaders into the realm of God. What one says is eclipsed by what one does, and precedence into the realm of God is contingent on change (μεταμέλομαι, *metamelomai* [21:29, 32]). To have witnessed radical change among the disreputable as a result of John's righteousness should have provoked a chain reaction of change among Jesus' questioners but apparently failed to do so (21:32). The importance of this parable of reversal is at least twofold: first, it unsettles assurance about precedence in(to) the reign of God; and second, in view of the burden of the succeeding parable of the Vineyard Tenants with which this parable is conjoined, such unsettling of assurance continues to apply to whomsoever inherits divine reign once it is retracted from the Jewish religious leaders. The reign of God "belongs" to those who produce *its* fruit (21:43), which implies that no particular ethnicity can claim divine reign for itself, even after its withdrawal from the Jewish leadership in charge of the temple.

Turning to the parable of the Vineyard Tenants, its interpretation depends on answers given to various thorny questions, including what type of parable it is and whether the parable in its entirety, including its evident allusions to Isa 5:1–7 and the stone citation with which it currently concludes,

---

5. This is evident from the identical summaries of their respective messages (Matt 3:2; 4:17) and other close overlaps in their teaching, some of which are noted in chapter 9, below.

6. According to Snodgrass, *Stories with Intent*, 266, the parable of Two Sons is a juridical parable because it provokes self-condemnation on the part of its hearers. More prominent in the two main textual forms of the parable (Vaticanus or Sinaiticus) is the motif of reversal, however. (Cf. Matt 19:30; 20:16; Mark 10:31; Luke 13:30.) On variant textual forms of this parable and their interpretive impact, see Foster, "A Tale of Two Sons."

can be traced back to Jesus. In Matthew's version of the parable, there is also an important textual issue with potentially profound source-critical significance, namely, whether or not Matt 21:44 is original or an early interpolation (from Luke 20:18). The version of the parable in the Gospel of Thomas 65–66 and its place in the tradition history of this parable is yet another crucial issue. In view of the key concern of this chapter, however, the focal question is: does this parable in its canonical variations envisage God retaliating violently to those opposed to the divine will? Only insofar as other interpretive issues bear on this question are they considered here.[7]

There can be few scholars who have devoted as much attention to Jesus' parable of the Vineyard Tenants as Klyne Snodgrass and John Kloppenborg, each of whom has written full-length monographs (as well as several shorter studies) on this single parable.[8] On most of the relevant interpretive issues, Snodgrass and Kloppenborg disagree, with Snodgrass defending the essential authenticity of the parable in something close to its canonical form(s) and Kloppenborg arguing that the synoptic versions of the parable are at least three elaborations removed from the original parable, which was probably closer in its basic structure to the version of the parable in the Gospel of Thomas.[9] In *Stories with Intent*, Snodgrass touches briefly on the affirmation of divine violence in response to the recalcitrant violence of the tenants, effectively dismissing this feature as peripheral to the parable's central concern.[10] For Kloppenborg, by contrast, the depiction of divine violence in this parable is important for at least two reasons: first, its lack of realism in

---

7. Among the range of views on this parable, some consider that expressions of divine violence in its canonical versions are later accretions to Jesus' original parable and therefore do not reflect his own theology. None of the interpretive issues identified above can be resolved conclusively, however, and answers to several of them inevitably reflect deep-seated assumptions of various kinds. For a survey of scholarly answers given to major research questions relating to this parable, see Lanier, "Mapping the Vineyard."

8. See, e.g., Snodgrass, *Parable of the Wicked Tenants* (1983); Snodgrass, "Recent Research" (1998); Snodgrass, *Stories with Intent*, 276–99; Kloppenborg, *Tenants in the Vineyard* (2006), preceded by several related journal articles.

9. For Kloppenborg, the (dual) transmission history of this parable is essentially as follows: Jesus' original parable, which Kloppenborg does not claim to be able to recover, except its basic structure; then two pre-Gospel elaborations, one pre-Thomasine and one pre-Markan; followed by two further independent elaborations, Thomas and Mark; and finally, two post-Markan elaborations by Matthew and Luke. For arguments in favor of Lukan influence on the Thomasine version of this parable, see Gathercole, "Luke in the *Gospel of Thomas*," 127–31; Gathercole, *Composition of the Gospel of Thomas*, 188–94. In defense of Thomasine dependence on all three Synoptic versions of this parable, see Meier, *Marginal Jew*, 5:115–24, 166–72.

10. Snodgrass, *Stories with Intent*, 289.

sociocultural context enables one to attribute this parabolic detail to later redaction; and second, it compounds the paradoxical reality that although the early Jesus movement was largely peaceable it also continued to envisage God as liable to resort to violence, especially on its own behalf.[11]

In an illuminating study of "The Representation of Violence in Synoptic Parables," Kloppenborg examines violent imagery associated with divine agency in parables of Jesus contained within Mark, Q, and Matthew. He focuses on parables of Jesus for two reasons: first, these parables at least "begin as generally realistic narratives" and thereby provide windows into the dynamics of ordinary life in the ancient world, including routine displays of force and violence; and second, these parables are "plastic" insofar as they are malleable to address new historical circumstances.[12] For Kloppenborg, this combination of realism and interpretive artifice within recorded parables of Jesus provides the attentive interpreter with a means of discriminating between realistic and "imaginary" violence attributed to divine agents, which may in turn serve as a criterion for discerning development (later application) within particular parables.[13] In short, the further removed from Jesus, the more his parables ascribe unrealistic or "imaginary" violence to God or God's agents.

With reference both to parables of Jesus in Matthew's Gospel and to expectations of eschatological condemnation in certain Qumran texts, Kloppenborg acknowledges that one way of demarcating between unacceptable and acceptable violence is to differentiate between what is permissible for people in the here and now and what is deemed necessary as integral to divine or divinely authorized eschatological judgment. Yet, according to Kloppenborg, such an eschatologically focused demarcation overlooks other displays of divine or divinely authorized violence in the synoptic tradition: "the destruction of demons, and especially parabolic discourse that reflects on divine violence in causing the destruction of Jerusalem."[14] Whether or not one should envisage exorcisms by Jesus as expressions of violence, especially since Jesus' exorcisms are generally presented as

---

11. See Kloppenborg, *Tenants in the Vineyard*, 346–47; Kloppenborg, "Representation of Violence in Synoptic Parables," 332–36, 343–51.

12. Kloppenborg, "Representation of Violence," 325.

13. Ibid., 326. (Although Kloppenborg takes care to discipline his appraisal of the distinction between realistic and "imaginary" violence by attending to documented cases of force and violence in antiquity, the distinction is not absolute. For example, even if irregular, violent "self-help" of the kind envisaged of the vineyard owner in the parable of the Vineyard Tenants is not historically inconceivable.)

14. Ibid., 328.

expulsions of oppressive demonic forces from their human habitations,[15] Kloppenborg's reference to the parabolic association between the destruction of Jerusalem and divine violence is particularly pertinent. Rather than differentiating between illegitimate and legitimate violence on the basis of eschatology, Kloppenborg proposes a simpler demarcation based on descriptions of warfare in classical Greek and Roman sources: the ordinary or more restrained violence on the part of humans and the extraordinary or extreme violence of gods and heroes.[16]

Kloppenborg's alternative means of differentiating between forms of violence deserves careful consideration, especially since he acknowledges that Greek and Roman depictions of warfare differed. Although he is correct that the fundamental distinction within the Gospel tradition is between divine or divinely authorized violence and non-authorized human violence, it is not self-evident that Greco-Roman sources provide the most apposite analogies for discriminating between conceptions of violence in the Gospels. Biblical and post-biblical texts, especially apocalyptic texts, should surely be given priority when studying the conceptual matrix within which to evaluate depictions of violence in the Gospel tradition(s). In this connection, although Kloppenborg is correct that eschatology is not the sole basis for evaluating depictions of violence within the Gospels, its close association with hopes of ultimate resolution implies that eschatology remains a significant determinant in reserving for God a range of violent means proscribed for human beings.

Previewing his discussion of representations of violence in Mark, Q, and Matthew, Kloppenborg signals a certain escalation in "imaginary" or divine violence, especially from Mark to Matthew and not only in relation to depictions of eschatological resolution. "Matthew and probably Mark," he writes, "are both able to imagine terrible violence purveyed by the deity

---

15. Kloppenborg, ibid., 330–31, correctly observes that "Markan metaphors ascribe to [Jesus] the power to torture and destroy demons," but whether he is ever depicted as doing so is unclear. The pigs of Mark 5:1–20 drown, but one wonders whether this confrontation was understood to have involved the destruction of "Legion." Jesus' parabolic warning in Matt 12:43–45 and Luke 11:24–26 indicates that evicted demons are not necessarily destroyed, and Mark 9:21–22 suggests that a malevolent spirit might deliberately seek to destroy its host by throwing the person into fire or water, presumably without suffering destruction itself. For a perspicacious discussion of Mark 5:1–20 in apocalyptic perspective, see Shively, *Apocalyptic Imagination*, 172–83. "The pigs rush into the sea so that these new hosts are destroyed," she writes, "and the unclean spirits are sent to a place that prevents their influence over human beings and points to their future judgment" (180).

16. Kloppenborg, "Representation of Violence," 328–30.

The Parable of the Vineyard Tenants 141

in historical time."[17] Although Kloppenborg discusses a range of texts from Mark, Q, and Matthew, I here narrow the focus to his appraisal of the parable of the Vineyard Tenants, paying particular attention to the depiction of divine vengeance in this parable.

Regarding Mark's version of the parable, Kloppenborg begins by drawing attention to its various realistic elements. Indeed, despite evidence of literary license, Kloppenborg adjudges Mark 12:1-8 to be largely realistic. "In sum," he affirms, "the scenario depicted in Mark 12:1-8 (and *Gos. Thom.* 65) is well within the realm of the imaginable."[18] By contrast, what Mark 12:9 asserts about the response of the vineyard owner to the killing of his son is deemed unrealistic. This is because such a response takes for granted three points that are not inevitable. First, it presumes that the vineyard owner would naturally take action himself against the tenants, even though documentary evidence indicates that such action on the part of landowners was not self-evident. Second, it takes as given that if the owner did take action himself to recover his property, he would succeed, an assumption no ancient hearer would necessarily share. And third, it assumes that the vineyard owner was entitled to take whatever action was necessary to repossess his land, whereas such "self-help" was illegal according to relevant contemporary law codes of the region.[19]

Responding to Kloppenborg, Snodgrass concedes that contemporary laws prohibited self-help, but he nevertheless counters that the vineyard owner's response in Mark 12:9 is broadly believable because laws are instituted to address existing problems. Laws limiting self-help existed precisely because persons in the vineyard owner's position were known to have reacted in similar ways.[20] For Kloppenborg, however, this misses the principal point. "It is not that such resorts to self-help may not have occurred," he grants. "The point is that Mark 12:9 does not betray the least embarrassment or interest in justifying what in a depiction of actual events was in fact clearly an illegal resort to force."[21]

---

17. Ibid., 330.

18. Ibid., 333. (Behind the remarks on the parable of the Vineyard Tenants in this essay stands the wealth of relevant historical data, prodigious research, and sagacious source- and historical-critical judgment found in Kloppenborg, *Tenants in the Vineyard*.)

19. Kloppenborg, "Representation of Violence," 334.

20. Snodgrass, *Stories with Intent*, 291-92.

21. Kloppenborg, "Representation of Violence," 334-35. In a footnote to this clarification, Kloppenborg asserts: "It is the *naive confidence* reflected in v. 9 rather than the action itself which indicates that the story is no longer speaking of a vineyard owner, but is speaking of God."

As one follows Kloppenborg further, however, it becomes evident that the question of whether Mark 12:9 is realistic or not is bound up with whether or not Jesus' original parable alluded to the Song of the Vineyard in Isa 5:1–7 and would have been perceived as doing so by his original hearers. Certainty on this point eludes interpreters, but in a series of studies culminating in *The Tenants in the Vineyard* Kloppenborg has set out his reasons for maintaining that Isaiah's Song of the Vineyard was not evoked by Jesus' original parable. In its synoptic form, the parable undoubtedly alludes to Isa 5:1–7,[22] but this is a later adaptation in light of two critical events: the crucifixion of Jesus at the instigation of temple authorities and the subsequent destruction of Jerusalem and the temple. In other words, the synoptic presentation of this parable reflects crucial events in the life of the primitive Jesus movement. Jesus' original parable was closer in form and content to its Thomasine version (*Gos. Thom.* 65).

As carefully considered as Kloppenborg's judgment on Mark 12:9 is, is it possible within a first-century Israelite context to discount Isa 5:1–7 as the intertext for Jesus' original parable? In a teaching setting unrelated to viticultural training, even as general an opening to a parable as "Someone had a vineyard" might well evoke the "classic" Song of the Vineyard, especially if, as the synoptic tradition affirms, the setting of Jesus' parable was the temple precincts. Within a Jewish context, would not the Song of the Vineyard be as deeply ingrained within people's collective psyche as actual viticultural experience? If so, then Jesus' original hearers might well have recognized his parable of the Vineyard Tenants as a twist on an old tale, an improvisation of an old song.[23]

In Isaiah's Song of the Vineyard, the vineyard symbolizes Israel, which faces judgment for failing to produce the right kind of grapes (justice; righteousness).[24] The parable of the Vineyard Tenants evokes the prophetic

22. The opening to Luke's version of the parable less obviously alludes to Isa 5:1–7, but for ears familiar with Israel's Scriptures, it would still have resonated with this earlier text (among others).

23. Whatever one decides about the authenticity of this parable of Jesus, its interpretive dynamic is decisive. The Song of the Vineyard is not only recalled but also reinterpreted. See Black, *Mark*, 250–51. For the difference it makes, or should make, to hear Jesus' parable of the Vineyard Tenants as echoing a vibrant biblical tradition in which Israel is variously represented by a vineyard, see Sabin, *Reopening the Word*, 84–90.

24. Some who distinguish between an original version of the parable of the Vineyard Tenants and its synoptic variations contend that the parable as originally formulated by Jesus was less explicitly about the relation between God and Israel and more concerned to display tensions caused by social inequities relating to land ownership and use. Since justice concerns were integral to the faith traditions of Israel, one should not demarcate too sharply between these interpretive options. Nevertheless, in view of this parable's evident echo of the Song of the Vineyard in Isa 5:1–7, its primary focus is

Song of the Vineyard to signal that its subject is the relation between God and Israel,[25] but its improvisation on an old song reveals that divine judgment is reserved for the vineyard's tenants (the Jewish religious leadership in Jerusalem) rather than the vineyard as a whole. This is transparent enough from the parable itself, at least in its synoptic variations, but it is reinforced by roughly contemporaneous non-Christian Jewish interpretations of Isaiah's Song of the Vineyard. As Dale Allison points out, a Qumran fragment (4QBenediction or 4Q500) associates the imagery of Isaiah's Song of the Vineyard with the Temple in Jerusalem, and the somewhat later (post-70 CE) Aramaic Isaiah *Targum* shifts the focus of the Hebrew text from Israel as a whole to Jerusalem and the temple.[26] This militates against a totalizing interpretation of the parable as signifying God's rejection of Israel as a whole.[27] So, although certainty is out of reach, it is at least conceivable within a first-century Israelite matrix that Jesus himself meant to say something about divine displeasure toward Israel's caretakers. If this is not a reckless inference, one hesitates to divorce from Jesus' original parable some such resolution as one finds in Mark 12:9 (and parallels).

I would prefer to be able to claim with confidence that the words attributed to Jesus in Mark 12:9 (and parallels) do not derive from Jesus. That would make it possible to distance Jesus from a troubling text. Even though I consider it probable that the Synoptic Gospels are indirectly related by virtue of their common dependence on an earlier shared source, a "Proto-Mark," source-critical analysis of this parable does not compel the conclusion that the substance of Mark 12:9 was absent from this more primitive source. On such an assumption, however, Mark 12:9 likely matches the wording of the shared source closely and may be read in more benign terms than the parallels in either Matt 21:40–41 or Luke 20:15b–16. For example, whereas in different ways both Matthew and Luke envisage Jesus as enquiring what the master of the vineyard will do *to the recalcitrant tenants*, Mark (probably reflecting "Proto-Mark") presents Jesus asking in more general terms what the master of the vineyard will do (without reference to the tenants, even if in response to their provocative actions). "How will the vineyard owner respond?" is how one might paraphrase Mark 12:9a. Moreover, although it is generally accepted that Mark depicts Jesus as answering his own question, as in Luke 20:16, both the unique Lukan addition (20:16b) and Matthew's

---

almost certainly theological, even if the expectation of just social relations within Israel is an integral dimension of the rationale for divine judgment (Isa 5:7).

25. See Snodgrass, *Stories with Intent*, 288.

26. Allison, *Scriptural Allusions*, 43–47.

27. For a contrasting viewpoint, see Marcus, *Mark 8–16*, 805–8, 813–14.

placement of the response to Jesus' question in the collective mouth of his interlocutors suggest that Mark 12:9b might be read—or might once have been read—as words of Jesus' hearers rather than his own.[28] This may not be the most natural reading of Mark 12:9, but it is a possible reading, especially in view of what follows in 12:10–11, which focuses solely on status reversal, not vengeance, and hence may be understood as a counter-question to the seemingly self-evident response to the earlier question in 12:9a. Indeed, although the opening words of Mark 12:10 are routinely understood as interrogative in construction, "Have you not read this scripture . . . ?," the sentence need not be read as a question and might even be understood as a counter-assertion that negates the retributive affirmation voiced in 12:9b. Such interpretive suggestions can only be made tentatively, however, and are unlikely to prove persuasive to those who operate with different source-critical (or ideological) assumptions.

Although I remain unconvinced that Mark 12:9 could not be part of Jesus' original parable, Kloppenborg's judgment that this is a "natural" conclusion to the parable (in its Markan or synoptic form) precisely because of its Isaian intertext seems at first sight to be compelling. Perceived as a story about Israel's God's response to recalcitrant caretakers, such a response makes sense because "God is unfettered by human prohibitions of self-help."[29] In other words, the violent response of the vineyard owner is presumed to be acceptable precisely because the vineyard owner represents God. According to Kloppenborg,

> The significance of this conclusion should not be missed. At a crucial point in his narrative, Mark moved beyond metaphors based on the "realistic" norms of force attested in the experiences of Mediterranean persons, and invokes a discourse of a *divine being using lethal force* in punishing enemies. Mark 12:9 does not involve the destruction of demons, but imagines the killing of humans, as 12:12 makes clear, Jesus' opponents. Mark 12:1–9 shifts registers to the realm of the gods and their ability to use force out of proportion with what humans could muster. This is the *only* point in Mark's narrative where the divine explicitly intervenes or is imagined to intervene with such deadly force to kill human opponents.[30]

---

28. For a similar suggestion, see Evans, *Mark 8:27–16:20*, 236. See also Decker, *Mark 9–16*, 112: "It is possible that the answer beginning here is offered by the crowd rather than Jesus (if so, Jesus' words resume in v. 10), but it seems more likely that Jesus both asks (v. 9a) and answers (v. 9b) the question." Cf. Hooker, *Gospel according to St Mark*, 276, who suggests that Mark 12:9b may be a later addition.

29. Kloppenborg, "Representation of Violence," 335.

30. Ibid., 336 (emphasis original).

For Kloppenborg, the significance of Mark 12:9 is that it reveals the evangelist to have "shifted registers" to the divine realm so as to invoke divine vengeance. Such violence as Mark 12:9 envisages is acceptable precisely because it is *divine* violence. Yet Kloppenborg's final observation gives one pause. If the resolution to the parable of the Vineyard Tenants in Mark 12:9 is the sole occasion within the entire Gospel in which God is envisaged to use deadly force against human beings, might that not signal that there is more (or in this case, less) to this resolution than first meets the eye? Kloppenborg's conclusion is premised on the perceived acceptability of divine violence in circumstances within which human violence is proscribed. Such logic finds support from within the biblical tradition, but that does not necessarily imply that it was wholly shared by Mark. Before pursuing this point, however, Kloppenborg's reflections on Matthew's version of this parable merit brief consideration.[31]

Kloppenborg's discussion of Matthew's version of the parable of the Vineyard Tenants emphasizes Matthew's allegorizing enhancements and, as an aspect of this, his intensification of depictions of divine vengeance. Assuming Matthew's redactional use of both Mark and Q, Kloppenborg envisages Matthew compounding displays of divine violence in his sources both by juxtaposing the parables of the Vineyard Tenants and the Wedding Banquet (as part of a triptych of parables in Matt 21:28–22:14) and also by ratcheting up verbal descriptions of divine violence found in both sources. In the case of the parable of the Vineyard Tenants, Matthew converts ἀπολέσει (*apolesei*, "he will destroy") into the more florid and vindictive phrase, κακοὺς κακῶς ἀπολέσει αὐτούς (*kakous kakōs apolesei autous*, "he will viciously destroy the vicious [lot of] them"). This tit-for-tat wordplay appears often in ancient Greek sources. "But when the phrase is used in connection with actions of a deity, as it is by Matthew," according to Kloppenborg, "it conjures up images of spectacular and extravagant violence and destruction."[32] As for the parable of the Wedding Banquet, adapted from Q (cf. Luke 14:16–24), Matthew adds the bellicose detail that the king's fury was vented by sending armed forces to destroy (ἀπώλεσεν, *apōlesen*) those murderers and to burn their city (22:7).[33] The parable is made even more

---

31. Since Kloppenborg's essay appears within a volume of studies on Matthew and Mark, he does not attend to Luke's version of this parable. Rather, between his discussions of violence in Mark and violence in Matthew, he examines the more realistic depictions of violence in parables attributable to Q (ibid., 336–42).

32. Ibid., 345. Kloppenborg translates Matthew's phrase as "he shall put them to a miserable death." My translation tries to capture both the play on words and its violent connotation.

33. Matthew 22:7 is regularly appealed to as evidence that the evangelist was aware

grim and gruesome by virtue of Matthew's distinctive ending, in which a rounded-up guest without a wedding garment is evicted to the outer darkness, a place of wailing and teeth-grinding (22:13).[34] According to Kloppenborg, "Matthew displays a strong apologetic interest in these two parables [Matt 21:33–22:14], providing an etiology of the destruction of the temple and the devastation of Jerusalem. For Matthew, the two parables offer an explanation of the temple's demise: God's demand for righteousness was ignored, God's repeated invitations to the Kingdom were rejected, and God's son and his prophets were killed. Under such circumstances, vengeance was inevitable."[35]

Kloppenborg's discussion of Matthew's version of the parable of the Vineyard Tenants and accompanying parables is largely compelling, although in this particular study he fails to draw attention to the potentially significant detail that the verdict of Matt 21:41, "he will viciously destroy the vicious [lot of] them," is not voiced by Jesus but by his interlocutors. This might be read as but another occasion on which Matthew narrates Jewish people calling down divine judgment on their own heads, as in the (infamous) acceptance of responsibility for the death of Jesus by Jewish people as a whole in Matt 27:24–25. Nevertheless, in Matt 21:43, which is unique to Matthew, Jesus' non-parabolic restatement of the divine response echoes his interlocutors' intuition about the vineyard (now the realm of God) being transferred to others, but he does not explicitly reiterate their expectation of vindictive vengeance.[36] Of course, if the uncompromising words of Matt 21:44 are original, they restore a sense of divine forcefulness to the parable's application, although Snodgrass notes that Matt 21:44 is a "proverbial warning" rather than a "sentence of destruction," as in 21:41.[37]

---

of Jerusalem's destruction and regarded that event in terms of divine judgment. Kloppenborg shares this view.

34. Kloppenborg, "Representation of Violence," 346. For Kloppenborg, Matt 22:11–14 is yet another parable conjoined by Matthew to the parable of the Wedding Banquet. The imagery of Matt 22:13 appears redundantly in this Gospel to signify the anguish associated with either exclusion from divine presence or (usually fiery) punishment (8:12; 13:42, 50; 22:13; 24:51; 25:30).

35. Ibid. (For a discussion of Matthew's version of the parable of the Vineyard Tenants as epitomizing the Deuteronomistic conception of Israel's history, involving repeated rejection of God's prophets, see Turner, *Israel's Last Prophet*, 225–51.)

36. On Matt 21:43, see Stanton, *Gospel for a New People*, 151: "This verse is probably the clearest indication in the gospel that the Matthean community saw itself as a separate and quite distinct entity over against Judaism."

37. Snodgrass, *Stories with Intent*, 686n186. Snodgrass thinks it likely that Matt 21:44 belongs to the original text of Matthew's Gospel, whereas Kloppenborg considers it to be a later assimilation to Luke 20:18. See Kloppenborg, *Tenants in the Vineyard*, 194–96, and also Meier, "Parable of the Wicked Tenants," 133–35. Despite

Even if such considerations mildly mitigate the violent tone of Matthew's version of this parable, there is little doubt that Matthew reckoned with divine vengeance. Both divine violence within history and eschatological vengeance are integral to his theological vision. Although Kloppenborg argues cogently for such a conclusion with respect to Matthew (and hints at a similar conclusion for Luke), he ultimately places responsibility for such alignment of the divine with overwhelming violence on Mark's shoulders. Hard on the heels of his discussion of the juxtaposed parables in Matt 21:33–22:14, within which he perceives "an etiology of the destruction of the temple and the devastation of Jerusalem," he writes:

> Mark's editing of the parable of the Tenants thus played a crucial role in the development of this fantasy of divine violence. It is worth noting that of all the synoptic parables, *only* Mark's Tenants, Matthew's Tenants and Banquet, and Luke's Entrusted Money [19:11–27] conclude with the wholesale slaughter of opponents. Since both Matthew's Banquet and Luke's Entrusted Money are found in the immediate context of their retellings of the Tenants, we must conclude that it was Mark's story of divine violence that provided the template for the development of later fantasies of divine vengeance. Mark's account of divine violence is understated: It occurs in a single verb, ἀπολέσει. But this is all it took to encourage Matthew and Luke to produce much more detailed accounts of divine violence. It might also be noted in passing that this exercise of divine force is *not* restricted to the End times but is, instead, an expression of lethal force by the deity *in* history.[38]

This is a remarkable paragraph for a number of reasons. First, Mark is held accountable for disturbing emphases developed by later redactors and indeed by later interpreters who were much more likely to have been

---

source-critical and theological-moral reasons for disputing the textual integrity of Matt 21:44, the manuscript evidence for doing so is inconclusive, if not relatively weak. If held to belong to the original text of Matthew, Matt 21:44 and Luke 20:18 comprise a significant agreement between Matthew and Luke against Mark, which on the two-document hypothesis is a problem for the alleged independence of Matthew and Luke. On my preferred theory of the common dependence of all three Synoptics on some form of "Proto-Mark," the substance of Matt 21:44, if original to Matthew's Gospel, was probably part of the parable of the Vineyard Tenants in "Proto-Mark" but omitted by Mark. Luke, by contrast, probably omitted the substance of Matt 21:42c and Mark 12:11 to reinforce the destructiveness of the rejected stone following its rehabilitation to the role of chiefstone. In Lukan perspective, the scriptural citation and its potentially destructive implications are uttered in response to the dismay expressed by Jesus' opponents to the resolution of the parable (20:16b).

38. Kloppenborg, "Representation of Violence," 346–47 (emphasis original).

influenced by Matthew or Luke. Mark's editing of a realistic parable of Jesus by introducing the (relatively restrained) element of unrealistic or mythical divine vengeance is responsible for subsequent elaborations of what Kloppenborg terms "this fantasy of divine violence." Indeed, Kloppenborg feels free to describe the entire historical development of the Christian association between the divine and destructive powers as "the Markan trajectory."[39]

Second, much is inferred from the observation that only a few parables (presumably also including Luke's version of the parable of the Vineyard Tenants) envisage the "wholesale slaughter of opponents." Although such a description might be apposite for Matthew's parable of the Wedding Banquet, it is somewhat exaggerated in relation to the synoptic versions of the parable of the Vineyard Tenants, within which divine violence is threatened to come on but a few—the tenants, not the vineyard as a whole, as in the original song or *mashal*. As for Luke's parable of the Throne Claimant (discussed earlier in chapter 2), it is by no means clear that the slaughter with which the parable ends represents divine violence. Even if Kloppenborg's observation is accepted as largely accurate, other parables within the synoptic tradition conclude with representations of divine violence that are no less stark and severe.[40]

Third, it is undeniable that Matthew's parable of the Wedding Banquet is found in the same literary context as the parable of the Vineyard Tenants, but the same can hardly be said for Luke's parable of the Throne Claimant (or Entrusted Money). Admittedly, it is not too far removed, but its location prior to Jesus' entry into Jerusalem rather than subsequent to it weakens Kloppenborg's inference that, since both these parables occur in the *immediate* context of the parable of the Vineyard Tenants, "we must conclude that it was Mark's story of divine violence that provided the template for the development of later fantasies of divine vengeance." This is overstatement, especially if the ending to Luke's parable of the Throne Claimant does not depict *divine* violence (as I argue in chapter 2).

As a result, if a source is to be held accountable for later excesses, why must the Markan source rather than Q or "M" (material unique to Matthew) be considered solely responsible? Kloppenborg is undoubtedly correct that,

---

39. Ibid., 347n81. Cf. Kloppenborg, *Tenants in the Vineyard*, 7–31, esp. 28: "Mark's version of the Tenants is the originating point in the long line of interpretation, stretching into the nineteenth century, which encodes an ideology of the domination of unruly powers by legitimate power." Probably informing Kloppenborg's interpretive judgment on this point is the importance he attaches to the anti-temple theme in Mark 11–15. See Kloppenborg, "*Evocatio deorum* and the Date of Mark," esp. 427–28, 447–50.

40. See, e.g., Reid, "Violent Endings in Matthew's Parables." Cf. Kloppenborg, "Representation of Violence," 347–50, where such parables are discussed as threats for underperforming insiders.

within the gospel tradition, "it is in Matthew that we see the widest development of scenarios of lethal violence."[41] Surely, then, Matthew is accountable for his own sins. If earlier tradition must share the blame, however, Q or "M" resourced Matthew's retributive or vindictive mind-set as much or even more richly than Mark's single intimation of divine vengeance—and that within parabolic mode.

This brings us back to the expression of divine violence in Mark's version of the parable of the Vineyard Tenants. Although there may be a hint of divine vengeance in Mark 12:9, several considerations mitigate the forcefulness of this resolution to the parable. First, whether or not Kloppenborg is correct that the substance of Mark 12:9 was added to Jesus' original parable, the question and response in this verse is part and parcel of Mark's version of this parable. In other words, it belongs to the symbolic story being told by Jesus. Second, Jesus asks only what the vineyard owner will do, not what the landowner will do "to those tenant vinedressers" (Matt 21:40) or "to them" (Luke 20:15b). And in response, if indeed Mark 12:9b is Jesus' response to his own question, his choice of verb to describe what the vineyard owner will do, ἀπόλλυμι (*apollumi*, "destroy"), is different from the verb used for the various killings by the vineyard tenants, ἀποκτείνω (*apokteinō*, "kill" or "murder"). This hints at a perceived distinction between legitimate and illegitimate violence, which suggests that ἀπόλλυμι is perhaps more open to symbolic interpretation than either ἀποκτείνω or its synonyms, θανατόω (*thanatoō*) or φονεύω (*phoneuō*).[42] Such considerations are not especially weighty, especially since ἀπόλλυμι is the verb used in Matt 21:41 and 22:7, but they do reinforce the point that Mark 12:9 is parabolic and hence symbolic, not prosaically descriptive of either historical or predicted events.

Furthermore, the scriptural citation in Mark 12:10–11, which serves as the *nimshal* or interpretive application to the preceding *mashal* (parable),[43] emphasizes reversal rather than retribution. Indeed, this understates the reality that the scriptural citation speaks only of reversal (the stone rejected by builders has been divinely restored as the chiefstone) and omits any reference to divine punishment, retribution, or vengeance. Missing from Mark's version of this parable is anything like the note in Luke 20:18 (and perhaps also in Matt 21:44) about the disastrous consequences for any who should happen either to fall on this stone or to have it fall on them. In other words, Mark considered it unnecessary to reinforce this parable's resolution

---

41. Kloppenborg, "Representation of Violence," 351.

42. For a different inference based on the same observation, see France, *Gospel of Mark*, 461.

43. See, e.g., Marcus, *Mark 8–16*, 814; Yarbro Collins, *Mark*, 547–48.

in 12:9 with a severe proverbial warning. Thus his interpretive application of the parable stresses divine judgment as reversal rather than as vengeful retribution,[44] which is precisely how Mark's story of Jesus unfolds. For Kloppenborg, the note in Mark 12:12 that Jesus' interlocutors perceived that he had directed this parable against them clarifies that 12:9 envisages the divine slaughter of Jesus' opponents.[45] In light of the intervening scriptural citation, however, that is not an assured inference. As Adela Yarbro Collins points out, "In Mark . . . the citation of v. 23 of the psalm [117:23 LXX] has an emphatic position in the rhetorical conclusion of the parable. In the psalm, what is marvelous is the striking reversal in the situation of the one who was surrounded by enemies and near death. By the power of God he could celebrate a victory. Similarly, in Mark what is marvelous is the radical change in the status of Jesus from one who was rejected and shamefully treated to the exalted Son of Man [cf. Mark 8:31; 9:31; 10:33–34; 14:62]."[46]

With the benefit of hindsight, Mark's readers might have read 12:12 alongside 12:9 as Kloppenborg does. If so, however, nothing else in Mark's narrative reinforces such an association between literal violence against persons and divine action in relation to Jesus. What is marvelous in Markan perspective is God's reversal of the ramifications of human recalcitrance rather than divine retaliation provoked by human violence, even if Mark 12:9 makes room for the divine prerogative to avenge. Perhaps in this particular instance, as elsewhere, Mark has been read in light of more explicit associations between God and violence in other Gospel texts.[47]

---

44. Cf. Neville, "Moral Vision and Eschatology," 374, where I float the suggestion that Mark 12:10 might be read epexegetically in relation to 12:9 to signal that the mode of "destruction" is divine reversal of human rejection. However tenuous that might seem to be at the exegetical level, it nevertheless evinces Mark's counterintuitive theological-moral vision.

45. Kloppenborg, "Representation of Violence," 336.

46. Yarbro Collins, *Mark*, 549.

47. Lest I be accused of anachronistically attributing to Mark moral sensibilities compatible with my own or with what I consider to be the moral meaning of Jesus' mission and message *in toto*, I am aware of that interpretive pitfall. As in my earlier discussions of Markan eschatology, however, I have found it necessary, in light of Mark's own Christologically (re-)configured moral vision, to push back against interpreters who read Mark on the basis of how his Gospel was (allegedly) read by Matthew or Luke (or even later readers). See Neville, "Moral Vision and Eschatology," and *A Peaceable Hope*, 45–87. (Incidentally, if aversion to violence is a criterion for determining that someone's interpretive grappling with a Gospel parable of Jesus is anachronistic, what is one to say about interpretive maneuvers designed to show that disconcerting features in canonical versions of a parable were probably absent from Jesus' original version of the parable?)

CONCLUDING COMMENTS

Although Matthew's (and indeed Luke's) version of the parable of the Vineyard Tenants seems to envisage God retaliating with overwhelming violence against those violently opposed to the divine will, Mark's version of this parable precludes such a straightforward conclusion. Following Kloppenborg, Ernest van Eck affirms that Mark's version of the parable of the Vineyard Tenants envisages violent human recalcitrance provoking divine or divinely authorized violence.[48] Although this is a possible reading of Mark 12:9 taken in isolation, Mark's version of the parable as a whole resists such a singular interpretation: first, by its evident allusion to the Song of the Vineyard in Isaiah 5, which recalls a long-standing but also fraught relational history between God and Israel that is not easily ended; second, by its depiction of the vineyard owner's repeated and apparently foolish efforts to retrieve his share of the vineyard produce, which reflects divine patience and forbearance;[49] and third, by the interpretation of the parable in Mark 12:10-11, which replaces the rasping note of retribution with reversal.

Put differently, although Mark's Gospel as a whole is relatively free of representations of divine or divinely authorized violence, Mark 12:9 apparently envisages divine destruction of recalcitrant rebels. That this is the sole such expression of divine violence against people in this Gospel provokes one to ponder, however, especially in light of the synoptic parallels to this parable, which in contrasting ways evidently envisage more vehement divine vengeance (see Matt 21:41a; Luke 20:18). Comparatively speaking, then, Mark's parabolic expression of divine retaliation is restrained. Furthermore, various other features of Mark's version of this parable reinforce this more "restrained" reading, none more so than the interpretive application in Mark 12:10-11, in which the divine prerogative to avenge is construed as reversal of rejection.

---

48. Van Eck, "Jesus and Violence," 120.

49. Cf. Donahue, *Gospel in Parable*, 52–55, where the suggestion is made that Jesus' original parable evoked the prophetically perceived "pathos" of God's patient pursuit of humanity and should therefore be known as the parable of "the Patient Vineyard Owner."

7

Provocation at Passover

(JOHN 2:13–22)

NONE OF THE GOSPEL accounts ever so much as suggests that Jesus' temple actions harmed or injured either human or non-human life. That is important to appreciate at the outset, whatever one decides about how forceful or provocative Jesus' behavior in the temple may have been. Nevertheless, in relation to the question of the moral value and validity of violence, the Johannine account of Jesus' provocation in the temple has received careful attention because it details Jesus constructing a whip of cords and apparently using it in connection with his expulsion of animals—and perhaps people—from the temple precincts (John 2:14–16).[1] Since the turn of the millennium, this episode in the Fourth Gospel has been subjected to careful scrutiny by some who regard it as evidence of Jesus' use of violence and also by others who consider it to be compatible with a nonviolent profile for Jesus. Although other studies might have been examined, those discussed in what follows have been selected because they focus attention on moral dimensions of Jesus' temple actions, especially in the Johannine version of this incident.

---

1. See Van der Watt and Kok, "Violence in a Gospel of Love," 168–69: "With only two possible exceptions [in the Fourth Gospel], Jesus and his disciples never use physical violence. The exceptions are when Peter cuts off the ear of Malchus (John 18:10), and the cleansing of the temple (John 2:13–17)." In a note on these exceptions, however, Van der Watt and Kok acknowledge that "Jesus' violent behaviour . . . is difficult to judge," by which they mean that his temple action might have been experienced as symbolically illustrative rather than violent.

In 2003 Mark Bredin, author of a book on nonviolent Christology in Revelation,[2] turned his attention to the Johannine account of Jesus' provocation in the temple, focusing on the question: "does the Johannine Jesus in the temple exemplify the nonviolent revolutionary of peace?"[3] Bredin's study is informed by a Girardian analysis of the interrelation between violence and sacrifice, the result of which is a somewhat one-sided and overly negative appraisal of the temple in Jerusalem as the seat of oppression and violence. Fundamental to Bredin's argument, however, is the perception that the account in John 2:13–22 alludes to various biblical and post-biblical traditions responsible for the Johannine depiction of Jesus' actions in the temple.

Key biblical and post-biblical traditions identified by Bredin as influencing the Johannine account of Jesus' provocation in the temple include the following: first, various traditions relating to Isaac as both a faithful witness and prototype of the suffering servant, such that Jesus as "Lamb of God" (John 1:29, 36) can be understood as a new Isaac;[4] second, Malachi 3:1, in which the Lord (or his messenger) comes to the temple in judgment, leading Bredin to propose that Jesus is presented as the figure of Mal 3:1;[5] third, Psalm 69:9 (LXX 68:10), explicitly referenced in John 2:17, which for Bredin explains the uniquely Johannine detail regarding the whip, that is, the whip bespeaks Jesus' zeal;[6] and fourth, the prophetic oracle of Zechariah 12–14, which concludes with the expectation that the eschatological day of the Lord will be marked by the absence of traders in the house of the Lord of hosts and thereby provides the backdrop to Jesus' words to the dove-sellers in John 2:16 not to make of his Father's house a "house of trade."[7]

2. Bredin, *Jesus, Revolutionary of Peace*.
3. Bredin, "John's Account of Jesus' Demonstration," 44.
4. Ibid., 45–46; cf. Bredin, *Jesus, Revolutionary of Peace*, 84–89.
5. Bredin, "John's Account of Jesus' Demonstration," 46.
6. Ibid., 47. Bredin actually makes a double inference on the basis of the biblical allusion in John 2:17. The whip is included to emphasize Jesus' zeal, and livestock are included to account for the whip.
7. Ibid., 47–48. Zechariah 12:10 refers to a figure pierced by the inhabitants of Jerusalem, for whom they will mourn as for an only child, leading Bredin to conclude that the Fourth Evangelist has the whole of Zechariah's closing oracle in mind. It is significant that both Mark and John seem to allude to this final saying of Zechariah, which looks forward to the ritual restoration of the temple. On the history of the interpretation of Zech 14:21, which prophesies that on the eschatological day of the Lord of hosts either "Canaanites" or "traders" or "Canaanites as traders" (see Hos 12:7; Zeph 1:11; Ezek 17:4; Prov 31:24; Job 41:6; probably also Zech 11:7, 11) will be absent from the temple, see Marcus, "No More Zealots." If Marcus interprets Mark correctly, the Markan version of Jesus' disruption to trade in the temple cannot be read as presenting Jesus in Zealot-like terms.

For Bredin, the web of intertextual associations "underwriting" John 2:13–22 lead to the conclusion that Jesus' actions in the temple precincts are to be understood as attacking temple sacrifice. "For John," according to Bredin, "things had to be put right in Jerusalem. Jesus' action was to announce the end of the sacrificial system, and replace it with a sanctified life much like that of the figure in Zechariah 12:10 or the suffering servant of Isaiah 53. This figure is also the new Isaac, the better Isaac. Tradition relates Isaac to the Passover lamb and the lamb in Isaiah 53. Jesus replaces this."[8] In a show of force that reveals his zeal for faithful, true, and just worship within his Father's house, Jesus challenges the violence inherent in the sacrificial system of the temple cult. In so doing, Jesus (in Johannine perspective) effectively replaces the temple and thereby serves to exemplify a mind-set that repudiates scapegoating as a means to re-establish peace, whether with God or within social relations. As such, according to Bredin, "Jesus is the nonviolent revolutionary of peace par excellence."[9]

Bredin does well to attend to intertextual allusions in John 2:13–22, but one wonders whether the Girardian framing of his discussion does not lead him to present temple sacrifice in terms that are too negative. Toward the end of his study, moreover, Bredin notes, with apparent approval, that "Girard suggests that Jesus' concern with the violence in society and where it will end, justifies the vehemence and brutality with which he sometimes acted . . . ."[10] Jesus' provocation in the temple undoubtedly displays a certain vehemence, but no biblical tradition envisages Jesus acting with brutality. The basic problem with this apparent justification of Jesus' vehemence, however, is that it seems to accept that violence may be overcome by its own means. Furthermore, Bredin does little to grapple with the latent supersessionism inherent within his remarks about Jesus replacing the temple, which historically has had such a lamentable legacy.

In 2004 J. Harold Ellens appealed to Jesus' provocation in the temple as clear evidence of "the violent Jesus."[11] Written in a lively style, Ellens's argument is somewhat shrill in tone, prone to overstatement (alongside occasional misstatement), and indeed rather reckless regarding particulars. That said, however, Ellens raises an important point, which cannot be sidestepped simply by drawing attention to (alleged) weaknesses in his argument.

---

8. Ibid., 49.
9. Ibid., 50.
10. Ibid., 49–50. (For a Girardian reading of Mark's version of the temple incident, see Hamerton-Kelly, *Gospel and the Sacred*, 15–22.)
11. Ellens, "Violent Jesus," 15–37.

Speaking of the temple incident, Ellens writes: "The truth is that Jesus had one of his fits of violence. These happened more frequently than Christian tradition is willing to acknowledge."[12] In defense of this assertion, Ellens contextualizes Jesus within the matrix of apocalyptic Judaism. This is neither idiosyncratic nor indefensible. It soon becomes clear, however, that Ellens regards the apocalyptic mind-set as imbalanced. In his view, Jewish religion in Jesus' day comprised two major types: non-apocalyptic, which included Pharisees, Sadducees, elders, and scribes, and apocalyptic Judaism, with its dualistic worldview in which human life is perceived to be engaged in a cosmic conflict between forces of good and forces of evil. The first of these he describes as "rational Judaism," the second as "rather neurotic hysteric Apocalyptic Jews, who imagined all sorts of supernatural things happening or about to happen in life and history."[13] During the Second Temple period, especially from its Hellenistic phase, apocalyptic Judaism was characterized by antipathy to the temple. Jesus, or at least the Jesus movement responsible for keeping his memory alive, emerged from apocalyptic Judaism rather than "rational Judaism," which largely explains Jesus' apocalyptic outlook and his hostility toward the temple in Jerusalem. Hence, Ellens's (sketchy) discussion of Jesus' provocation in the temple occurs under the heading, "Jesus as Apocalyptic Jew." [14]

Ellens refers to Gospel texts but not attentively. At one point he harmonizes the synoptic and Johannine presentations of the temple incident, whereas at another he characterizes the Johannine interpretation of Jesus' saying about raising the temple as a "lame rationalization."[15] His basic justification for describing Jesus' temple action as a "violent cleansing" is that Jesus was an apocalyptic Jew motivated by an "intrinsic spirituality," that is, one whose religious understanding led him to perceive the temple worship of the time to be formal and functional, focused on external ritual. As a result, "Jesus came to the temple with his Essene-like hostility toward the temple, grounded in the conviction that the priesthood currently in charge at the temple was inauthentic, and so the entire enterprise of the temple

---

12. Ibid., 16. In support of this assertion, Ellens points to John 2:3–4, Mark 8:27–33, John 9:1–34, and Mark 3:33 as other "fits of inappropriate response to people" on the part of Jesus. Note the slippage from "fits of violence" to "fits of inappropriate response to people." (A little later in this chapter by Ellens, one learns that he sees John 9 as an occasion when Jesus was more concerned to provoke the Pharisees than to restore sight to a blind man.)

13. Ibid., 22–23.

14. Ibid., 24–27. Ellens writes as though he is addressing the historical Jesus, but one wonders whether he is really concerned with the depiction of Jesus passed on by his apocalyptically minded followers.

15. Ibid., 24–25.

program and its liturgies was impure, ground and trunk, root and branch."[16] As part of his broader concern to counter Christian interpretations of this event that effectively slander Judaism and Jewish worship,[17] Ellens's positive assessment of the reason for the presence of sacrificial animals and coin-changers within the temple precincts is commendable. From both the tone and content of his chapter, however, one wonders whether, in trying to be fair to the Judaism(s) of Jesus' day, he has been unfair to Jesus, or at least the various Gospel writers' depictions of Jesus' provocation in the temple.

After summarizing two contrasting psychological appraisals of Jesus' provocation in the temple, which effectively cancel each other out, Ellens returns to the theme of antipathy toward the temple and indeed toward rational forms of Judaism on the part of apocalyptic Jews. This, for Ellens, is the shaping influence on Jesus' mind-set and best explains his violent behavior in the temple. "Thus," he writes, "we are forced to conclude that Jesus' violence in the temple was simply an expression of the worldview he had developed over his life time of identification with the various forms of Apocalyptic Judaism, all part of the theological strata of Galilee in his time."[18] Ellens considers that Jesus progressively identified himself *with* the apocalyptic Son of humanity and then *as* the apocalyptic Son of humanity but met with persistent misunderstanding on the part of those whom he sought to reach with his vision of divine reign. In this state of mind, he found himself in the temple. Here is Ellens' description of what transpired:

> He walked into the temple for the third time in three days [sic], trying to find a place of tranquility in which to pray and an audience with whom he could discuss the coming kingdom of God. All he could see was the hated priests in their formalistic rituals. All he could hear was the bawling of the cattle. All he could smell was the odors of the stable. All he could think was how everything was going to hell. He cracked. He picked up a riding crop or bullwhip and started to abuse those most available, expending his long-anguished anger, his weariness with the spiritual mediocrity of human life, and his obsessive need to feel the power of his delusional vision of the triumphal Son of Man realized in the here and now.[19]

---

16. Ibid., 26. Ellens attributes his distinction between intrinsic and extrinsic spirituality to William James and Gordon Allport. These are helpful distinctions, but it is doubtful whether they shed light on Jesus' provocation in the temple.

17. Ibid., 36.

18. Ibid., 30.

19. Ibid., 32.

Even allowing for historical imagination and admissible hyperbole, it is difficult to see in this summary description much more than eisegesis. It is certainly hard to reconcile Ellens's imaginative reconstruction with any of the Gospel accounts of Jesus' provocation in the temple. Nevertheless, his attention to the shaping influence of apocalyptic thought-forms on Jesus and his earliest followers deserves to be taken seriously.

To conclude his chapter on "The Violent Jesus," Ellens ruminates on the violent church that came after Jesus and took its inspiration from Jesus' action in the temple. During nearly three centuries of vulnerability, most of Jesus' followers followed his example of nonretaliation during his passion and death. After its alliance with the Roman Empire, however, the church reclaimed the "model" of Jesus' violence in the temple as and when it served its purposes.[20] In other words, the scriptural record of Jesus' provocation in the temple is not merely an incident in the life of Jesus but also a moral "script" subsequently re-enacted by others, allegedly in Jesus' name and for his sake.

In 2009 the scenario of contrasting conclusions drawn from Jesus' provocation in the temple was replayed in two differently focused studies by Jennifer Glancy and Clayton Croy.[21] Like Ellens, Glancy sees in the Johannine version of Jesus' temple action an expression of violence that effectively triggers the violence later inflicted on Jesus in the passion narrative. "According to the Fourth Gospel," she writes, "Jesus' history of violence, a history that culminates in the violence of crucifixion, begins in Jerusalem when Jesus picks up [sic] a whip to clear the temple."[22] On the basis of Jesus' response to the request for an authorizing sign, "Destroy this temple, and in three days I will raise it" (John 2:18–19), Glancy discerns a narrative correlation between Jesus' violent provocation in the temple and his crucifixion, written against the backdrop of the relatively recent destruction of Jerusalem and its temple. Antagonism triggered by Jesus' violence in the temple leads to the violent destruction of Jesus himself, which is interpreted as prefiguring the destruction of the temple and its displacement (or replacement) by Jesus. Seen in this light, Jesus' provocation in the temple is not only violent in and of itself but also sows the seeds of later violence.

At times Glancy sounds like Ellens, albeit more restrained rhetorically. A distinctive and illuminating feature of her study, however, is her attention to corporeality and spatiality, bodies and space, with particular reference

---

20. Ibid., 32–34.

21. Glancy, "Violence as Sign in the Fourth Gospel," 100–117; Croy, "Messianic Whippersnapper," 555–68.

22. Glancy, "Violence as Sign," 100.

to the narrative interplay in the Fourth Gospel between the body of Jesus, including his bodily actions, and the sacred space of the temple. Glancy makes the perceptive point that violence not only damages bodies but may also damage space, especially space with representational significance. According to Glancy, "Violence rearranges space, at least temporarily. Whip in hand, Jesus briefly reconfigured the space of the temple. In the aftermath of the razing of the Roman temple Christian memory connected the story of Jesus' body to the history of the temple. A history of a body propelled a particular telling of the history of a sacred space."[23]

Glancy's discussion of Jesus' temple provocation in the Fourth Gospel emphasizes four main points. First, by virtue of its narrative setting in the Fourth Gospel, the temple incident is the event that provokes hostility between Jesus and Jewish authorities. It is undoubtedly a provocation, and it is Jesus who provokes. Furthermore, although the temple incident is not the catalyst for Jesus' arrest, as seems to be the case in the synoptic tradition, the meeting of the Sanhedrin after the raising of Lazarus expresses concern that, as a result of Jesus' many signs, his following might increase to the point that the Romans will destroy both the temple and the Jewish nation (John 11:45–53). As Glancy comments, "The history of violence in the Fourth Gospel continues to intercalate violence implicating Jesus with violence implicating the temple."[24]

Second, Glancy responds to Bredin's argument that Jesus' provocation in the temple is nonviolent by challenging his contention that the designation of his temple action as nonviolent is premised on the violence and oppression of the temple itself. For Glancy, even if one accepts that Jesus was authorized to act as he is said to have done, that does not make his action nonviolent.[25]

Third, Glancy takes up the question whether Jesus may be understood to have used his whip on four-legged animals only but not on people. Although she overstates the extent to which Johannine specialists consider πάντας (*pantas*, all) in John 2:15 to include the people selling cattle and sheep, she correctly points out the inherent ambiguity of this description. If the evangelist had intended to depict Jesus using a whip to drive out four-legged animals only, such an intention could have been expressed with far less ambiguity. Moreover, Glancy raises the legitimate question whether

---

23. Ibid., 104. (Although not Glancy's inference, one might correlate what she says about violence rearranging or reconfiguring space with the perception that space is susceptible to violation.)

24. Ibid., 106.

25. Ibid., 107–8.

sellers can be imagined to have stood by while their livestock (and livelihood!) was driven away.[26]

Fourth, Glancy focuses on the discomfiting image of Jesus brandishing a *flagellum*, even if makeshift and lacking the sharp tips that made such a whip an instrument of torture. In this connection, she draws attention to the report in John 19:1 that Pilate whipped Jesus. Even if understood to mean that Pilate had Jesus flogged rather than that he whipped Jesus himself, Glancy's observation is disconcerting: "It's somehow easier to imagine Jesus than Pilate with a whip in hand."[27] It is certainly striking that the evangelist used a loanword from the Latin, τό φραγέλλιον (*to phragellion*), to describe the whip Jesus constructed, but did not use the cognate verb to describe the whipping he received from Pilate.

In support of Glancy's case that Jesus' provocation in the temple, as recounted in the Fourth Gospel, triggers a trajectory of violence in which the fate of Jesus and the fate of the temple intersect, she identifies Jesus' violent action in the temple as a Johannine sign. Various events within the Fourth Gospel are narrated as signs (σημεῖα, *sēmeia*), including the transformation of water into wine at the wedding in Cana (2:1–11), the healing of a boy from Capernaum (4:46–54), the healing of a lame man at Bethesda (5:1–9a), the feeding of five thousand and subsequent walking on water (6:1–21), the healing of a man born blind (9:1–9), and the raising of dead Lazarus (11:1–44). Jesus is said to have done many other signs, however, not only those not included in the Fourth Gospel (20:30) but also others alluded to within the narrative. John 2:11 designates Jesus' wine sign as the beginning of his signs, and immediately after the temple incident the evangelist speaks of many in Jerusalem believing in Jesus when they saw the signs he was doing (2:23). In John 3:2 Nicodemus also refers to "these signs" done by Jesus as evidence of divine presence. Even within the temple episode, Jesus is asked for a sign to authorize his actions (2:18). One way to read Jesus' response to this request for a sign is to understand the resurrection of Jesus as the culmination of his signs, prefigured by the sign of his raising of Lazarus from the dead. For Glancy, however, Jesus' provocation in the temple is one of his Jerusalem signs—indeed, the only one narrated—and his violent eviction of animals and people from the temple is, ironically, the self-revelatory sign itself, which in turn prefigures Jerusalem's destruction. In short, divinely sanctioned and motivated violence is a revelatory sign that attracts believers. Even in the wake of the raising of Lazarus, which seems to galvanize the resolution to kill Jesus, the Sanhedrin is made aware of "many

---

26. Ibid., 109–110.
27. Ibid., 111.

signs" done by Jesus in or near Jerusalem, not only his raising of Lazarus, which would hardly provoke the Romans to destroy the Jewish "holy place." "The first of those signs," according to Glancy, "was Jesus' whip-wielding outburst at the temple. The actions set in place by the Sanhedrin are designed to make sure that Jesus cannot continue performing signs, but the Johannine audience knows that the Roman army nonetheless destroyed the temple."[28] By seeing Jesus' provocation in the temple as a Johannine sign, Glancy's proposed correlation between Jesus' violent action in the temple, the violence associated with Jesus' death by crucifixion, and Rome's violent destruction of Jerusalem and the temple is further strengthened.

Glancy is not the first to identify the Johannine narration of Jesus' provocation in the temple as one of his signs. If it is one of the signs narrated within the Fourth Gospel, however, its revelatory character must surely be discerned from the words of Jesus in response to a request for a sign: "Destroy this temple and in three days I will raise it" (2:19). As with the other narrated signs within the Fourth Gospel, raising what has been destroyed relates to what enhances, sustains, or restores life, not with violent destruction itself. This tells against Glancy's thesis that Jesus' violence per se is a Johannine sign and, as such, plays a triggering role in the history of violence that extends at least to Rome's destruction of Jerusalem.

Glancy's study seems premised on accepting Jesus' provocation in the temple as a violent incident, even though no account of this episode indicates that anyone (or even any animal) suffers harm. That Jesus' action in the temple is a provocation raises the moral question of whether any such provocation must bear some responsibility for violent responses it provokes, but that is significantly different from the close associations Glancy draws between Jesus' temple action, his violent execution, and Rome's destruction of the temple. It might well be appropriate to describe Jesus' temple action as a violation of sacred space, but it probably goes too far to say, "The Gospel of John twins the history of Jesus' body with the history of the temple."[29] Even so, that Glancy is able to present a cogent case for reading John 2:13-22 as "a violent epiphany"[30] gives one pause. Although I remain unpersuaded that Jesus' provocation in the temple may legitimately be described as a violent incident, nevertheless certain aspects of the presentation of this episode within the Synoptic and Johannine Gospels have made it possible for it to be construed as violent no less than provocative.

28. Ibid., 115.
29. Ibid., 116.
30. Ibid.

Whereas Ellens and Glancy effectively presume that the Johannine account of Jesus' provocation in the temple depicts a violent Jesus, Croy focuses on the uniquely Johannine detail that underwrites that presumption—whether or not Jesus used a whip on people. His aptly titled study, "The Messianic Whippersnapper," presents evidence of various kinds to support the conclusion that John 2:14–16 does not envisage Jesus whipping people out of the temple. In an opening section, Croy addresses the unease caused by the reference to Jesus constructing and using a φραγέλλιον (*phragellion*), a Greek loanword from the Latin *flagellum*. Although this Greek noun appears nowhere else in the New Testament (or in the Septuagint), the cognate verb, φραγελλοῦν (*phragelloun*), appears in Matt 27:26 and Mark 15:15 to describe the scourging of Jesus prior to his crucifixion. Within the context of Roman imperialism, the choice of this particular Latin loanword must have triggered associations of oppression, brutality, and violent punishment. In Croy's view, however, the narrative diffuses such associations by making clear that Jesus could not have constructed a *flagellum* proper, which ordinarily comprised a leather thong or thongs and was often "enhanced" with metal or bone thong tips. Indeed, John 2:15 explicitly states that Jesus constructed his makeshift whip "from cords" (ἐκ σχοινίων, *ek schoiniōn*). In other words, any such whip made *in situ* could not have been particularly damaging.[31]

Croy also raises the important textual note that although the most widely used critical editions of the New Testament do not present ὡς φραγέλλιον (*hōs phragellion*) as the original reading in John 2:15, there are good text-critical reasons for considering this reading original, not least because it is the reading found in the two oldest witnesses.[32] John 2:15 would then begin as follows: "He made something like a *flagellum* from [rattan or rope] ties . . . ." This clearly conveys a different image. Although Croy seems to agree with Bruce Metzger that, if original, ὡς would not have been deliberately dropped by scribes, this overlooks the church's "peacemaking" with state-sanctioned violence in the post-Constantinian period. In other words, further to Croy's important text-critical observations, it is possible to offer a credible reason for the deliberate omission of an incidental qualifier in the interests of portraying Jesus as one willing to use force. Subsequent appeal to this text in support of the church's use of force is corroborating, albeit not conclusive, evidence for such an editorial amendment.[33]

31. Croy, "Messianic Whippersnapper," 556–57.

32. Ibid., 557. Cf. Metzger, *Textual Commentary*, 173. See also Wasserman, "Lectio vehementior potior," 228–29.

33. An influential example is Augustine's appeal to John 2:15 to authorize violence against Donatist Christians, on which see Alexis-Baker, "Violence, Nonviolence and

The bulk of Croy's study is devoted to the question of whether Jesus, having constructed a makeshift whip, used it on people as well as livestock. "There is enough textual ambiguity on this point that the commentators are divided," he writes, "although the majority seem inclined toward Jesus' application of the whip to persons as well as animals."[34] The textual ambiguity to which Croy refers largely comprises two grammatical cruxes: first, whether the phrase in John 2:15, "the sheep and the cattle," is an appositive; and second, whether the same mixed-gender phrase refers back to and thereby circumscribes the masculine pronoun πάντας (*pantas*, all) earlier in the sentence.

The first issue, whether the phrase relating to the sheep and cattle is appositional, has to do with whether this phrase both parallels and qualifies πάντας earlier in the sentence. If so, the phrase, "both the sheep and the cattle," describes the constituent parts of the "all" driven from the temple, presumably with the makeshift whip constructed by Jesus. Croy is compelling on this point, and he supports his grammatical argument with additional arguments based on logic and narrative flow. Logically, the appositional phrase is made up of two kinds of animals that would ordinarily be herded by using a whip, sheep and cattle. The whip is not used on doves. Moreover, in terms of narrative flow, Jesus' words to the dove-sellers in John 2:16 take for granted that neither they nor their doves had been driven out of the temple at the lash of a whip. Croy says that the same applies to the money-changers, whose coins were scattered when Jesus overturned their tables. As he summarizes, "The structure of vv. 15–16 thus implies a threefold strategy: (1) Jesus drove off the livestock with the whip, an action that effectively routed the sellers; (2) he overturned the tables of the money changers and spilled their coinage on the ground; and (3) he ordered the sellers of doves to take them away, presumably by carrying off their cages."[35]

Croy recognizes that his reconstruction of Jesus' provocation in the temple according to John 2:13–22 fills gaps in the narrative—one being that the text never explicitly states that Jesus used the whip on anything. Nevertheless, he considers his reconstruction to be guided by the text, including explicit details and implied features. For Croy, a possible weakness relates to "grammatical concord," that is, whether the author would have used the masculine pronoun πάντας to refer solely to animals. Before turning to Croy's discussion of this grammatical point, however, it is perhaps worth pointing out that his inference based on narrative flow can be turned against

---

the Temple Incident," 79–81, discussed below.

34. Croy, "Messianic Whippersnapper," 559.

35. Ibid., 563.

him. John 2:14 indicates that within the temple precincts Jesus found sellers of cattle, sheep, and doves along with coin-changers. That Jesus scatters the coins of the money-changers and speaks to the dove-sellers after driving out the "all" of John 2:15 might be taken to imply that the sellers of livestock must have been among the "all" driven out by the messianic whippersnapper. Moreover, one wonders whether the description in John 2:14–16 is intended to be read in strict chronological sequence. It is at least conceivable that the evangelist intended to describe the scene in broad brushstrokes, without concern for chronological precision. This is not to argue in favor of envisaging Jesus applying his whip to the sellers of livestock, who might well be imagined to have kept track of their cattle and sheep as they were herded out of the temple. The point, rather, is that not too much may be inferred on the basis of narrative flow.

Croy's argumentation with respect to whether the mixed-gender phrase, "both the sheep (neuter) and the cattle (masculine)," refers back to the masculine pronoun πάντας is intricate. This is because both grammatical and biological gender must be considered in relation to people and animals. On the basis of numerous examples, Croy comes to a nuanced conclusion that seems unimpeachable: "John 2:15 is hard to fit into any of the patterns because it is so complex: a masculine pronoun (πάντας) preceded by five possible antecedents of various genders (sellers, cattle, sheep, doves, money changers) and followed by a likely appositional construction of two genders (sheep and cattle). What can be confidently asserted is that the gender of πάντας does *not* exclude the possibility that the phrase τά τε πρόβατα καὶ τοὺς βόας [both the sheep and the cattle] refers back to it."[36]

On grammatical and syntactical grounds, Croy convincingly demonstrates that John 2:14–16 may legitimately be interpreted to mean that Jesus used his makeshift whip on four-legged animals only and not on people. He also shows that the grammatical evidence marshaled in his essay converges with other kinds of corroborating evidence, which include: the nonviolent depiction of Jesus elsewhere in the Gospel tradition; narrative sequence; and "the logic of the scene," which for Croy relates to those people referred to after Jesus is said to have driven larger animals out of the temple with a whip.[37] Although I am in basic agreement with Croy, it is nevertheless the case that each of his converging lines of evidence is either ambiguous or subjective. With regard to grammatical and syntactical details, Croy has shown that it is possible to interpret John 2:14–16 to mean that Jesus did not use his whip on people, but he has not demonstrated that it is impossible to envisage Je-

36. Ibid., 566.
37. Ibid.

sus applying his whip to at least some people. As for his appeal to the general depiction of Jesus as nonviolent toward people, that depends to some extent on his definition of violence. Even more subjective is his appeal to narrative flow and the logic of the scene. For example, despite the strength of Croy's argument for interpreting the phrase, τά τε πρόβατα καὶ τοὺς βόας [both the sheep and the cattle], as appositional, it is difficult to imagine livestock sellers simply standing by or following Jesus demurely as he herded their animals out of the temple. Without some prior arrangement,[38] Jesus could not have driven animals out of the temple unimpeded. If that be granted, it is difficult to imagine Jesus' makeshift whip failing to make contact with people no less than their animals.

Croy concludes his study with "a patristic coda" in which he shows that Cosmas Indicopleustes, an Egyptian monk, merchant, and geographer from the sixth century, argues against reading John 2:14–16 to mean that Jesus lashed people with his whip.[39] It is profoundly important that earlier expositors interpreted the Johannine version of this incident in this way, but perhaps Croy pays too little attention to the fact that Cosmas had to contest another interpretation of this incident, which envisaged Jesus lashing people with his whip. The text itself is ambiguous and therefore inevitably open to interpretation.[40]

In view of the interpretive imperative, Andy Alexis-Baker's survey of the history of interpretation of the temple incident, especially in Johannine perspective, is significant.[41] Aware that Jesus' provocation in the temple has been appealed to in order to justify violence on the part of Christians, especially those in positions of power, Alexis-Baker argues that this was a development in the reception history of this episode. "Indeed," according to Alexis-Baker, "the tradition that interprets Jesus' activity [in the temple] as nonviolent is older than that which uses it to justify violence."[42] Prior to Origen, it would seem, most pre-Constantinian patristic writers appealed to John 2:16 or 2:19 to discredit charging money for ministry or to defend

38. Unlike the synoptic accounts of Jesus' provocation in the temple, John 2:14 opens by narrating that Jesus *found* in the temple the sellers of cattle and sheep and doves and also money-changers, rather than that he *saw* them and then acted. It would be too much of a stretch, however, to argue from this that Jesus might have staged this event.

39. Croy, "Messianic Whippersnapper," 566–67.

40. See Wasserman, "*Lectio vehementior potior,*" 230.

41. Alexis-Baker, "Violence, Nonviolence and the Temple Incident in John 2:13–15," 73–96. (An error in the article title makes it appear that Alexis-Baker examines only a snippet of this Johannine pericope, but he treats the whole of John 2:13–25 as a single passage.)

42. Ibid., 74.

Jesus' divinity or the resurrection of the body. With Origen, however, most critical issues raised by differences between the various accounts of Jesus' provocation in the temple are noted and addressed. Recognizing that differences between the various (and varied) accounts cannot be harmonized at the historical level, Origen interprets the incident spiritually. Especially with respect to Jesus' use of a whip, Origen considers it unlikely that Jesus could have driven out such a large number of animals or that he could have whipped people without being restrained. Moreover, such an action is uncharacteristic of Jesus. As a result, Origen interprets the text allegorically, such that the whip represents Jesus' words driving out what is harmful to one's soul or the church.[43]

In the late fourth century, John Chrysostom addressed concerns about the historicity of the Johannine version of Jesus' actions in the temple, especially since Jesus' use of a whip on people in this episode conflicts with his behavior in other circumstances. Moreover, the response of others to Jesus in this episode seems at odds with more vehement reactions to less provocative actions elsewhere. John Chrysostom's response is to defend the historicity of the event, emphasizing the risk attached to Jesus' confrontation of rich and powerful people, but to urge his audience to imitate the disciples, who allegedly gave alms, rather than to make use of whips.[44]

Next in historical succession comes Cosmas Indicopleustes from the mid-sixth century, who directly addresses the question of whether Jesus whipped people. He argues that Jesus whipped irrational animals and threw down lifeless matter (coins and tables) but by contrast chastised rational beings with words, not with a whip.[45] Not long after Cosmas, a certain Barhadbesabba records an incident in which Theodore of Mopsuestia is recalled as rebuking Rabbula for defending an accusation that he had hit priests by appealing to Jesus' example of hitting people in the temple. Theodore is remembered as repudiating the view that Jesus hit people with a whip, affirming instead that the whip was reserved solely for cattle and sheep.[46] "Thus from Origen in 250 CE to Barhadbesabba in 598 CE, several reading strategies emerged to interpret Jesus' action in the temple as physically

---

43. Ibid., 75–76.

44. Ibid., 76–77.

45. Ibid., 77–78. Cf. Croy, "Messianic Whippersnapper," 566–67, who points out that Cosmas envisaged Jesus using a three-tiered approach in accordance with a three-fold ontological hierarchy: "inanimate creation, animate but irrational creatures, and animate and rational human beings."

46. Alexis-Baker, "Violence, Nonviolence and the Temple Incident," 78. Alexis-Baker places this event at a synod held in Constantinople in 394 CE, two centuries before Barhadbesabba's written record of it.

nonviolent."⁴⁷ Alexis-Baker readily recognizes that Origen was forced to allegorize or spiritualize the temple incident to interpret Jesus' whipping action as nonviolent toward people. Given Origen's scholarly credentials, however, it probably deserves to be emphasized that, at the literal or lexical level, he read John 2:14–16 to mean that Jesus applied the whip to people no less than to cattle and sheep. Furthermore, each and every example cited of a nonviolent interpretation of Jesus' provocation in the temple is given in response to what would seem to be the "default" position, namely, that Jesus whipped the sellers of cattle and sheep along with their livestock.

Roughly three centuries after the publication of the Fourth Gospel, Augustine appealed to Jesus' use of the whip in the temple to answer this question by the Donatist, Petilian: "Where is your Christianity, if you not only do violence and put to death but also order these things to be done?" In reply, Augustine writes: "The Lord Christ drove out the shameless merchants from the temple with whippings. . . . So we find Christ a persecutor. . . . Christ even bodily persecuted those whom he expelled from the temple with whippings."⁴⁸ Although later writers such as Cosmas Indicopleustes and Barhadbesabba argued for an alternative reading of the Greek text of John 2:14–16, Augustine's interpretation was to prevail in later centuries. This is partly because of his influential homilies on the Fourth Gospel,⁴⁹ but probably also because he represented an interpretive position that was compatible with and supportive of the post-Constantinian state-church alliance.

During the medieval period, Jesus' provocation in the temple was appealed to in order to combat simony within the church (by force if necessary) and to justify armed aggression against external enemies. Alexis-Baker draws attention to such notables as Pope Gregory VII, Peter Damian, Bruno of Segni, and, perhaps most notably, Bernard of Clairvaux, whose notorious defense of the Knights Templar compared their use of the sword against pagans with Jesus' use of the whip against merchants.⁵⁰ As for the reformation period, Alexis-Baker briefly reminds readers of Calvin's defense of his role in the execution of Michael Servetus for heresy on the grounds that Jesus' use of a whip in the temple reveals that he put aside his meekness to deal with certain kinds of recalcitrance.⁵¹ In this connection, Alexis-Baker might have noted that Calvin the exegete makes little of Jesus' zeal-fuelled actions within the temple except to warn individuals without public author-

47. Ibid., 79.
48. Ibid., 79–80.
49. Ibid., 81.
50. Ibid., 81–84.
51. Ibid., 85.

ity against imitating Jesus by acting forcefully for corrective purposes.[52] He might also have mentioned that Luther's sermons on John's Gospel reveal that Luther envisaged Jesus as applying his makeshift whip to people, even if most attention is devoted to explaining this use of force by Jesus along salvation-historical lines and within the framework of Luther's two-realms theory, with Jesus' temple actions interpreted as being in accordance with the Law of Moses and temporal authority so as to demonstrate his own authority over both secular and spiritual realms. Like Calvin, however, Luther makes it clear that Jesus' conduct within the temple is not to be emulated, except for the sake of punishment on the part of a person with secular authority.[53] For Alexis-Baker's purposes, however, it suffices to show, with reference to two recent statements, that the prevalent view since Augustine still has currency in defense of Christian resort to violence in certain circumstances and under certain conditions.[54]

After surveying major trends in the interpretation of John 2:14–16 from Origen to Calvin, Alexis-Baker addresses textual, exegetical, and interpretive issues relevant to the question of whether this passage depicts Jesus acting violently by using a whip on people. First, he concurs with those who argue that Jesus' makeshift whip could not have been a *flagellum* proper; it most likely comprised animal bedding, fodder, or ropes and therefore cannot be construed as capable of inflicting serious injury.[55] Second, on the question of whether πάντας (*pantas*, all) in John 2:15 refers solely to the cattle and sheep or also includes their sellers, he takes a more decisive position than Croy on the former option. Jesus applied his makeshift whip only to four-legged animals. This is largely because Alexis-Baker considers the τε . . . καί (*te . . . kai*) phrase in John 2:15 to be a clear example of a partitive appositive, that is, one that identifies the constituent parts of a larger whole. In short, the masculine πάντας in John 2:15 could conceivably cover all antecedent nouns from 2:14 but the appositional τε . . . καί phrase restricts the "all" driven from the temple by means of a whip to sheep and cattle.[56]

---

52. In Calvin's published commentaries on the New Testament, see his exegetical comments on John 2:12–17 and on the synoptic versions of this episode in Matt 21:10–22; Mark 11:11–24, and Luke 19:39–40, 45–48.

53. See Luther's seventeenth sermon on the Gospel of John in *Luther's Works*, vol. 22, 217–28.

54. Alexis-Baker, "Violence, Nonviolence and the Temple Incident," 85–86. At this point, Alexis-Baker cites Glancy's study, discussed above, and also notes various commentators on the Fourth Gospel who consider that John 2:15 depicts Jesus as driving people as well as livestock out of the temple with a whip (Barrett, Beasley-Murray, Brown, Lindars, McHugh, Moloney).

55. Ibid., 88–89.

56. Ibid., 88–92.

Convinced that the Greek text of John 2:14–16 does not envisage Jesus applying his whip to people, Alexis-Baker ponders whether the Johannine version of the temple incident might be less vehement than the synoptic version(s). This he does in conversation with Richard Bauckham's thesis that the Fourth Gospel was written for an audience larger than a "Johannine community" that was therefore probably familiar with Mark's Gospel. On Bauckham's view, the Johannine version of the temple incident should be understood as correcting the Markan version. For Alexis-Baker, John 2:15 corrects the Markan version of Jesus' provocation in the temple by clarifying that Jesus did not drive sellers and coin-changers from the temple violently. "If this suggestion is plausible," he writes, "then John's passage would be even more intentionally nonviolent than the Synoptics because John intentionally added the partitive appositive construction to clarify ambiguities in Mark and the other Gospels."[57]

That the Johannine version of Jesus' provocation in the temple might present Jesus in a less vehement light than the synoptic depiction is a rather counterintuitive proposition. Quite apart from the plausibility of Bauckham's thesis, it is difficult to read John 2:14–16 as correcting Mark 11:15–16 (and/or its synoptic parallels) in the way Alexis-Baker suggests. Introducing a whip into the episode might well be linked to a desire to clarify that only four-legged animals were forcibly expelled from the temple. If this was the evangelist's intent, however, one must conclude that it was something of a botched effort. Such a Johannine "correction" would actually constitute a contradiction of the Markan version, since on Alexis-Baker's reading of John 2:14–16 Jesus does not drive anyone out of the temple, only animals. More importantly, however, if John 2:14–16 was written to ameliorate the apparent aggression of Jesus depicted in Mark 11:15–16, this could have been done much more clearly. Within the synoptic tradition, any "casting out" effected by Jesus—even from the temple (Matt 21:12; Mark 11:15; Luke 19:45)—is apparently done verbally (e.g., Matt 8:16; Mark 5:40; 7:26; 9:25–29; Luke 9:40),[58] so if the Johannine version of the temple incident is to be accepted as correcting the synoptic version, it is not for the purpose of presenting a less vehement Jesus.

Alexis-Baker concludes his study by contending that Jesus' provocation in the temple provides no precedent for Christian participation in killing or warfare, although he allows that this incident might be used to justify "acts

---

57. Ibid., 93–94. Alexis-Baker cites Bauckham, "John for Readers of Mark," 159–60.
58. Cf. Matt 12:28/Luke 11:20, in which Jesus claims to expel demons by the Spirit or finger of God. This claim reinforces the authority of Jesus' word.

of civil disobedience, property tampering and even acts to restrain evil."[59] He also defends Jesus against the potential charge of treating animals violently, since his makeshift whip could not have inflicted any serious harm and actually prevented their slaughter, at least temporarily.[60] Although I am less confident than Alexis-Baker that close exegesis of the Greek text of John 2:14–16 rules out the possibility that Jesus might have struck some people with a whip, he is nevertheless correct in what he infers from this passage. The desire to rationalize Christian resort to violence might well lead one to seek legitimization from John 2:14–16, but this passage does not depict Jesus harming people or animals.

Most of the studies surveyed above focus on the Johannine version of Jesus' provocation in the temple. Even Ellens's study clearly appeals to specifically Johannine features for rhetorical force. In *Killing Enmity*, however, Thomas Yoder Neufeld's discussion of Jesus' provocation in the temple adopts a broader perspective, although he naturally addresses some of the same issues and responds on various points to most of the authors surveyed above.[61] Yoder Neufeld characterizes what Jesus is remembered to have done in the temple as a "prophetic parabolic act,"[62] which leads to an appraisal not only of what Jesus is alleged to have done but also of what his "parabolic act" signified at the time and what it means today. Although impossible to separate from Jesus' specific actions in the temple and more difficult to pin down with any precision, the meaning of Jesus' provocation in the temple is more significant in relation to the spiritual and/or moral evaluation of violence. For this reason, Yoder Neufeld's discussion is invaluable.

After describing the essential features of the temple episode in both its Markan and Johannine versions, Yoder Neufeld pauses to sum up how critical this biblical event has been and continues to be in relation to the moral validity of violence: "The Christian tradition has historically used the incident to justify violence. Today it frequently serves to implicate Jesus in violence, and thus to discredit his supposed non-violence."[63] Perceived as a violent episode in the life of Jesus, the temple incident serves the interests either of those who seek to justify violent aggression in Jesus' name or of those who seek to discredit Jesus—or the biblical portrait of Jesus—as morally

---

59. Alexis-Baker, "Violence, Nonviolence and the Temple Incident," 95.

60. Ibid., 94, 96.

61. Yoder Neufeld, *Killing Enmity*, 57–72. (See also Yoder Neufeld, *Recovering Jesus*, 219–20, 233–36.)

62. Yoder Neufeld, *Killing Enmity*, 57. Two pages later, this event is described as a "prophetic symbolic act."

63. Ibid., 59.

authoritative or exemplary. For those who take their moral bearings from Jesus as he is displayed in the Gospels, much is at stake.

Concerning what Jesus actually did in the temple, Yoder Neufeld focuses on three points: first, whether the use in all four biblical accounts of the Greek verb ἐκβάλλειν (*ekballein*, to cast out) implies violent expulsion from the temple; second, whether in the Johannine account Jesus uses his makeshift whip on people as well as on livestock; and third, the forcefulness of Jesus' accompanying sayings provided as warrant for his temple provocation. Regarding the first point, Yoder Neufeld acknowledges that ἐκβάλλειν may mean no more than "to send out." In view of this verb's widespread association within the synoptic tradition with expulsion of demonic forces, however, Yoder Neufeld considers that its use by all four Gospel writers implies at least forcefulness on Jesus' part. "Such use of the term is 'nonviolent' only if one does not share a world view in which divine judgement or life-and-death struggles with demons are experiential realities," he writes. "In keeping with how *ekballō* is most often used, we should take 'throwing out' as carrying an unambiguous implication of forceful expulsion of persons and their business from the temple precincts."[64] In short, Jesus' temple action is characterized by the evangelists as a forceful "cleansing" comparable to Jesus' exorcisms of unclean spirits.

On the question of whether, in the Johannine version of this incident, Jesus uses his makeshift whip on people as well as on livestock, Yoder Neufeld concurs with the view that the whip constructed *in situ* could not have been capable of causing injury and also that it was in all likelihood used only on the cattle and sheep. Like Bredin, Croy, and Alexis-Baker, he considers that the reference to a whip in John 2:14–15 is but a natural complement to the reference to cattle and sheep, which do not feature in the synoptic versions of this event. Yet the exorcistic coloring of the incident in all four accounts overshadows Yoder Neufeld's determination to draw the sting from the Johannine reference to a whip. After opining that the whip of John 2:15 should be considered as little more than an innocuous instrument for "shooing animals," he writes: "At the same time, 'throwing out' cautions us not to downplay the forcefulness or the disruptiveness of Jesus' actions as depicted by the evangelists."[65] In other words, associations created by the way in which Jesus' provocation in the temple is characterized by all four Gospel writers are perhaps more significant for the ethical evaluation of this incident than this or that particular detail, however important it may be to address such details. Even if this is not quite what Yoder Neufeld means, I

64. Ibid., 60.
65. Ibid., 61.

consider this to be part of the interpretive challenge. The impression created by a narrative account may be something more than the sum of its constituent semantic parts, and affective elements of a text are not susceptible to neat and tidy exegesis. The use of terminology suggestive of "exorcism" in relation to Jesus' provocation in the temple cannot be contained. Nor indeed can associations evoked by the fourth evangelist's use of the loan word φραγέλλιον (*phragellion*), exegetical qualifications notwithstanding, or his comment that what Jesus did in the temple reminded his disciples of a scriptural text relating to religious zeal (John 2:17, echoing Psalm 69:9 [68:10 LXX]).

Yoder Neufeld's reflections on what Jesus is recalled to have said in conjunction with what he purportedly did in the temple reinforce the complexity of the interpretive challenge posed by the temple incident. "He is remembered as 'throwing out' while quoting words from the prophets of Israel. . . . Jesus and his contemporaries would have perceived prophetic words of condemnation as far graver and more fearsome than any use of a whip made of the straw lying around."[66] This is a crucial point all too easily overlooked. In relation to the question of the moral validity of violence, interpreters of the temple incident naturally focus on what Jesus did. Why he did what he did is critical for moral evaluation of what he did, however, and why he did what he did is only explicable with reference to what he purportedly said. This does not necessarily put us in touch with Jesus' own intention, but it does provide access to the respective evangelists' understanding(s) of the event, which is what counts for moral appraisal of Jesus' provocation in the temple. Moreover, as Yoder Neufeld points out, if Jesus' actions and words are understood as prophetic, his utterances are themselves acts.[67]

In view of the inherent plausibility of perceiving Jesus' provocation in the temple as prophetic and hence symbolic, with both his actions and his accompanying words understood as imbued with performative force, the question that arises is the likely implication or meaning of Jesus' prophetic provocation. Yoder Neufeld considers there to be general scholarly agreement on the symbolic nature of Jesus' temple action, evocative of prophetic demonstrations in the Hebrew Bible, but little agreement on precisely what his prophetic provocation symbolized. Before outlining different proposals, however, he points out that to read Jesus' temple provocation in light of prophetic precursors raises the possibility that "what seems to our eyes

---

66. Ibid., 61.

67. Ibid., 62. (From the perspective of speech-act theory, the prophetic words of judgment expressed by Jesus may be regarded as judgment enacted by being articulated, comparable to the performative efficacy of Jesus' words of exorcism within the synoptic tradition. See Thiselton, *New Horizons*, 286.)

like violence and hostility might well have been understood as the grammar of urgency. The vehemence of the action and the words are within the 'language set' of biblical prophetic demonstrations."[68] In other words, if understood as prophetic by his contemporaries, Jesus' vehemence in this instance would have been recognized as signifying something urgent and pressing rather than violent. This is a worthwhile observation, especially at the exegetical level. There is nothing in any of the Gospel accounts to suggest that Jesus' provocation in the temple was physically injurious to anyone or any living thing. Even when questioned by Jewish religious authorities, the issue is Jesus' authority or religious authorization for what he has done, not any injury or damage he has caused. Important as this is at the exegetical level, however, the point remains that the reception history of this incident shows it to have played an inauspicious role in validating violence.

Since the meaning of Jesus' symbolic prophetic provocation is decisive for ascertaining whether or not it serves to authorize violence in certain circumstances, Yoder Neufeld's survey of scholarly opinion helpfully categorizes the plethora of proposals into six, with some overlap between some of them.[69] First, Jesus' provocation symbolized the need to purify the temple on account of its profanation by corrupt commerce, even though a certain level of commercial activity was needed to make the necessary tithes and sacrifices. Second, rather than a prophetic protest against commercial exchange in the temple, Jesus' action is to be seen as condemning the temple and its hierarchy for their role in the systemic oppression of the majority of Israelites who lived at subsistence level. Jesus' prophetic provocation symbolized divine judgment on the temple for its complicity in economic violence. Third, Jesus' temple action symbolized forthcoming divine judgment on the temple, in part for its sanctioning of violent resistance to Roman rule, and thereby forecast its rejection in favor of himself as its replacement. Fourth, understood within the framework of Jewish apocalyptic eschatology, Jesus' provocation in the temple anticipated its destruction as part of the imminent advent of divine reign. For some who advocate this interpretation, the temple's destruction is but the prelude to God's eschatological temple, which is implicit in Jesus' symbolic action. Fifth, what Jesus did and said in the temple symbolized its destruction simply because its

---

68. Yoder Neufeld, *Killing Enmity*, 62.

69. Ibid., 62–65. (For some alternative categorizations of scholarly proposals regarding the probable symbolic meaning of Jesus' temple action, see Ådna, "Jesus and the Temple," 2654–65; Ådna, "Temple Act," 949–51; Chanikuzhy, *Jesus, the Eschatological Temple*, 150–83; Perrin, *Jesus the Temple*, 88–92; Snodgrass, "Temple Incident," 462–74. Both Ådna and Perrin subdivide the various proposals they survey into non-eschatological and eschatological interpretations.)

purported role of mediating between God and people conflicted with Jesus' view that people could enjoy unmediated access to God. Sixth and finally, Yoder Neufeld refers to Glancy's argument that Jesus' temple action was a deliberate violation of sacred space and hence reflective of an inherently violent mind-set.

Only after considering the symbolic meaning of Jesus' prophetic provocation in the temple does Yoder Neufeld address the question: was Jesus violent? This is sagacious because it is not simply whether or not any particular action of Jesus can be said to be violent that determines whether Jesus' provocation in the temple authorizes violence for those who take their moral bearings from the life story of Jesus. If what Jesus did and said are deemed not to be violent per se but are premised on divine violence in one way or another, or if they provoke violent associations that inevitably color how the Gospel accounts are received, such considerations bear on the moral appraisal of this episode with respect to violence. This is not always appreciated, but Yoder Neufeld is attuned to this dimension of things.

Regarding Jesus' specific actions, it is clear that Yoder Neufeld does not think that anything Jesus did could be described as violent in and of itself. He seems to accept that the event was small-scale enough not to provoke immediate arrest, and he doubts that any account envisages Jesus striking, let alone injuring, people during the course of this event. Despite his inclinations in this regard, he accepts, as I think one must, that the Markan and Johannine accounts are somewhat ambiguous about whether Jesus' physical actions were violent to some degree or may have been perceived as such.[70] Even if perceived as such, however, it warrants reiterating that no account of this episode so much as hints in the direction that any person or animal was hurt, maimed, or injured as a result of Jesus' actions.

What, then, of what Jesus is remembered as saying? In light of Yoder Neufeld's appreciation that, if perceived as prophetic, Jesus' utterances might well have been considered more forceful than his actions, his question of whether Jesus' words should be considered as violent is not an idle one. According to Yoder Neufeld, "In narrating this episode the evangelists clearly believed that there was a direct connection between Jesus' words of warning and prediction and the actual destruction of Jerusalem and its temple by the Romans some decades later, even if at some points they ascribe that prophecy to false witnesses (Mark 14.57–58). From that perspective Jesus' words might be understood not as 'only words' and thus not 'real' violence

---

70. Yoder Neufeld, *Killing Enmity*, 65.

but, given who is saying them, and to what power they are connected, as an exercise of violence itself."[71]

These are troubling lines, not because they attribute to Jesus prescience regarding the temple's imminent destruction but because they infer that the words of Jesus accompanying his dramatization of destruction relate that anticipated destruction to divine judgment. In other words, understood as prophecy, Jesus' rationale for his provocation in the temple is to be read as a prophecy of divine judgment construed as destruction. Yoder Neufeld mitigates the force of his inference by saying that such a prophecy of judgment was intended to provoke change so that judgment might be averted. Only after the event of Jerusalem's destruction and hence the absence of the change called for to avert it was the prophecy itself seen as forecasting an inevitable outcome.

It is clear that Yoder Neufeld has reflected long and hard on this matter. Indeed, his brief ruminations on how the vehement Jesus can be enlisted in the service of anti-Judaism once this incident is read in isolation from the Jewish prophetic tradition, in which the purpose of prophecy is to provoke change, are perspicacious.[72] It seems to me, however, that in thinking about the temple incident Yoder Neufeld has overread the sayings remembered as providing the rationale for Jesus' disruptive actions. The sayings of Jesus recalled in conjunction with his temple actions evidently provide the rationale for those actions, and they certainly evoke prophetic texts. But it stretches the evidence too far to say that the evocation of prophetic texts to provide the rationale for Jesus' actions in the temple constitutes a prophecy of the temple's destruction conceived as divine judgment. One cannot help but suspect that in considering Jesus' sayings in the temple incident, Yoder Neufeld has taken into account all of Jesus' sayings relating to the temple within the Gospels. At this point in the respective narrative accounts, however, what Jesus says apparently explains what he does, whether in the synoptic or Johannine tradition, but in and of themselves they do not comprise prophecies of divine destruction, even if they express divine displeasure with aspects of temple worship. If Jesus' prophetic words are themselves speech-*acts* no less than his symbolic actions, then what he does and says within the temple precincts intrinsically constitute (the extent of) his prophetic judgment. This is especially meaningful in relation to the Johannine account of the temple incident, which in narrative terms occurs in relatively close proximity to the Gospel's prologue, wherein Jesus is conceived as the definitive speech-act of God (John 1:1–18; cf. Gen 1:1–2:3; Isa 55:6–11).

71. Ibid., 66.
72. Ibid., 66–67.

As the creative and prophetic self-expression of God in human form, what Jesus does and what Jesus says *already* instantiates and effectuates divine judgment.[73] Seen through the interpretive lens provided by the Gospel's prologue, what Jesus does and says within the temple might be said to provoke self-judgment on the part of "the Jews," but his actions and words are not presented as presaging the temple's destruction. To the contrary, this incident is explicitly associated with Jesus' own death, which in Johannine terms is the focal point of divine judgment no less than divine life-giving (see John 12:20–36).

After considering whether either Jesus' actions within the temple or accompanying sayings can be construed as violent, Yoder Neufeld ponders the view, proffered on various grounds, that Jesus deliberately engineered his own demise and in doing so drew others into a spiral of violence that he himself provoked. Some see this as a result of Jesus' conviction of his own role in salvation history, others in terms of Jesus' psychological development. Yoder Neufeld is correctly skeptical of psychological explanations of Jesus' provocation in the temple, but he perhaps does Ellens an injustice by addressing his appraisal of the "violence" of Jesus in the temple principally, if not solely, in psychological terms.[74] Yoder Neufeld thinks it plausible that Jesus may have anticipated his premature death in pursuit of his mission but considers this to be quite different from any kind of alleged death wish on his part.

On the interpretive implications of Jesus' provocation in the temple, Yoder Neufeld begins by pointing out that, for the evangelists, Christology rather than moral instruction was uppermost in their minds when narrating this incident. Nevertheless, he accepts that all the Gospel writers envisaged Jesus' behavior as exemplary, thereby requiring an appraisal of "whether this episode encourages violence or encourages resolute confrontation with violence."[75] Yoder Neufeld conducts his own appraisal by asking how Jesus' provocation in the temple corresponds in a moral sense with his instruction on nonretaliation and love of enemies (the focus of the second chapter of Yoder Neufeld's book). For Yoder Neufeld, Jesus' teaching on nonretaliation

---

73. For my understanding of the moral meaning of the Logos-become-flesh presented in the Johannine prologue and also of the distinctively Johannine notion of divine judgment, see Neville, *A Peaceable Hope*, 177–216. In the synoptic tradition, one could make a similar case by focusing on the burden of Jesus' message: if, in the mission of Jesus, the reign of God is present or impinges on the present, then judgment pronounced by Jesus may be perceived as judgment enacted by Jesus, especially in view of the Gospel writers' "divine identity" Christology (on which see Bauckham, *God Crucified, passim*).

74. Yoder Neufeld, *Killing Enmity*, 67–69.

75. Ibid., 71.

is analogous to Jesus' "acted parable of judgment" in the temple because they may be read as "evocative mini-parables of ingenuity in the face of oppression."[76] In other words, there is moral coherence between Jesus' provocation in the temple and his teaching on nonretaliation insofar as in each instance accepted norms are challenged. As for whether Jesus' temple actions correspond in a moral sense with love for enemies, Yoder Neufeld's brief response is that if such is the case, "such love is intelligible only within biblical narratives in which prophetic anger and rage are experienced, even if only with the benefit of long hindsight, as the sometimes fierce and terrifying love of a divine covenant partner."[77] In the main, Yoder Neufeld addresses this profoundly perplexing issue with sensitivity and insight, but his concluding hermeneutical reflections on Jesus' provocation in the temple are perfunctory and ultimately too tentative. I think he sees in Jesus' temple action moral authorization to confront oppressive powers, but whether, in his view, such confrontation allows for degrees of violence depending on the circumstances is unclear to me. As for whether Jesus' temple action is morally compatible with loving enemies, Yoder Neufeld evades the issue. "If so," he writes, "such is not a quiet and gentle love."[78] This moves in the direction of redefining love to make room for "tough love," especially of the divine kind attested to in the prophetic tradition. Even though Yoder Neufeld does not envisage Jesus conducting himself violently in the temple, he nevertheless seems intent on making room for the possibility that Jesus' actions and words bespeak divine judgment of a kind that is violent if prophetic warning does not provoke change.

David Rensberger's 2014 study of "Jesus's Action in the Temple" begins by drawing attention to the way in which this incident's "afterlife," especially in visual media, routinely displays Jesus as lashing out against money changers and livestock vendors in righteous rage. In other words, a debatable feature in only one of the Gospel accounts of Jesus' provocation in the temple became central to the interpretation of this incident, even among many biblical scholars. As Rensberger observes, "This widespread image of whip-cracking rage presents obvious problems for a shalom-centered understanding of Jesus. . . . If Jesus acted violently on his (justifiable) anger, what is to prevent Christians of any period from doing likewise when provoked by injustice or sacrilege?"[79] Contrary to the common tendency to appeal to this single episode as undermining the peaceful tenor of Jesus'

---

76. Ibid.
77. Ibid., 71–72.
78. Ibid., 71.
79. Rensberger, "Jesus's Action in the Temple," 180.

mission and message, Rensberger acknowledges the peaceable character of Jesus' mission as a whole and therefore seeks to interpret the temple incident as cohering with that broader context. This might be construed as tendentious, but Rensberger is both conscious of his own leanings and exegetically disciplined. "I will be privileging textual details in an effort to avoid importing familiar visual and homiletic representations," he advises.[80]

Rensberger accepts the historicity of Jesus' provocation in the outer court of the temple, albeit relatively limited in scale and immediate effect. In his view, it was in all likelihood a dramatic symbolic disruption within the temple precincts but not a disturbance that brought temple activities to a standstill. Reminiscent of biblical records of symbolic actions by various prophets from centuries past, Jesus' behavior in the temple should be understood in symbolic terms, although Rensberger does not think it possible to identify with precision what Jesus intended to convey by his symbolic actions.[81] His concern is whether either John or Mark's account of the temple incident depicts it in violent terms.

Regarding the version of this episode in the Fourth Gospel, Rensberger focuses on the distinctive feature of the whip of cords, which, he insists, is inseparable from the cattle and sheep that are also distinctive to the Johannine account of this event. Persuaded by Croy's argument, Rensberger concludes that "John shows Jesus using the *flagellum* on animals, not on people."[82]

Turning to Mark's version of the temple incident, which is accepted as the basis for both Matthew and Luke's accounts, Rensberger focuses on two points: first, the detail common to all four canonical accounts that Jesus is reported to have "imposed his will on people" by various means; and second, the common assumption that the conduct of Jesus in the temple was motivated by anger.[83] On the first point, Rensberger contends that ἐκβάλλειν (*ekballein*), the verb used in all four accounts to describe Jesus' act of expulsion, has a wide range of connotations and is not inherently violent or forceful. Correct as he may be that the use of this verb does not necessarily imply the use of force, the point remains that it may denote more than the authority of verbal commands—as clearly evidenced in John 2:15! Moreover, combined with Jesus' action of overturning tables and stools, his expulsion of people involved in temple-related transactions takes on a certain forcefulness and

---

80. Ibid., 181.
81. Ibid., 182–84.
82. Ibid., 186.
83. Ibid., 186–89.

even coerciveness. That said, Rensberger is correct that none of the Gospel accounts indicates that Jesus' conduct caused harm or injury.

As for the common assumption that Jesus' actions in the temple were motivated by (righteous) anger, Rensberger remarks that "the Gospels give no description of Jesus's emotions here. In the one incident in which readers are most inclined to see an angry Jesus, the Gospels themselves say nothing of the kind. They simply narrate a series of actions without mentioning emotion."[84] Correct as that may be at one level, John 2:17 needs to be addressed in this connection. This text, which follows Jesus' disruptive actions and his assertive words to dove-sellers, apparently provokes his disciples to recall the words of Psalm 69:9, "Zeal for your house will consume me." Zeal is not synonymous with righteous rage, but there are biblical precedents for relating the two, for example, the actions of Phinehas, whose zealous violence is validated and valorized in Jewish scripture and tradition (Numbers 25; Psalm 106:28–31; 1 Macc 2:19–28; Sirach 45:23–25). In light of John 2:17, then, to infer a wrathful motivation for Jesus' temple actions is at least understandable, if not required.[85] On the basis of the synoptic tradition, Rensberger is perhaps right to remark: "As a *symbolic* deed, the temple action would not have been a crazed outburst but coolly calculated and methodically executed."[86] The Johannine version of this episode is somewhat less susceptible to such a reading. Even so, Rensberger's study helpfully cautions against projecting violence onto textual accounts that make no explicit reference to violent conduct or injurious consequences.

CONCLUDING COMMENTS

In light of the restraint with which the Gospel writers recount Jesus' provocation in the temple, it is remarkable how frequently commentators describe his actions as "violent." Even in the Johannine version of this incident, to describe Jesus' actions as violent is to indulge in hyperbole. At the risk of counterbalancing hyperbole by means of redundancy, none of the Gospel writers envisages Jesus as inflicting harm or injury on persons or animals. There is an assertive, even forceful dimension to his actions, but his conduct is nonviolent and harmless.

---

84. Ibid., 188.
85. See Bryan, "Consumed by Zeal," in which a good case is made for comprehending the zeal that consumes Jesus to be the zeal of Jewish authorities to protect the existing temple, not Jesus' own zeal.
86. Rensberger, "Jesus's Action in the Temple," 189.

Although I find more persuasive the arguments of those who maintain that the temple incident in John 2:13–22 does not depict a violent Jesus, this is not a conclusion grounded in close exegesis alone. Regarding John 2:15a, I would prefer to affirm, with Willard Swartley, that "the particular *both-and* construction in Greek shows that Jesus used the whip on both the sheep and the cattle and not on the people."[87] On grammatical grounds alone, however, it is difficult to exclude a reading of this text that envisages people no less than livestock being evicted from the temple by a whip-brandishing Jesus.[88] Moreover, it needs to be recognized that at least some of the fourth evangelist's linguistic choices evoke violent associations, as evidenced by this narrated event's history of reception and effects.

Although the Johannine version of Jesus' temple provocation at Passover is not overtly violent in and of itself, questions nevertheless remain regarding the role of this incident for Christian moral evaluation of violence. For example, what is the moral value of provocation, symbolic or otherwise, if violent retaliation is the effect provoked? In such circumstances, is provocation that results in violence morally implicated in the violence provoked? Furthermore, if Jesus' provocation at Passover intentionally symbolized the destruction of the temple as an expression of divine judgment, the question of whether or not Jesus may have flicked anyone with a makeshift whip is trivial by comparison.

In *A Peaceable Hope* I make a case for reading the Fourth Gospel as a "nonviolent apocalypse."[89] For scholars like Ellens, an apocalyptic mind-set explains Jesus' violent outburst in the temple—an instance of *apocalyptic animosity*. Although an apocalyptic mind-set may find expression in violence (or projected violence), the Fourth Gospel itself composes evidence that an apocalyptic conception of reality may also find expression in the pursuit of peace—means no less than ends. Even so, the legacy of the Fourth Gospel is mixed with respect to violence, not so much because of its apocalyptic contextualization of Jesus' mission and message but rather because of its "replacement" theology grounded in an explicit "divine identity" Christology.[90] As Rudolf Schnackenburg avers in connection with the Johannine version of the temple incident, "The cleansing of the temple is meant to portray the abrogation of the Jewish cult by Jesus, and its replacement by himself and his community."[91] Understood this way, the story of Jesus' provocation at

---

87. Swartley, *John*, 100.

88. See, e.g., Brown, *Gospel according to John*, 1:114–15; Barrett, *Gospel according to St John*, 197–98; McHugh, *John 1–4*, 203–5.

89. See Neville, *A Peaceable Hope*, 177–216.

90. On "divine identity Christology," see Bauckham, *God Crucified*, passim.

91. Schnackenburg, *Gospel according to St John*, 1:356. For more recent discussions

Passover undoubtedly sowed the seeds of later violence, however nonviolent Jesus himself may have been and however nonviolently the temple incident may have been depicted in the Fourth Gospel. Interpretive engagement with the Fourth Gospel in peace perspective needs to continue to grapple with this Gospel's (apparent) replacement theology. For the purposes of this book, however, it is time to turn from a Gospel episode routinely read as implicating Jesus in violence to a notorious passage within which Jesus is presented as engaging in verbal violence.

---

of Jesus as the (new) temple or its replacement and/or fulfillment in the Fourth Gospel, see, e.g., Coloe, *God Dwells with Us*; Coloe, "Temple Imagery in John," 368–81; Kerr, *Temple of Jesus' Body*; Hoskins, *Jesus as the Fulfillment*; Chanikuzhy, *Jesus, the Eschatological Temple*, 233–329; Hays, *Echoes of Scripture*, 308–35.

8

The Rhetoric of Rage

(MATTHEW 23)

WITHIN THE GOSPELS, ONE of the things for which Jesus is remembered is his verbal vehemence. Some of his sayings were culturally shocking. To a (potential?) disciple who felt obliged to bury his father first, Jesus is recalled as saying, "Leave the dead to bury their own dead" (Matt 8:22; Luke 9:60). Other sayings seem deliberately offensive. In response to a non-Israelite woman's request for assistance for her demon-afflicted daughter, Jesus retorts, "It is not good to take children's bread and to throw it to the dogs" (Matt 15:26; Mark 7:27). Still other sayings are extreme, even if understood as hyperbole for pedagogical purposes: "If your eye or hand or foot entices you to sin, remove it!" (Matt 5:29-30; 18:8-9; Mark 9:43-48). Or, "No one who comes to me is able to be my disciple without hating each and every family member—and even one's own self!" (Luke 14:26; cf. Matt 10:37).

Beyond such provocative and hyperbolic sayings, there are others in which Jesus is recalled as being vitriolic. Although Jesus gained a reputation for acting compassionately toward many—especially those considered disreputable, dishonorable, or discredited—he is also remembered as expressing severe hostility toward opponents. In Matt 15:1-9 and Mark 7:1-13, in response to a relatively mild challenge, Jesus castigates Pharisees and scribes for elevating human traditions above divine commands. In Luke 11:37-52, after accepting the hospitality of a Pharisee and with little provocation, Jesus lambastes both Pharisees and scribes for perceived inconsistencies and faults.¹ According to John 8:44, Jesus identifies Jewish interlocutors as children of the devil, a murderer and the father of lies (and hence of liars).² But the invective against scribes and Pharisees in Matthew 23 is the most sustained diatribe of Jesus against Jewish opponents, the vehemence of which is reinforced by the reality that hostile polemic against Jewish authorities is a distinguishing feature of Matthew's Gospel.³ For this reason, the rhetoric of rage expressed in Matthew 23 is the concern of this chapter—indeed, its *concern* in a twofold sense: first as focus of attention and second as troubling content. The more time one spends with Matthew 23 and reflects on its disturbing history of effects, the more one appreciates Ulrich Luz's frank admission of how difficult he found it to identify with this Gospel passage: "in the woes discourse of chapter 23 I sometimes stood as interpreter in amazement before the text, and I sometimes wished that this chapter were not in the Bible."⁴

Various considerations of a historical-critical nature enable one to mitigate the verbal vehemence on display in Matthew 23. For example, it is reasonable to suppose that this *collection* of sayings reflects a life-setting later than that of Jesus. In other words, the vehement Jesus of Matthew 23 is to some extent Matthew's construct, even if some or most or even all of the sayings themselves are traceable to Jesus. It is also important to interpret slanderous sayings such as are found in Matthew 23 within their sociocultural context. Polemics between rival schools of thought were apparently commonplace in the ancient Mediterranean world; indeed, the closer rival groups were to each other, the more vituperative the invective tended to be. One has only to recall that within Jewish tradition prophetic denunciations against fellow Israelites were often no less cutting than against outsiders or oppressors. Such mitigating considerations are undoubtedly important, but in light of the reception history of texts such as those collected together in Matthew 23 and the (mis)use of such texts to justify slurs, violence, and pogroms against Jews, something more is needed to address such texts in theological and ethical perspective. The vehement Jesus of Matthew 23 (and of other similar texts) has authorized too much terror for far too long,

---

1. This is the Lukan "parallel" to Matt 23:1-36, which is regularly regarded as reflecting more closely Matthew's source material. In Luke 11:37-52 Jesus first castigates Pharisees (11:39-44), then scribes (11:46-52). On the significance of the original (or even purported) audience for interpreting such challenging texts, see Allison, *Resurrecting Jesus*, 47-55.

2. Strangely, this libel occurs within the context of Jesus' discussion with Jews who believed him (see John 8:30-31). Also relevant is the pattern of usage within the Fourth Gospel of the often derogatory expression, "the Jews."

3. See Hagner, *Matthew 1-13*, lxxii.

4. Luz, *Matthew 21-28*, xv.

especially by reinforcing negative and indeed false stereotypes of Pharisees in particular and Jews en masse. In this chapter, therefore, in addition to surveying considerations that mitigate the vehemence of Jesus' tirade in Matthew 23, I consider it important to address the hostile Jesus of Matthew 23 by means of intratextual critique.[5] In light of past wrongs authorized by texts such as one finds in Matthew 23, intratextual critique is but one drop in an oversized bucket, but it does at least challenge immoral authorization on the basis of equally authoritative biblical texts.

MATTHEW 23: LITERARY CONTEXT, STRUCTURE, CONTENT, AND "CHARACTER"

By any measure, Matthew 23 is a striking section within the first canonical Gospel. With the exception of its brief narrative introduction, which identifies Jesus' audience as the crowds and his disciples (23:1),[6] this passage comprises what purports to be direct discourse by Jesus. Much of what Jesus says is stridently polemical, especially the distinctive "woes" uttered toward (rather than simply against) scribes and Pharisees. What marks out this section of Matthew's Gospel is not simply its hostile content and strident tone but also its prolonged polemic. The vehemence of this passage is not occasional but rather sustained and hence reflective of deep discord. As such, it disturbs in part because it is such a prominent feature of Matthew's Gospel, not a trivial or incidental aberration within its larger narrative framework.

Matthew 23 occurs within this Gospel's Jerusalem section, following Jesus' all-disturbing entry into Jerusalem, his eviction of all from within the temple precincts, and his healing of the blind and lame within the temple (21:1–16). When Jesus next comes to the temple, he is challenged by chief priests and elders on the source of his authority for doing what he has been doing (21:23–27). This establishes an atmosphere of conflict and contestation between Jesus and various groups or groupings of Jewish religious authorities: chief priests and elders (21:23); chief priests and Pharisees (21:45–46); Pharisees and Herodians (22:15); Sadducees (22:23–33); and

---

5. I am conscious of other means of responsible interpretive engagement with troubling texts such as Matthew 23, e.g., Bakhtin's notion of dialogic truth, which might appeal more to some than my use of intratextual critique. In 2015, well after putting what I had thought to be the finishing touches on this chapter, two important studies on Matthew 23 were published: Esler, "Intergroup Conflict and Matthew 23," and Turner, *Israel's Last Prophet*.

6. See Esler, "Intergroup Conflict," 41, 44, for whom this double audience reveals that Matthew addresses two different time frames—crowds of Israelites during Jesus' public mission and Christ-followers contemporaneous with the evangelist himself.

Pharisees alone (22:34–45). Leading up to Matthew 23, then, Jesus provokes hostility from various groups within the religious hierarchy and repeatedly bests any who challenge him. In literary terms, therefore, the ferocity of Jesus in Matthew 23 is prepared for by the ambience of hostility established since Jesus' disruptive entry into Jerusalem.

Although there is broad agreement on literary connections between Matthew 23 and what precedes it, there is considerable debate on the relation between the discourse material in Matthew 23 and the so-called eschatological discourse in Matthew 24–25. Although the bulk of both Matthew 23 and Matthew 24–25 comprises discourse material, there is considerable reluctance to treat all three chapters as one single, climactic discourse. For reasons set out by Vicky Balabanski, Eugene Boring, and Jason Hood, however, Matthew 23 should probably be interpreted as the first main part of the fifth and final discourse in this Gospel.[7]

In view of the clear pattern of alternation between narrative and discourse material in Matthew's Gospel, it seems prima facie reasonable to treat Matthew 23 as part of Jesus' final discourse because no significant narrative section interposes between chapters 23 and 24. For many, however, the shift in narrative setting from temple to Mount of Olives in Matt 24:1–3 and the change in audience from crowds and disciples (23:1) to disciples alone (24:3) are sufficient grounds for concluding that Matt 24:3 marks the beginning of an entirely new discourse. As Balabanski, Boring, and Hood point out, however, both a comparable change in narrative setting and a comparable narrowing of audience occur also in Matt 13:1–53, the third of Matthew's five major discourses (see esp. 13:36).[8] If such shifts do not break Matt 13:1–53 into two separate discourses, there is no reason why they should do so in Matthew 23–25. As Hood observes, "A pure discourse, free from narrative elements and audience shifts, is not a Matthean *desideratum*."[9]

Focused as his study is on the relation between Matthew 23 and 24–25, Hood offers further arguments for treating the whole of Matthew 23–25 as one discourse. Among his various additional arguments, the following are especially noteworthy. First, Hood demonstrates how closely the content of Matthew 23 relates to what follows in chapters 24–25. He even contends that the thematic connections between Matthew 23 and what follows are closer than those between this section and the controversy material in the

---

7. Balabanski, *Eschatology in the Making*, 135–39; Boring, "Gospel of Matthew," 428–29; Hood, "Matthew 23–25." For counter-considerations, see Turner, *Israel's Last Prophet*, 271–72.

8. Balabanski, *Eschatology in the Making*, 135–36; Boring, "Gospel of Matthew," 428; Hood, "Matthew 23–25," 530–31.

9. Hood, "Matthew 23–25," 531.

two chapters that precede it, even though this goes beyond what is necessary for his larger argument.[10] Second, Hood follows David Garland in seeing Matthew 23 as providing negative hortatory instruction, albeit not only for (later) disciples but also for non-Christian Jews in Matthew's day (represented by the crowds of Matt 23:1).[11] Jesus' castigations of scribes and Pharisees serve as negative warnings for Christian disciples of Matthew's day, who are subject to the same kinds of temptations as any scribe or Pharisee and hence also subject to similar judgment visited upon Jerusalem. Seemingly directed at scribes and Pharisees, the criticisms of Jesus in Matthew 23 are mainly for the benefit of later Christians, as well as for potential disciples among non-Christian Jews.[12]

Third, finally, and perhaps most importantly from a moral perspective, Hood draws attention to a series of significant literary correspondences between Matthew's final and first discourses, especially those between the woes of Matt 23:13–36 and the beatitudes of 5:3–12.[13] Beyond these crucial intratextual connections, however, Hood also draws attention to other parallels between the first and final discourses, for example, the contrast between the wise and foolish in the latter part of each discourse and the datum that both discourses conclude with parables warning of inevitable judgment. For Hood, such literary and thematic correspondences between the final and first discourses in Matthew's Gospel lead to the conclusion that "Matthew intends his readers to interpret the last discourse in light of the first."[14] Whether Matthew's compositional intentions are quite so trans-

10. Ibid., 532–33 and also 537–40 (on compositional considerations holding the entirety of Matthew 23–25 together). See also Stanton, *Gospel for a New People*, 165.

11. Hood, "Matthew 23–25," 535–37. Cf. Garland, *Intention of Matthew 23*; Garland, *Reading Matthew*, 232–33. See also Balabanski, *Eschatology in the Making*, 137–38, for whom one implication of interpreting Matthew 23 as integral to the final discourse in the Gospel is to read Jesus' invective within this section as targeting hypocrites within Matthew's circle such as "the apparently successful prophets reflected in Matt. 7:15–23 and 24:5, 11, 24." Balabanski is supported in this respect by Combrink's sociorhetorical interpretation of Matthew 23, according to which its reproaches are best understood as "the rhetoric of apostrophe that amounts to addressing the actual audience of the disciples in an indirect manner by ostensibly addressing somebody else." See Combrink, "Shame on the Hypocritical Leaders in the Church," 1–35 (33).

12. At one level, this is an enticing explanation of the function of Jesus' diatribe against scribes and Pharisees in Matthew 23. Taking the harsh criticisms of Jesus as an opportunity for self-appraisal is perhaps the most noble means of reception, but that is unlikely to have been its sole or even primary intended function. See Stanton, *Gospel for a New People*, 146–68.

13. Hood, "Matthew 23–25," 540–42. (Although not referred to by Hood, the correspondences between Matthew's beatitudes and woes have been appraised in social-scientific perspective by K. C. Hanson in a study examined later in this chapter.)

14. Ibid., 541.

parently evident is open to question, but Hood's interpretive inference is nevertheless insightful. Indeed, as will become clear in due course, certain correspondences between Matthew's first and final discourses are critical for my own appraisal of the rhetoric of rage in Matthew 23.

There is a discernible three-part structure to Matthew 23, even though it is not entirely clear where the second subsection ends. As is generally agreed, the first subsection comprises Matt 23:1-12. The second composes Jesus' seven woes apparently directed toward scribes and Pharisees who are no longer present at the narrative level (see 23:1).[15] This subsection must therefore extend beyond Matt 23:30, but precisely to what point is disputed. Perhaps, as both Luz and Davies and Allison envisage, the second subsection ends at 23:33, with the remainder of the chapter comprising two triadic subunits.[16] Yet Matt 23:36 begins with the solemn formula, ἀμὴν λέγω ὑμῖν (*amēn legō humin*; truly, I say to you), and the remainder of the saying has a concluding ring to it. Furthermore, as Luz himself points out, the woes in Matt 23:13-33 most obviously recall the Hebrew prophetic tradition, in which woes are inevitably associated with pronouncements of judgment. Although none of the individual woes is paired with a pronouncement of judgment, the series as a whole prepares for an oracle of judgment, which is duly uttered no later than at Matt 23:36 (but may begin as early as at 23:31).[17] In Matt 23:37, moreover, Jesus directly addresses Jerusalem for the first time, and the tone shifts from one of castigation to something closer to regretful reproach tinged, perhaps, with a hint of hope. As a result of these considerations, it seems reasonable to extend the second subsection of this passage to 23:36,[18] with the third subsection comprising the disconsolate address to Jerusalem in 23:37-39. Even if not incontestable, Matthew 23 subdivides into three uneven sections: 23:1-12, 13-36, 37-39.[19]

---

15. An eighth woe was at some point interpolated either after or before Matt 23:13. In the Textus Receptus, it appears at Matt 23:14. See Metzger, *Textual Commentary*, 50.

16. Luz, *Matthew 21-28*, 92-93; Davies and Allison, *Gospel according to Saint Matthew*, 3:311.

17. See Luz, *Matthew 21-28*, 112, where he writes: "Thus the entire succession of woes is aimed at the pronouncement of judgment in vv. 34-39." Although not decisive, I incline to the view that the pronouncement of judgment begins at 23:31 and concludes at 23:36, with 23:37-39 effecting a shift in form and function.

18. Cf. Hagner, *Matthew 14-28*, 673-78, where Matt 23:34-36 is designated an "appendix to the seventh woe." If I correctly comprehend Combrink on the argumentative texture and pattern of Matthew 23, his analysis of this passage as a chreia elaboration supports my structural delimitations. See Combrink, "Shame on the Hypocritical Leaders in the Church," 14-26.

19. So also Turner, *Israel's Last Prophet*, 270. In narrative terms, Jesus' omen in Matt 23:38, "Look, your house is left to you deserted," is paralleled by his own final

On this literary subdivision, the first subsection of Matthew 23 begins the fifth and final major discourse of the Gospel. Addressing both crowds and his disciples, Jesus begins by recognizing the teaching authority of scribes and Pharisees but promptly warns against following their example—for three reasons: first, there is a mismatch between their teaching and their conduct; second, they burden others but are unwilling to share the load; and third, their conduct is calculated to make an impression.[20] Jesus' audience, by contrast, is challenged to adopt a countercultural, non-hierarchical, and hence non-competitive social stance, according to which service for the benefit of others is recognized as genuine greatness. The first subsection of Jesus' final discourse concludes with an apposite assurance of reversal, probably to be understood in terms of eschatological judgment even though the first half of this saying rings true as a sociocultural inevitability in an agonistic social order. Were this the extent of Jesus' critique of scribes and Pharisees, one might well interpret his invective as preparing for his exhortation to integrity, mutual service, and humility. Alas, this is but the beginning of woes.

The second subsection comprises seven slanders against scribes and Pharisees. Not only is Jesus' tirade in this subsection scathing but it is also indiscriminate. Jesus is here remembered as being both defamatory and prone to indulging in generalizations; he is not recalled as excoriating scribes and Pharisees if and when there is a mismatch between their word and their way but rather as denouncing such opponents en masse. By virtue of their identification (by Matthew in the main) as opponents of Jesus, they are ipso facto hypocrites, persons of perdition, blind bumblers, morons, indeed, a clutch of venomous snakes. Not only do they refuse entry into God's heavenly reign but they bar entry to others; they multiply their shortcomings among their disciples; not only do they bind and loose with respect to obfuscating oaths but their casuistic reasoning is misguided; they tithe herbs in accordance with the Torah but neglect weightier obligations of Jewish Law; they attend to externals but lack moral integrity by virtue of their greed, self-indulgence, and indeed lack of regard for the Torah; and despite their apparent honoring of past prophets, they really belong to the line of those who shed the blood of the prophets. The woes of Jesus in Matt 23:13–36 compose an intemperate assault, culminating in the ominous prophecy that the history of bloodshed perpetuated by the scribes and Pharisees will be avenged on "this generation," that is, Israelite contemporaries of both Jesus

---

departure from the temple in 24:1.

20. See Boring, "Gospel of Matthew," 431.

and the first generation of his disciples.[21] As Luz summarizes, "The line of argument of Matt 23:32–36 is as follows: Since by abusing, persecuting, and murdering the prophets, wise men, and scribes sent by Jesus, you *now* have filled the measure of the biblical fathers who murdered the prophets and righteous from Abel to Zechariah, all blood—including the blood that they shed—comes upon you, 'this generation.'"[22]

Matthew 23 and hence the first main part of the fifth and final discourse in the Gospel ends with a mournful reproach against Jerusalem that serves also as a conditional prophecy of judgment followed by redemption.[23] According to Boring, "For Matthew and his community, these words [of Matt 23:38] and the following explicit prediction of the Temple's destruction functioned as an apologetic, explaining how the destruction of the Temple fit into the divine program as a punishment for the people's sins in rejecting the prophets, including Jesus and the Christian prophets of the final generation. . . ."[24]

The caustic character of Jesus' diatribe in Matthew 23 is evident from the preceding overview, but how serious is the moral—and hence interpretive—challenge posed by this Gospel passage? Within a sociocultural context characterized by honor/shame dynamics, denunciations of the kind uttered by Jesus in his woes against scribes and Pharisees have been shown to have been customary in contemporary polemics. Even when Jesus' rhetoric of rage is comprehended within its sociocultural context, however, its moral seriousness is brought into stark relief by other contextual considerations. For example, however commonplace demeaning insults may have been in ancient polemical discourse, they could also provoke a spiral of escalating intensity that might well result in bloodshed, which in turn was likely to provoke violent retaliation.[25] Moreover, according to John Kloppenborg, within the ancient Mediterranean world "even rhetorical speech

---

21. See Davies and Allison, *Gospel according to Saint Matthew*, 3:319.

22. Luz, *Matthew 21–28*, 155. On Matt 23:36, Luz wrestles with the notion of collective guilt implicit in this pronouncement of judgment, which contradicts the theological insight of prophetic precursors (Jer 32:29–30; Ezekiel 18). On the history of the interpretation of Matt 23:35, see Gallagher, "Blood from Abel to Zechariah."

23. Here I follow Allison, "Matt 23:39," 75–84; Davies and Allison, *Gospel according to Saint Matthew*, 3:319–25. In favor of interpreting Matt 23:39 as an oracle of unconditional salvation beyond judgment, see Stanton, *Gospel for a New People*, 247–51. Stanton reads this oracle as a reiteration of the Deuteronomistic pattern of sin followed by exile (curse or judgment) followed in turn by return (blessing or salvation).

24. Boring, "Gospel of Matthew," 438.

25. See the reading scenario on "honor and violence" in Malina and Rohrbaugh, *Social-Science Commentary*, 372.

was conceived as a form of violence."[26] In certain respects, then, the reception history of Matthew 23 mirrors the conflictual ethos that accounts for this biblical passage.

Furthermore, texts of the time witness to an appreciation that since words may wound they are subject to moral appraisal. Indeed, one of the thematic connections between the letter of James and Matthew's Gospel is a common concern for careful speech. The speech ethic of James 3 resonates with the teaching of Jesus in the Sermon on the Mount (5:8, 14–16, 21–22, 33–48; 6:7–8; 7:1–12), which is further reinforced by Matt 12:33–37, especially this concluding pronouncement by Jesus: "I tell you that on the day of judgment people will account for each and every worthless word they might utter. For on the basis of your words you will be vindicated, and on the basis of your words you will be condemned."[27] Since such texts bespeak a concern for the content, character, and consequences of human speech, interpretive regard for the damaging effects of verbal violence cannot be considered anachronistic, nor can such invective simply be discounted on the basis of contextual considerations. Even so, the historical and sociocultural context of the polemic one finds in Matthew 23 is noteworthy.

"ANTI-JUDAIC" INVECTIVE IN HISTORICAL AND SOCIOCULTURAL PERSPECTIVE

The theme of "anti-Judaism" in the Gospels, as well as in other parts of the New Testament, has been thoroughly explored in recent decades. Here I do no more than to survey some of the more important historical and sociocultural considerations that contribute to clearer perspective and enhanced understanding of "anti-Judaic" invective such as one finds in Matthew 23. Whether "anti-Judaic" is the most appropriate adjective to describe such invective within the New Testament remains an open question, especially since most, if not all, of the New Testament authors were *Jewish* Christians. Within the scholarly literature on this topic, however, "anti-Judaism" seems to be considered the least unfortunate term for vilification within New

---

26. Kloppenborg, "Representation of Violence," 324.

27. On moral dimensions of human speech in James 3, see, for example, Painter and deSilva, *James and Jude*, 112–26. Commenting on James 3:1, Painter draws parallels between its warning to teachers and Jesus' invective against scribes and Pharisees for failing in their responsibility as teachers (Matthew 23). See also Allison, *Epistle of James*, 514–15.

Testament texts directed against Jewish opponents for perceived failures and shortcomings.[28]

In discussions of anti-Judaism within the New Testament, scholars routinely refer to Luke Timothy Johnson's 1989 study of the New Testament's anti-Jewish slander within the context of ancient polemical conventions.[29] Revisiting this topic in "Anti-Judaism and the New Testament," Johnson's introductory paragraph articulates this blunt observation: "Christianity's long history of anti-Jewish behavior cannot be separated from the portrayal of Jews in the New Testament. And no discussion of the New Testament with respect to Judaism can be isolated from the ways in which the Christian canon can continue to foster attitudes and actions dangerous to Jews."[30] In other words, certain texts held by Christians to be sacred words of life are nevertheless implicated in death-dealing.

At the outset, Johnson differentiates between historical, exegetical, and hermeneutical concerns.[31] At the historical level, one must evaluate how accurately the New Testament portrays Jewish attitudes and actions, especially toward Jesus and early Christians. The exegetical challenge is to comprehend the meaning and significance of New Testament statements regarding Jews, especially in relation to "the rhetoric of community formation in antiquity." Finally, the hermeneutical challenge concerns how such texts are to be understood and received today. Although Johnson allows "an obvious connection between these levels of concern," he warns against confusing them.

Among various factors that contribute to the complexity of considering anti-Judaism in the New Testament, Johnson highlights "the overwhelmingly Jewish character of the New Testament compositions themselves.

---

28. See, e.g., Farmer, ed., *Anti-Judaism and the Gospels*; Bieringer, Pollefeyt, and Vandecasteele-Vanneuville, eds., *Anti-Judaism and the Fourth Gospel*; Fredriksen and Reinhartz, eds., *Jesus, Judaism, and Christian Anti-Judaism*; Donaldson, *Jews and Anti-Judaism in the New Testament*; and Johnson, "Anti-Judaism and the New Testament." Cf. Esler, "Intergroup Conflict," 38–40, for whom "anti-Judean" in an ethnic sense would seem to be a more historically accurate term.

29. Johnson, "New Testament's Anti-Jewish Slander." For an entirely negative evaluation of Johnson's study, see Avalos, *Bad Jesus*, 182–88. Despite the validity of some of Avalos's criticisms at a philosophical level, I consider Johnson's work on New Testament expressions of anti-Judaism to be historically illuminating and hermeneutically helpful.

30. Johnson, "Anti-Judaism and the New Testament," 1609. See also Esler, "Intergroup Conflict," whose study seems motivated by concerns similar to those expressed by Johnson, albeit focused on Matthew 23 interpreted in terms of intergroup conflict within the conceptual framework of social identity theory. Although Esler's article complements and thereby reinforces much that one finds in Johnson's studies, he makes no reference to either study by Johnson.

31. Johnson, "Anti-Judaism and the New Testament," 1609–10.

Whatever the New Testament has to say about 'the Jews,' it does so not from a detached position, but from a place within the complex conversation that was first-century 'Judaism.'"[32] Part of the difficulty of evaluating anti-Judaic sentiment within the New Testament is that when such sentiments were codified in writing, they expressed a claim to represent the faithful continuation of Israel's religious heritage. Crucial in this respect is the comparative evaluation of New Testament writings in relation to (other) Jewish sources for constructing formative Judaism contemporaneous with emerging Christian groups. With respect to the Gospels, whatever may be established regarding their material connections to the historical figure of Jesus, the selection and shaping of their respective contents reflects the circumstances in which they were composed. "With respect to what the gospels report concerning Jews," according to Johnson, "this means that the struggles of nascent Christian communities with 'the Synagogue down the street' between 50–90 affect the selection and shaping of traditions concerning Jesus' interaction with Jews in 28–30."[33] Such awareness does not resolve historical questions regarding Jesus, but to appreciate that anti-Judaic invective in the Gospels emerged from sociocultural contexts characterized by conflict is nevertheless illuminating for interpretation.[34]

Having outlined the complex nature of the issues relating to anti-Judaism and the New Testament, Johnson addresses three dimensions of the topic: first, negative historical and narrative roles ascribed to Jews within the New Testament; second, rhetorical vilification of Jews; and third, New Testament affirmations suggestive of a supersessionist attitude toward Israelite tradition. On the first point, Johnson rightly distinguishes between possible historical actions by Jews against Jesus and early (Jewish) Christians on one hand and narrative portrayals of such actions on the other.[35] Johnson accepts that some Jews were involved in both the death of Jesus and the persecution of early followers of Jesus, but it is the totalizing and undifferentiated narrative depiction of Jewish hostility to Jesus and his earliest followers that, in Johnson's view, borders on "anti-Judaism."

Johnson's treatment of rhetorical vilification of Jews within the New Testament summarizes his 1989 study, "The New Testament's Anti-Jewish Slander and the Convention of Ancient Polemic," in which such hostile rhetoric is examined in sociocultural context with reference to a range of

---

32. Ibid., 1611.
33. Ibid., 1614.
34. With respect to Matthew 23, see especially Esler, "Intergroup Conflict," 38–59.
35. Johnson, "Anti-Judaism and the New Testament," 1616. (This section of Johnson's study deserves greater attention than can be given to it here.)

contemporaneous Jewish and Hellenistic texts. For Johnson, although negative characterizations of Jews may be found in Paul, in both Luke and John's Gospels, and also in Revelation, a "classic example" of slander against Jewish opponents is Matthew 23.[36] To understand the function of such invective in its historical context, Johnson makes six principal points.[37] First, within the New Testament at least, hostile rhetoric against opponents was the defensive language of a relatively powerless and occasionally persecuted minority, a situation that likely exacerbated verbal venom. Second, within a messianic movement that was marked by diversity and hence controversy from the outset, much hostile rhetoric was directed against others within the movement, with non-Christian opponents "addressed only indirectly."[38] Third, moreover, the evident diversity within early Christianity reflected and indeed contributed to significant diversity among first-century Israelites. Seen in correct historical perspective, according to Johnson, "the Christian claims about the way to read Torah and the proper understanding of God's Temple represent only one more voice in an already contentious conversation."[39]

Having shown that hostile rhetoric within the New Testament is the language of a relatively powerless and variegated minority movement within a much larger but nevertheless diverse religious tradition, Johnson next situates such slander within the social setting of rival schools of thought. His fourth point, then, is that the best sociocultural framework for making sense of slander within the New Testament is to envisage diverse Jewish and Jewish-Christian groups as rival philosophical schools, whose principal concern during the Hellenistic period was the moral life. "Over the centuries," according to Johnson, "a stereotyped polemic developed in which such disputes found conventional expression. This is the context, and these are the conventions, that best explain the language about Jews in the New Testament."[40] Following on from this, Johnson's fifth point is that disputes between rival schools of thought typically resorted to denigrating the character of one's opponents: "Such charges became standard, so that certain things were said about all opponents. Their teaching was self-contradictory,

---

36. Ibid., 1620–21; Johnson, "New Testament's Anti-Jewish Slander," 420.

37. Johnson, "Anti-Judaism and the New Testament," 1622–34. (For complementary observations from the perspective of social identity theory, see Esler, "Intergroup Conflict.")

38. Johnson, "Anti-Judaism and the New Testament," 1624; Johnson, "New Testament's Anti-Jewish Slander," 426.

39. Johnson, "Anti-Judaism and the New Testament," 1625; cf. Johnson, "New Testament's Anti-Jewish Slander," 427.

40. Johnson, "Anti-Judaism and the New Testament," 1628; cf. Johnson, "New Testament's Anti-Jewish Slander," 430.

or trivial, or led to bad morals. Their behavior could be criticized in two different ways. Either they preached but did not practice (showing they were hypocrites), or they lived as they taught, and their manner of life showed the falsity of their doctrines (like the Epicureans). Certain vices were indiscriminately applied to opponents on every side: they were all lovers of pleasure, lovers of money, lovers of glory."[41]

Not only were such hostile accusations conventional but their purpose was not so much to refute their opponents as to discredit them in the eyes of those in one's own philosophical school. For Johnson, this explains the secondary, literary use of such polemics against opponents for protreptic purposes, that is, to encourage certain behaviors or adherence to a particular way of life. Indeed, according to Johnson, such a protreptic purpose is to be seen in Matthew 23. "Its literary and rhetorical function is turned inward to Matthew's messianic readers," he writes. "Matthew's attack on Scribes and Pharisees is an attack on rival *teachers*, and serves to frame the positive instructions on messianic disciples (*mathetai* = students) in 23:8–11."[42]

Johnson's sixth and final point regarding anti-Judaic slander is that it is characteristic not only of rival non-Jewish philosophical schools but also of Jewish literature of the period, particularly Hellenistic Jewish texts. Not only did cultured Jews such as Josephus and Philo vilify non-Jews but they also slandered fellow Jews, as occasion required. Although direct documentary evidence for first-century Palestinian Judaism is limited apart from some apocalyptic texts such as the Parables of Enoch and 4 Ezra, the Qumran library, Josephus, and the New Testament itself, Johnson considers the available evidence suggestive of "the same sort of many-voiced and contentious polemic" found in the diaspora, against both outsiders and fellow Israelites.[43]

From his sociocultural investigation of anti-Judaic vilification within the New Testament, Johnson draws four conclusions: first, such verbal vitriol is more intelligible because it was commonplace; second, by comparison with both Hellenistic conventions and contemporaneous intra-Jewish slander, rhetorical vilification within the New Testament is relatively mild; third, the conventional nature of such rhetorical slander signals little more than that those vilified are opponents with different viewpoints; and fourth,

---

41. Johnson, "Anti-Judaism and the New Testament," 1629; cf. Johnson, "New Testament's Anti-Jewish Slander," 432.

42. Johnson, "Anti-Judaism and the New Testament," 1630; cf. Johnson, "New Testament's Anti-Jewish Slander," 433.

43. Johnson, "Anti-Judaism and the New Testament," 1632; cf. Johnson, "New Testament's Anti-Jewish Slander," 437. On factions and factionalism within Second Temple Judaism, see also Dunn, *Jesus Remembered*, 265–86.

"grasping the historical situation and social setting within which such language was shaped helps us understand it as a function of community-identification among disputants to a shared tradition."[44]

After a final section in which Johnson considers literary data within the New Testament suggestive of a supersessionist mind-set, and within which he reiterates the importance of being sensitive toward both historical context and narrative portrayal,[45] his conclusion is fourfold: first, it is anachronistic to describe any New Testament text as "anti-Jewish"; second, even though anti-Judaic invective within the New Testament is not anti-Jewish per se, it has been used to denigrate Jewish tradition and to vilify Jews en masse; third, historical, social, and rhetorical forms of analysis are the best means of interpreting anti-Judaic invective within the New Testament; and fourth, the interpretive task of grappling with such anti-Judaic slander nevertheless remains "a difficult challenge for Christian readers."[46]

Johnson helpfully places Jesus' rhetoric of rage in historical and sociocultural context, which mitigates its vehemence somewhat. Even so, the vilification of opponents en masse, as Jesus is depicted as doing in Matthew 23, is starkly at odds with Matthew's portrayal of Jesus as an authoritative teacher concerned with the morality of words as well as of deeds. "The importance of speech ethics for Matthew makes the question of the woes in Matthew 23 much more urgent," as Lorenzo Scornaienchi points out.[47] For Scornaienchi, the resolution of this intratextual tension resides in the prophetic characterization of Jesus by Matthew and the prophetic character of the woes in Matthew 23: "Jesus is presented by Matthew as a prophet who condemns this generation responsible for the catastrophe of the war. In a Jewish context, this is not aggressive language that would contradict the rigid speech ethic in the Sermon on the Mount. It is expected that a prophet will speak dramatically and denunciate injustice."[48]

The portrayal of Jesus as a prophet by Matthew (no less than by Luke) is undoubtedly an important consideration when interpreting the intemperate denunciations of Jesus against scribes and Pharisees in Matthew 23.[49] As is

---

44. Johnson, "Anti-Judaism and the New Testament," 1633–34; cf. Johnson, "New Testament's Anti-Jewish Slander," 441.

45. Johnson, "Anti-Judaism and the New Testament," 1635: "The gospels are written out of a context of intense conflict and competition with rival forms of Jewish conviction."

46. Ibid., 1637–38.

47. Scornaienchi, "Controversy Dialogues," 309–321 (319). Scornaienchi is dismissive of Johnson's way of addressing Matthew's anti-Judaic polemic, but he oversimplifies Johnson's multifaceted argument.

48. Ibid., 320.

49. This is the burden of the book by Turner, *Israel's Last Prophet*. Although Israel's

so often the case, however, Scornaienchi's designation of Jesus as a prophetic figure in Matthew's Gospel fits Jesus within the framework of a prophetic type without asking whether, in adopting a prophetic persona, Jesus (even according to Matthew) might also have reshaped it. Regarding Matthew's own conception of Jesus as a prophet, Scornaienchi may be correct. Yet the tension between authoritative moral teacher and woe-pronouncing prophet within Matthew's Gospel is not thereby relieved, especially if one accepts as determinative certain Christological convictions distinctive to Matthew, for example, the affirmation about Jesus articulated in the Gospel's narrative opening proper—Emmanuel (1:18–25). For Matthew, Jesus is not only an Israelite descended from Abraham, not only the messianic Son of David, not only another Moses (moral teacher and prophet), but also the personal locus of divine presence for salvation from sins. Such a conviction sits uneasily alongside the invective of Matthew 23.

Yet another distinctive feature of Matthew's Christology further tightens the tension between discrepant depictions of Jesus within his Gospel, as Luz explains: "Matthew formulates his own anti-Jewish words in the name of the exalted Lord Jesus. Matthew sees Jesus, the Son of Man and Judge of the World, as an absolute authority. The fact that this Jesus has formulated them gives the harsh judgments against Israel more weight than parallel Jewish texts. Matthew works through his conflict with Israel in the name of Jesus the exalted Son of Man. This renders his anti-Judaism more fundamental and far-reaching than the sectarian Jewish polemics in which it is rooted."[50] In other words, Matthew's exalted Christology overrides contextual factors that make comprehensible much of the content and tone of Matthew 23.

Among the valuable points made by Johnson is his observation that what the Gospels recount regarding Jesus was invariably affected by religious conflict in later decades. Although almost every word of Matthew 23 is attributed to Jesus, it is commonly acknowledged that even if some or most or even all of the sayings in this chapter are traceable to Jesus in some form, their present formulation, agglutination, and contextualization owe much to the evangelist. In other words, from this first section of the fifth and final discourse in Matthew's Gospel, it is difficult to tease out what goes back to Jesus beyond the reminiscence that he sometimes engaged in debate with Jewish religious leaders. Some would go so far as to say that nothing in Matthew 23 derives from Jesus, others that isolated sayings of Jesus have been reformulated, elaborated, or adapted to address new

---

prophetic traditions are important for understanding both Jesus and Matthew's portrayal of Jesus, one must be careful about appealing to such traditions. See Levine, "Anti-Judaism and the Gospel of Matthew," 12–26.

50. Luz, "Anti-Judaism in the Gospel of Matthew," 259.

circumstances, others still that Matthew or an earlier compiler's role was largely that of bringing together thematically related and formally similar sayings of Jesus.⁵¹ Whichever of these alternative reconstructions reflects historical circumstances most closely, it is widely (albeit not unanimously) accepted that the sayings attributed to Jesus in Matthew 23 address a post-70 CE life-setting in which they serve the evangelist's purpose of defining his own—and his own Jewish-Christian community's—self-understanding in light of recent developments within formative Judaism. In their present form and narrative context, therefore, the sayings of Jesus in Matthew 23 are best appraised in relation to the life-setting of the evangelist, especially in light of the historical reality that their lethal legacy is largely the result of their Matthean "preservation" and transmission.

For F. W. Beare, however, differentiating between Jesus and Matthew is irrelevant for assessing the content of Matthew 23. As he asserts, "In such a compilation, no purpose is served by attempting to distinguish between sayings that may be authentic utterances of Jesus and sayings which were produced in the early church after his death and resurrection. They are all, 'authentic' or not, intended by Matthew to be received as instruction delivered by Christ the risen Lord to Christian believers, not as historical records of words spoken by Jesus several decades before the Gospel was published."⁵²

Some might consider it difficult to sustain Beare's contention regarding Matthew's alleged equation between sayings of the risen Lord (presumably uttered by Christian prophets) and sayings of the historical Jesus. Notwithstanding one's view on this disputed matter, Matthew's placement of sayings attributed to Jesus within his final discourse undoubtedly led to an understanding on the part of readers that such sayings were integral to his authoritative body of teaching to be transmitted to the nations (Matt 28:18-20). Indeed, as Sean Freyne points out, this concluding commission alludes to Jesus' various teachings throughout the Gospel, especially within the five major discourses, all of which are now categorized as *commands* to be taught, irrespective of the form in which they are expressed earlier in the Gospel.⁵³ Consequently, in light of reprehensible stages in the reception history of sayings such as those concentrated in Matthew 23, it is a salutary, if not necessary, dimension of the interpretive task to read such sayings in

---

51. Within this paragraph, all references to Jesus are to the historical Jesus. Depending on one's view of Christian prophecy, however, yet another viewpoint is that the various woes found in Matthew 23 are sayings of the risen Jesus articulated by early Christian prophets. See Boring, *Continuing Voice of Jesus*, 213–16, 254–55.

52. Beare, *Gospel according to Matthew*, 446.

53. Freyne, "Vilifying the Other," 119–20.

light of the evangelist's life-setting. Without exaggerating the significance of differentiating between Jesus and Matthew,[54] it is nevertheless important to attend to the role Matthew gives to such sayings as are found in this section of the fifth and final discourse in his Gospel.

INTRATEXTUAL TENSION AND INTERPRETIVE IMPLICATIONS

One of the consequences of recognizing Matthew 23 as part and parcel of the fifth and final discourse in the Gospel is to make more noticeable certain correspondences between the final discourse and the first discourse, the so-called Sermon on the Mount in Matthew 5–7. Perhaps the most prominent of such correspondences is the negative correlation between the beatitudes in Matt 5:3–12 and the contrasting woes in 23:13–36. That blessings and woes are contrasting formulations is well illustrated by the way in which four makarisms are counterbalanced by four contrasting woes in Luke 6:20–26. The negative correlation between the beatitudes that begin Jesus' Sermon on the Mount and the woes that comprise a significant part of the opening section of Jesus' final discourse is significant in its own right. Beyond that literary and thematic significance, however, such resonances between the first and final discourses invite interpretive appraisal of intratextual dissonance between the two discourses.

In *Recovering Jesus*, Thomas Yoder Neufeld's discussion of the Sermon on the Mount takes a brief "detour" following his treatment of the so-called antitheses in Matt 5:21–48 to consider three texts in apparent conflict with Jesus' exhortation to nonretaliation and love of enemies. The three texts are Matt 10:34, Luke 22:36–38, and the temple episode recounted in all four canonical Gospels.[55] The rhetoric of rage on display in Matthew 23 does not feature in this "detour," however, despite its apparent tension with Jesus' instruction in the Sermon on the Mount. For Willard Swartley in *Covenant of Peace*, by contrast, this is the major intratextual pressure point in Matthew's Gospel. A significant proportion of his chapter on Matthew is devoted to the peacemaking implications of the Sermon on the Mount, but within the context of that discussion he devotes attention to the question of consistency between Jesus' teaching on love of enemies and his verbal vehemence toward Jewish opponents. "How does Jesus' command to love enemies

---

54. Later in this chapter, I return to the question of distinguishing between Jesus and Matthew in dialogue with John Dominic Crossan.

55. Yoder Neufeld, *Recovering Jesus*, 218–20. (These texts are addressed elsewhere in this book.)

correlate with Matthew's portrait of Jesus speaking harsh (violent?) words against the Pharisees?" Swartley asks. "Are Jesus' teachings in the Sermon contradicted by his own words and actions?"[56]

While considering Matthew's narrative world as a context for moral dimensions of discipleship, Richard Hays identifies literary evidence of hostility toward Jewish synagogues as a salient feature of this Gospel. According to Hays, "The battle between Matthew's community and emergent rabbinic Judaism has left indelible scars upon Matthew's Gospel, in the form of scathing prophetic denunciations of the scribes and Pharisees. *Matthew's text provides no clues about how this implacable hostility toward the traditional representatives of Israel is to be integrated with Jesus' teaching concerning the love of enemies.*"[57]

Both Hays and Swartley identify the tension between Jesus' teaching on love of enemies and his verbal vehemence against scribes and Pharisees as a significant interpretive problem with profound ethical implications. In this regard they are not alone. Hays's description of Jesus' rhetoric of rage as "scathing prophetic denunciations of the scribes and Pharisees" matches Swartley's resolution of this interpretive dilemma. For Swartley, Jesus' confrontational invective against scribes and Pharisees is best understood as intra-Jewish critique in the tradition of the Hebrew prophets, whose harsh criticisms were generally directed against Israel's leaders and intended to provoke change. "Read as intra-Jewish polemic," Swartley writes, "Matthew 23 does not sanction ethnic hatred, and, specifically, not discrimination against Jews. The 'woes' of Matthew 23 fall under the rubric of Jesus' prophetic word as judgment on his own people, and specifically the leaders, not all Israel."[58]

Swartley draws upon an important body of scholarship that has placed Matthew's Gospel within the socioreligious framework of formative Judaism in the aftermath of the temple's destruction. In such a setting, narrated hostility toward scribes and Pharisees reflects a contest between rival claimants for recognition as faithful guardians of Israelite traditions. Competing claims between rival contenders for the inheritance of Israel account for

56. Swartley, *Covenant of Peace*, 68. (For Swartley, Matthew 23 is the prime example of apparently unloving speech on the part of Jesus toward opponents, but he also notes other instances: 8:10–12; 12:36–45; 16:4; 21:43.)

57. Hays, *Moral Vision*, 109 (emphasis mine). Matthew may not have provided explicit clues for resolving this intratextual tension, probably because he was insensitive to it, but the burden of my argument in this chapter is that he did provide resources for grappling with it, even if inadvertently.

58. Swartley, *Covenant of Peace*, 70. Swartley's viewpoint is reinforced by Turner, *Israel's Last Prophet*. Cf., however, Levine, "Anti-Judaism and the Gospel of Matthew," 12–26.

expressions of hostility. Addressing the issue of "anti-Judaism and ethnic conflict," Hays foregrounds the importance of scholarly reappraisals of the relation between formative Judaism and emergent Christianity. His summary of the scholarly consensus features the following four points: first, first-century Judaism was characterized by diversity of conviction and expression; second, early Christianity began as yet another sectarian movement within variegated Judaism; third, the biblical Gospels were written during the late first century when the early Christian movement's relation to formative Judaism was increasingly under question as a result of much greater responsiveness to the Christian message among non-Jews than among Jews; and fourth, New Testament texts that reflect anti-Judaic hostility should, in light of the first three points, be understood as expressions of "sibling rivalry."[59] In short, Hays and Swartley (among many others) concur with Johnson that expressions of "anti-Judaism" within the Gospels are best understood as but one side of *intra-Jewish* polemics.

As helpful as such considerations are at the interpretive level, they do not finally relieve the moral tension arising from the contrast between Jesus' distinctive injunction to love enemies and Jesus' rhetoric of rage, both of which feature prominently in Matthew's Gospel. Words wound, which is precisely why they are used to vilify others. Moreover, in a cultural environment centered on honor and shame, such vilification was designed to enhance one's own honor at the expense of another's. In short, at both the cultural and the interpersonal levels, wounding words are incompatible with loving enemies. Indeed, words that wound perpetuate enmity rather than dissolve it. As a result, although considerations of the kind articulated by Johnson, Hays, and Swartley (among others) make the vehement Jesus of Matthew 23 more comprehensible in sociocultural perspective, the acute moral tension that such interpreters correctly perceive remains.[60]

For Hays, expressions of anti-Judaism within New Testament texts bring to the surface a crucial question of method in relation to New Testament theology and ethics: "How do we deal with the diversity of the New Testament witnesses in a case where different texts stand fundamentally in tension with one another?"[61] Naturally, as Hays himself appreciates, this methodological matter is pressing only for those who accept the normative

---

59. Hays, *Moral Vision*, 409–10.

60. On reflection, I doubt that it is possible or even desirable to massage away the moral tension caused by the discrepancy between Jesus' command to love enemies and his caustic castigations of scribes and Pharisees. At times, I wonder whether a better interpretive response is to underscore this discrepancy as an inherent dialectical tension within Matthew's Gospel, indeed, within the Jesus tradition.

61. Hays, *Moral Vision*, 408.

status of the Bible for ethics. Moreover, it is clear that, for Hays, the diversity within the New Testament to which he calls attention is diversity between biblical texts (or corpora) in their entirety, not diversity *within* biblical texts. This is why he illustrates the methodological problem caused by such diversity by discussing four prominent New Testament writers: Paul, Luke, Matthew, and John.[62] When Hays compares these writers in canonical context, he finds it impossible to harmonize their differences, leading him to aver that "we must let the tensions stand."[63] This in turn leads him to the conclusion that in view of incompatible differences between Paul, Luke, Matthew, and John on the relation between the church and Israel, a theological choice must be made in favor of one over the other witnesses. In this instance, Hays chooses Paul over Luke, Matthew, and John as the *determinative canonical measure* for Christian attitudes and actions toward Jews.[64] This choice is buttressed by reasoning that is both sagacious and sensitive to nuance, but the perceived necessity of choosing between alternatives in light of evident "intracanonical tensions," a phrase used by Hays while introducing the synthetic task,[65] is not only the crucial point but one that may be adapted analogously.

If, within the collection of texts that compose the New Testament, tensions between texts (or corpora) must be permitted to stand such that one must inevitably select between alternative perspectives, might not such an interpretive procedure also be applicable at the intratextual level, that is, in relation to tensions inherent *within* individual texts? In other words, might not Hays's synthetic task apply also to intractable tensions internal to texts such as Matthew's Gospel, quite apart from tensions between Matthew and Paul, or between Matthew and Mark, or Luke, or John?

For Hays, the synthetic task in his interpretive process is concerned to discern coherence between diverse canonical witnesses.[66] Having given due diligence to hearing any individual biblical text on its own terms, one must then confront the question of coherence between biblical texts. Indeed, in Hays's view, canonical coherence is determinative for upholding the New Testament as normative for theological ethics. Cognizant that the synthetic task is beset by subjectivity and methodological indeterminacy, Hays nevertheless considers it to be essential to the interpretive process,

---

62. Hays, *Moral Vision*, 411–28. For Hays, the second, synthetic task of New Testament ethics is to read any individual biblical text in canonical context.

63. Ibid., 429.

64. Ibid., 430.

65. Ibid., 5.

66. Ibid., 187–92.

provided it is undertaken inductively, carefully, humbly, and with openness to critique and correction from others. To this end, he proposes three procedural guidelines and, beyond these, three "focal images" for discerning canonical coherence within the collection of New Testament texts.[67]

Hays's three procedural guidelines are the following. First, to avoid proof-texting, the full range of canonical witnesses must be considered. Second, tensions between texts must not be dissolved, massaged away, or forcibly harmonized; rather, such tensions must be permitted to stand. Here Hays presages the point, later reiterated in relation to anti-Judaism, that there are issues on which intractable tension between canonical texts is best addressed by selecting between alternative canonical voices. And third, Hays exhorts attention and sensitivity to literary genre or form. Of these three proposed guidelines, the second and third are as pertinent to intratextual tensions as to the synthetic task of discerning coherence between discrepant canonical witnesses. Especially the second guideline, to resist harmonizing tensions, is hermeneutically helpful at the intratextual level.

As for Hays's three focal images—community, cross, and new creation—some such means of discerning unity within plurality or coherence within diversity (or discrepancy) seems inescapable if one is to engage in responsible biblical interpretation. Bible readers *inevitably* privilege certain texts over others, interpreting biblical texts according to self-interest or present-day commonplaces or inherited doctrinal grids. All too often, such interpretations are claimed to be "plain readings" or defended on the basis of the perspicuity of Scripture. Ever since the articulation of the interpretive rule of faith by Irenaeus in the late second century, however, there has been a better way—better because it is more self-aware and hence more honest and more disciplined, more attentive to the need for critical theological appraisal of the Bible as a whole, and more attuned to what is at stake in identifying and applying such an interpretive norm.[68] Whether or not one set of focal images or one interpretive rule or one canon within the canon suffices for all interpretive challenges, nevertheless Hays is surely correct that some such norm is necessary to negotiate interpretive challenges responsibly. Such an interpretive rule is also applicable at the intratextual no less than the intracanonical level. In other words, when wrestling with tensions within texts no less than between texts, an important aspect of the interpretive process is to measure texts against one's normative interpretive

---

67. Ibid., 193–205.

68. See Irenaeus, *Adversus haereses* 1.10. See also Augustine's interpretive rule of love articulated in his *De doctrina christiana* 1.84–85, 95–96; 3.54, as well as the analogous "rule of moral-theological adjudication" elaborated by Cosgrove, *Appealing to Scripture*, 2–4, 154–80.

rule, which both derives from Scripture taken as a whole and encapsulates a coherent theological vision. At the intracanonical level, Hays himself appeals to the consistent New Testament perspective on the morality of violence to relativize Matthew and John's (apparent) anti-Judaism.[69] Done with care, what Hays does at the intracanonical level may also be done at the intratextual level.

READING MATTHEW 23 IN LIGHT OF THE SERMON ON THE MOUNT

As indicated earlier, one consideration in favor of accepting Matthew 23 as integral to the Gospel's fifth and final discourse relates to various correspondences between the final discourse (inclusive of chapter 23) and the first discourse, the so-called Sermon on the Mount. Boring notes the correspondence in length between the first and final discourses, provided Matthew 23 is accepted as part of the final discourse, but he also points to other thematic and literary correspondences: "Whereas the Sermon on the Mount begins with blessings, this speech begins with woes (5:1–12 = 23:13–33); both speeches involve a mountain on which Jesus sits to teach, with crowds and disciples as hearers (5:1; 7:29 = 23:1; 24:3); in the closing scene of each speech, false disciples say 'Lord, Lord' and are told 'I never knew you' (7:21–27 = 25:11)."[70] Hood surveys various other literary interconnections between various parts of Matthew's final discourse (inclusive of chapter 23) and the Sermon on the Mount. These include: the contrast between true and false teaching and practice; attention to aspects of Jewish law and religious devotion; the almost exclusive use of the term "hypocrite" within Matthew's first and final discourses; the presence of judgment parables at or near the respective conclusions of each discourse, in which the criterion for judgment is obedience to Jesus' teaching; the contrast between the wise and the foolish toward the end of each discourse, which overlaps with Boring's observation about those who cry out, "Lord, Lord"; and finally the inclusion of warnings against false prophets in both discourses.[71] On the basis of such

---

69. Hays, *Moral Vision*, 434: "Having been given a general mandate to love enemies and eschew violence, we hardly need a set of rules specifying that the prohibition of violence applies also to violence against Jews." Hays makes a comparable point when viewing anti-Judaic texts in Matthew and John through the lens of his focal image of the cross (431–33).

70. Boring, "Gospel of Matthew," 428. (The motif of Jesus sitting to teach on a mountain has been appealed to as evidence against seeing Matthew 23 as the beginning of Matthew's final discourse.)

71. Hood, "Matthew 23–25," 541.

literary links between the first and last of Matthew's discourses, Hood infers that the evangelist intended his audience to interpret the final discourse in light of the first.

If one narrows the focus to correspondences between Matthew 23 alone and the Sermon on the Mount, the quantum of literary and thematic resonances remains remarkable. The most obvious are the inverse parallels between the beatitudes at the beginning of the Sermon on the Mount and the catalog of woes that dominate Matthew 23.[72] For understandable reasons, the beatitudes of Matt 5:1–12, especially within the setting of the Sermon on the Mount, have received much scholarly attention. An illuminating study from a sociocultural perspective is that by K. C. Hanson, "How Honorable! How Shameful! A Cultural Analysis of Matthew's Makarisms and Reproaches." Attending to dimensions of the ancient Mediterranean sociocultural milieu dominated by honor and shame, Hanson's essay examines the relation between makarisms and woes, on one hand, and blessings and curses, on the other. His differentiations between blessings and makarisms and also between curses and woes are noteworthy, but his explication of makarisms and woes in sociocultural terms is especially significant. At heart, according to Hanson, a makarism expresses the public validation of some experience, behavior, or attitude as honorable and hence worthy of emulation.[73] By contrast, within a sociocultural context centered on honor and shame, woes or reproaches seek to undermine the status and social standing of another person or group. Only by successfully countering the challenge represented by another's reproach was it possible to avoid social humiliation, that is, loss of status and respect in the only estimation that mattered—the estimation of others.

Having argued that makarisms and woes are inversely related, one being the antithesis of the other, Hanson not only analyzes the form of Matthew's makarisms (5:3–10) and woes (23:13–36) but also comments on the compositional function of their respective placements within the Gospel.[74] Complementing his formal and structural analyses of these makarisms and woes, Hanson draws attention to multiple contrasts in content between them by means of a two-column chart:[75]

---

72. Note, too, parallels of various kinds between the opening subsection of Matthew 23 and the central section of the Sermon on the Mount concerned with practices of piety such as almsgiving, prayer, and fasting (6:1–18). See Davies and Allison, *Gospel according to Saint Matthew*, 3:266.

73. Hanson, "How Honorable!," 90.

74. Ibid., 99–103. (Hanson considers the ninth makarism of Matt 5:11–12 to have been added to an original list of eight or perhaps even seven.)

75. Ibid., 102. (Cf. Malina and Rohrbaugh, *Social-Science Commentary*, 330–31.)

206 The Vehement Jesus

Makarisms (Matt 5:3–12)	**Reproaches** (23:13–31)
honoring	shaming
third-person formulations	second-person formulations
addressed to disciples	addressed to opponents
opens public ministry	closes public ministry
"theirs is the kingdom of the heavens" (3, 10)	"you shut the kingdom of the heavens" (13)
"hunger and thirst for righteousness" (6)	"outwardly appear righteous" (28)
"merciful . . . receive mercy" (7)	"neglected mercy" (23)
"pure of heart" (8a)	"impure" (27)
"see God" (8b)	"swear by God's throne" (22)
"sons of God" (9)	"son of Gehenna" (15)
"so they persecuted the prophets" (12)	"sons of those who killed the prophets" (31)

Many of these inverse parallels in content are striking. Especially important (for my purposes), however, are Hanson's comments on the narrative placement of Matthew's makarisms and woes. Regarding the makarisms in Matt 5:3–10, he writes: "Other than the two summary statements (4:17, 23), the 'Sermon on the Mount' is the first of Jesus' public teaching in the Gospel; this places particular emphasis on this series of makarisms as the inauguration of Jesus' message. The makarisms are the opening of the sermon and therefore set the tone for the whole."[76] Moreover, according to Hanson, since makarisms are essentially attributions of honor, the makarisms that open the Sermon on the Mount at the beginning of Jesus' teaching mission should be understood as a "programmatic value statement."[77]

As for the narrative placement of the woes or honor-challenging reproaches in Matt 23:13–36, Hanson observes: "The placement of the reproaches by the evangelist is pivotal: they form the conclusion to the public ministry of Jesus. They are introduced with: 'Then Jesus said to the crowds and his disciples' (23:1). Following the series of reproaches, Jesus teaches only his disciples. . . . Thus the makarisms in Matthew 5 and reproaches in 23 form an inclusion on Jesus' public ministry."[78] In narrative terms, these are significant observations with invaluable interpretive implications. For Hanson, these are expressed in terms of honor and shame, antithetical appraisals of value that open and close the public mission of Jesus and thereby express both positive and negative values in light of divine reign. The ma-

76. Ibid., 100.
77. Ibid.
78. Ibid., 102.

karisms express and encourage "positive ideals of the kingdom," whereas the woes or withering reproaches look back upon opposition to Jesus by the scribes and Pharisees and effectively condemn it by holding it up to public ridicule.[79]

As illuminating as Hanson's study is, his investigation of Matthew's makarisms and reproaches seems to overlook one decisive point. Although he demonstrates that these makarisms and woes are antithetically related, with the makarisms expressing a "programmatic value statement," he apparently ignores the counter-cultural force of the specific content of Jesus' makarisms. Whether this is a consequence of an analytical mind-set intent on maximizing points of contact between biblical texts and their sociocultural context(s) is impossible to say, but Hanson's culturally oriented approach to Matthew's makarisms and reproaches majors on how both make sense within the cultural context of their day without drawing attention to the way in which Jesus' makarisms challenge central cultural values. In Hanson's abstract, one reads: "These forms [makarisms and reproaches] are part of the word-field and value system of honor and shame, the foundational Mediterranean values; they exemplify the agonistic nature of Mediterranean culture."[80] In other words, these *forms of speech* make best sense within a competitive cultural context characterized by verbal challenges intended to enhance one's own honor at the expense of others. This makes good contextual sense. On examination, however, the *content* of at least some of Jesus' makarisms (honor ascriptions) challenge social values of his day (no less than ours),[81] whereas his reproaches seem merely to buy into the competitive cultural conventions of his day, even if in content some are premised on values honored in his makarisms. Jesus made use of conventional forms of speech but also filled such wineskins with new wine—at least in his makarisms. For this reason, the hermeneutical value of Hanson's study goes beyond his own insightful inferences.

Formal, thematic, and linguistic resonances between Matthew's first and final discourses lead Hood to the conclusion that Matthew 23 should be interpreted in light of the Sermon on the Mount. For similar reasons,

---

79. Ibid., 103.

80. Ibid., 81. (See also his third conclusion on page 104.)

81. See Neyrey, *Honor and Shame*, 163–228; Malina and Rohrbaugh, *Social-Science Commentary*, 40–41. In this connection, see also the illuminating discussion of Matt 23:8–12 by Esler, "Intergroup Conflict," 45–50. This segment of Matthew 23, which immediately precedes the condemnatory woes against scribes and Pharisees in 23:13–36, most evidently addresses Matthew's own Messiah-movement contemporaries and culminates in a twofold pronouncement (23:12) that articulates what Esler describes as "a radical rejection of prevailing modes of conduct in the honor and shame culture that was pervasive in the ancient Mediterranean" (50).

albeit more deeply grounded in contextual sociocultural analysis, Hanson adjudges the makarisms of Matthew 5 to express a "programmatic value statement." As such, they articulate a programmatic moral vision not only for the Sermon on the Mount but for the Gospel as a whole. On narrative grounds alone, it may be one-sided to argue that Matthew 23 should be interpreted in light of the Sermon on the Mount, as if reading narrative texts were solely a unidirectional exercise. If theological and moral vision is taken into account, however, Hood's interpretive suggestion has much to commend it because the rhetoric of rage in Matthew 23 is discrepant in both content and tone from the theological and moral vision of Jesus expressed in the Sermon on the Mount. In short, intratextual tension provokes interpretive grappling.

"A foolish consistency is the hobgoblin of little minds, adored by little statesmen and philosophers and divines."[82] In view of this dictum penned by Ralph Waldo Emerson, the crucial question regarding Matthew's portrait of Jesus is whether or not the expectation of moral consistency inherent in my discomfiture with Matthew 23 in light of the Sermon on the Mount is foolish. In this connection, one must be wary of appraising a text from antiquity in accordance with anachronistic post-Enlightenment criteria.[83] In this case, however, it is Matthew's Gospel itself that raises the expectation of moral coherence on the part of Jesus.

Within the Gospel according to Matthew, one of the most caustic and cutting insults is to label an opponent a "hypocrite." Most of Jesus' castigations of scribes and Pharisees in Matthew 23 are punctuated by this insulting labeling (23:13, 15, 23, 25, 27, 29). In Jesus' or Matthew's day, hypocrisy may have meant more than consistency between what one said and what one did, between appearance and reality, but it did not mean less than that fundamental level of coherence.[84] Thus, the use of this label signals that the criterion of moral coherence is intrinsic to the Gospel and indeed to Matthew's description of the moral shape of Jesus' mission and message. In short, interpretive appraisal of Matthew's presentation of Jesus according to the criterion of moral coherence is neither anachronistic nor inapposite.

---

82. Emerson, "Self-Reliance." For commentary on this remark, see Joseph, *Nonviolent Messiah*, 84–85. In context, according to Joseph, Emerson equates "foolish consistency" with unreflective conformity to social convention.

83. I am grateful to Thorwald Lorenzen for reminding me of this. For a similar caution, see Allison, *Resurrecting Jesus*, 49.

84. On different nuances regarding the meaning of "hypocrisy" in Matthew's Gospel, see Garland, *Intention of Matthew 23*, 91–123, and Tuckett, "Matthew and Hypocrisy." See also Weinfeld, "Charge of Hypocrisy," who argues that most accusations of hypocrisy in Matthew 23 emerge from Jewish tradition.

Sadly, however, the use by Matthew's Jesus of this label (among others) against opponents undermines the moral consistency on which the label itself is premised.

In their retrospect on Matthew's Gospel, Davies and Allison surmise that alongside the "rabbinic" influence on Matthew—that is, his faithful preservation of sayings of Jesus—one also detects the influence of the Hellenistic tradition that emphasized congruity between what a teacher taught and how a teacher lived. Socrates was the great exemplar, but Philo affirmed the same of Moses, as did Matthew of Jesus.[85] Within the same section on genre and moral instruction, they advance the view that one reason for the biographical features of Matthew's Gospel is the evangelist's conviction that Jesus was the moral model par excellence. "This," they say, "is why there is in our Gospel a multitude of obvious connexions between Jesus' words and his deeds."[86] Of the many examples they cite of such congruity, most specific teachings "fulfilled" by Jesus later in the narrative are from the Sermon on the Mount, including no fewer than three from the Beatitudes (meekness, mercifulness, and enduring persecution for the sake of righteousness). Complementing their view that such positive correlations between Jesus' words and deeds illustrate a concern to present Jesus as moral exemplar, Davies and Allison appeal to Matthew's use of the language of "righteousness" and "hypocrisy." Whereas the Pharisees are characterized as hypocrites because of a "disjunction between word and deed" and hence serve as negative moral examples, "Matthew's Jesus ... is the antithesis of all this."[87]

Would that this were always so! Davies and Allison are correct regarding Matthew's concern to compose congruence between Jesus' words and deeds, but this is only the positive part of the picture. There is a darker side, as Allison himself recognizes and addresses in his later study, "Deconstructing Matthew," which opens with these words: "The Gospel of Matthew often seems to speak against itself. Its Jesus can say one thing and then do another, as when he forbids demeaning another as a 'fool' (5:22) and then upbraids the scribes and Pharisees as 'fools' (23:17)."[88] In this sagacious study, Allison identifies various tensions within Matthew's Gospel and then offers a fivefold typology, with some appraisal, of ways in which such tensions have been addressed in the history of interpretation. Addressing a range of Matthean inconcinnities, he nevertheless recognizes that "those between

---

85. Davies and Allison, *Gospel according to Saint Matthew*, 3:710–11.

86. Ibid., 3:714–15.

87. Ibid., 3:716–17.

88. Allison, *Studies in Matthew*, 237–49. (Within this study Allison acknowledges that, when writing his ICC Commentary on Matthew, he sought maximum coherence within the Gospel.)

word and deed are especially challenging because Matthew . . . is much concerned to correlate Jesus' actions with his imperatives. . . . Matters seem all the worse because, for the evangelist, hypocrisy, the disjunction between speech and behavior, is the sin Jesus denounces most."[89]

If I understand Allison correctly, he considers the intratextual tension between Jesus' moral imperatives in the Sermon on the Mount and his invective in Matthew 23 as best addressed by accepting that Matthew, shaped as he was by Jewish tradition, depicted Jesus occasionally acting contrary to his teaching in response to competing obligations. Occasional inconsistencies between teaching and behavior reflect the complex exigencies of human life in which competing moral obligations must be prioritized rather than harmonized, with the result that some such ethical imperatives are sometimes broken but not thereby annulled. In other words, the cruciality of the content of Jesus' criticisms against religious opponents legitimizes the anger and invective in Matthew 23, even though both contradict his own moral instruction. Put succinctly, wrath is wrong except when it is righteous.[90] Allison does not necessarily embrace this interpretive resolution, but he thinks Matthew may have held some such view.

I see no reason to demur from Allison's historically oriented apology for Matthew, which finds coherence within (apparent) contradiction on context-sensitive grounds. Nevertheless, were it possible to summon up Matthew's ghost and put present-day concerns to him, as Allison himself conjectures on occasion, is it imaginable that Matthew would consider this defense sufficient in light of the reception history of his witness to Jesus? As impossible as this question is to answer, so also is our capacity to read Matthew's Gospel as if its checkered history of reception had not occurred. As a result, although it is possible to critique aspects of Matthew's presentation of Jesus on the basis of criteria external to his moral vision, perhaps some deference is shown to Matthew by employing a method of intratextual critique—in short, by pitting Matthew's Jesus against Matthew's Jesus.

As happens from time to time, one finds that someone else has trumped one's hand before it has been played. Intratextual as well as intrabiblical critique is part and parcel of how I wrestle with Matthew's violent eschatology in *A Peaceable Hope*,[91] and it was my intended means for coming to grips with Jesus' rhetoric of rage in Matthew 23. In *The Power of Parable*, however, John Dominic Crossan has pipped me to the post, critiquing the "rhetorical violence" of Matthew's Jesus in light of the so-called antitheses of Matthew

---

89. Allison, *Studies in Matthew*, 240–41.
90. Ibid., 246–48.
91. See Neville, *A Peaceable Hope*, 17–44.

5.[92] Crossan is rather more confident than I about attributing the Gospel's "rhetorical violence" solely to Matthew rather than (partly) to Jesus, but his basic interpretive maneuver is to probe and indeed to magnify the discrepancy between Jesus' teaching in part of the Sermon on the Mount and his verbal violence in Matthew 23. There is much to learn from Crossan, even if he effectively rescues Jesus by drowning Matthew.

Crossan's discussion of rhetorical violence in Matthew's Gospel begins with the question of whether the evident violence directed against Jesus within Matthew's Gospel is counterbalanced by violence on Jesus' part. Prima facie, Crossan's question seems to demand a negative response until he raises the prospect of how violence is defined. "Are there various types, dimensions, and modes of violence?" he asks, and in answer to this question he proposes that human violence may proceed from ideological through rhetorical to physical violence.[93] To think less of others than one thinks of oneself leads to speaking of others in dehumanizing ways, which leads in turn to acting violently and sometimes even lethally against such persons. Although not an immutable sociological law, Crossan's proposal regarding the escalation of violence matches historical experience. And it leads Crossan to put his question about violence on the part of Matthew's Jesus more sharply: "Is there ideologically grounded rhetorical violence *by* Jesus in Matthew's parable gospel?"[94]

Having rephrased his question regarding violence on the part of Jesus in Matthew's Gospel, Crossan's answer is twofold and apparently paradoxical: on one hand, Jesus is not rhetorically violent, but, on the other hand, he most certainly is.[95] Focusing initially on the Sermon on the Mount, especially the first and last of the so-called "antitheses," Crossan identifies decisive texts in which Jesus' instructions prohibit verbal vitriol directed against others. In the first "antithesis," Jesus intensifies the prohibition against murder by warning against both anger and demeaning insults: "You have heard that it was said to people of old, 'Do not murder. Whoever murders will be subject to judgment.' But I say to you that everyone who is wrathful against his brother will be subject to judgment; whoever utters an insult against his brother will be subject to the Sanhedrin; whoever says 'Fool' will be subjected to the Gehenna of fire" (Matt 5:21–22).

---

92. Crossan, *Power of Parable*, 177–95. "Rhetorical Violence" is Crossan's title for his chapter on Matthew's Gospel.

93. Ibid., 181.

94. Ibid., 182 (emphasis original). By "parable gospel," Crossan designates the four biblical Gospels as complex mixtures of historical reminiscence and theological interpretation in narrative form.

95. Ibid., 182–87.

Crossan observes that here, "anger, insult, and name-calling are solemnly condemned with escalating divine judgments."[96] This probably overstates things, but there is an escalation from (a) judgment to (b) official sanction at the highest human level to (c) what would seem to be divine condemnation to hell. Crossan might also have pointed out that in this threefold escalation, the third and most severely sanctioned speech event is nonrestrictive, like the ancient prohibition against murder. Lest one seek to find wriggle room within Jesus' intensification of this ancient prohibition by pointing to the restriction, in the case of anger and of insult, when directed against family members or kin, the harshest judgment is reserved for the nonrestrictive warning against denigrating another—any other—as a fool.

As for the sixth and final "antithesis," in which Jesus extends the command to love so as to incorporate both enemies and prayer for persecutors, Crossan brings out the important point that the rationale for Jesus' expansive love command derives from an expansive conception of the character of God, whose "perfection" consists in providing for all. Hence, for Crossan, "Jesus solemnly forbids any *rhetorical* violence in the opening frame of those six moral escalations and any *ideological* violence in their closing frame."[97] In other words, Jesus' opening "antithesis" precludes the rhetoric of rage or insult, and his final "antithesis" provides the rationale for prohibiting such verbal vehemence by undermining ideological chauvinism on theological grounds.

For Crossan, however, this is only one part of the picture, and glimpses of a darker part of the picture appear within the Sermon on the Mount immediately after the "antitheses" of Matthew 5. Although his primary evidence for the presence of rhetorical violence in Matthew's Gospel occurs in chapter 23, nevertheless Crossan perceives within the threefold use of the term "hypocrites" in Jesus' teaching on almsgiving, prayer, and fasting in Matt 6:1–18 seeds that later flower into the stinging invective of Matthew 23. He then lists the litany of libels on the lips of Jesus in Matt 23:13–36. On six occasions, Jesus insults scribes and Pharisees as "hypocrites" (23:13, 15, 23, 25, 27, 29). On five occasions, he castigates their blindness (23:16, 17, 19, 24, 26). In Matt 23:17, he goes so far as to address them as μωροὶ καὶ τυφλοί (*mōroi kai tuphloi*), a phrase often translated as "blind fools" but which might be more accurately rendered as "morons and blind bumblers!" The first of these insults (μωρέ, *mōre*) is precisely that affirmed by Jesus to put one at risk of condemnation to hell (5:22), yet within Matthew's Gospel he is the only person to use it against opponents. Within the invective of

---

96. Ibid., 184.
97. Ibid., 185.

Matthew 23, scribes and Pharisees are also characterized as sons of Gehenna (23:15), as being like whitewashed tombs (23:27), as sons of murderers of the prophets (23:31), and as the spawn of serpents destined for hell (23:33). In short, in stark contrast to both the spirit and even the letter of Matt 5:21–22, the verbal vitriol of Matthew 23 is wrathful, redundantly insulting, and even involves using the F word ("Fool" or "moron"). Little wonder, then, that Crossan highlights the "glaring discrepancy" between the Jesus of Matthew 5 and the Jesus of Matthew 23: "Jesus opens by absolutely forbidding ideologically based rhetorical violence, but closes by doing himself precisely what he has earlier forbidden."[98]

Crossan continues by constructing an argument to demonstrate that the "glaring discrepancy" between the Jesus of Matthew 5 and the Jesus of Matthew 23 is neither isolated nor random but endemic to this Gospel. To this end, he presents a series of case studies to show that Matthew invariably depicts Jesus as more vehement than the sources from which he drew (Mark and Q). Time and again, he shows that where Matthew can be seen to have found vehement or threatening rhetoric in his sources, he invariably adopts it and often escalates it, sometimes exponentially. A case in point is Matthew's adoption (from one occurrence in Q) of the phrase, "There (in the outer darkness), there will be wailing and the grinding of teeth" (Matt 8:11–12; Luke 13:28–29), which Matthew then employs a further five times in parables that feature eschatological vengeance (13:42, 50; 22:13; 24:51; 25:30).[99] Even apart from Crossan's source-critical convictions, Matthew's Gospel undoubtedly presents a more verbally vehement Jesus than his synoptic counterparts. Beyond this, however, Crossan ties the rhetorical violence of Matthew's Jesus to the way in which Matthew intensifies within his passion narrative Jewish culpability for the death of Jesus, most notoriously when he recounts the Jewish people as a whole crying out to Pilate, "His blood upon us and upon our children" (27:24–25).

Ultimately, for Crossan, something must yield. There is no satisfactory harmonization of the "glaring discrepancy" between Matthew's two contrasting profiles of Jesus. No less than other New Testament scholars, he appreciates that the rhetorical violence of Matthew's Jesus reflects Matthew's own post-temple, *intra-Jewish* conflict with formative Pharisaic Judaism. Nevertheless, in light of the intratextual tension he discerns within Matthew's Gospel, which in his view exposes Jesus himself to the charge of hypocrisy, Crossan resolves things this way: "The Jesus of Matthew is regularly and rhetorically violent, but that is not Jesus himself; it is Matthew who

98. Ibid., 186–87.
99. Ibid., 187–93.

is speaking."[100] Not Jesus himself but his interpreter Matthew is responsible for Jesus' rhetoric of rage.

Crossan writes winsomely as well as provocatively, but on reflection one wonders whether his resolution to the problem of rhetorical violence in Matthew's Gospel is not too tidy. Even apart from the question of whether his characterization of the Gospels as *essentially* parabolic is sustainable, there is the further matter of Crossan's confidence about attributing *all* the verbal vehemence in Matthew's Gospel to the evangelist, even though he acknowledges the presence of some rhetorical violence in Matthew's sources, most notably within Q, which for Crossan is both a gospel (not merely a sayings source) and earlier than Mark. In other words, Matthew's vehement Jesus is not his own creation but rather his intensification of a feature already present in his sources. It is striking that in Crossan's section on this particular point, he neglects to mention that, although not as extensive as the catalog of woes in Matthew 23, there are partial parallels in Luke 11:37–52, which most proponents of the two-document hypothesis would attribute to Q. If the vehement Jesus is present already in Q, how can Crossan so confidently demarcate between Jesus and Matthew on this point?[101]

Although I demur from Crossan's scapegoating of Matthew to preserve a congenial portrait of Jesus, I concur that Matthew's discrepant profiles of Jesus provoke an interpretive choice. Matthew undoubtedly enhanced the vehemence of Jesus, but the "glaring discrepancy" between the Jesus of Matthew 5 and the Jesus of Matthew 23 calls for theological-moral-interpretive discernment. With those who discern a compelling theological-moral vision in the programmatic teaching of Jesus in Matthew 5, I read the caustic castigations of Jesus by its interpretive light.[102] In other words, the vehement Jesus of Matthew 23 is in certain respects "pre-restrained" by the rigorous but also life-enhancing Jesus of Matthew 5.

---

100. Ibid., 195.

101. This is a question Crossan does not address here, but the answer is probably to be found in his chronological stratification of the Jesus tradition as a whole and also of Q, according to which an apocalyptic layer in Q is secondary to a sapiential layer. See Crossan, *Historical Jesus*, xxvii–xxxiv (prologue) and 427–50 (appendix 1); Crossan, *Birth of Christianity*, 91–149; 237–344.

102. See Neville, *A Peaceable Hope*, 254, where I give reasons for describing the moral vision of Jesus in Matthew 5 as a "treasure text." See also Neville, "Moral Vision of Jesus in Matthew 5."

CONCLUDING COMMENTS

Only with hesitancy do I conclude this chapter, knowing full well that so much more could and should be said. Cognizant, too, that but a few perspectives pertaining to the topic of this chapter have been given their due, I must nevertheless rest content to reiterate distinctive features of this discussion, which emerge from seeking to understand Matthew's Gospel not only in its historical, sociocultural, and religious context but also in light of its negative history of effects. Matthew is not responsible for all that has been done in the name of the vehement Jesus he portrayed. In light of the litany of anti-Jewish horrors that comprise part of the reception history of Matthew's Gospel, however, it is necessary to think more deeply on the reality that its description of Jesus' rhetoric of rage not only grates on post-Shoah sensitivities but also militates against clear and compelling moral imperatives ascribed to Jesus within the selfsame narrative—and in a programmatic way.

In *Jews and Anti-Judaism in the New Testament*, Terence Donaldson discusses the various perspectives of Matthew, Luke, John, and Paul according to their respective locations on three analytical axes: first, the self-understanding or self-definition of each writer in relation to first-century Judaism, as that may be discerned from their writings; second, the social location of these authors and their intended audiences relative to their Israelite contemporaries or, more simply, the degree of closeness or distance from Judaism; and third, the rhetorical character of these respective texts in relation to first-century Jewish contemporaries.[103] With regard to each of these somewhat overlapping axes, Donaldson demonstrates that to determine where to place Matthew's Gospel is neither a simple nor a straightforward exercise. Although Donaldson does not himself map Matthew against his three analytical axes, it is probably incumbent on me to do so, if only to be transparent about my (current) interpretive presumptions.

With respect to the first axis, Matthew's self-definition relative to his Israelite heritage, I consider Matthew to be so deeply indebted to Israelite biblical tradition as to make it difficult to decide whether to describe him as a Jewish Christian or a Christian Jew. Either way, his convictions regarding Jesus as the Jewish Messiah put him at odds with Jews who did not share such convictions. As a result, Matthew probably saw himself and those for whom he wrote as the legitimate heirs of Israel's religious heritage, over against representatives of what we now describe as formative Judaism in the aftermath of the Roman destruction of the temple in Jerusalem.[104] In other

---

103. Donaldson, *Jews and Anti-Judaism*, 28–29.

104. This assessment probably applies even if Matthew's Gospel is dated to before the destruction of Jerusalem in 70 CE, although I consider Matthew's contentiousness

words, Matthew saw himself and those for whom he wrote in competition with other representatives of his own Israelite heritage—rabbis, scribes, and Pharisees associated with "their synagogues" (4:23; 9:35; 10:17; 12:9; 13:54; cf. 7:29; 13:52; 23:1–36)—yet from a vantage point outside (non-Christian) Jewish assemblies. The hostility and hurt reflected in Matthew's invective suggest that a rupture has already occurred, without concession on either side that the other's leaders are legitimate preservers and transmitters of Israel's religious traditions. In religious terms, Matthew's self-definition is "Jewish"; in sociological terms, however, his stance is at least one step removed from Jews of his day, as is evident from distinctive features of his post-resurrection account (28:11–15).

As for the social location of Matthew's Gospel, it is impossible to speak definitively about its geographical place of origin. Syrian Antioch seems a reasonable inference from the available evidence, but such evidence is slim and inconclusive. Although I find it difficult to envisage Matthew and those for whom he wrote as inhabiting a recognized niche within the confines of post-70 CE formative Judaism, Matthean Christianity was nevertheless self-consciously Jewish (obedient to Torah, *as interpreted by Jesus Messiah*) and still considered itself the legitimate inheritor and interpreter of Israel's religious heritage. To a non-Jewish outsider, the Matthean ἐκκλησία (*ekklēsia* [16:18; 18:17]) might have seemed indistinguishable from the nearby synagogue, but it is difficult to envisage members of either assembly being welcome at the other—except perhaps as a result of desertion or exclusion from the other.[105] Non-Jewish members were apparently welcome in the Matthean *ekklēsia*, provided they were willing to adopt a way of life in line with the Torah *as interpreted by Jesus Messiah*.

Regarding the rhetorical function of Matthew's apparently anti-Judaic texts, Donaldson surveys several approaches.[106] One is to envisage Matthew as principally concerned to vilify Jewish people of his day, either as a whole or with a particular focus on Jewish leaders. Another is to interpret apparently anti-Judaic texts as intended for Matthew's in-group, with a view to "reinforcing a sense of group identity and solidarity among the members."[107] A variation on this second approach is to differentiate between Matthew's characterizations of Jewish leaders and other Israelites, the purpose of which

---

toward scribes and Pharisees in particular to indicate a later date when such a pairing might reasonably be expected to have been at the forefront of reconfiguring Israelite religious traditions from being temple centered to being (even more) Torah oriented.

105. Crucial for the question of the relation between Jewish synagogue and Matthean *ekklēsia* is that in Matt 16:18 Jesus speaks of constructing "*my* assembly."

106. Donaldson, *Jews and Anti-Judaism*, 52–53.

107. Ibid., 52. (Broadly speaking, this is the position of Johnson, outlined above.)

is understood to have been to encourage the latter to join the Christian community as interpreted by Matthew. At the other end of this spectrum of approaches is the view that invective of the kind one finds in Matthew 23 is primarily directed inward to warn disciples of Jesus against adopting attitudes and behaviors associated with scribes and Pharisees. Importantly, none of the approaches surveyed by Donaldson envisages Matthew's primary purpose as being to provide a historically accurate record of Jesus' stance toward fellow Israelites, especially Jewish leaders. Rather, the rhetoric of rage attributed to Jesus reflects Matthew's own life-setting and concerns.

I am not entirely sure where to place Matthew on any of Donaldson's three overlapping analytical axes, but I accept that Matthew 23 reflects the Gospel writer's sociocultural context and concerns. Matthew 23 does not provide a clear window onto Jesus but rather reconfigures Jesus to address a later life-setting characterized by conflict between *ekklēsia* and synagogue, both of which claimed to be legitimate guardians and faithful interpreters of Israel's religious traditions.

Although the apparently anti-Judaic invective of Matthew 23 is mitigated to some degree by interpreting this passage in historical and sociocultural perspective, there is no escaping the moral seriousness of the picture of Jesus painted by this passage. As in other contemporaneous texts, Matthew's Gospel itself testifies to an awareness of the damaging effect of verbal abuse. Since this is a point of deep dissonance between Jesus' diatribe in Matthew 23 and his moral teaching in the Sermon on the Mount, interpretive appraisal of Jesus' rhetoric of rage in light of his own moral vision displayed in Matthew's primary and programmatic discourse seems both reasonable and responsible. Whether or not Matthew himself intended his fifth and final discourse to be interpreted in light of his first discourse, various correspondences between his first and final discourses facilitate such a moral-interpretive appraisal.[108] In view of seemingly intractable intratextual tensions *within* Matthew's Gospel, I interpret the vehement Jesus of Matthew 23 in light of the visionary Jesus of Matthew's Sermon on the Mount, especially the challenging beatitudes and rigorous "antitheses" of Matthew 5, which together compose a compelling, if counterintuitive, theological-moral vision of life in anticipation of God's heavenly reign.

---

108. Cf. Nolland, "Gospel of Matthew and Anti-Semitism," 163: "the Matthew who gives us chap. 23 also gives us the clearest window onto Jesus' vision of love of enemies, which is clearly something Matthew has reflected deeply on, not simply reproduced traditions about. He is committed to a fundamental openness to the hostile other." I am not so confident about the inference Nolland makes about Matthew's "fundamental openness to the hostile other," but his preceding insight is decisive.

9

Teleological Terror

By "TELEOLOGICAL TERROR" I mean the threat of what John J. Collins has termed "eschatological vengeance."[1] In the biblical tradition, the prospect of future divine recompense features in the later prophetic and apocalyptic literature of the Second Temple period and is also prevalent in various New Testament writings, including the Gospels. Divine judgment conceived in solely retributive terms is terrifying for two reasons: first, it envisages a form of judgment that severs persons irredeemably from the source of life, God the creator; and second, it is generally imagined as involving incessant torment of one kind or another. There are also two reasons why the prospect of such terror is teleological: first, such retributive vengeance is foreseen to occur at the end or termination (τέλος, *telos*) of the present age; and second, it is often invoked for ethical effect and is thus intended to serve as teleological moral motivation.

In this chapter I revisit the central concern of *A Peaceable Hope*, in which I wrestle with theological and moral dimensions of eschatological vengeance in the canonical Gospels, Acts, and Revelation. Although present to some degree in all four biblical Gospels, teleological terror in the remembered teaching of Jesus is largely restricted to the Gospels according to Matthew and Luke. Among the four Gospels, the threat of eschatological vengeance for the purpose of encouraging good and proper behavior in the present is especially prominent in Matthew's Gospel.

Although the threat of eschatological vengeance is usually invoked to provoke moral reappraisal and behavioral change, it is itself morally ambivalent, even perturbing. Even if the prospect of divine retribution in the

1. Collins, *Does the Bible Justify Violence?* 21–27.

long run enables some to eschew vengeance here and now, it may also have the opposite effect. Furthermore, the mind-set inculcated by the prospect of eschatological vengeance, whether for others or for oneself, is probably not the healthiest in either psychological or moral terms. The expectation that God will ultimately right wrongs by means of overwhelming retributive violence also does damage to God's reputation—in the sense of people's image of God. And finally, if God's final resort is to vengeance, is that not, for people of faith, an ultimate validation of violence?

I have come to regard the expectation of teleological terror as theologically and morally corrosive, but that should not be taken to mean that the theological concept of divine judgment is no longer necessary or meaningful. To equate judgment with retributive justice is historically comprehensible but biblically and theologically problematic. In biblical perspective, divine judgment cannot be divorced from God's redemptive work. As a result, divine judgment has more to do with overturning the way things are than with retribution for the wrongs that have led to the way things are; it is more about righting than requiting wrongs. There may well be a retributive dimension to divine judgment—but hopefully within the larger context of God's reclamation, restoration, and transformation of all that is.

TELEOLOGICAL TERROR IN MATTHEAN PERSPECTIVE

No sooner has Matthew's story of Jesus begun than he narrates an episode of indiscriminate slaughter. Troubled at the prospect of the birth of a potential rival as "king of the Jews," Herod (known to history as Herod the Great) orders the slaughter of all the boys of Bethlehem two years old and under. This, according to Matthew, fulfilled what had been uttered by the prophet Jeremiah:

> A voice in Rama was heard,
>> much weeping and mourning;
> Rachel weeping for her children,
>> and not willing to be consoled because they no longer are. (Matt 2:18)

This violent episode provoked by the birth of Jesus reflects the historical realities of the day, even if the story itself is more theological commentary than historical reminiscence.[2] In narrative terms, it sets the tone for all that follows. Matthew makes a point of depicting Jesus as a gentle and even

---

2. On Matthew's reference to Rachel's lament as a comforting "metaleptic trope," see Hays, *Reading Backwards*, 41–43.

humble Messiah,³ but he also describes the mission of Jesus as provoking hostile responses, which in turn must be judged. God's saving initiative in Jesus—thereby fulfilling the promise of *Immanu-el* (1:21-23)—is peaceful, but the hostility and indeed violence provoked by the mission of Jesus will ultimately be recompensed. Echoing the bitter weeping of Rachel for her erased children, Matthew's record of the teaching of Jesus makes much of the bitter weeping awaiting all those either hostile to God's initiative in Jesus or ultimately judged by God to be unfaithful, unrighteous, or evil.

Before launching into his account of the teaching and healing ministry of Jesus, Matthew takes time to summarize the mission and message of his forerunner, John the Immerser. For Matthew, John's role is to prepare the way of the Lord by means of baptism, presumably understood as cleansing for sins confessed (3:1-6). Yet prior to his description of the baptism of Jesus by John (3:13-17), he devotes even more space to the vehement teaching of John focused on invective against Pharisees and Sadducees and on future fire (3:7-12). Moreover, what he predicts about his more powerful successor indicates that the one to come will not only echo his own warnings of judgment but will also execute such judgment.

Although Matthew does not present Jesus as executing judgment in his historical ministry, nevertheless he does envisage that Jesus will ultimately exact vengeance on the recalcitrant. This is prepared for in two main ways: first, by recording Jesus' teaching as echoing John's in various respects; and second, by postponing what John affirms about the judging role of Jesus to his future eschatological *parousia*. In Matthew's Gospel, there are various points of contact between the message of John and the teaching of Jesus. The most important of these is that Matthew's summary of the message of Jesus (4:17) is *identical* with his summary of the proclamation of John (3:2). The teaching of Jesus also echoes John's on various specific points. Like John, Jesus castigates Jewish religious leaders as the "offspring of vipers" (3:7; 12:34; 23:33). Jesus never reiterates John's use of the phrase, "the coming wrath" (3:7), but he certainly echoes John's warning about the fiery fate of fruitless trees (3:10; 7:19!) and the fiery destiny for whatever is discarded after harvest (3:12; 13:37-43). The prominent motif of "fire" in what Matthew records of John's teaching is, if anything, even more prominent and menacing in the teaching of Jesus (5:22; 7:19; 13:40, 42, 50; 18:8, 9; 25:41). For both John and Jesus, according to Matthew, the fire of divine punishment is incessant ("unquenchable" for John, "eternal" for Jesus). Whereas John thought that the one coming after him would cleanse by fire, however, Jesus is presented as envisaging a postponement of fiery retribution until

---

3. See Theissen, *Gospel Writing*, 59-63.

the end of the age, when the angels of the Son of humanity will separate the righteous from the unrighteous and consign the latter to hellfire. This postponement notwithstanding, it is nevertheless clear that for Matthew there is substantial continuity not only between Jesus and prophetic figures of old but also between Jesus and John, especially in relation to eschatological judgment.

Eschatological judgment is a prominent theme in Matthew's presentation of Jesus' teaching. The motif of the "day" of judgment first appears toward the conclusion of the Sermon on the Mount, where Jesus warns that failure to do the will of God will result in exclusion from God's heavenly kingdom (7:21–23). This is reinforced by the comparison between the fate of houses built either on rock or sand when tested by floods and storms (7:24–27). This is the note on which the Sermon on the Mount ends—a note reinforced and intensified in later discourses, especially Matthew 13 and 23–25.

At various points, Jesus warns of eschatological judgment for spurning him, his message, or that of his messengers. In Matt 10:12 he sends out the Twelve with a word of peace on their lips. Although he counsels retreat if his apostles are not welcomed, he also utters the solemn warning that towns inhospitable to the Twelve will face a worse fate on the "day of Judgment" than the land of Sodom and Gomorrah (10:11–15). Similar warnings are directed at the unresponsive towns of Chorazin, Bethsaida, and Capernaum. Things will be worse for the inhabitants of these towns on the "day of Judgment" than for those dwelling in Tyre, Sidon, and indeed Sodom (11:20–24). Much the same is said of this generation for failing to respond appropriately to Jesus (12:38–42; cf. 23:29–36), and in Matt 12:36–37 Jesus teaches that the "day of Judgment" is a time of appraisal for words no less than for deeds.

Such warnings of accountability on the eschatological day of Judgment may be disconcerting, especially when the judgment to be meted out is envisaged as more severe than what Sodom and Gomorrah experienced. Even so, the primary function of such warnings is to underscore the gravity of failing to respond positively to the mission and message of Jesus and his emissaries. On the assumption that Jesus is *Immanu-el*, God with us, to reject Jesus is a serious choice with grave, indeed, incalculable ramifications.

The prospect of universal eschatological judgment is not, in itself, odious, but the way in which Matthew describes the teaching of Jesus regarding the "day of Judgment" is theologically and morally disturbing. This is because he so often presents Jesus as anticipating eschatological judgment in excessively severe and exclusively retributive terms. Admittedly, this is not the whole picture, but in broad Matthean perspective the judgment about which Jesus warns is eschatological divine vengeance—teleological terror. This is best illustrated with reference to imagery associated with eschatological judgment and parables of Jesus relating to that "day."

Figurative Language Associated with Eschatological Judgment

In the second episode after the conclusion to the Sermon on the Mount, a centurion notifies Jesus of his paralyzed servant lying at home, "terribly tormented" (δεινῶς βασανιζόμενος, *deinōs basanizomenos* [8:6]). In the exchange that follows, Jesus is astounded by the centurion's level of trust and warns fellow Israelites that although many will come from east and west to sit at the messianic banquet with the patriarchs of Israel in the kingdom of the heavens, the children of that kingdom will be cast into the outer darkness, where there will be wailing and teeth-grinding (8:10–12). In this passage, Jesus forewarns fellow Israelites not only of possible exclusion from the heavenly kingdom to which they naturally belong but also of the kind of torment that had moved him to offer healing to the centurion's servant. This might seem a far-fetched inference from this passage alone, but the image of outer darkness as a site of wailing and teeth-grinding recurs in Matthew's Gospel in ways that reinforce its association with divine retributive violence.

Among the biblical Gospels, the phrase, "wailing and teeth-grinding," occurs outside of Matthew's Gospel once only in Luke's parallel to Matt 8:11–12. In Luke 13:22–30 Jesus responds to a question about whether salvation is restricted to a few by indicating that many will find themselves outside the reign of God, wailing and grinding their teeth at the sight of the patriarchs and prophets of Israel inside God's kingdom. The passage concludes with a solemn saying of reversal: "And behold, there are last ones who will be first; there are first ones who will be last" (13:30). In context, therefore, the wailing and teeth-grinding of those who find themselves shut out of God's kingdom betokens their chagrin. No doubt the phrase hints at punishment, but that is not its primary connotation.

Things are otherwise in Matthew's deployment of the phrase. First, "wailing" recalls Rachel's bitter weeping for her deceased children (2:18, citing Jer 31:15) at the culmination of Matthew's initial story of indiscriminate violence. This association between the experience of overwhelming violence and the response of inconsolable weeping reverberates through Matthew's later uses of this term. As it happens, he makes use of the clause, "There, there will be wailing and teeth-grinding," five further times in a series of (predominantly eschatological) parables (13:42, 50; 22:13; 24:51; 25:30). Moreover, most occurrences of this clause relate either to exclusion (outer darkness) or to torment (fire) as the mode of retribution. The one exception is the conclusion to the eschatological parable of the Waiting Slave, who is diced in two and finds his dismembered self with the hypocrites, a place of wailing and teeth-grinding no less than outer darkness or fire (24:48–51). So, not only does the phrase, "wailing and teeth-grinding," occur with relative frequency throughout Matthew's Gospel but it is also invariably associated with retributive judgment. As Blaine Charette observes, "Whatever the origin or tradition history of the declaration, it is quite clear that in Matthew's Gospel it fulfils an important function as a solemn refrain underscoring the distress experienced by the cursed in the place of future punishment."[4] Such imagery alone says much about Matthew's mind-set.

The impression formed by the repetition of the imagery of "wailing and teeth-grinding" on the part of those foreseen to be either banished from the divine presence or consigned to pyro-torment is further reinforced by a series of eschatological parables to which such imagery provides the grisly punch line. There are four such parables, the final two of which lead up to and prepare for the scenario of final judgment at the conclusion of Matthew's eschatological discourse. These are the twin parables of the Tares and Dragnet in Matthew's parable discourse (chapter 13) and the parables of the Waiting Slave and the Talents in Matthew's eschatological discourse (chapters 23–25).[5]

The collection of parables in Matthew 13:1–53 composes the third of five discourses of Jesus in the Gospel. If the final comparison in 13:52 between a scribe trained in accordance with the reign of the heavens and a householder who brings both new and old treasures from the storehouse is discounted as a parable, there are seven separate parables of God's heavenly reign within this discourse, along with two explanations for speaking in parables (13:10–17, 34–35). Five of the parables (Mustard Seed, Leaven, Treasure, Pearl, and Net) are brief comparisons that offer glimmers of insight into God's heavenly reign, although the culminating parable of the Net recapitulates the parable of the Tares using different imagery and thereby reinforces its essential impact. The first two parables of the Sower and the Tares are the most developed analogies, and both are given allegorical

---

4. Charette, *Theme of Recompense*, 140. Charette relates this expression to the misery associated with "the torments of eternal punishment" (141). Furthermore, "the outer darkness," a phrase distinctive to Matthew, signifies banishment from the light of divine presence (142–43).

5. The parable of the Wedding Banquet (22:1–14) concludes with an inappropriately attired guest being bound and cast out into outer darkness, where there is wailing and teeth-grinding. Although a parable of judgment, possibly directed against the Jewish leadership and Jerusalem, it is not obviously a parable of *eschatological* judgment.

interpretations within the discourse. Although the parable of the Sower is given primacy within this discourse, it is to some extent upstaged by the parable of the Tares in two respects: first, the parable of the Tares itself along with its later interpretation is substantially longer (132 + 125 words) than the parable of the Sower and its interpretation (87 + 128 words); and second, the parable of the Tares is the only one about which the disciples request an explanation of its meaning (13:36). This might simply be a compositional transition after the shift of audience at this point in the discourse. But in view of Jesus' statement in 13:11, "To you it has been given to know the mysteries of the reign of the heavens, but to them [the crowds; cf. 13:1–2, 34] it has not been given," it would seem that the disciples' request for an explanation of the parable of the Tares (but not those of the Mustard Seed or Leaven) indicates Matthew's concern that it be clearly comprehended. Its "reiteration" in the culminating parable of the Net—the third longest parable in the collection of seven (seventy-one words)—strengthens this supposition.

In Matt 13:37–43, the parable of the Tares is given a focus-shifting allegorical interpretation.[6] The person who sowed good seed is the Son of humanity; the field in which good seed is sown is the world; and the good seed sown (and presumably harvested) represent the children of divine reign. By contrast, the tares represent the children of the evil one, planted by the devil. The harvest represents the end of the age and the harvesters angels. According to the end-time scenario depicted by this interpretation of the parable of the Tares, angels sent by the Son of humanity will first sort out from the righteous both what causes people to fall away and those who behave contrary to Torah, then cast both into the furnace of fire, precisely like the tares in the parable are bundled to be burnt.

The same end-time scenario recurs in the parable of the Net (13:47–50), which also receives a brief interpretation along the lines of the interpretation given to the parable of the Tares. Several phrases found in the interpretation of the parable of the Tares reappear in the interpretation of the parable of the Net: "This is how things are at the culmination of the age" (13:40, 49); "They [angels] will cast them [the unrighteous] into the furnace of fire" (13:42, 50); and "There [in the furnace of fire], there will be wailing and teeth-grinding" (13:42, 50). For those with ears to hear (13:43b), Matthew's Jesus takes pains to repeat himself. Both the space given to the parable of the Tares and its interpretation and also the culminating role of the parable of the Net, which recalls the parable of the Tares, leave the audience of this discourse with a dominant impression of God's heavenly reign.

---

6. Snodgrass, *Stories with Intent*, 196, 211.

Although other things are affirmed about divine reign, what stands out is its uncompromising entry requirements and its retributive recompense for those ultimately deemed unworthy.

The remaining parables of eschatological judgment in Matthew's Gospel appear at the end of the fifth discourse in the narrative (24:45–25:46).[7] The parable of the Unforgiving Slave in Matt 18:23–35 ends on the note of violent judgment, but the eschatological dimension is not pronounced, which is why this parable is discussed in chapter 2. Matthew's fifth and final discourse section is contextually parallel to the eschatological discourses of Mark 13 and Luke 21, meaning that it occurs in the same relative context in all three Synoptic Gospels—a few days after Jesus' arrival in Jerusalem and immediately before Jesus instructs his disciples to prepare for Passover. In at least three respects, however, this discourse section in Matthew's narrative is distinctive: first, the note of hostility and impending judgment for both the current generation of Israelites and for Jerusalem itself is heightened by the vehement invective of Jesus in Matthew 23 (see chapter 8 above), which precedes and builds up to the specifically eschatological material in chapters 24–25; second, within this discourse only Matthew records the disciples and Jesus explicitly referring to the *parousia* of Jesus or the Son of humanity at the culmination of the age (24:3, 27, 37, 39); and third, although all three evangelists punctuate their respective eschatological discourses with parabolic conclusions, Matthew goes to extremes in this respect by including various analogies and parables both to reinforce the indeterminacy of the Son of humanity's *parousia* (24:36–25:13) and also to characterize that day as one of final judgment (24:45–25:46). In these (and other) ways, Matthew makes of Jesus' fifth and final discourse something as weighty and memorable as his Sermon on the Mount.[8]

The bracketing function of Matt 24:36 and 25:13, at which points Jesus asserts that it is impossible to know the day or the hour of the Son of humanity's *parousia*, makes it possible to interpret all that falls between these asseverations as principally concerned to warn of the need for watchfulness in view of the reality that the timing of the *parousia* is indecipherable (see

---

7. Strictly speaking, the scenario of final judgment in Matt 25:31–46 is not a parable, but it contains parabolic features.

8. The double setting of Matthew's final discourse is probably also significant. Whereas the Mount of Olives is the setting for Mark 13 and the temple provides the setting for Luke 21, the temple is the setting for the first part of Matthew's fifth discourse directed against both the Jewish leadership and Jerusalem, and the Mount of Olives is the setting for the more explicitly eschatological part of the discourse. For an audience cognizant of both Jewish tradition and recent Judean history, these two settings evoke powerful associations.

also 24:42, 44).[9] Even so, the comparison between the *parousia* of the Son of humanity and the days of Noah (24:37–39) and the contiguous parables of the Waiting Slave and Ten Bridesmaids (24:45–25:13) seem concerned with more than the matter of the impossibility of knowing precisely when the *parousia* might occur. Watchfulness involves more than simple readiness.

The comparison between the *parousia* of the Son of humanity and the days of Noah in Matt 24:37–39 reads as follows:

> For as the days of Noah were, so will the arrival [*parousia*] of the Son of humanity be. For as, in the days before the cataclysm, they were eating and drinking, marrying and marrying off, until the day Noah entered into the big box, and they were unaware until the cataclysm came and swept them all away, the arrival [*parousia*] of the Son of humanity will occur in the same way.

According to W. D. Davies and Dale Allison, "Noah's contemporaries . . . were remembered as great sinners who did not foresee God's wrath. . . . Sometimes the flood was a prototype of the last judgment or end of the world. . . . But our saying goes its own way in focusing neither upon the sins of Noah's generation nor his righteousness but upon the unexpected nature of the cataclysm that overtook the world while people went about their daily business unawares."[10]

Davies and Allison correctly identify the primary emphasis of this comparison: the utter unpredictability of the Son of humanity's *parousia*. Given how familiar Jesus or Matthew's audience would have been with the story of Noah, however, this principal point could have been made without belaboring the cataclysmic consequences of the flood. In the days of Noah, unawareness of impending calamity resulted in wholesale devastation. It is hardly possible, especially in light of the analogy's larger literary context, that Matthew was unconcerned to underscore the analogy's retributive associations. The Son of humanity's *parousia* may be unpredictable with respect to timing but not, for Matthew, with respect to ominousness.

---

9. Although the impossibility of knowing the timing of the Son of humanity's *parousia* seems to be the basic burden of Matt 24:36–25:13, it is possible to read 24:36 in particular as concerned with more than the timing of the *parousia*. What follows focuses on the matter of timing, but 24:36 reads: "Now with respect to that day and hour, nobody knows—neither the angels of the heavens nor the Son—except the Father alone." This applies to every aspect of that day and hour, not only to its timing. As a result, this implies that everything presaged about the *parousia* in Matthew's Gospel, whether attributed directly to Jesus or to Matthew (or to both), is not knowledge-in-advance but vision subject to divine revision.

10. Davies and Allison, *Gospel according to Saint Matthew*, 3:380. Although said specifically of Matt 24:37, it applies to the entire analogy.

If the retributive dimension is secondary in the Noah analogy, it comes to the fore in the parable of the Waiting Slave (24:45–51). It is not entirely clear whether the parable envisages one slave only or two. The introduction of the adjective κακός (*kakos*, bad, evil, or even irresponsible) in Matt 24:48 hints at a second slave, but this qualifier may be based on how the slave already mentioned decides to treat fellow slaves after determining that his master is delayed. Like its close parallel in Luke 12:41–46, this parable is apparently a warning to those within the community of faith with leadership responsibilities. Building upon a study by Otto Betz, Snodgrass draws attention to parallels between this parable and Psalm 37 and concludes from this that "Jesus' parable looks like an eschatological version of Psalm 37 applied to disciples through use of the servant imagery."[11] Concern with timing appears at Matt 24:48 but only in relation to the rationale for the waiting slave's aggressive and indulgent behavior. The point of the parable is that bad leadership will result in a bad end. Although the parable indicates that the master's return will occur at an unexpected time, emphasis is given to the vengeance visited on the irresponsible slave.[12] The slave is sliced in two and dispatched to "hypocrite hell," where (as the reader has come to expect) there will be wailing and teeth-grinding (24:51). Even when seen to reinforce the moral imperatives of responsible and careful leadership, to associate the *parousia* of the Son of humanity with such vindictive vengeance is theologically disturbing and morally corrosive because such associations inculcate a retributive mind-set precisely on the part of those in positions of power.

Although the parable of the Ten Bridesmaids (25:1–13) more obviously emphasizes the need for watchful readiness in light of the unpredictability of the Son of humanity's *parousia*, its disconcerting ending is reminiscent of the strident conclusion to the Sermon on the Mount. The unprepared and hence foolish bridesmaids illustrate the words of Jesus in Matt 7:21–23; not everyone who says "Lord, Lord" will be granted entry into God's heavenly reign. They also parallel the foolish man who failed to build his house on a foundation of rock, since they fail (in the envisaged future) to act on Jesus' instruction to be watchful (7:24–27). By virtue of its thematic and verbal echoes of the strong note of judgment on which the Sermon on the Mount

---

11. Snodgrass, *Stories with Intent*, 502.

12. Although the punishment inflicted on this slave seems extreme to Western readers today, such brutality toward slaves was commonplace in antiquity (and not unknown today). For the view that Matthew's slave parables not only reflect but also reinforce the classical ideology of slavery, with ramifications for the God-image they project, see Glancy, "Slaves and Slavery," 67–90.

ends, the parable of the Ten Bridesmaids functions as a warning of judgment, even if the note of retributive violence is muted.

Both the nature of the introduction to the parable of the Talents in Matt 25:14 and its present context suggest that this parable might also be intended to reinforce the need for watchful readiness in light of the unpredictability of the Son of humanity's *parousia* (24:36, 42, 44; 25:13).[13] Like the parable of the Waiting Slave, however, this parable, which also features slaves, seems to have other, larger concerns. The note of timing is sounded at Matt 25:19, but otherwise it does not feature. Much more dominant is the matter of whether or not the master's slaves have advanced the master's interests (and interest!). This lengthy and well developed parable begins with the master apportioning talents to slaves according to their (perceived) strength or capabilities (δύναμις, *dunamis*). Like the cruel and indulgent slave two parables earlier, the slave who did nothing with his master's single talent apart from preserving it is deemed irresponsible and is therefore stripped of his talent and consigned to outer darkness, where there will be wailing and teeth-grinding (25:30). Thus this parable is concerned more with responsibility than with readiness—not to mention the retribution that awaits the irresponsible!

The fifth and final discourse in Matthew's Gospel comes to its climactic crescendo in the scenario of final judgment (25:31–46). By virtue of its placement as the climax to Matthew's culminating discourse, this scenario was clearly intended to create—and clearly has created—a lasting impression. Each of Matthew's five discourses ends on the note of judgment,[14] and his final discourse ends by depicting final and indeed inscrutable judgment. More than this, however, this final scenario of eschatological judgment reinforces earlier indications throughout Matthew's Gospel that divine judgment equates to teleological terror, even though it also reinforces the noble notion that all are answerable to the judge of all for how we have responded to the needs of the most vulnerable.

This scenario of the final judgment of the nations reiterates the idea that judgment entails discriminating between the righteous and the unrighteous, only at this time according to the criterion of whether or not the needs of the "least significant" have been attended to.[15] Those judged not to have served the needs of the "least significant," and hence those of the en-

---

13. Matthew 25:13 may be seen to introduce the parable of the Talents no less than to conclude the parable of the Ten Bridesmaids.

14. See Schnelle, *Theology of the New Testament*, 460.

15. It is impossible to be certain, but I incline to the view that by the "least significant" (25:40, 45) Matthew here has all humanity in view, not merely the lowly members of his own community.

throned Son of humanity, are sent away to the "eternal fire" prepared for the devil and his angels (25:41, 46). This scenario closely matches that depicted in the two parables of the Tares and the Net (13:24–30, 36–43, 47–50). According to this end-time scenario, divinely authorized judgment by the Son of humanity takes into account the vulnerable and the lowly but also consigns the self-absorbed to the perdition of "eternal punishment." Ultimately, according to Matthew's record of Jesus' instruction regarding the *parousia* at the end of the age, the Son of humanity will resort to eschatological vengeance, not judgment more in keeping with the character of Jesus, Immanuel. Within the Gospel according to Matthew, the eschatological parables of Jesus instill teleological terror.

The figurative language associated with eschatological judgment in Matthew's Gospel signals an expectation of divine vengeance. That such language is symbolic is significant. Although we might wish that Matthew (or Jesus before him) had spoken about eschatological judgment in more measured or nuanced terms, the reality is that the language of hope within the biblical tradition is inescapably visionary and symbolic. This applies even to eschatological sayings that are neither parabolic nor obviously figurative.

The *Parousia* of the Son of Humanity

Within Matthew's Gospel is a series of sayings of Jesus regarding the future advent of the Son of humanity. The texts are these: 10:23; 16:27–28; 24:27, 30–31, 37, 39, 44; 26:64. In the eschatological discourse, three of these sayings refer specifically to the *parousia* of the Son of humanity (24:27, 37, 39). This part of the discourse is in response to the twofold question of disciples: "Tell us, when will these things occur, and what is the sign of your *parousia* and culmination of the age?" (24:3). The "these things" to which they refer echoes the ambiguous "all these things" of 24:2, which Jesus apparently relates to the impending destruction of the buildings that comprise the temple. The disciples' twofold question suggests that they relate the impending destruction of the temple complex to the *parousia* of Jesus. Implicit within their question, in any case, is a coalescing of the *parousia* of Jesus with the end of the age. One wonders why the precise term *parousia* appears first of all on the lips of the disciples. In light of the use of this same term by Jesus later in the discourse alongside the imagery of "coming" (ἔρχομαι, *erchomai* [24:30, 44; also 24:42]), it seems safe to regard both the "coming" and the *parousia* of the Son of humanity as equivalent for Matthew, including elsewhere in his Gospel. Furthermore, the saying of Matt 24:42 no less than the prompting question of the disciples indicates that Matthew identifies Jesus with the coming Son of humanity. In Matthean perspective, therefore, sayings of Jesus regarding the future advent of the Son of humanity are promises of his own return.

To address all of the questions raised by Matthew's future-oriented Son of humanity sayings would require a book-length study. Here the focus is on whether or not such sayings reinforce the tenor or tone of the figurative language used within Matthew's Gospel to depict eschatological judgment.

The unparalleled saying of Matt 10:23, in which Jesus solemnly assures his twelve disciples that they will not have reached all Israelite towns before the Son of humanity comes, is especially enigmatic. By its association with other future-oriented Son of humanity sayings, it may intimate judgment; on the face of it, however, that is neither its emphasis nor its most perplexing aspect. But because it is impossible to read this particular saying as referring to the *parousia* without accepting that Jesus was mistaken, some interpret this saying as a reference to the destruction of Jerusalem construed as divine judgment. On this view, the imminent future advent of the Son of humanity equates to the "coming" of the Son of humanity in or by means of the judgment of Jerusalem.[16] Such interpreters thereby color this saying as referring to vindictive vengeance of the kind visited on Jerusalem by Roman forces. In other words, to protect Jesus from the charge of being mistaken (or perhaps Matthew from the charge of inaccurate transmission of a dominical saying), this particular interpretation gives to this saying a vehemence (along with a correspondingly vengeful interpretation of divine judgment) that is prima facie absent.

The note of judgment is explicit in Matt 16:27–28. Compared to the parallel sayings in Mark 8:38–9:1 and Luke 9:26–27, the note of recompense on the basis of deeds is one of two distinctive features of these coupled sayings in their Matthean form (16:27b);[17] the other is the recasting of a saying regarding the imminent perception of the reign of God in terms of the coming Son of humanity (16:28b). Relative to its Markan and Lukan contextual parallels, therefore, this pair of sayings explicitly characterizes the coming of the Son of humanity as a time of judgment in the form of individual recompense. The form or nature of such judgment is not specified, however, and there is no indication that judgment is necessarily violent or strictly retributive. Such associations are perhaps inevitable, given the imagery with which Matthew depicts divine judgment elsewhere, but in 16:27–28

---

16. See, e.g., Hagner, *Matthew 1–13*, 278–80; Gibbs, *Jerusalem and Parousia*, 65–76.

17. See Travis, *Christ and the Judgement*, 224–25.

the prospect of judgment at the coming of the Son of humanity is affirmed without giving grounds for teleological terror.

The forward-looking instruction of Jesus in Matthew 24 concerns both the destruction of Jerusalem and the *parousia* of Jesus as the eschatological Son of humanity. It is difficult, however, to determine whether certain parts of this instruction relate to one of these events alone and, if so, which parts relate primarily to the *parousia*. Critical to an understanding of this chapter as a whole is the meaning of Matt 24:29–31, in which Jesus foresees cosmic catastrophe immediately following the affliction apparently associated with the lead-up to the destruction of Jerusalem, which gives way in turn to the advent of the Son of humanity and related events. Many see this passage as referring to the return of Jesus as the judging Son of humanity, but some consider it (along with 24:32–34) to be metaphorical language signifying the exaltation of Jesus as the Son of humanity, of which the destruction of Jerusalem is its most salient historical manifestation.[18]

Until Matt 24:27, much of Jesus' instruction in this chapter comprises warnings of what must occur before his arrival at the end of the age so that his disciples are not deluded. The indeterminate time leading up to (but not necessarily signaling) the end will be characterized by upheaval, persecution, tribulation, and false messianic and prophetic claims. The ambiguity of all such circumstances and events implies that none in itself nor any of them together signals the end precipitated by the *parousia*. Rather, as the lightning analogy of 24:27 clarifies, the *parousia* of the Son of humanity will be unmissable and unmistakable.

Because of the verbal and thematic connections between Matt 24:30, where the Greek term *parousia* does not occur, and 24:3, 27, 37, and 39, where it does, many interpret the reference to seeing the Son of humanity coming on the clouds of heaven as a reference to the *parousia*. R. T. France (among others) accepts Matt 24:27 as a parenthetical reference to the return of Jesus, but the absence of the term *parousia* at 24:30 (alongside other considerations) leads him to deny that anything prior to 24:36 (apart from 24:27–28) relates to the end.[19] If he is correct, the coming of the Son of humanity on the clouds of heaven in Matt 24:30 refers to the exaltation of Jesus, confirmed by the destruction of Jerusalem and the growth of the early church. Matthew 24:29–31 may not refer to *end-time* judgment, according to France,[20] but it does refer to divine judgment in the form of Jerusalem's

---

18. A long-standing advocate of this view is R. T. France. See France, *Gospel of Matthew*, 889–931. See also Gibbs, *Jerusalem and Parousia*, esp. chap. 6.

19. France, *Gospel of Matthew*, 891–93.

20. Ibid., 919–28.

destruction, perhaps as the pattern for eschatological judgment at the *parousia*.[21]

If Matt 24:30–31 foresees the *parousia* of the Son of humanity without using that specific term,[22] however, the note of eschatological judgment is sounded but muted. Following the signs of cosmic collapse described in Matt 24:29, which will immediately follow the earlier tribulation of indeterminate duration, the sign of the Son of humanity will appear in the sky. What comprises this heavenly sign is not specified, but the lightning analogy of Matt 24:27 suggests that the coming Son of humanity is his own heavenly sign. Perhaps echoing this earlier assurance that the *parousia* of the Son of humanity will be unmistakable, Jesus here says that all the tribes of the earth will lament the appearance of the sign of the Son of humanity even as they see the Son of humanity coming on the clouds of heaven with power and glory. The text reads: "And then *the sign of the Son of humanity will appear in heaven*, and then *all the tribes of the earth will lament*, and they will see the Son of humanity coming upon the clouds of heaven with power and much glory."[23] According to Matthew, Jesus foresees the coming of the Son of humanity as provoking universal distress. As Walter Wink comments, "Whereas Mark's 'coming' of the son of the man was an occasion for rejoicing at deliverance from tribulation, Matthew has added 'then all the tribes of the earth will mourn' (24:30), shifting the focus to an adverse judgment that will overtake the enemies of the son of the man."[24]

Although Wink is correct to draw attention to the difference in tone between Matt 24:30 and its Markan (or Lukan) parallel, it is not as though Matthew makes a point of stressing that the apprehension of all human tribes was for good reason. Certainly the majesty of the coming Son of humanity is emphasized, and Matt 24:31 affirms that he will dispatch his angels with a trumpet blast. Although this might intimate an interpretation along the lines of eschatological battle, there is no description of eschatological battle. Rather than engage in battle, the marshaled angelic host

---

21. To be fair to France, his interpretation of Matthean eschatology does not draw parallels between the destruction of Jerusalem and eschatological judgment. Hagner does not accept France's interpretation of Matt 24:29–31, but his understanding of Matthean eschatology makes much of a perceived typological association between the destruction of Jerusalem and eschatological judgment, with Jerusalem's destruction anticipating or prefiguring final judgment. See Hagner, "Matthew's Eschatology," 61–70; Hagner, *Matthew 14–28*, 485–87, 708–717.

22. See also Matt 24:42–44, esp. 24:44, which France accepts as a reference to the *parousia* even though that specific term is not used. See France, *Gospel of Matthew*, 941–43.

23. The italicized phrases are unique to Matthew.

24. Wink, *Human Being*, 170.

embarks on a gathering exercise, bringing together the Son of humanity's chosen ones from the four winds. In line with Matt 16:27–28 but in contrast to figurative language associated with eschatological judgment elsewhere in the Gospel, neither the coming Son of humanity nor his gathering angels pursue eschatological vengeance. There is an intimation of judgment but without conveying the impression that such judgment is inescapably violent or irredeemably retributive. This observation needs to be held in balance with the point that much of the remainder of this discourse continues in such a way as to characterize the judgment of the Son of humanity as eschatological vengeance for those on his wrong side.

Of all the future-oriented Son of humanity sayings in Matthew's Gospel, the one at 26:64 is perhaps most amenable to an interpretation along the lines of exaltation rather than the *parousia*. Evidence from the second century, however, suggests that this saying was then understood as referring to the return of Jesus following his exaltation.[25] Facing a hostile Sanhedrin intent on finding evidence to secure his punishment by death, Jesus here utters an enigmatic saying that affirms his imminent vindication but not necessarily his vindictiveness. This is undoubtedly an expression of confidence in divine judgment, but the saying does not characterize divine judgment in such a way that it must be construed as vengeance. In this sense, it is of a piece with other future-oriented Son of humanity sayings in the Gospel, which do not paint lurid scenarios of eschatological vengeance.

TELEOLOGICAL TERROR IN LUKAN PERSPECTIVE

Unlike Matthew, Luke does not open his Gospel by foregrounding hostility to the birth of Jesus. To the contrary, the births of both John and Jesus occasion wonderment, joy, and hope. The note of impending judgment features in Luke's record of John's preaching no less than in Matthew's, but it is softened somewhat by John's civil response to the crowd's question about how they should respond to his stern warnings (3:7–18). Despite Luke's tightening of the bonds between John and Jesus by intercalating stories about their conceptions, births, and personal development, he does not present Jesus as echoing John's strident preaching. With the exception of Jesus' parable of the rich man who ignored his poor neighbor Lazarus (16:19–31) and the

---

25. For a brief discussion of evidence from Hegesippus and Justin Martyr, see Neville, *A Peaceable Hope*, 75–76. According to Graham Stanton, moreover, an early form of the "two advents" schema found in Justin and in later Christian apologists is present in Matthew's Gospel as a means of countering Jewish criticisms that the mission of Jesus failed to fulfill biblical prophecies regarding the promised Messiah. See Stanton, *Gospel for a New People*, 185–91; Stanton, "Two Parousias of Christ," 183–95.

analogical reference to the destruction of Sodom (17:28–30), the threat of hellfire is well nigh missing from Jesus' teaching. Indeed, at a crucial juncture in Luke's narrative, Jesus repudiates the suggestion of James and John that fiery judgment should be called down from heaven upon inhospitable Samaritan villagers (9:51–55). Moreover, in light of what transpires at Pentecost in Acts 2:1–4, John's prophecy that his more powerful successor will baptize with the Holy Spirit and with fire may be seen as interpreted by Luke in wholly positive terms. At one point, Luke recalls Jesus as identifying the purpose of his mission in terms of casting fire upon the earth (12:49), but in context this enigmatic saying probably forecasts the hostile reaction inevitably provoked by his mission.[26]

As in Matthew, however, so also at various points in Luke, Jesus warns of future judgment for failing to respond positively to himself, his message, or that of his messengers. Luke's distinctive record of the mission of the Seventy-Two contains the warning that on "that Day" things will be worse for unwelcoming towns than for Sodom (10:10–12). Warnings against the Galilean towns of Chorazin, Bethsaida, and Capernaum are also found in this context (10:13–16). Luke also records Jesus' warnings against "this generation" for seeking a sign; for failing to recognize that something greater than Solomon and Jonah is present, this generation will be condemned at "the Judgment" by the queen of the south and the men of Nineveh (11:29–32). Even so, although the threat of judgment constitutes a visible and meaningful thread in the fabric of Jesus' teaching, as Luke presents it, it is neither so prominent nor so vehement as in Matthew's presentation of Jesus' mission and message.

Beyond these more general warnings of eschatological judgment, the Gospel according to Luke contains three blocks of future-oriented teaching relating to the arrival of the Son of humanity: 12:35–48; 17:20–37; and 21:5–36.[27] The last of these is contextually parallel to the eschatological discourse of Jesus in Matthew 24 and Mark 13, but the earlier two also contain conceptual and verbal parallels with the one eschatological discourse in Matthew and, to a lesser extent, in Mark. For whatever reason, Luke apparently presents Jesus as addressing the eschatological horizon on three

---

26. See comments on this passage in chapter 1, above.

27. Many would add to these passages the distinctively Lukan parables of the Persistent Widow (18:1–8) and the Throne Claimant (19:11–28). Although Luke 18:8 features the prospect of the coming Son of humanity, its relation to the preceding parable seems secondary and the parable itself serves a purpose different from 17:22–37. My reasons for interpreting the parable of the Throne Claimant as probably unrelated to the return of Jesus are set out in chapter 2, above.

separate occasions, not only during his final week in Jerusalem but also on two separate occasions en route to Jerusalem.

Luke 12:35–48

The various parabolic sayings in Luke 12:35–48 emphasize vigilant readiness for the arrival of the Son of humanity. The passage begins by sounding the note of vigilance and continues by underscoring the joy experienced by servants who are ever-ready to welcome home their master from a wedding feast. Far from emphasizing the threat of retribution for failing to be ready, the first part of this larger passage dwells on both the delight and the surprise in store for those who are ready. Readiness is rewarded not only by approval but by a sociocultural turning of the tables in which the returning master takes the place of the slaves and serves them at table! Although implausible in sociocultural perspective (see Luke 17:7–10), this eschatological expectation is fully in keeping with how Jesus characterizes his status among his friends at his final meal with them (22:27). In other words, in this parabolic exhortation to vigilance, the returning master turns the tables on those waiting for him in precisely the way Jesus characterizes his mission as one of service. Although the image of a break-in in Luke 12:39 is somewhat jarring, it simply reinforces the motif of unexpected arrival for which one must always be prepared.

Admittedly, the sociocultural tables are turned because the master finds his slaves alert and ready for his return. The important point, however, is that this passage gives primacy to the blessings associated with eschatologically oriented readiness. Only in response to Peter's question about whether Jesus' parable is addressed to his disciples or to everyone does Jesus reinforce his call for readiness with a more ominous warning about the consequences of abusing responsibility. In what follows, the parabolic setting of a master's household is maintained, but the focus clearly shifts from readiness to responsible leadership. A makarism matching that of Luke 12:37 is recorded in 12:43, except that the latter slave is blessed if his master returns to find him attending to his responsibilities rather than keeping watch. If, as a result of his master's delay, however, the slave mistreats those under his management and overindulges his appetites, he will receive retribution that kills and consigns the victim to the fate of the faithless. This somber warning of violent payback for irresponsible leadership is carried over into Luke 12:47–48, albeit with consideration for levels of culpability.

The parable of the waiting slave in Luke 12:39–46 closely parallels Matt 24:43–51, but Luke's inclusion of Peter's query, "To us or to all?" (12:41), more obviously relates the grim warnings of violent retribution in Luke 12:45–48 to those with leadership responsibilities within the community of faith. Such warnings of inevitable payback for failure to exercise leadership responsibly and with due care reveals deep concern for people without power. Nevertheless, the image of a punitive master who deals in dicing no less than drubbing so easily inculcates a retributive mind-set in leaders confident that they are in the right and bear responsibility for making things turn out right. The moral bearing of this parable is therefore double-sided. Given the placement of this parable after the earlier exhortation to readiness in Luke 12:35–40, however, it may be seen as the shadow side of an entirely positive, albeit surprising, prospect of eschatological reversal.

Luke 17:20–37

Like Luke 12:39–46, Luke's second block of eschatological teaching in 17:20–37 contains significant thematic and verbal points of contact with the eschatological discourse in Matthew 24.[28] Yet such parallels are arranged differently, as this table reveals:

Luke	Matthew
17:20–22	—
17:23	24:23
17:24	24:27
17:25	—
17:26–27, 30	24:37–39
17:31	24:17–18
17:33	10:39
17:34–35	24:40–41
17:37b	24:28

Insofar as the material in Luke 17:20–37 parallels Matthew's version of the so-called Synoptic Apocalypse, of which Luke 21:5–36 is the contextual parallel, the eschatological material in Luke 17 and 21 might be seen as literary "doublets."

Within what Jesus here foresees in connection with the day (or days) of the Son of humanity, both the twofold comparison with the days of Noah and Lot and the birds-of-prey saying with which this section ends (17:37) have an ominous ring to them. Like Matt 24:37–39, Luke 17:26–27 compares the days of the Son of humanity to the days of Noah. To reinforce the

---

28. Luke 17:23 and 31 also contain verbal parallels to Mark 13:21 and 15–16, respectively. The Matthean parallel to Luke 17:33 is 10:39.

burden of this analogy, however, Luke supplements it with the comparable analogy of Sodom's destruction in the days of Lot (17:28–29). "In accordance with such (events) will the day of the Son of humanity be revealed," Luke records Jesus as saying (17:30). Robert Tannehill's appraisal of Luke 17:26–30 demonstrates that the primary effect of the two analogies relating the past days of Noah and Lot to the future day(s) of the Son of humanity is to underscore the unanticipated interruption of the normal rhythm of daily life. The explicit focus of these parallel sayings is not the wickedness of Noah and Lot's contemporaries—and hence their deserved punishment—but rather the unexpected interruption of daily routines.[29] In short, the principal concern of these analogies is to forewarn: expect the unexpected!

Tannehill may be correct about the primary purpose of the analogies of Noah and Lot, but surprising unexpectedness is not their sole lasting effect. Together with the doubling of the analogies, the exact repetition of the note of total destruction in Luke 17:27 and 29 indicates that divine retribution analogous to the wholesale punishments associated with the biblical stories of Noah and Lot is at least part of their impact. As Tannehill concedes, "The nature of the interruption is not specified. It is hidden behind the biblical images. But it is destructive for those whose life is wrapped up in the activities of heedless people."[30] Although nothing definite is said about the specific form of destruction associated with the future day(s) of the Son of humanity, nevertheless the analogies of Noah and Lot foreshadow near-indiscriminate divine retribution. Even the subsequent warning of Luke 17:31–32 intimates devastation no less than urgency. Preservation from destruction might be possible provided one does not falter—like Lot's wife! The day(s) of the Son of humanity will not only come without warning but will also bring calamity and devastation for the unprepared.

Many consider the warning of divine retribution implicit within the Noah and Lot analogies to be present in the concluding saying: "Wherever the body, there also will eagles be gathered" (17:37b). Darrell Bock follows I. H. Marshall by reading this saying as emphasizing the finality of divine judgment intimated in the preceding images of division (17:34–35):

> Judgment will be visible, universal, and permanent. . . . Vultures gather to feed off the dead bodies. . . . This point that once judgment is rendered it is final seems the most likely sense. . . . All will see the judgment's horrific finality. . . . The graphic and emotive image of vultures is a warning that the return will be a grim affair. The return of the Son of Man saves some but permanently

---

29. Tannehill, *Sword of His Mouth*, 118–22.
30. Tannehill, *Luke*, 261.

condemns others. The return will be what was longed for in 17:22, but when it comes it will mean ultimate judgment for those who are not prepared. This is classic day-of-the-Lord warning to the unprepared.[31]

Since the theme of judgment implicitly pervades much of this passage, Bock may well be correct to interpret the saying with which it ends as foreboding grisly judgment.[32] Although the imagery may be suggestive of judgment, the primary point of the saying is probably to reinforce the lightning saying of Luke 17:24. In Matt 24:26-28 these sayings occur in immediate succession, whereas Luke seems to have used the two sayings to enclose Jesus' teaching regarding the future day(s) of the Son of humanity. Although the latter saying is more ominous, it probably parallels the lightning saying in meaning, especially if it envisages birds of prey circling in flight, thereby comprising parallel signs in the sky. No less than when lightning illuminates the entire sky, the day(s) of the Son of humanity will be as unmistakable as the presence (and perhaps even the location) of a body from circling birds of prey.

In my earlier discussion of this passage, I pondered whether Luke 17:22-37 might relate more to the passion of Jesus than to his *parousia*.[33] This was largely on the basis of Jesus' seemingly context-alien sayings in Luke 17:25 and 33, which together echo Luke 9:18-27. Although I retained an eschatologically oriented reading of Luke 17:22-37, it was an interpretation in which the later passage (17:22-37) is understood in light of the earlier one (9:18-27). In two carefully reasoned studies, however, T. J. Lang argues that Jesus' discourse in Luke 17:22-37 does not look forward to his *parousia*.[34] In the first of these studies, Lang addresses interpretive challenges associated with references to multiple "days" of the Son of humanity (17:22, 26), an expression unique to Luke, alongside references to his (singular) "day," and he also proposes that Luke 17:22 should be read as *antanaclasis*, "which is a type of rhetorical wordplay where the same (or a similar) term is repeated,

---

31. Bock, *Luke 9:51—24:53*, 1440; cf. Marshall, *Gospel of Luke*, 669.

32. See Bridge, "Where the Eagles Are Gathered," whose book-length study of this enigmatic saying emphasizes deliverance rather than retribution. Even for Bridge, however, Luke 17:37b is a text of deliverance only because it holds out this promise for "survivors" rather than "victims" of eschatological retribution.

33. See Neville, *A Peaceable Hope*, 129-36. Neither Luke nor Mark employs the term *parousia*, but the future coming of the Son of humanity and the return of the ascended Jesus belong to Luke's convictional framework, probably as the same hoped-for event (although this is somewhat controversial).

34. Lang, "Reading Luke 17.22 as Antanaclasis" (2011); Lang, "Luke 17:37 and the Arrest of Jesus" (2013).

but in different senses."[35] For Lang, the two different verbal expressions of sight perception in Luke 17:22, ἰδεῖν (*idein*) and ὄψεσθε (*opsesthe*), should be understood differently along the following lines: "Days are coming when you will desire to *witness* one of the days of the Son of humanity and not *comprehend* it as such."[36] On such a reading of Luke 17:22, Lang proposes that the remainder of Jesus' discourse in Luke 17 is not about the *parousia* but rather a warning to his disciples about their future failure to *perceive* his passion as integral to his identity and mission.

Building on his detailed treatment of Luke 17:22, Lang's slightly later study of Luke 17:37 proposes that the enigmatic saying, "Wherever the body, there also will eagles be gathered," foreshadows the arrest of Jesus in Luke 22, when Jesus himself (the "body") is surrounded by captivating forces ("eagles"). To demonstrate the *prima facie* plausibility of his proposed referents for both the "body" and "eagles" in this saying, Lang appeals to cross-cultural literary and linguistic evidence from antiquity, including biblical and post-biblical literary data.[37] Especially noteworthy is that subsequent to the reference to the "body" in Luke 17:37, every further reference to "body" in Luke's narrative refers to the (dead) body of Jesus (22:19; 23:52, 55; 24:3, 23), although each such reference makes this identification explicit. Moreover, Lang demonstrates that the theme of the disciples' inability to perceive suffering as inherent—because (divinely) necessary—to the Son of humanity's identity and mission is a recurring Lukan leitmotif (see 9:44–45; 18:31–34; 24:13–35).[38] As a result, Lang's proposed interpretation of Luke 17:22–37 deserves careful consideration, especially in view of his determination to respect Luke's own redactional concerns and hence the potential distinctiveness of Lukan eschatology.

To test his reading of Luke 17:22, Lang offers an "interpretive sketch" of the larger discourse, 17:20–37, as concerned with the passion (rather than the *parousia*) of Jesus.[39] It would seem that, for Lang, Luke 17:22–37 relates *either* to the passion *or* to the *parousia* of Jesus; he does not consider whether this passage might best be understood in a way that mediates between these stark alternatives. Furthermore, he avers that "if not approached from the perspective of a Gospel synopsis, there is not a single image, term or expression that necessarily signals to the reader that the topic of the discourse is

---

35. Lang, "Reading Luke 17.22 as Antanaclasis," 283.

36. Although not an instance of exact verbal repetition, Luke 17:22 is a case of the repetition of the same, albeit differently inflected, lexeme. See Lang, "Reading Luke 17.22 as Antanaclasis," 288.

37. Lang, "Luke 17:37 and the Arrest of Jesus," 324–27.

38. Lang, "Reading Luke 17.22 as Antanaclasis," 289–90.

39. Ibid., 290–98; Lang, "Luke 17:37 and the Arrest of Jesus," 327–35.

the end-time return of the Son of Man."[40] Although well aware that close verbal and conceptual parallels to Luke 17:22–37 appear in Jesus' discourse on the *parousia* in Matthew 24, Lang asserts that such parallels do not recur in Luke 21. "There are certainly some general parallels between the two discourses [Luke 17:20–37; 21:5–36]," he concedes, "but the parallels are not enough to require their equation. They are simply two different discourses about two different eschatological events of cosmic proportions."[41]

The parallels between Luke 17:20–37 and 21:5–36 may not be close enough to "require their equation," but they are probably close enough to envisage a connection between them, especially when one recalls that the motif of readiness for the (returning) Son of humanity features as early as Luke 12:35–40, well before 17:20–37. In narrative terms, it is difficult to read Luke 17:20–37 without reference to—that is, as not reminiscent of—12:35–40, and it is even more difficult to read Luke 21:5–36, especially 21:25–36, as unrelated to and hence not reminiscent of the two earlier passages. All three passages anticipate something future on the part of the Son of humanity. The motif of the *coming* of the Son of humanity may not feature in Luke 17:20–37, as it does in 12:40 and 21:27, but it does occur at 18:8, which leads some scholars to treat 18:1–8 as part of the larger discourse beginning at 17:20.[42] Although the focus of this parable of the Persistent Widow differs from the particular concerns of the preceding discourse, the close proximity of Luke 18:8b to 17:20–37 hints at a thematic connection.

It is also noteworthy that heavenly imagery features both in Luke 17:20–37 and in 21:5–36, earlier to symbolize how unmistakable the Son of humanity will be on his day (17:24) and later as portents preceding the coming of the Son of humanity (21:25–27). Although Lang asserts that the language of the "day" or "days" of the Son of humanity, so prominent in Luke 17, is "conspicuously absent" from Luke 21,[43] this overlooks the association in 21:34–36 between "that Day" and standing before the Son of humanity, which must surely relate to the deliverance drawing near at the coming of the Son of humanity in 21:27–28. The expression, "days of the Son of humanity," is indeed missing from the eschatological discourse of Luke 21,[44] but it is more difficult to affirm the absence of the "day of the

---

40. Lang, "Reading Luke 17.22 as Antanaclasis," 290.
41. Ibid., 291.
42. See, e.g., Carroll, *Luke*, 345–57.
43. Lang, "Reading Luke 17.22 as Antanaclasis," 291.
44. For those who interpret the coming of the Son of humanity as referring to the destruction of Jerusalem, the "days of vengeance" in Luke 21:22 are in some sense "days of the Son of humanity." For Ryan Juza, however, the "days of the Son of humanity" comprise the period of rejection and suffering experienced by both Jesus and

Son of humanity," which seems clearly to refer to his return. As a result, it is hardly far-fetched to equate "the day of the Son of humanity's disclosure" (17:30) with "the coming of the Son of humanity on a cloud with power and much glory" (21:27).

In this connection, it is noteworthy that the expression, "days are coming," appears not only in Luke 17:22 but also in 21:6. The same expression also appears much earlier in Luke 5:35, at which point Jesus forewarns that days are coming when the bridegroom will be taken away from his companions so that then they will fast in those days.[45] It is difficult to decide whether "days are coming" in Luke 5:35 refers to the time of Jesus' suffering and death or beyond it, but in 21:6 this expression undoubtedly points beyond events recounted within Luke's narrative—in this case, the destruction of the temple a generation after Jesus. In view of other parallels between the discourses in Luke 17 and 21, the days said to be coming in 17:22 might also point beyond the bounds of the Gospel narrative to something as yet unrealized at the time when the Gospel was written.

Yet another conceptual similarity between the two discourses in Luke 17 and 21 is the relation between what is anticipated of the Son of humanity and what is said about the reign of God. Lang accepts that what is said about the reign of God in Luke 17:20–21 is "topically related" to what follows regarding the Son of humanity in 17:22–33.[46] In Luke 21:25–36 the nearness of the reign of God parallels the nearing of deliverance associated with the coming of the Son of humanity, thereby displaying yet again a close connection between what is affirmed of both the Son of humanity and the reign of God.[47]

In light of the various conceptual parallels between Luke 17:20–37 and 21:5–36, one hesitates to dissociate one from the other (or either of these later passages from 12:35–40).[48] Lang may be correct that Luke 17:22–37

---

his witnesses leading up to the destruction of Jerusalem, interpreted as the revelatory and indeed condemnatory "day of the Son of humanity." See Juza, "One of the Days," 575–95. For those who accept Luke 21:27 as intimating the destruction of Jerusalem, Juza's interpretation of Luke 17:22–37 is difficult to dismiss.

45. For Carroll (*Luke*, 349), "Luke 17:22 repeats the point Jesus made in 5:34–35," thus referring to a time in the (near) future when the disciples will experience the absence of Jesus.

46. Lang, "Reading Luke 17.22 as Antanaclasis," 291.

47. A similar close relation between what is affirmed of the coming Son of humanity and the reign of God appears also in Luke 9:26–27, part of a passage with close resonances to Luke 17:22–37.

48. Luke 12:35–40 hardly features in Lang's two studies on Luke 17:22–37, although a footnote within his 2013 study draws attention to thematic similarities between the discourses in Luke 12 and Luke 17, primarily in support of his contention that such

relates to the passion of Jesus, but it is rather more difficult to affirm that it bears no relation to the *parousia* of Jesus.

There is much to appreciate in Lang's rereading of Luke 17:22-37, but I am yet to be persuaded that this passage is unrelated to the *parousia*. Lang offers a possible, perhaps even plausible, reading of Luke 17:23-25, but his interpretation of several features of these verses as referring to aspects of Luke's passion narrative seems strained. For example, in light of the way in which Luke 17:23 echoes 17:21, Lang's reading of this verse as presaging, but also warning against, the disciples' abandonment or betrayal of Jesus later in the narrative is not so convincing as to trump more traditional readings. Nor, it seems to me, is the burden of the lightning analogy in 17:24 "suddenness," as Lang avers without argument,[49] but rather unmistakable transparency. As a result, it is difficult to follow Lang in reading the lightning analogy as referring to the crucifixion of Jesus.

Moreover, although the passion prediction of Luke 17:25 is crucial to Lang's interpretation, the way in which this saying begins, πρῶτον δὲ δεῖ (*prōton de dei* . . .), makes room not only for Lang's reading, in which suffering and rejection precede the Son of humanity's crucifixion (or postresurrection appearances), but also for a more traditional reading in which the Son of humanity's suffering and death must precede his more glorious appearance. "By only mentioning suffering and rejection as what 'must come first' (πρῶτον δὲ δεῖ)," according to Lang, "the text remains open to the possibility that the crucifixion itself, or what follows from it, corresponds to the metaphor in v. 24."[50] In support of this claim, Lang notes that Luke's other passion predictions make reference to the Son of humanity's death and resurrection, but the textual evidence cited in support of this observation (Luke 9:22; 18:31-34; 24:7) is incomplete. First, it is doubtful, on Lang's reading of Luke 17:22-37 as directed to the disciples of Jesus within the Gospel, that 24:7 counts as a passion prediction. And second, if Luke 9:44 is taken to be a passion prediction that echoes 9:22, as it surely must, then 17:25 may also be read as intimating the Son of humanity's death.[51] As a result, perhaps the best commentary on the passion prediction of Luke 17:25 is 24:26, in which the risen Jesus poses the rhetorical question: "Was

---

teaching is directed toward the disciples within Luke's narrative. See Lang, "Luke 17:37 and the Arrest of Jesus," 322.

49. Lang, "Reading Luke 17.22 as Antanaclasis," 293; Lang, "Luke 17:37 and the Arrest of Jesus," 327-30.

50. Lang, "Reading Luke 17.22 as Antanaclasis," 294.

51. Luke 9:44-45 is important for Lang's interpretation of Luke 17:22 as *antanaclasis*. (See also Luke 12:50 and 13:32-33, two implicit passion predictions that also precede 17:25.)

it not necessary that the Messiah suffer these things and [only then] enter into his glory?"

For Lang, the passion prediction of Luke 17:25 is not out of place because its context concerns not the *parousia* but "the coming apocalypse of the Son of Man in his suffering."[52] Perhaps so, but it is no less plausible to read Luke 17:25 as reinforcing the burden of other passion predictions within Luke's narrative that the suffering and death of the Son of humanity is the necessary precondition for his "day of disclosure" (17:30). No doubt "the apocalypse of the Son of Man *begins with the passion*,"[53] as Lang expresses the upshot of his argument in his concluding remarks, but that does not necessarily imply that Luke 17:22–37 is solely concerned with the passion.

Much also depends on what is made of the differences between the varied expressions, "one of the days of the Son of humanity" (17:22), his "day" (17:24, 30), and "the days of the Son of humanity" (17:26). For Lang,

> The "days of" expressions in vv. 26 and 28 indicate the time just prior to and including the departure of the representative figure [Noah, Lot], and "the day" (vv. 27 and 29) is the departure itself, which initiates the divine judgment and redemption. Extending this comparison to the "days of"/"day of" the Son of Man, the time prior to and including the departure of the Son of Man is the time prior to and including the rejection and suffering of the Son of Man in Jerusalem, and so the earthly ministry of Jesus. The "day of the Son of Man," or "the day when the Son of Man is revealed" (17.30), corresponds to the day that begins with the night of Jesus' arrest and departure (Lk. 22)—the event which inaugurates the passion that the Son of Man is destined to endure.[54]

In short, the comparisons with "the days" of Noah and Lot leading up to "the day" of their respective escapes are determinative for making sense of "the days of the Son of humanity" leading up to his "day."

Also important for Lang is that "the day" of both Noah and Lot is characterized as a departure, rather than as a return.[55] Here, however, Lang's interpretive agenda seems to blur his exegetical vision. Lot may have departed from Sodom, but Noah went into the boat. What these respective comparisons emphasize is the all-encompassing destruction that *came* (the cataclysmic flood) or *came down from heaven* (fire and sulfur) on the day

---

52. Lang, "Reading Luke 17.22 as Antanaclasis," 294.
53. Ibid., 298 (emphasis mine).
54. Ibid., 294.
55. Ibid., 294–95; Lang, "Luke 17:37 and the Arrest of Jesus," 331n28.

that Noah entered the boat and Lot left Sodom. As a result, the day of the disclosure of the Son of humanity in Luke 17:30 would seem to be more closely related to his final, all-encompassing retribution than to his disclosure as one who must suffer violence and death.

Based in part on similar imprecision regarding the eschatological "day" or "days" in 1 Enoch 96:8, I previously accepted these related expressions in Luke 17:22-30 as largely synonymous or at least as too ambiguous to differentiate with any clarity. On further reflection, however, I have come to a different view.[56]

Among the traditional materials at his disposal, Luke was familiar with Son of humanity sayings with different emphases. Whether he was familiar with Mark's Gospel or, as I think more likely, an earlier source shared by all three authors of the Synoptic Gospels, Luke was aware of Son of humanity sayings that featured his authority (Mark 2:10, 28), other sayings that focused on the Son of humanity's suffering, death, and resurrection (Mark 8:31; 9:31; 10:33-34), and future-oriented sayings that anticipated the Son of humanity's coming with power and/or glory (Mark 8:38; 13:26; 14:62). He was also familiar with Son of humanity sayings that summed up the purpose of his earthly mission (Mark 10:45; Luke 19:10). Reflecting on such similar sayings with varied emphases, Luke may well have categorized them accordingly, thereby anticipating the more recent threefold classification of such sayings. In an eschatologically charged setting, within which biblical "day of the Lord" imagery was applied to different phases of Jesus' mission *as a whole*, Luke might well have considered each such phase as one of several "days of the Son of humanity." Especially in relation to future-oriented Son of humanity sayings, such a view helps to make sense of the peculiarly Lukan notion of multiple "days of the Son of humanity," any one of which might be distinguished from others.[57] "One of the days of the Son of humanity" might refer to his death and/or resurrection, whereas another might refer to his coming in glory, whether understood as his ascension

---

56. Although I came to this view while reflecting on Lang's two studies, in one respect I concur with Juza, "One of the Days," 575-81, namely, by understanding the *days* (plural) of the Son of humanity as a series of related, albeit distinct, days associated with Jesus as the Son of humanity. In certain respects but for different reasons, my suggested interpretation also resonates with that of Leaney, *Gospel according to St. Luke*, 68-72, 229-32. To be clear, however, I demur from both Leaney and Juza that Luke 17:22-37 relates to the destruction of Jerusalem.

57. This view does not make as much sense of Son of humanity sayings focused on Jesus' historic mission, but Luke speaks of "days of the Son of humanity" only with reference to the future. In this connection, it is notable that in various ways Luke 17:22-37 echoes 9:18-27, which contains initial references to two different future-oriented Son of humanity sayings (9:22, 27). See Neville, *A Peaceable Hope*, 134-36.

or return (or indeed both). In Luke's understanding, perhaps the passion/death of Jesus, his resurrection, his ascension to the right hand of God (see Acts 2:33; 7:55–56!),[58] and his return are all decisive "days" of the Son of humanity, any one of which might be designated "one of the days of the Son of humanity."

In relation to Luke 17:22, such a view facilitates the following readings. On Lang's interpretation of this saying as an instance of *antanaclasis*, one might understand the Lukan Jesus as saying that days are coming when the disciples will want to witness one of the days of the Son of humanity but will fail to perceive it as such because they are looking for a day of glory, not his day of suffering and death, which they will witness but also fail to perceive as one of his indispensable days. By contrast, if Luke 17:22 is not understood as an instance of *antanaclasis*, the disciples will neither truly nor fully witness one of the days of the Son of humanity for one of two reasons: either because they will abandon Jesus, having failed to comprehend that suffering and death are integral to one of his divinely determined days;[59] or because they desire to see one of his glorious days without witnessing his day of suffering and death. On such a view, to decide on whether or not Luke 17:22 is an instance of *antanaclasis* is not determinative for reading the remainder of the discourse as focused solely on Jesus' passion. In Luke 17:22-37 the suffering and death of Jesus is undoubtedly in view—but (probably) as the divinely ordained precondition for subsequent, more glorious days of the Son of humanity, which are either recounted or anticipated in Luke's Gospel and Acts.

If, despite Lang's argument to the contrary, Luke 17:30 relates to the *parousia* rather than to the passion of the Son of humanity—albeit *only after and beyond* his experience of suffering and death—this implies that 17:31-35 also relates to the *parousia*. Although the phrase, "on that night," in Luke 17:34 is difficult to explain, except perhaps as a Lukan variation or deliberate evocation of 12:35-40, 17:31-32 tethers the remainder of this discourse to the preceding part. Like Luke 17:25, 17:33 seems intrusive in this context—except as a reminder (see 9:23-26) that willingness to lose one's life out of loyalty to Jesus and his way is the sole means to ultimate preservation. Luke 17:31-32 might seem to suggest the possibility of escape on the day of the disclosure of the Son of humanity, but 17:33 suggests that Jesus' counterintuitive recipe for preserving one's life remains in place, *then*

---

58. In light of what is affirmed of Jesus in Acts 2:33, perhaps Pentecost might also be considered "one of the days of the Son of humanity."

59. Luke 24:21 and Acts 1:6 might lend support to this latter reading of Luke 17:22, but Luke 23:49a suggests that the disciples of Jesus do witness the crucifixion of Jesus, albeit from afar.

as now. This interpretation seems no less compelling than Lang's reading, in which the instructions of Jesus are understood to forecast events narrated in Luke 22, "when Jesus is divided from his disciples, and they are divided from each other."[60]

As much as any particular text within Luke 17, the culminating saying of Jesus seems to anticipate his passion. In answer to this question from his disciples, "Where, Lord?" Jesus replies, "Where so ever the body, there also will eagles be gathered" (17:37). It is tempting to interpret this saying as foreshadowing Jesus' own crucifixion, with the body his own tortured body surrounded by Roman soldiers. As earlier indicated, Lang considers "the body" of this saying to signify Jesus' own body, albeit at his arrest by hostile (but non-Roman) forces, represented by the biblical image of eagles. "Understanding that the division depicted in vv. 34–35 is a prediction related to [the disciples]," Lang writes, "their question concerns the place where this division will occur."[61] But if Luke 17:34–35 presages universal judgment, as Lang concedes, to interpret Jesus' answer as forecasting his arrest is too restrictive and also unrelated to location. Lang assumes that Jesus' response dignifies his disciples' question focused on locality, the question of *where*, but whether that can be assumed is uncertain. It is not as though the disciples are presented by Luke as routinely perspicacious. Especially in relation to the Son of humanity's necessary suffering, they are obtuse (9:44–45; 18:31–34), a point emphasized by Lang. Thus their question might as well relate to the saying in Luke 17:30 or to the saying in 17:24 or to both, and Jesus' response might simply reiterate how unmistakable that day of the Son of humanity will be and thereby signal how superfluous the question is.

If, as Matthew 24:26–28 suggests, Luke found among the traditions available to him both the lightning and eagles analogies side by side as related and hence mutually interpreting sayings, his bracketing of much of the discourse material in 17:22–37 between these two sayings (17:24, 37) can be seen as purposive and meaningful. In response to the disciples' redundant question, which is provoked by all that Jesus has been saying and thereby reinforces the obtuseness of the disciples implicit in Jesus' opening observation (17:22), Jesus reiterates in 17:37 the burden of 17:24 while also

60. Lang, "Reading Luke 17.22 as Antanaclasis," 297. Cf. Lang, "Luke 17:37 and the Arrest of Jesus," 333: "With Jesus' arrest and departure 'in that night,' the comparisons made in 17:26–30 begin to take place within the world of the narrative." Regarding Luke 17:35, however, Lang concedes in his earlier and more detailed study that this image of two women grinding grain "must be taken in a more general sense as an illustration of the coming judgment, inaugurated by the cross, that extends across humanity" (297). In his slightly later study, Lang says something similar about *both images of division* in 17:34–35 (334). In my view, this concession is applicable to the passage as a whole.

61. Lang, "Luke 17:37 and the Arrest of Jesus," 334.

intimating the suffering and death of the Son of humanity (17:25) that must precede the subsequent unmistakable day of the (heavenly) disclosure of the selfsame Son of humanity. In other words, perhaps the concluding eagles saying was intended by Luke not only to reinforce the sense of the lightning saying but also to evoke Jesus' suffering as the necessary precondition for that (yet future) unmistakable day.

On reflection, as suggestive and appealing as Lang's rereading of Luke 17:20–37 is, it would seem that this passage looks beyond the passion of Jesus to his *parousia*. Perhaps better, it looks forward to the *parousia* through (perception patterned on) the passion of Jesus. In this sense, Luke 17:22–37 envisages Jesus as looking to the future with what might be described as bifocal vision—in the short term, to the suffering triggered by abandonment and betrayal on the part of his disciples, but also beyond that "day" to another promised "day" of the Son of humanity as yet unfulfilled. With John Carroll, whose understanding of this passage has also been influenced by Lang's rereading, I accept that "the discourse of 17:22–37 foreshadows the events of the Passion Narrative," but also that "the passion drama does not exhaust the meaning potential of the discourse: there is eschatological remainder . . . ."[62] Were Lang's rereading to prove correct, that would draw the sting from Luke's most vehement text of teleological terror, but it would seem that the evangelist of peace held out the prospect of eschatological vengeance on the day of the disclosure of the Son of humanity.

Luke 21:5–36

No less than the content of Matthew 24 and Mark 13, the eschatological discourse of Jesus in Luke 21 is well nigh inscrutable from an interpretive perspective. Here my focus is on the extent to which the judgment foreshadowed in this chapter is cause for teleological terror. Much mayhem is forecast in Luke 21 but, perhaps surprisingly, not in relation to the Son of humanity's arrival. Although the teaching of Jesus in Luke 21 generally reinforces previously articulated eschatological themes and emphases, eschatological expectation in this teaching block differs in one important respect—the absence of eschatological vengeance explicitly associated with the arrival of the Son of humanity. The Son of humanity is expected to come with power and glory (21:27) but not with exterminating sword or punishing staff (cf. 12:45–48a); the coming of the Son of humanity brings a day of deliverance (21:28), not days of destruction (cf. 17:27, 29).

---

62. Carroll, *Luke*, 353.

Such an interpretive appraisal is based in part on dissociating the heavenly signs of Luke 21:25-28 from the prediction of Jerusalem's destruction (21:20-24). Because there is no clearly defined demarcation between the prediction of Jerusalem's trampling by Gentiles and the forecast of heavenly signs, some consider the heavenly signs of Luke 21:25-28 as both biblical imagery for, and theological commentary on, Jerusalem's destruction. Perhaps the most high-profile proponent of this perspective is N. T. Wright, who regards the destruction of Jerusalem as the historical demonstration of God's vindication of the mission and message of Jesus by means of his exaltation.[63] There is something to be said for this reading of Luke's eschatology, and I readily concede that my disagreement with this viewpoint is partly conditioned by theological and ethical considerations.[64] Either to equate or to parallel the carnage associated with the destruction of Jerusalem with divine vindication of Jesus seems theologically incongruous to me. Without textual grounding for an alternative view, however, I might grudgingly have to accept that Wright and others interpret Luke correctly on this point.

The textual basis for dissociating the arrival of the Son of humanity from Jerusalem's destruction is Luke 21:10-11. For the following reasons, I read these verses as a parenthetical preview of what must precede the Son of humanity's arrival on a cloud with power and much glory.[65] First, only Luke records Jesus as referring to heavenly signs so early in the discourse (cf. Matt. 24:7-8; Mark 13:8). Second, Luke's uniquely intrusive introduction to Jesus' words at the beginning of 21:10, including its phrasing, suggests that what follows serves as a summary. Third, in 21:11 the double use of the enclitic particle τε (*te*) along with καί (*kai*) couples together (a) great earthquakes with famines and plagues and (b) terrors with great signs from the heavens. And finally, the continuation of the discourse in 21:12, "Before all these things, however . . . ," reads like a backtracking resumption. The opening section of Jesus' response to the question posed in 21:7 concludes with the words, "for these things must occur first, but the end is by no means imminent" (21:9). Immediately thereafter the words of 21:10-11 interrupt the flow of the discourse thus far to form a new beginning: "At that time he was saying to them, 'People groups will rise against people groups and

---

63. See Wright, *Jesus and the Victory of God*, chapters 8 and 13; and Wright, *Challenge of Jesus*, chapters 2 and 5.

64. For many advocates of an exaltation interpretation of Luke 21:27 (and parallels), however, there are apologetic reasons for holding to such a viewpoint, the most significant of which is to protect Jesus from the charge of false prophecy.

65. I am indebted to John Carroll for this view of Luke 21:10-11. See Carroll, *Response to the End*, 112, where he identifies Luke 21:9-11 as "an overview of the entire eschatological scenario." Cf. Carroll, *Luke*, 415-16.

kingdoms against kingdoms; not only will there be great earthquakes but also, from place to place, famines and plagues, not only terrors but also great signs from heaven.'"

Instead of identifying only the "beginning of end-time labor pains" (Matt 24:8; Mark 13:8) at this early point in the discourse, in Luke's reconfigured presentation Jesus previews the full sweep of events preceding the coming of the Son of humanity. Read as an eschatological preview, the summary in Luke 21:10–11 compensates in advance, so to speak, for the absence in 21:25 of an explicit distancing of heavenly signs from the destruction of Jerusalem. This is important not only for chronological but also for theological reasons because many see in the description of Jerusalem's destruction (21:20–24) something of a template for eschatological judgment. In other words, the "days of vengeance" visited upon Jerusalem comprise a precursor to eschatological vengeance! Luke 21:25–36 undoubtedly affirms judgment at the coming of the Son of humanity, but the theme of judgment is not presented in such a way that it must be construed as vengeance. Rather, in tandem with the countercultural scenario forecast in 12:35–40, "Luke's programmatic statement on eschatology" in 21:25–36 enunciates an end-expectation more in keeping with focal features of Jesus' historic mission as recorded by Luke—redemption, reversal, and restoration.[66]

CONCLUDING INTERPRETIVE IMPLICATIONS

The rather different eschatological emphases of Matthew and Luke reflect differences that obtain more broadly across the New Testament. The violent imagery with which final victory over evil is depicted in the Revelation to John reinforces the prospect of teleological terror evidenced in Matthew's Gospel, but both the Gospels according to Mark and John and also the Acts of the Apostles mute the motif of eschatological vengeance even more than does Luke's Gospel. Moreover, although the prospect of final judgment features in all four canonical Gospels, only in two of them does the prospect of such judgment threaten teleological terror, and only in Matthew is eschatological vengeance a major motif. Indeed, on close inspection, Gospel texts in which Jesus looks forward to the coming—or, in Matthew, to the *parousia*—of the Son of humanity frequently fail to feature divine retributive violence. Since it was clearly possible to narrate the story of Jesus without featuring ultimate violence on his part, despite his own violent death,

---

66. The phrase, "Luke's programmatic statement on eschatology," derives from Carroll, *Response to the End*, 103–104, to describe the discourse of Luke 21:5–36 in its entirety.

the degree to which eschatological vengeance features within the Gospels would seem to reflect the mind-sets and circumstances of these respective witnesses to Jesus' mission and message. In other words, although divine judgment is intrinsic to the Jesus story, the prospect of eschatological vengeance is but one conceptualization of divine judgment, not its defining determination. This raises a significant exegetical no less than interpretive issue—the nature of divine judgment. There are biblical reasons for the ready association between divine judgment and retributive violence, but end-expectation in the Gospels (as well as elsewhere in the New Testament) also provides grounds for dissociating divine judgment from eschatological vengeance. The apparent default setting that divine judgment necessarily implies violent retribution needs to change.

Related to this is the scholarly prejudice that apocalyptic thought patterns are inherently violent and vindictive. One often encounters the supposition that eschatological vengeance is but the concomitant expression of an apocalyptic vision of reality. Granted that an apocalyptic worldview may—and often does—find expression in texts of teleological terror, certain Gospel texts nevertheless destabilize such a ready association between apocalyptic and violence. Some apocalyptic texts served a militant ideology, whereas others were written in the service of a non-militant ideological stance, as John J. Collins has shown.[67] Analogously, in my view, apocalyptic eschatology may be premised on divine *shalom* no less than on divine violence, as evidenced in at least two of the canonical Gospels by virtue of an apparent conceptual renovation of apocalyptic eschatology in light of the mission and message of Jesus. In all four biblical Gospels, theological reflection on the mission and message of Jesus was facilitated by apocalyptic thought forms, and in the Gospels according to Mark, Luke, and John, such thought forms were largely reconfigured under the impress of the story of Jesus. One such reconfiguration was to move toward dissociating divine action from violence.

In the synoptic tradition, moreover, there is a discernible correlation between parabolic form and violent eschatology. When Jesus is remembered as warning about final judgment in parables, such parabolic texts often envisage final judgment in violent terms. This is especially evident in Matthew's Gospel, which among the Gospels depicts eschatological events in the most violent and retributive ways. When Jesus is recalled as presaging end-time events in more prosaic language, however, as in the non-parabolic sections of the so-called eschatological discourse in Matthew 24, Mark 13, and Luke 21, the future arrival of the Son of humanity is described largely

---

67. Collins, "From Prophecy to Apocalypticism," esp. 158–59.

in positive or non-retributive terms. For example, although the coming of the Son of humanity in Matt 24:27–31 is envisaged along the lines of mustering for eschatological battle, no battle ensues and no violence is visited on lamenting tribes of the earth. As outlined above, however, Matthew's eschatological discourse continues with a series of *parables* that envisage the day of the Son of humanity as *Doomsday*, not only for those deemed to be evil, wicked, or unrighteous but also for insiders judged to be unfaithful.

Admittedly, non-parabolic eschatological instruction is no less figurative or symbolic than parabolic teaching. Like prophetic insight,[68] eschatological foresight in visionary and intuitive, not empirical-in-advance, so to speak.[69] Even so, the difference between parabolic and non-parabolic eschatological discourse does seem to parallel, broadly speaking, the distinction between violent and nonviolent eschatology. If this correlation holds generally within the synoptic tradition, perhaps the perception that Jesus' parabolic eschatological teaching tends to make use of more violent imagery than his non-parabolic eschatological instruction provides further interpretive leverage for tempering texts of teleological terror. After all, parables provoke rather than preach, tease rather than tutor, inspire rather than instruct, and destabilize rather than indoctrinate. Rather than drawing clearly circumscribed sense delimitations, parables open up indeterminate horizons of meaning potential. In short, parables invite audience participation to probe meaning, not least their own.

Especially with respect to violent eschatology in Matthew's Gospel, then, not only can one say that eschatological vengeance is largely a Matthean feature, relative to his canonical counterparts; not only can one say that violent eschatology is theologically and morally incongruous with Matthew's *own* account of Jesus' historic mission and message; but one can also say that, relative to non-parabolic eschatological teaching recounted by Matthew (no less than his synoptic counterparts), most texts of teleological terror are parabolic and therefore susceptible to interpretation more in theological tune with the life story of *Immanu-el* as narrated by Matthew himself, regarding which he is in much closer concert with his biblical counterparts.

Some interpreters may be nonplussed by the claim that, within the non-parabolic sections of the so-called synoptic eschatological discourse, the future arrival of the Son of humanity is described largely in positive or non-retributive terms. For some, references to the coming of the Son of humanity in Matthew 24, Mark 13, and Luke 21 are understood to signify

---

68. See Meyer, *Aims of Jesus*, 246–47.
69. See Allison, *Historical Christ*, 97–98.

divine vindication of Jesus by means of exaltation, which is paralleled and thereby mundanely manifested by Jerusalem's destruction. By virtue of intertextual associations with prophetic texts, the imagery of cosmic collapse serves as theological commentary on the epochal significance of Jerusalem's destruction construed as divine judgment. On this reading, the association between the coming of the Son of humanity and violent retribution is integral and inextricable, although this is generally neither acknowledged nor addressed.

This reading of future-oriented or "apocalyptic" Son of humanity texts has been subjected to close and careful scrutiny by Edward Adams,[70] whose critique is instructive and, to my mind, largely persuasive. Reflecting on the interpretive question Adams addresses has reinforced a related but altogether different interpretive conviction. For over a century, New Testament scholars have been keenly aware of the close relation between eschatology and ethics—or, more precisely, between eschatological expectation and ethical exhortation. By and large, ethical exhortation within New Testament texts has been understood to be conditioned by eschatological expectation. Where eschatological expectation and ethical exhortation are related within the Gospels and the wider New Testament, however, that conventional description of the relation between eschatology and ethics deserves closer scrutiny, especially when divine violence plays a role in end-expectation. In such circumstances, moral appraisal of the validity and value of violence deserves to play a role in evaluating eschatological expectations no less than the more conventional evaluation of the moral implications of eschatological convictions.

In conclusion, without attempting to tame Gospel texts of teleological terror, close study of such texts nevertheless raises both implicit and explicit interpretive implications. First, contrary to the common misconception that texts of terror inhabit only the Old Testament rather than the New, texts of teleological terror comprise but one category of violent texts within the Gospels and the wider New Testament, depending to some extent on how violence is defined. Second, although some eschatological texts within the Gospels (and indeed elsewhere in the New Testament) seem to anticipate divine vengeance, others do not, a literary datum that unsettles any inevitable association between divine judgment and violence. Third, related to the reality that not every eschatological text in the Gospels anticipates divine vengeance is the positive correlation, especially in Matthew's Gospel, between parabolic form and violent eschatology, which opens up room for interpretive discernment. A fourth interpretive issue is whether, as I infer,

---

70. Adams, *Stars Will Fall from Heaven*, 1–181.

a peaceable eschatological hope is compatible with an apocalyptic vision of reality. Fifth, for those who interpret Gospel texts concerning the coming of the Son of humanity as either non-eschatological or eschatological in the sense that they signify the vindication of Jesus as messiah by means of Jerusalem's destruction, the onus is not only to persuade on that particular point but also to show how such an understanding of divine action coheres with the intuition articulated by the Gospel authors that the historic mission of Jesus provides a window into the very nature or character of God. Sixth, and related to the theological interpretation of Jesus' mission and message in the Gospels and elsewhere in the New Testament, the relation between eschatology and ethics requires reconsideration. It is inadequate merely to ascertain how eschatological convictions impact on moral exhortation. In New Testament theology and ethics, the question of whether eschatological expectations cohere with theologically grounded moral convictions also needs to be addressed. In other words, interpretive discernment and choice on the basis of theological-moral criteria are integral—rather than an impediment—to responsible exegesis. In line with this—and on the basis of conclusions reached in earlier chapters of this book—I continue to hold that the moral character of Jesus' historic mission and message serves as an interpretive criterion for evaluating and indeed contesting Gospel (and other New Testament) texts of teleological terror.

Concluding Remarks

THE VEHEMENT JESUS? ALLOWING for the subtle distinction posited in my introductory chapter between *vehemence* and *violence*, the basic argument of this book is that the vehement Jesus of the biblical Gospels is nevertheless the peaceful Jesus. Indeed, insofar as distributive or restorative justice is integral to both the procuration and preservation of peace, Gospel depictions of the vehement Jesus might well be indispensable to his peaceable profile.

No less counterintuitively, at various points in the preceding chapters I maintain that an apocalyptic vision of reality is compatible with, even indispensable to, the peaceful persona and proclamation of Jesus. In chapter 1, for example, I follow in the footsteps of those who argue that the declaration of Jesus in Matt 10:34, "Do not suppose that I have come to sow peace upon the earth; I have not come to sow peace but rather a sword," is best comprehended within the ideological matrix of apocalyptic eschatology. Beyond that perception, however, I also argue that an apocalyptic mind-set or vision of reality is indispensable for interpreting Matt 10:34 in accord with a peaceable conception of Jesus' mission and message. Similarly, in connection with Jesus' curious command in Luke 22:36 that his disciples purchase swords, I consider that the presumption of an apocalyptic mind-set on the part of Jesus and Luke—or Jesus as portrayed by Luke—is decisive for interpreting this instruction in peaceful terms.

Such a viewpoint is at odds with much that is asserted about apocalyptic eschatology or an apocalyptic vision of reality. As illustrated in chapter 7, which is devoted to a discussion of recent discourse on the Johannine depiction of the temple incident, Jesus' disruptive demeanor within the temple precincts is frequently taken to reflect a mind-set shaped by apocalyptic eschatology, according to which his actions anticipate divine judgment in the form of destruction. Similarly, Jesus' "violent" attack on temple trade is sometimes judged to be an expected, if not inevitable, expression of his apocalyptic mentality. Although I accept that apocalyptic eschatology or an apocalyptic mind-set frequently finds expression in stark descriptions of vindictive violence, the point remains that three of the biblical Gospels, and especially the Gospels according to Mark and John, retain an apocalyptic vision of reality while reconfiguring the relation between divine disclosure (apocalypse) and violence.

At times during the course of this book, I cautiously distance certain depictions of the vehement Jesus from the historical figure of Jesus himself. In chapter 2, for example, I concur with those who hold that Matt 18:35 is probably a *Matthean* application of the preceding parable of the Unforgiving Slave. This concluding inference seems to provide a portal into Matthew's own retributive mind-set, in accordance with which he both received and interpreted the story of Jesus. Within the Gospel tradition, the vehement Jesus is, to a significant extent, a Matthean construct. Not entirely, however. In sayings about the destruction of Jerusalem attributed to Jesus by Luke, analyzed and appraised in chapter 3, we seem occasionally to encounter Luke's rather than Jesus' own viewpoint on the judgment of Jerusalem.

Within this exercise in New Testament theology and ethics, however, distancing Gospel depictions of the vehement Jesus from Jesus himself is a subsidiary interpretive maneuver. More important is interpretive engagement by means of intratextual critique, whereby disconcerting dimensions of a Gospel writer's portrait of Jesus are appraised in light of determinative features of the same evangelist's Christology and moral vision. In chapter 3, for example, Lukan texts that construe Jerusalem's destruction in terms of divine judgment are evaluated not only against the backdrop of Israel's prophetic heritage but also in light of Luke's peaceful Christological and moral convictions, shaped as these were by traditions about Jesus known to Luke and also by his own reflection on these traditions. In this connection, the preceding discussion of the parable of the Throne Claimant in chapter 2 also plays a role by demonstrating, on the basis of decisive theological and ethical emphases within Luke's Gospel, that it is possible to read this parable in such a way that it reflects neither on Jesus nor on God. Rather, it more plausibly mirrors the machinations associated with conventional modes of ruling that are inimical to the reign of God as displayed in Jesus' mission and message. If so, however, such an interpretation has a bearing on whether or how one views the destruction of Jerusalem and its temple as a mundane manifestation of divine judgment.

In various ways, intratextual critique plays a crucial role in several other chapters—from adventuring an alternative interpretation of Mark's narrative framing of the temple incident by the cursing and withering of a hapless fig tree (chapter 5) to reading Matthew 23 in dialogue with the moral vision of the beatitudes in Matthew 5 (chapter 8) to appraising texts of teleological terror in light of the peaceable character of Jesus' historic mission and message (chapter 9). No doubt there are other ways of addressing such troubling texts, if indeed they are perceived as perplexing, but I leave appraisal of this mode of interpretive grappling—whether it be sound or unsound—to those willing to taste and thereby test its fruit (see Matt 7:15-20; Luke 6:43-45).

Of all the troubling texts considered in this book, those that come closest to implicating Jesus in violence are texts that testify to his wounding words. The available evidence suggests that Jesus was remembered as one who used forceful and confronting speech. At various points within the Gospels, most noticeably in the vehement invective against scribes and Pharisees found in Matthew 23, Jesus is recalled as engaging in abusive slander that many would now characterize as verbal violence. Whether or not Jesus' characterization in Matthew 23 accurately reflects the character of the historical figure of Jesus is difficult to determine, but it seems likely that Jesus did sometimes engage in verbal polemics. The Gospel writers seem unabashed by this, but the Gospel writer who depicts Jesus most vehemently in this respect also presents Jesus as sensitive to the morality of speech. In other words, within Matthew's Gospel there is discord between Jesus' teaching on careful speech and his own verbal vehemence. Moreover, among early Christian communities concerned to take their moral bearings from Jesus, evidence suggests a heightened level of consciousness about the damaging effect of insulting invective. Despite his profoundly peaceful theology, the apostle Paul seems to have considered it necessary or at least defensible to castigate fellow Christians, as in his letter to the Galatians, but both James 3 and Eph 4:15 signal that early followers of Jesus recognized moral constraints on their speech no less than on other aspects of their conduct, even when considered to constitute a witness to truth. Thus, the canonical testimony to Jesus' rhetoric of rage is out of kilter with other features of his moral legacy.

At times, then, the vehement Jesus reflects the mind-sets of his earliest interpreters; at others, however, the vehement Jesus gestures to his wild "untamability." Though merciful, the Jesus of the Gospels is not at our mercy, and though peaceful, the Jesus of the Gospels nevertheless disturbs our equanimity and passivity. In the words of Dale Allison, "A domesticated Jesus who sounds like us, makes us comfortable, and commends our opinions is no Jesus at all."[1] The vehement Jesus exhibits the conviction that proximity to Jesus implies one's undoing—for good, but one's undoing nonetheless. Although I continue to consider troubling certain Gospel texts explored in

---

1. Allison, *Historical Christ*, 90.

this book, wrestling with these texts has made me more, not less, attached to them. Having grappled with them, they maintain their grip on my life and moral identity. Despite their vexing features, I comprehend better why these texts in their respective narrative contexts have sustained no less than challenged would-be disciples for two millennia.

Bibliography

Adams, Edward. *The Stars Will Fall from Heaven: Cosmic Catastrophe in the New Testament and Its World*. Library of New Testament Studies 347. London: T & T Clark International, 2007.

Ådna, Jostein. "Jesus and the Temple." In *Handbook for the Study of the Historical Jesus, Volume 3: The Historical Jesus*, edited by Tom Holmén and Stanley E. Porter, 2635-75. Leiden: Brill, 2011.

———. "Temple Act." In *Dictionary of Jesus and the Gospels*, 2nd ed., edited by Joel B. Green, Jeannine K. Brown, and Nicholas Perrin, 947-52. Downers Grove, IL: InterVarsity, 2013.

Aichele, George. "Jesus' Violence." In *Violence, Utopia, and the Kingdom of God: Fantasy and Ideology in the Bible*, edited by Tina Pippin and George Aichele, 72-91. London: Routledge, 1998.

Alexis-Baker, Andy. "Violence, Nonviolence and the Temple Incident in John 2:13-15." *Biblical Interpretation* 20 (2012) 73-96.

Allison, Dale C., Jr. *Constructing Jesus: Memory, Imagination, and History*. Grand Rapids: Baker Academic, 2010.

———. *A Critical and Exegetical Commentary on the Epistle of James*. International Critical Commentary. London: Bloomsbury T&T Clark, 2013.

———. *The End of the Ages Has Come: An Early Interpretation of the Passion and Resurrection of Jesus*. Philadelphia: Fortress, 1985.

———. "The Eschatology of Jesus." In *The Encyclopedia of Apocalypticism, Volume 1: The Origins of Apocalypticism in Judaism and Christianity*, edited by John J. Collins, 267-302. New York: Continuum, 2000.

———. *The Historical Christ and the Theological Jesus*. Grand Rapids: Eerdmans, 2009.

———. "How to Marginalize the Traditional Criteria of Authenticity." In *Handbook for the Study of the Historical Jesus, Volume 1: How to Study the Historical Jesus*, edited by Tom Holmén and Stanley E. Porter, 3-30. Leiden: Brill, 2011.

———. *The Intertextual Jesus: Scripture in Q*. Harrisburg, PA: Trinity, 2000.

———. *Jesus of Nazareth: Millenarian Prophet*. Minneapolis: Fortress, 1998.

———. "Matt 23:39 = Luke 13:35b as a Conditional Prophecy." *Journal for the Study of the New Testament* 18 (1983) 75-84.

———. *The New Moses: A Matthean Typology*. Minneapolis: Fortress, 1993.

———. "Q 12:51-53 and Mark 9:11-13 and the Messianic Woes." In *Authenticating the Words of Jesus*, edited by Bruce Chilton and Craig A. Evans, 289-310. Leiden: Brill, 1999.

———. "Rejecting Violent Judgment: Luke 9:52–56 and Its Relatives." *Journal of Biblical Literature* 121 (2002) 459–78.
———. "Response to Rafael Rodríguez, 'Jesus as his Friends Remembered Him: A Review of Dale Allison's *Constructing Jesus*.'" *Journal for the Study of the Historical Jesus* 12 (2014) 245–54.
———. *Resurrecting Jesus: The Earliest Christian Tradition and Its Interpreters*. New York: T & T Clark International, 2005.
———. *Scriptural Allusions in the New Testament: Light from the Dead Sea Scrolls*. North Richland Hills, TX: BIBAL, 2000.
———. *Studies in Matthew: Interpretation Past and Present*. Grand Rapids: Baker Academic, 2005.
Arens, E. *The ΗΛΘΟΝ-Sayings in the Synoptic Tradition: A Historico-critical Investigation*. Göttingen: Vandenhoeck & Ruprecht, 1976.
Ashton, John. *Understanding the Fourth Gospel*. 2nd ed. Oxford: Oxford University Press, 2007.
Aslan, Reza. *Zealot: The Life and Times of Jesus of Nazareth*. Sydney: Allen & Unwin, 2013.
Avalos, Hector. *The Bad Jesus: The Ethics of New Testament Ethics*. The Bible in the Modern World 68. Sheffield: Sheffield Phoenix, 2015.
Bailey, Kenneth E. *Poet & Peasant and Through Peasant Eyes: A Literary-Cultural Approach to the Parables of Luke*. Combined edition. Grand Rapids: Eerdmans, 1983.
Balabanski, Vicky. *Eschatology in the Making: Mark, Matthew and the Didache*. Society for New Testament Studies Monograph Series 97. Cambridge: Cambridge University Press, 1997.
Bammel, Ernst. "The Revolution Theory from Reimarus to Brandon." In *Jesus and the Politics of His Day*, edited by Ernst Bammel and C. F. D. Moule, 11–68. Cambridge: Cambridge University Press, 1984.
Barrett, C. K. *The Gospel according to St John: An Introduction with Commentary and Notes on the Greek Text*. 2nd ed. London: SPCK, 1978.
Barton, Stephen C. *Discipleship and Family Ties in Mark and Matthew*. Society for New Testament Studies Monograph Series 80. Cambridge: Cambridge University Press, 1994.
———. "Why Do Things Move People? The Jerusalem Temple as Emotional Repository." *Journal for the Study of the New Testament* 37 (2015) 351–80.
Bauckham, Richard. *God Crucified: Monotheism and Christology in the New Testament*. Grand Rapids: Eerdmans, 1998.
———. "John for Readers of Mark." In *The Gospels for All Christians: Rethinking the Gospel Audiences*, edited by Richard Bauckham, 147–71. Grand Rapids: Eerdmans, 1998.
Beare, Francis Wright. *The Gospel according to Matthew: Translation, Introduction and Commentary*. Oxford: Blackwell; New York: Harper & Row, 1981; reprinted by Hendrickson, 1987.
Beasley-Murray, G. R. *Jesus and the Kingdom of God*. Grand Rapids: Eerdmans, 1986.
Berger, Klaus. "Der 'brutale' Jesus." *Bibel und Kirche* 51 (1996) 119–27.
Bermejo-Rubio, Fernando. "Jesus and the Anti-Roman Resistance." *Journal for the Study of the Historical Jesus* 12 (2014) 1–105.
———. "(Why) Was Jesus the Galilean Crucified Alone? Solving a False Conundrum." *Journal for the Study of the New Testament* 36 (2013) 127–54.

Bieringer, Reimund, Didier Pollefeyt, and Frederique Vandecasteele-Vanneuville, editors. *Anti-Judaism and the Fourth Gospel*. Louisville: Westminster John Knox, 2001.

Biggar, Nigel. "Against Christian Pacifism." In *In Defence of War*, 16–60. Oxford: Oxford University Press, 2013.

———. "The New Testament and Violence: Round Two." *Studies in Christian Ethics* 23 (2010) 73–80.

———. "Specify and Distinguish! Interpreting the New Testament on 'Non-violence.'" *Studies in Christian Ethics* 22 (2009) 164–84.

Black, C. Clifton. *Mark*. Abingdon New Testament Commentary. Nashville: Abingdon, 2011.

———. "Shouting at the Legally Deaf: Sin's Punishment in the Gospels." *Interpretation* 69 (2015) 311–22.

Black, Matthew. "'Not peace but a sword': Matt 10:34ff; Luke 12:51ff." In *Jesus and the Politics of His Day*, edited by Ernst Bammel and C. F. D. Moule, 287–94. Cambridge: Cambridge University Press, 1984.

Bock, Darrell L. *Luke 1:1–9:50*. Baker Exegetical Commentary on the New Testament. Grand Rapids: Baker, 1994.

———. *Luke 9:51–24:53*. BECNT. Grand Rapids: Baker, 1996.

Borg, Marcus J., and John Dominic Crossan. *The Last Week: What the Gospels Really Teach about Jesus's Final Days in Jerusalem*. New York: HarperSanFrancisco, 2006.

Boring, M. Eugene. *The Continuing Voice of Jesus: Christian Prophecy and the Gospel Tradition*. Louisville: Westminster John Knox, 1991.

———. "The Gospel of Matthew: Introduction, Commentary, and Reflections." In *The New Interpreter's Bible*, edited by Leander E. Keck, et al., 8:87–505. Nashville: Abingdon, 1995.

———. *Mark: A Commentary*. The New Testament Library. Louisville: Westminster John Knox, 2006.

Böttrich, Christfried. "Jesus und der Feigenbaum: Mk 11:12–14, 20–25 in der Diskussion." *Novum Testamentum* 39 (1997) 328–59.

Bovon, François. *Luke 1: A Commentary on the Gospel of Luke 1:1–9:50*. Translated by Christine M. Thomas. Hermeneia. Minneapolis: Fortress, 2002.

———. *Luke 2: A Commentary on the Gospel of Luke 9:51–19:27*. Translated by Donald S. Deer. Hermeneia. Minneapolis: Fortress, 2013.

———. *Luke 3: A Commentary on the Gospel of Luke 19:28–24:53*. Translated by James Crouch. Hermeneia. Minneapolis: Fortress, 2012.

Brandon, S. G. F. *Jesus and the Zealots: A Study of the Political Factor in Primitive Christianity*. Manchester: Manchester University Press, 1967.

Bredin, Mark R. *Jesus, Revolutionary of Peace: A Nonviolent Christology in the Book of Revelation*. Carlisle, Cumbria: Paternoster, 2003.

———. "John's Account of Jesus' Demonstration in the Temple: Violent or Nonviolent?" *Biblical Theology Bulletin* 33.2 (2003) 44–50.

Brenneman, Laura L. "Peace and Violence across the Testaments." In *Struggles for Shalom: Peace and Violence across the Testaments*, edited by Laura L. Brenneman and Brad D. Schantz, 1–10. Eugene, OR: Pickwick, 2014.

Brenneman, Laura L., and Brad D. Schantz, editors. *Struggles for Shalom: Peace and Violence across the Testaments*. Studies in Peace and Scripture 12. Eugene, OR: Pickwick, 2014.

Bridge, Steven L. *"Where the Eagles Are Gathered": The Deliverance of the Elect in Lukan Eschatology*. Journal for the Study of the New Testament Supplement Series 240. London: Sheffield Academic Press, 2003.

Brown, Raymond E. *The Death of the Messiah: From Gethsemane to the Grave*. 2 volumes. New York: Doubleday, 1994.

———. *The Gospel according to John*. 2 volumes. Anchor Bible. Garden City, NY: Doubleday, 1966–70.

Brown, Robert McAfee. *Religion and Violence*. 2nd ed. Philadelphia: Westminster, 1987.

Brown, Scott G. "Mark 11:1–12:12: A Triple Intercalation?" *Catholic Biblical Quarterly* 64 (2002) 78–89.

Bryan, Steven M. "Consumed by Zeal: John's Use of Psalm 69:9 and the Action in the Temple." *Bulletin for Biblical Research* 21 (2011) 479–94.

Bultmann, Rudolf. *History of the Synoptic Tradition*. Rev. ed. Translated by John Marsh. Oxford: Basil Blackwell, 1963.

Burkett, Delbert. *Rethinking the Gospel Sources: From Proto-Mark to Mark*. New York and London: T & T Clark International, 2004.

———. "The Return of Proto-Mark: A Response to David Neville." *Ephemerides Theologicae Lovanienses* 85 (2009) 117–34.

Byrne, Brendan. *A Costly Freedom: A Theological Reading of Mark's Gospel*. Collegeville, MN: Liturgical, 2008.

———. *The Hospitality of God: A Reading of Luke's Gospel*. Collegeville, MN: Liturgical, 2000.

Camara, Helder. *Spiral of Violence*. London: Sheed and Ward, 1971.

Campbell, D. Keith. "NT Scholars' Use of OT Lament Terminology and Its Theological and Interdisciplinary Implications." *Bulletin for Biblical Research* 21 (2011) 213–26.

Carlson, John D. "Religion and Violence: Coming to Terms with Terms." In *The Blackwell Companion to Religion and Violence*, edited by Andrew R. Murphy, 7–22. Chichester: Wiley-Blackwell, 2011.

Carroll, John T. *Luke: A Commentary*. The New Testament Library. Louisville: Westminster John Knox, 2012.

———. *Response to the End of History: Eschatology and Situation in Luke–Acts*. SBL Dissertation Series 92. Atlanta: Scholars, 1988.

Carroll, Robert P. "Surplus Meaning and the Conflict of Interpretations: A Dodecade of Jeremiah Studies (1984–95)." In *Recent Research on the Major Prophets*, edited by Alan J. Hauser with schuyler kaufman, 195–216. Sheffield: Sheffield Phoenix, 2008.

Carter, Warren. "Constructions of Violence and Identities in Matthew's Gospel." In *Violence in the New Testament*, edited by Shelly Matthews and E. Leigh Gibson, 81–108. New York: T & T Clark International, 2005.

———. "Jesus' 'I have come' Statements in Matthew's Gospel." *Catholic Biblical Quarterly* 60 (1998) 44–62.

———. *Matthew and the Margins: A Socio-Political and Religious Reading*. Sheffield: Sheffield Academic Press, 2000.

———. "Resisting and Imitating Empire: Imperial Paradigms in Two Matthean Parables." *Interpretation* 56 (2002) 260–72.

Chance, J. Bradley. *Jerusalem, the Temple, and the New Age in Luke–Acts*. Macon, GA: Mercer University Press, 1988.

Chanikuzhy, Jacob. *Jesus, the Eschatological Temple: An Exegetical Study of Jn 2,13–22 in the Light of the Pre-70 C.E. Eschatological Temple Hopes and the Synoptic Temple Action.* Leuven: Peeters, 2012.

Charette, Blaine. *The Theme of Recompense in Matthew's Gospel.* Journal for the Study of the New Testament Supplement Series 79. Sheffield: JSOT, 1992.

Clough, David. "On the Relevance of Jesus Christ for Christian Judgements about the Legitimacy of Violence: A Modest Proposal." *Studies in Christian Ethics* 22 (2009) 199–210.

Collins, John J. *Does the Bible Justify Violence?* Minneapolis: Fortress, 2004.

———. "From Prophecy to Apocalypticism: The Expectation of the End." In *The Encyclopedia of Apocalypticism, Volume 1: The Origins of Apocalypticism in Judaism and Christianity*, edited by John J. Collins, 129–61. New York: Continuum, 2000.

Coloe, Mary L. *God Dwells with Us: Temple Symbolism in the Fourth Gospel.* Collegeville, MN: Liturgical, 2001.

———. "Temple Imagery in John." *Interpretation* 63 (2009) 368–81.

Combrink, H. J. Bernard. "Shame on the Hypocritical Leaders in the Church: A Socio-Rhetorical Interpretation of the Reproaches in Matthew 23." In *Fabrics of Discourse: Essays in Honor of Vernon K. Robbins*, edited by David B. Gowler, L. Gregory Bloomquist, and Duane F. Watson, 1–35. Harrisburg, PA: Trinity, 2003.

Conzelmann, Hans. *The Theology of St Luke.* Translated by Geoffrey Buswell. London: Faber & Faber, 1960.

Cosgrove, Charles H. *Appealing to Scripture in Moral Debate: Five Hermeneutical Rules.* Grand Rapids: Eerdmans, 2002.

Crossan, John Dominic. *The Birth of Christianity: Discovering What Happened in the Years Immediately After the Execution of Jesus.* New York: HarperSanFrancisco, 1998.

———. "Divine Violence in the Christian Bible." In *The Bible and the American Future*, edited by Robert L. Jewett, with Wayne L. Alloway Jr. and John G. Lacy, 208–236. Eugene, OR: Cascade, 2009.

———. "Eschatology, Apocalypticism, and the Historical Jesus." In *Jesus Then and Now: Images of Jesus in History and Christology*, edited by Marvin Meyer and Charles Hughes, 91–112. Harrisburg, PA: Trinity, 2001.

———. *The Historical Jesus: The Life of a Mediterranean Jewish Peasant.* New York: HarperSanFrancisco, 1991.

———. *How To Read the Bible and Still Be a Christian: Struggling with Divine Violence from Genesis through Revelation.* New York: HarperOne, 2015.

———. *The Power of Parable: How Fiction by Jesus Became Fiction about Jesus.* New York: HarperOne, 2012.

Croy, N. Clayton. "The Messianic Whippersnapper: Did Jesus Use a Whip on People in the Temple (John 2:15)?" *Journal of Biblical Literature* 128 (2009) 555–68.

Culy, Martin M. "Series Introduction [to the Baylor Handbook on the Greek New Testament]." In *Mark 1–8: A Handbook on the Greek Text* by Rodney J. Decker, ix–xiii. Waco, TX: Baylor University Press, 2014.

Culy, Martin M., Mikeal C. Parsons, and Joshua J. Stigall. *Luke: A Handbook on the Greek Text.* Baylor Handbook on the Greek New Testament. Waco, TX: Baylor University Press, 2010.

Davies, W. D., and Dale C. Allison Jr. *A Critical and Exegetical Commentary on the Gospel according to Saint Matthew*. 3 volumes. International Critical Commentary. Edinburgh: T&T Clark, 1997.

Dear, John. "Didn't Jesus Overturn Tables and Chase People Out of the Temple with a Whip?" In *A Faith Not Worth Fighting For: Addressing Commonly Asked Questions about Christian Nonviolence*, edited by Tripp York and Justin Bronson Barringer, 184–91. Eugene, OR: Cascade, 2012.

Decker, Rodney J. *Mark 1–8: A Handbook on the Greek Text*. Baylor Handbook on the Greek New Testament. Waco, TX: Baylor University Press, 2014.

———. *Mark 9–16: A Handbook on the Greek Text*. BHGNT. Waco, TX: Baylor University Press, 2014.

Denton, Donald L., Jr. *Historiography and Hermeneutics in Jesus Studies: An Examination of the Work of John Dominic Crossan and Ben F. Meyer*. Journal for the Study of the New Testament Supplement Series 262. London: T & T Clark International, 2004.

Desjardins, Michel. *Peace, Violence and the New Testament*. Sheffield: Sheffield Academic Press, 1997.

De Villiers, Pieter G. R. "Hermeneutical Perspectives on Violence in the New Testament." In *Coping with Violence in the New Testament*, edited by Pieter G. R. de Villiers and Jan Willem van Henten, 247–73. Leiden: Brill, 2012.

De Villiers, Pieter G. R., and Jan Willem van Henten, editors. *Coping with Violence in the New Testament*. Leiden: Brill, 2012.

Donahue, John R. *The Gospel in Parable: Metaphor, Narrative, and Theology in the Synoptic Gospels*. Philadelphia: Fortress, 1988.

Donaldson, Terence L. *Jews and Anti-Judaism in the New Testament: Decision Points and Divergent Interpretations*. London: SPCK, 2010.

Dowd, Sharyn. *Prayer, Power, and the Problem of Suffering: Mark 11:22–25 in the Context of Markan Theology*. Society of Biblical Literature Dissertation Series 105. Atlanta: Scholars, 1988.

Dowling, Elizabeth V. *Taking Away the Pound: Women, Theology and the Parable of the Pounds in the Gospel of Luke*. Library of New Testament Studies 324. London: T & T Clark International, 2007.

Downing, F. Gerald. "Dale Martin's Swords for Jesus: Shaky Evidence?" *Journal for the Study of the New Testament* 37 (2015) 326–33.

Dunn, James D. G. *Christianity in the Making, Volume 1: Jesus Remembered*. Grand Rapids: Eerdmans, 2003.

Edwards, James R. *The Gospel according to Luke*. Grand Rapids: Eerdmans, 2015.

Ellens, J. Harold. "The Violent Jesus." In *The Destructive Power of Religion: Violence in Judaism, Christianity, and Islam, Volume 3: Models and Cases of Violence in Religion*, edited by J. Harold Ellens, 15–37. Westport, CT: Praeger, 2004.

Emerson, Ralph Waldo. "Self-Reliance" (1841). In *The American Scholar. Self Reliance. Compensation*. New York: American Book Company, 1893.

Esler, Philip F. "God's Honour and Rome's Triumph: Responses to the Fall of Jerusalem in 70 CE in Three Jewish Apocalypses." In *Modelling Early Christianity: Social-Scientific Studies of the New Testament in Its Context*, edited by Philip F. Esler, 239–58. London: Routledge, 1995.

———. "The Incident of the Withered Fig Tree in Mark 11: A New Source and Redactional Explanation." *Journal for the Study of the New Testament* 28 (2005) 41–67.

———. "Intergroup Conflict and Matthew 23: Towards Responsible Historical Interpretation of a Challenging Text." *Biblical Theology Bulletin* 45 (2015) 38–59.

Evans, Craig A. *Mark 8:27–16:20*. Word Biblical Commentary. Nashville: Thomas Nelson, 2001.

———. "Temple Action of Jesus." In *The Routledge Encyclopedia of the Historical Jesus*, 634–37. New York: Routledge, 2010.

Eve, Eric. *Behind the Gospels: Understanding the Oral Tradition*. London: SPCK, 2013.

Farmer, William R., editor. *Anti-Judaism and the Gospels*. Harrisburg, PA: Trinity, 1999.

Ferguson, Everett. *The Rule of Faith: A Guide*. Eugene, OR: Cascade, 2015.

Finsterbusch, Karin. "Violence against Judah and Jerusalem: The Rhetoric of Destruction within Jeremiah 1–6." In *Encountering Violence in the Bible*, edited by Markus Zehnder and Hallvard Hagelia, 79–93. Sheffield: Sheffield Phoenix, 2013.

Fisk, Bruce N. "*See My Tears*: A Lament for Jerusalem (Luke 13:31–35; 19:41–44)." In *The Word Leaps the Gap: Essays on Scripture and Theology in Honor of Richard B. Hays*, edited by J. Ross Wagner, C. Kavin Rowe, and A. Katherine Grieb, 147–78. Grand Rapids: Eerdmans, 2008.

Fitzmyer, Joseph A. *The Gospel according to Luke (I–IX): Introduction, Translation, and Notes*. Anchor Bible. Garden City, NY: Doubleday, 1981.

———. *The Gospel according to Luke (X–XXIV): Introduction, Translation, and Notes*. Anchor Bible. Garden City, NY: Doubleday, 1985.

Foster, Paul. "A Tale of Two Sons: But Which One Did the Far, Far Better Thing? A Study of Matt 21.28–32." *New Testament Studies* 47 (2001) 26–37.

France, Richard T. *The Gospel of Mark: A Commentary on the Greek Text*. New International Greek Testament Commentary. Grand Rapids: Eerdmans, 2002.

———. *The Gospel of Matthew*. New International Commentary on the New Testament. Grand Rapids: Eerdmans, 2007.

Fredriksen, Paula. "Arms and the Man: A Response to Dale Martin's 'Jesus in Jerusalem: Armed and Not Dangerous.'" *Journal for the Study of the New Testament* 37 (2015) 312–25.

———. *Jesus of Nazareth, King of the Jews: A Jewish Life and the Emergence of Christianity*. New York: Knopf, 1999.

———. "The Historical Jesus, the Scene in the Temple, and the Gospel of John." In *John, Jesus, and History, Volume 1: Critical Appraisals of Critical Views*, edited by Paul N. Anderson, Felix Just, and Tom Thatcher, 249–76. Atlanta: Society of Biblical Literature, 2007.

Fredriksen, Paula, and Adele Reinhartz, editors. *Jesus, Judaism, and Christian Anti-Judaism: Reading the New Testament after the Holocaust*. Louisville: Westminster John Knox, 2002.

Fretheim, Terence E. "Violence and the God of the Old Testament." In *Encountering Violence in the Bible*, edited by Markus Zehnder and Hallvard Hagelia, 108–27. Sheffield: Sheffield Phoenix, 2013.

Freyne, Sean. "Vilifying the Other and Defining the Self: Matthew's and John's Anti-Jewish Polemic in Focus." In *"To See Ourselves as Others See Us": Christians, Jews, "Others" in Late Antiquity*, edited by Jacob Neusner and Ernest S. Frerichs, 117–43. Chico, CA: Scholars, 1985.

Funk, Robert W., Roy W. Hoover, and the Jesus Seminar. *The Five Gospels: The Search for the Authentic Words of Jesus*. New York: Macmillan, 1993.

Funk, Robert W., and the Jesus Seminar. *The Acts of Jesus: The Search for the Authentic Deeds of Jesus*. New York: HarperSanFrancisco, 1998.
Gallagher, Edmon L. "The Blood from Abel to Zechariah in the History of Interpretation." *New Testament Studies* 60 (2014) 121–38.
Garland, David E. *The Intention of Matthew 23*. Studien zum Neuen Testament 52. Leiden: Brill, 1979.
———. *Reading Matthew: A Literary and Theological Commentary*. Macon, GA: Smyth & Helwys, 1993.
Garrett, Susan R. *The Demise of the Devil: Magic and the Demonic in Luke's Writings*. Minneapolis: Fortress, 1989.
Gaston, Lloyd. *No Stone on Another: Studies in the Significance of the Fall of Jerusalem in the Synoptic Gospels*. Supplements to *Novum Testamentum* 23. Leiden: Brill, 1970.
Gathercole, Simon J. *The Composition of the Gospel of Thomas: Original Language and Influences*. Society for New Testament Studies Monograph Series 151. Cambridge: Cambridge University Press, 2012.
———. *The Gospel of Thomas: Introduction and Commentary*. Texts and Editions for New Testament Study 11. Leiden: Brill, 2014.
———. "Luke in the *Gospel of Thomas*." *New Testament Studies* 57 (2011) 114–44.
———. *The Preexistent Son: Recovering the Christologies of Matthew, Mark, and Luke*. Grand Rapids: Eerdmans, 2006.
Geddert, Timothy J. *Mark*. Believers Church Bible Commentary. Scottdale, PA: Herald, 2001.
Gibbs, Jeffrey A. *Jerusalem and Parousia: Jesus' Eschatological Discourse in Matthew's Gospel*. Saint Louis: Concordia Academic Press, 2000.
Girard, René. *I See Satan Fall Like Lightning*. Translated and with a Foreword by James G. Williams. Maryknoll, NY: Orbis, 2001.
Glancy, Jennifer A. "Slaves and Slavery in the Matthean Parables." *Journal of Biblical Literature* 119 (2000) 67–90.
———. "Violence as Sign in the Fourth Gospel." *Biblical Interpretation* 17 (2009) 100–117.
Goodacre, Mark. "Criticizing the Criterion of Multiple Attestation: The Historical Jesus and the Question of Sources." In *Jesus, Criteria, and the Demise of Authenticity*, edited by Chris Keith and Anthony Le Donne, 152–69. London: T & T Clark International, 2012.
———. *Thomas and the Gospels: The Making of an Apocryphal Text*. London: SPCK, 2012.
Goodman, Martin. *Rome and Jerusalem: The Clash of Ancient Civilizations*. London: Allen Lane, 2007.
Gray, Timothy C. *The Temple in the Gospel of Mark: A Study of Its Narrative Role*. Tübingen: Mohr Siebeck, 2008.
Green, Joel B. *The Gospel of Luke*. New International Commentary on the New Testament. Grand Rapids: Eerdmans, 1997.
———. *The Theology of the Gospel of Luke*. Cambridge: Cambridge University Press, 1995.
Gundry, Robert H. *Mark: A Commentary on His Apology for the Cross*. Grand Rapids: Eerdmans, 1993.

Gurtner, Daniel M., and Nicholas Perrin. "Temple." In *Dictionary of Jesus and the Gospels*, 2nd ed., edited by Joel B. Green, Jeannine K. Brown, and Nicholas Perrin, 939–47. Downers Grove, IL: InterVarsity, 2013.

Hägerland, Tobias. "The Future of Criteria in Historical Jesus Research." *Journal for the Study of the Historical Jesus* 13 (2015) 43–65.

Hagner, Donald A. *Matthew 1–13*. Word Biblical Commentary. Dallas: Word, 1993.

———. *Matthew 14–28*. WBC. Dallas: Word, 1995.

———. "Matthew's Eschatology." In *To Tell the Mystery: Essays on New Testament Eschatology in Honor of Robert H. Gundry*, edited by Thomas E. Schmidt and Moisés Silva, 49–71. Journal for the Study of the New Testament Supplement Series 100. Sheffield: JSOT, 1994.

Hamerton-Kelly, Robert G. *The Gospel and the Sacred: Poetics of Violence in Mark*. Minneapolis: Fortress, 1994.

Hanson, K. C. "How Honorable! How Shameful! A Cultural Analysis of Matthew's Makarisms and Reproaches." *Semeia* 68 (1996) 81–111.

Hare, D. R. A. "The Lives of the Prophets: A New Translation and Introduction." In *The Old Testament Pseudepigrapha*, edited by James H. Charlesworth, 2:379–99. Garden City, NY: Doubleday, 1985.

Hatina, Thomas R. *In Search of a Context: The Function of Scripture in Mark's Narrative*. London and New York: Sheffield Academic Press, 2002.

Hauerwas, Stanley, and John Berkman. "Violence." In *Dictionary of Ethics, Theology and Society*, edited by Paul Barry Clarke and Andrew Linzey, 866–70. London: Routledge, 1996.

Hays, Christopher M. *Luke's Wealth Ethics: A Study in Their Coherence and Character*. Tübingen: Mohr Siebeck, 2010.

Hays, J. Daniel. "The Persecuted Prophet and Judgment on Jerusalem: The Use of LXX Jeremiah in the Gospel of Luke." *Bulletin for Biblical Research* 25 (2015) 453–73.

Hays, Richard B. *Echoes of Scripture in the Gospels*. Waco, TX: Baylor University Press, 2016.

———. *The Moral Vision of the New Testament—Community, Cross, New Creation: A Contemporary Introduction to New Testament Ethics*. San Francisco: HarperOne, 1996.

———. "Narrate and Embody: A Response to Nigel Biggar, 'Specify and Distinguish.'" *Studies in Christian Ethics* 22 (2009) 185–98.

———. *Reading Backwards: Figural Christology and the Fourfold Gospel Witness*. Waco, TX: Baylor University Press, 2014.

———. "The Thorny Task of Reconciliation: Another Response to Nigel Biggar." *Studies in Christian Ethics* 23 (2010) 81–86.

Herzog, William R., II. *Parables as Subversive Speech: Jesus as Pedagogue of the Oppressed*. Louisville: Westminster John Knox, 1994.

Holmén, Tom. "Authenticity Criteria." In *The Routledge Encyclopedia of the Historical Jesus*, 43–54. New York: Routledge, 2010.

Hood, Jason. "Matthew 23–25: The Extent of Jesus' Fifth Discourse." *Journal of Biblical Literature* 128 (2009) 527–43.

Hooker, Morna D. *A Commentary on the Gospel according to St Mark*. Black's New Testament Commentaries. London: A & C Black, 1991.

———. "Mark's Parables of the Kingdom (Mark 4:1–34)." In *The Challenge of Jesus' Parables*, edited by Richard N. Longenecker, 79–101. Grand Rapids: Eerdmans, 2000.

———. *The Signs of a Prophet: The Prophetic Actions of Jesus*. Harrisburg, PA: Trinity, 1997.

Horsley, Richard A. *Jesus and the Spiral of Violence: Popular Jewish Resistance in Roman Palestine*. Minneapolis: Fortress, 1993.

Hoskins, Paul M. *Jesus as the Fulfillment of the Temple in the Gospel of John*. Milton Keynes: Paternoster, 2006.

Jenkins, Philip. *Laying Down the Sword: Why We Can't Ignore the Bible's Violent Verses*. New York: HarperOne, 2011.

Jeremias, Joachim. *The Parables of Jesus*. 3rd rev. ed. Translated by S. H. Hooke. London: SCM, 1972.

Johnson, Luke Timothy. "Anti-Judaism and the New Testament." In *Handbook for the Study of the Historical Jesus, Volume 2: The Study of Jesus*, edited by Tom Holmén and Stanley E. Porter, 1609–38. Leiden: Brill, 2011.

———. *The Gospel of Luke*. Sacra Pagina. Collegeville, MN: Liturgical, 1991.

———. "The Lukan Kingship Parable (Lk. 19:11–27)." *Novum Testamentum* 24 (1982) 139–59.

———. "The New Testament's Anti-Jewish Slander and the Conventions of Ancient Polemic." *Journal of Biblical Literature* 108 (1989) 419–41.

Jones, Kenneth R. *Jewish Reactions to the Destruction of Jerusalem in A.D. 70: Apocalypses and Related Pseudepigrapha*. Leiden: Brill, 2011.

Joseph, Simon J. *The Nonviolent Messiah: Jesus, Q, and the Enochic Tradition*. Minneapolis: Fortress, 2014.

Josephus. *Jewish Antiquities*. 6 volumes. Translated by H. St. J. Thackeray, Ralph Marcus, and Louis H. Feldman. Loeb Classical Library. London: William Heinemann, 1930–65.

———. *The Jewish War*. 2 volumes. Translated by H. St. J. Thackeray. Loeb Classical Library. London: William Heinemann, 1927–28.

Juel, Donald. *Messiah and Temple: The Trial of Jesus in the Gospel of Mark*. Society of Biblical Literature Dissertation Series 13. Missoula, MT: Scholars, 1977.

Juza, Ryan P. "One of the Days of the Son of Man: A Reconsideration of Luke 17:22." *Journal of Biblical Literature* 135 (2016) 575–95.

Kattathara, Thomas. *The Snag of The Sword: An Exegetical Study of Luke 22:35–38*. Frankfurt am Main: Peter Lang, 2014.

Keck, Leander E. *Who Is Jesus? History in Perfect Tense*. Columbia, SC: University of South Carolina Press, 2000.

Keith, Chris. "The Narratives of the Gospels and the Historical Jesus: Current Debates, Prior Debates and the Goal of Historical Jesus Research." *Journal for the Study of the New Testament* 38 (2016) 426–55.

———. "Social Memory Theory and Gospels Research: The First Decade (Part One)." *Early Christianity* 6 (2015) 354–76.

———. "Social Memory Theory and Gospels Research: The First Decade (Part Two)." *Early Christianity* 6 (2015) 517–42.

Keith, Chris, and Anthony Le Donne, editors. *Jesus, Criteria, and the Demise of Authenticity*. London and New York: T & T Clark International, 2012.

Kerr, Alan R. *The Temple of Jesus' Body: The Temple Theme in the Gospel of John*. Journal for the Study of the New Testament Supplement Series 220. London: Sheffield Academic Press, 2002.

Kinman, Brent. "Parousia, Jesus' 'A-Triumphal' Entry, and the Fate of Jerusalem (Luke 19:28–44)." *Journal of Biblical Literature* 118 (1999) 279–94.
Kirk, J. R. Daniel. "Time for Figs, Temple Destruction, and Houses of Prayer in Mark 11:12–25." *Catholic Biblical Quarterly* 74 (2012) 509–27.
Kitchen, Merrill. "Rereading the Parable of the Pounds: A Social and Narrative Analysis of Luke 19:11–28." In *Prophecy and Passion: Essays in Honour of Athol Gill*, edited by David Neville, 227–46. Adelaide: Australian Theological Forum, 2002.
Kloppenborg, John S. "*Evocatio deorum* and the Date of Mark." *Journal of Biblical Literature* 124 (2005) 419–50.
———. "The Representation of Violence in Synoptic Parables." In *Mark and Matthew I. Comparative Readings: Understanding the Earliest Gospels in their First-Century Settings*, edited by Eve-Marie Becker and Anders Runesson, 323–51. Tübingen: Mohr Siebeck, 2011.
———. *The Tenants in the Vineyard: Ideology, Economics, and Agrarian Conflict in Jewish Palestine*. WUNT 195. Tübingen: Mohr Siebeck, 2006.
Koch, Klaus. "Is There a Doctrine of Retribution in the Old Testament?" In *Theodicy in the Old Testament*, edited by James L. Crenshaw, 57–87. Philadelphia: Fortress, 1983.
Kruger, H. A. J. "A Sword over His Head or in His Hand? Luke 22,35–38." In *The Scriptures in the Gospels*, edited by Christopher M. Tuckett, 597–604. Leuven: Leuven University Press, 1997.
Lampe, G. W. H. "The two swords (Luke 22:35–38)." In *Jesus and the Politics of His Day*, edited by Ernst Bammel and C. F. D. Moule, 335–51. Cambridge: Cambridge University Press, 1984.
Lang, T. J. "'Where the Body Is, There also the Eagles Will Be Gathered': Luke 17:37 and the Arrest of Jesus." *Biblical Interpretation* 21 (2013) 320–40.
———. "'You will desire to see and you will not see [it]': Reading Luke 17.22 as Antanaclasis." *Journal for the Study of the New Testament* 33 (2011) 281–302.
Lanier, Gregory R. "Luke's Distinctive Use of the Temple: Portraying the Divine Visitation." *Journal of Theological Studies* 65 (2014) 433–62.
———. "Mapping the Vineyard: Main Lines of Investigation Regarding the Parable of the Tenants in the Synoptics and *Thomas*." *Currents in Biblical Research* 15 (2016) 74–122.
Leander, Hans. *Discourses of Empire: The Gospel of Mark from a Postcolonial Perspective*. Semeia Studies 71. Atlanta: Society of Biblical Literature, 2013.
Leaney, A. R. C. *A Commentary on the Gospel according to St. Luke*. 2nd ed. London: Adam & Charles Black, 1966.
Le Donne, Anthony. *The Historiographical Jesus: Memory, Typology, and the Son of David*. Waco, TX: Baylor University Press, 2009.
Levine, Amy-Jill. "Anti-Judaism and the Gospel of Matthew." In *Anti-Judaism and the Gospels*, edited by William R. Farmer, 9–36. Harrisburg, PA: Trinity, 1999.
Longenecker, Bruce W. "Rome's Victory and God's Honour: The Jerusalem Temple and the Spirit of God in Lukan Theodicy." In *The Holy Spirit and Christian Origins: Essays in Honor of James D. G. Dunn*, edited by Graham N. Stanton, Bruce W. Longenecker, and Stephen C. Barton, 90–102. Grand Rapids: Eerdmans, 2004.
Luther, Martin. *Luther's Works, Volume 22: Sermons on the Gospel of St. John, Chapters 1–4*. Translated by Martin H. Bertram. Edited by Jaroslav Pelikan. Saint Louis: Concordia Publishing House, 1957.

Luz, Ulrich. "Anti-Judaism in the Gospel of Matthew as a Historical and Theological Problem: An Outline." In *Studies in Matthew*, translated by Rosemary Selle, 243–61. Grand Rapids: Eerdmans, 2005.

———. *Matthew 1–7: A Commentary*. Rev. ed. Translated by James E. Crouch. Hermeneia. Minneapolis: Fortress, 2007.

———. *Matthew 8–20: A Commentary*. Translated by James E. Crouch. Hermeneia. Minneapolis: Fortress, 2001.

———. *Matthew 21–28: A Commentary*. Translated by James E. Crouch. Hermeneia. Minneapolis: Fortress, 2005.

Macquarrie, John. *The Concept of Peace: The Firth Lectures 1972*. London: SCM, 1973.

———. "Peace." In *Dictionary of Ethics, Theology and Society*, edited by Paul Barry Clarke and Andrew Linzey, 634–38. London: Routledge, 1996.

Malina, Bruce J. *The Social Gospel of Jesus: The Kingdom of God in Mediterranean Perspective*. Minneapolis: Fortress, 2001.

Malina, Bruce J., and Richard L. Rohrbaugh. *Social-Science Commentary on the Synoptic Gospels*. 2nd ed. Minneapolis: Fortress, 2003.

Mann, C. S. *Mark: A New Translation with Introduction and Commentary*. Anchor Bible. Garden City, NY: Doubleday, 1986.

Manson, T. W. *The Sayings of Jesus*. London: SCM, 1957; first published in 1937 as Part II of *The Mission and Message of Jesus*.

Marcus, Joel. *Mark 1–8: A New Translation with Introduction and Commentary*. Anchor Bible. New York: Doubleday, 2000.

———. *Mark 8–16: A New Translation with Introduction and Commentary*. Anchor Yale Bible. New Haven, CT: Yale University Press, 2009.

———. "No More Zealots in the House of the Lord: A Note on the History of Interpretation of Zechariah 14:21." *Novum Testamentum* 55 (2013) 22–30.

Marshall, Christopher D. *Beyond Retribution: A New Testament Vision for Justice, Crime, and Punishment*. Studies in Peace and Scripture 5. Grand Rapids: Eerdmans, 2001.

———. *Compassionate Justice: An Interdisciplinary Dialogue with Two Gospel Parables on Law, Crime, and Restorative Justice*. Eugene, OR: Cascade, 2012.

Marshall, I. Howard. *The Gospel of Luke: A Commentary on the Greek Text*. New International Greek Testament Commentary. Exeter: Paternoster, 1978.

Martin, Dale B. "Jesus in Jerusalem: Armed and Not Dangerous." *Journal for the Study of the New Testament* 37 (2014) 3–24.

———. "Response to Downing and Fredriksen." *Journal for the Study of the New Testament* 37 (2015) 334–45.

Mason, Steve. *Josephus and the New Testament*. 2nd ed. Peabody, MA: Hendrickson, 2003.

Matera, Frank J. "Jesus' Journey to Jerusalem (Luke 9:51–19:46): A Conflict with Israel." *Journal for the Study of the New Testament* 51 (1993) 57–77.

Matson, David Lertis. "Pacifist Jesus? The (Mis)Translation of ἐᾶτε ἕως τούτου in Luke 22:51." *Journal of Biblical Literature* 134 (2015) 157–76.

Matson, Mark A. "The Temple Incident: An Integral Element in the Fourth Gospel's Narrative." In *Jesus in Johannine Tradition*, edited by Robert T. Fortna and Tom Thatcher, 145–53. Louisville: Westminster John Knox, 2001.

Mauser, Ulrich. *The Gospel of Peace: A Scriptural Message for Today's World*. Studies in Peace and Scripture 1. Louisville: Westminster John Knox, 1992.

McConville, J. Gordon. "Retribution in Deuteronomy: Theology and Ethics." *Interpretation* 69 (2015) 288–98.
McHugh, John F. *A Critical and Exegetical Commentary on John 1–4*, edited by Graham N. Stanton. London and New York: T & T Clark International, 2009.
McKnight, Scot. *Jesus and His Death: Historiography, the Historical Jesus, and Atonement Theory*. Waco, TX: Baylor University Press, 2005.
―――. "Jesus and Prophetic Actions." *Bulletin for Biblical Research* 10 (2000) 197–232.
McNicol, Allan J. "Response to Daryl D. Schmidt." In *Anti-Judaism and the Gospels*, edited by William R. Farmer, 111–19. Harrisburg, PA: Trinity, 1999.
McWhirter, Jocelyn. *Rejected Prophets: Jesus and His Witnesses in Luke–Acts*. Minneapolis: Fortress, 2013.
Meier, John P. *A Marginal Jew: Rethinking the Historical Jesus*. 5 volumes. New York: Doubleday, 1991–2001; New Haven, CT: Yale University Press, 2009–2016.
―――. "The Parable of the Wicked Tenants in the Vineyard: Is the Gospel of Thomas Independent of the Synoptics?" In *Unity and Diversity in the Gospels and Paul: Essays in Honor of Frank J. Matera*, edited by Christopher W. Skinner and Kelly R. Iverson, 129–45. Atlanta: Society of Biblical Literature, 2012.
Metzger, Bruce M. *A Textual Commentary on the Greek New Testament*. 2nd ed. Stuttgart: Deutsche Bibelgesellschaft, 1994.
Meyer, Ben F. *The Aims of Jesus*. London: SCM, 1979.
―――. *Reality and Illusion in New Testament Scholarship: A Primer in Critical Realist Hermeneutics*. Collegeville, MN: Liturgical, 1994.
Minear, Paul S. "A Note on Luke xxii 36." *Novum Testamentum* 7 (1964) 128–34.
Miquel, Esther. "The Impatient Jesus and the Fig Tree: Marcan Disguised Discourse against the Temple." *Biblical Theology Bulletin* 45.3 (2015) 144–54.
Neville, David J. "Calamity and the Biblical God—Borderline or Line of Belonging? Intratextual Tension in Luke 13." In *Bible, Borders, Belonging(s): Engaging Readings from Oceania*, edited by Jione Havea, David J. Neville, and Elaine M. Wainwright, 39–55. Atlanta: Society of Biblical Literature, 2014.
―――. "Love of Enemies, New Testament." *Encyclopedia of the Bible and Its Reception*, forthcoming.
―――. "Moral Vision and Eschatology in Mark's Gospel: Coherence or Conflict?" *Journal of Biblical Literature* 127 (2008) 359–84.
―――. The Moral Vision of Jesus in Matthew 5." *St Mark's Review* 227 (February 2014) 46–61.
―――. "Parable as Paradigm for Public Theology: Relating Theological Vision to Social Life." In *The Bible, Justice and Public Theology*, edited by David J. Neville, 145–60. Sheffield: Sheffield Phoenix, 2014.
―――. *A Peaceable Hope: Contesting Violent Eschatology in New Testament Narratives*. Studies in Peace and Scripture 11. Grand Rapids: Baker Academic, 2013.
―――. "The Phantom Returns: Delbert Burkett's Rehabilitation of Proto-Mark." *Ephemerides Theologicae Lovanienses* 84 (2008) 135–73.
―――. "Toward a Hermeneutic of Shalom: Reading Texts of Teleological Terror in Peace Perspective." *Word & World: Theology for Christian Ministry* 34 (Fall 2014) 339–48.
Neyrey, Jerome H. *Honor and Shame in the Gospel of Matthew*. Louisville: Westminster John Knox, 1998.

Nolland, John. "The Gospel of Matthew and Anti-Semitism." In *Built upon the Rock: Studies in the Gospel of Matthew*, edited by Daniel M. Gurtner and John Nolland, 154–69. Grand Rapids: Eerdmans, 2008.

———. *Luke 18:35–24:53*. Word Biblical Commentary. Dallas: Word, 1993.

Painter, John, and David A. deSilva. *James and Jude*. Paideia. Grand Rapids: Baker Academic, 2012.

Pao, David W., and Eckhard J. Schnabel. "Luke." In *Commentary on the New Testament Use of the Old Testament*, edited by G. K. Beale and D. A. Carson, 251–414. Grand Rapids: Eerdmans, 2007.

Parsons, Mikeal C. "The Place of Jerusalem on the Lukan Landscape: An Exercise in Symbolic Cartography." In *Literary Studies in Luke–Acts: Essays in Honor of Joseph B. Tyson*, edited by Richard P. Thompson and Thomas E. Phillips, 155–71. Macon, GA: Mercer University Press, 1998.

———. *Luke*. Paideia. Grand Rapids: Baker Academic, 2015.

———. *Luke: Storyteller, Interpreter, Evangelist*. Peabody, MA: Hendrickson, 2007.

Pate, C. Marvin, and Douglas W. Kennard. *Deliverance Now and Not Yet: The New Testament and the Great Tribulation*. Studies in Biblical Literature 54. New York: Peter Lang, 2003, 2005.

Pattison, Stephen. "The Shadow Side of Jesus." *Studies in Christian Ethics* 8.2 (1995) 54–67.

Perrin, Nicholas. *Jesus the Temple*. London: SPCK, 2010.

Pilch, John J. *A Cultural Handbook to the Bible*. Grand Rapids: Eerdmans, 2012.

Pitre, Brant. "Blessing the Barren and Warning the Fecund: Jesus' Message for Women Concerning Pregnancy and Childbirth." *Journal for the Study of the New Testament* 81 (2001) 59–80.

———. *Jesus, the Tribulation, and the End of Exile: Restoration Eschatology and the Origin of the Atonement*. Tübingen: Mohr Siebeck; Grand Rapids: Baker Academic, 2005.

Puskas, Charles B., and David Crump. *An Introduction to the Gospels and Acts*. Grand Rapids: Eerdmans, 2008.

Reid, Barbara E. "Violent Endings in Matthew's Parables and Christian Nonviolence." *Catholic Biblical Quarterly* 66 (2004) 237–55.

———. "Which God Is With Us?" *Interpretation* 64 (2010) 380–89.

Reiser, Marius. "Eschatology in the Proclamation of Jesus." Translated by Linda M. Maloney. In *Jesus, Mark and Q: The Teaching of Jesus and its Earliest Records*, edited by Michael Labahn and Andreas Schmidt, 216–38. Journal for the Study of the New Testament Supplement Series 214. Sheffield: Sheffield Academic Press, 2001.

———. *Jesus and Judgment: The Eschatological Proclamation in Its Jewish Context*. Translated by Linda M. Maloney. Minneapolis: Fortress, 1997.

Rensberger, David. "Jesus's Action in the Temple." In *Struggles for Shalom: Peace and Violence across the Testaments*, edited by Laura L. Brenneman and Brad D. Schantz, 179–90. Eugene, OR: Pickwick, 2014.

Rhoads, David. "The Ethics of Reading Mark as Narrative." In *Reading Mark, Engaging the Gospel*, 202–19. Minneapolis: Fortress, 2004.

Rodríguez, Rafael. "Authenticating Criteria: The Use and Misuse of a Critical Method." *Journal for the Study of the Historical Jesus* 7 (2009) 152–67.

———. "Jesus as his Friends Remembered Him: A Review of Dale Allison's *Constructing Jesus*." *Journal for the Study of the Historical Jesus* 12 (2014) 224–44.

Sabin, Marie Noonan. *Reopening the Word: Reading Mark as Theology in the Context of Early Judaism*. New York: Oxford University Press, 2002.
Sanders, E. P. *Jesus and Judaism*. Philadelphia: Fortress, 1985.
Schertz, Mary H. "Swords and Prayer." In *Struggles for Shalom: Peace and Violence across the Testaments*, edited by Laura L. Brenneman and Brad D. Schantz, 191–204. Eugene, OR: Pickwick, 2014.
Schmidt, Daryl D. "Anti-Judaism and the Gospel of Luke." In *Anti-Judaism and the Gospels*, edited by William R. Farmer, 63–96. Harrisburg, PA: Trinity, 1999.
———. "Luke's 'Innocent' Jesus: A Scriptural Apologetic." In *Political Issues in Luke-Acts*, edited by Richard J. Cassidy and Philip J. Scharper, 111–21. Maryknoll, NY: Orbis, 1983.
Schnackenburg, Rudolf. *The Gospel according to St John*. 3 volumes. Translated by Kevin Smyth et al. New York: Herder & Herder; Seabury; Crossroad, 1968–1982.
Schnelle, Udo. *Theology of the New Testament*. Translated by M. Eugene Boring. Grand Rapids: Baker Academic, 2009.
Schultz, Brian. "Jesus as Archelaus in the Parable of the Pounds (Lk. 19:11–27)." *Novum Testamentum* 49 (2007) 105–27.
Schweitzer, Albert. *The Quest of the Historical Jesus*. First complete [English] edition, edited by John Bowden. Translated by W. Montgomery, J. R. Coates, Susan Cupitt, and John Bowden. London: SCM, 2000.
Scobie, Charles H. H. "A Canonical Approach to Interpreting Luke: The Journey Motif as a Hermeneutical Key." In *Reading Luke: Interpretation, Reflection, Formation*, edited by Craig G. Bartholomew, Joel B. Green, and Anthony C. Thiselton, 327–49. Milton Keynes: Paternoster, 2005.
Scornaienchi, Lorenzo. "The Controversy Dialogues and the Polemic in Mark and Matthew." In *Mark and Matthew I. Comparative Readings: Understanding the Earliest Gospels in their First-Century Settings*, edited by Eve-Marie Becker and Anders Runesson, 309–321. WUNT. Tübingen: Mohr Siebeck, 2011.
Seccombe, David. "Incongruity in the Gospel Parables." *Tyndale Bulletin* 62.2 (2011) 161–72.
Seeley, David. "Jesus' Temple Act." *Catholic Biblical Quarterly* 55 (1993) 263–83.
———. "Jesus' Temple Act Revisited: A Response to P. M. Casey." *Catholic Biblical Quarterly* 62 (2000) 55–63.
Selby, Rosalind M. *The Comical Doctrine: An Epistemology of New Testament Hermeneutics*. Milton Keynes: Paternoster, 2006.
Senior, Donald. "The New Testament and Peacemaking: Some Problem Passages." *Faith and Mission* 4.1 (Fall 1986) 71–77.
Shirock, Robert J. "The Growth of the Kingdom in Light of Israel's Rejection of Jesus: Structure and Theology in Luke 13:1–35." *Novum Testamentum* 35 (1993) 15–29.
Shively, Elizabeth E. *Apocalyptic Imagination in the Gospel of Mark: The Literary and Theological Role of Mark 3:22–30*. Berlin: Walter de Gruyter, 2012.
Smith, Stephen H. "The Literary Structure of Mark 11:1–12:40." *Novum Testamentum* 32 (1989) 104–24.
Snodgrass, Klyne R. "Key Questions on the Parables of Jesus." *Review and Expositor* 109 (Spring 2012) 173–85.
———. *The Parable of the Wicked Tenants*. WUNT 27. Tübingen: J. C. B. Mohr, 1983.
———. "Recent Research on the Parable of the Wicked Tenants: An Assessment." *Bulletin for Biblical Research* 8 (1998) 187–216.

_____. *Stories with Intent: A Comprehensive Guide to the Parables of Jesus.* Grand Rapids: Eerdmans, 2008.

_____. "The Temple Incident." In *Key Events in the Life of the Historical Jesus: A Collaborative Exploration of Context and Coherence,* edited by Darrell L. Bock and Robert L. Webb, 429–80. Tübingen: Mohr Siebeck, 2009.

Snyder Belousek, Darrin W. *Atonement, Justice, and Peace: The Message of the Cross and the Mission of the Church.* Studies in Peace and Scripture 10. Grand Rapids: Eerdmans, 2012.

_____. *Good News: The Advent of Salvation in the Gospel of Luke.* Collegeville, MN: Liturgical, 2014.

Stanton, Graham N. *A Gospel for a New People: Studies in Matthew.* Louisville: Westminster John Knox, 1993.

_____. "The Two Parousias of Christ: Justin Martyr and Matthew." In *From Jesus to John: Essays on Jesus and New Testament Christology in Honour of Marinus de Jonge,* edited by Martinus C. de Boer, 183–95. Sheffield: JSOT, 1993.

Stein, Robert H. *Gospels and Tradition: Studies on Redaction Criticism of the Synoptic Gospels.* Grand Rapids: Baker, 1991.

Stone, Michael E., and Matthias Henze. *4 Ezra and 2 Baruch: Translations, Introductions, and Notes.* Minneapolis: Fortress, 2013.

Strauss, Mark L. *Jesus Behaving Badly: The Puzzling Paradoxes of the Man from Galilee.* Downers Grove, IL: InterVarsity, 2015.

Swartley, Willard M. *Covenant of Peace: The Missing Peace in New Testament Theology and Ethics.* Studies in Peace and Scripture 9. Grand Rapids: Eerdmans, 2006.

_____. *Israel's Scripture Traditions and the Synoptic Gospels: Story Shaping Story.* Peabody, MA: Hendrickson, 1994.

_____. *John.* Believers Church Bible Commentary. Harrisonburg, VA, and Waterloo, ON: Herald, 2013.

_____. "Peace and Violence in the New Testament: Definition and Methodology." In *Struggles for Shalom: Peace and Violence across the Testaments,* edited by Laura L. Brenneman and Brad D. Schantz, 141–54. Eugene, OR: Pickwick, 2014.

Talbert, Charles H. *Reading Luke: A Literary and Theological Commentary on the Third Gospel.* New York: Crossroad, 1982.

Tannehill, Robert C. "Israel in Luke–Acts: A Tragic Story." *Journal of Biblical Literature* 104 (1985) 69–85; reprinted in Tannehill, *The Shape of Luke's Story,* 105–124.

_____. *Luke.* Abingdon New Testament Commentary. Nashville: Abingdon, 1996.

_____. *The Shape of Luke's Story: Essays on Luke–Acts.* Eugene, OR: Cascade, 2005.

_____. *The Sword of His Mouth: Forceful and Imaginative Language in Synoptic Sayings.* Philadelphia: Fortress; Missoula: Scholars, 1975.

Telford, William R. *The Barren Temple and the Withered Tree: A Redaction-Critical Analysis of the Cursing of the Fig-Tree Pericope in Mark's Gospel and Its Relation to the Cleansing of the Temple Tradition.* Journal for the Study of the New Testament Supplement Series 1. Sheffield: JSOT, 1980.

Theissen, Gerd. *Gospel Writing and Church Politics: A Socio-rhetorical Approach.* Hong Kong: Theology Division, Chung Chi College, 2001.

Theissen, Gerd, and Dagmar Winter. *The Quest for the Plausible Jesus: The Question of Criteria.* Translated by M. Eugene Boring. Louisville: Westminster John Knox, 2002.

Thiselton, Anthony C. *New Horizons in Hermeneutics.* London: HarperCollins, 1992.

Tiede, David L. *Prophecy and History in Luke–Acts*. Philadelphia: Fortress, 1980.
Travis, Stephen H. *Christ and the Judgement of God: The Limits of Divine Retribution in New Testament Thought*. Revised edition. Milton Keynes: Paternoster, 2009.
Trocmé, André. *Jesus and the Nonviolent Revolution*. Translated by Michael H. Shank and Marlin E. Miller. Scottdale, PA: Herald, 1973.
Tuckett, Christopher M. *Luke*. Sheffield: Sheffield Academic Press, 1996.
_____. "Matthew and Hypocrisy." In *Jesus, Matthew's Gospel and Early Christianity: Studies in Memory of Graham N. Stanton*, edited by Daniel M. Gurtner, Joel Willitts, and Richard A. Burridge, 152–65. London and New York: T & T Clark International, 2011.
Turner, David L. *Israel's Last Prophet: Jesus and the Jewish Leaders in Matthew 23*. Minneapolis: Fortress, 2015.
Van der Watt, Jan, and Jacobus Kok. "Violence in a Gospel of Love." In *Coping with Violence in the New Testament*, edited by Pieter G. R. de Villiers and Jan Willem van Henten, 151–83. Leiden: Brill, 2012.
Van Eck, Ernest. "Do not question my honour: A social-scientific reading of the parable of the minas (Lk 19:12b–24, 27)." *HTS Teologiese Studies/Theological Studies* 67.3 (2011), Art. #977, 11 pages. DOI: 10.4102/hts.v67i3.977.
_____. "Jesus and Violence: An Ideological-Critical Reading of the Tenants in Mark 12:1–12 and Thomas 65." In *Coping with Violence in the New Testament*, edited by Pieter G. R. de Villiers and Jan Willem van Henten, 101–31. Leiden: Brill, 2012.
_____. "Social Memory and Identity: Luke 19:12b–24 and 27." *Biblical Theology Bulletin* 41 (2011) 201–212.
Van Henten, Jan Willem. "Religion, Bible and Violence." In *Coping with Violence in the New Testament*, edited by Pieter G. R. de Villiers and Jan Willem van Henten, 3–21. Leiden: Brill, 2012.
Verhey, Allen. "Neither Devils nor Angels: Peace, Justice, and Defending the Innocent: A Response to Richard Hays." In *The Word Leaps the Gap: Essays on Scripture and Theology in Honor of Richard B. Hays*, edited by J. Ross Wagner, C. Kavin Rowe, and A. Katherine Grieb, 599–625. Grand Rapids: Eerdmans, 2008.
Via, Dan O. *Divine Justice, Divine Judgment: Rethinking the Judgment of Nations*. Minneapolis: Fortress, 2007.
Wahlen, Clinton. "The Temple in Mark and Contested Authority." *Biblical Interpretation* 15 (2007) 248–67.
Walker, Peter W. L. *Jesus and the Holy City: New Testament Perspectives on Jerusalem*. Grand Rapids: Eerdmans, 1996.
Waltner Goossen, Rachel. "'Defanging the Beast': Mennonite Responses to John Howard Yoder's Sexual Abuse." *Mennonite Quarterly Review* 89 (2015) 7–80.
Wasserman, Tommy. "*Lectio vehementior potior*: Scribal Violence on Violent Texts?" In *Encountering Violence in the Bible*, edited by Markus Zehnder and Hallvard Hagelia, 216–34. Sheffield: Sheffield Phoenix, 2013.
Watson, Francis. *The Fourfold Gospel: A Theological Reading of the New Testament Portraits of Jesus*. Grand Rapids: Baker Academic, 2016.
_____. *Gospel Writing: A Canonical Perspective*. Grand Rapids: Eerdmans, 2013.
_____. "The Quest for the Real Jesus." In *The Cambridge Companion to Jesus*, edited by Markus Bockmuehl, 156–69. Cambridge: Cambridge University Press, 2001.
Weaver, Dorothy Jean. "'As sheep in the midst of wolves': Mission and peace in the Gospel of Matthew." In *Beautiful upon the Mountains: Biblical Essays on Mission,*

Peace, and the Reign of God, edited by Mary H. Schertz and Ivan Friesen, 123–43. Studies in Peace and Scripture 7. Elkhart, IN: Institute of Mennonite Studies; Scottdale, PA: Herald, 2003.

———. *Matthew's Missionary Discourse: A Literary Critical Analysis.* Journal for the Study of the New Testament Supplement Series 38. Sheffield: Sheffield Academic Press, 1990.

Wedderburn, Alexander J. M. *Jesus and the Historians.* WUNT 269. Tübingen: Mohr Siebeck, 2010.

Weinfeld, Moshe. "The Charge of Hypocrisy in Matthew 23 and in Jewish Sources." In *Normative and Sectarian Judaism in the Second Temple Period*, 279–85. London and New York: T & T Clark International, 2005.

Wells, Samuel. "Didn't Jesus Say He Came Not to Bring Peace, but a Sword?" In *A Faith Not Worth Fighting For: Addressing Commonly Asked Questions about Christian Nonviolence*, edited by Tripp York and Justin Bronson Barringer, 154–69. Eugene, OR: Cascade, 2012.

Wink, Walter. *The Human Being: Jesus and the Enigma of the Son of the Man.* Minneapolis: Fortress, 2002.

Wong, Solomon Hon-fai. *The Temple Incident in Mark 11,15–19: The Disclosure of the Marcan Faction.* Frankfurt am Main: Peter Lang, 2009.

Wright, N. T. *The Challenge of Jesus.* London: SPCK, 2000.

———. *Jesus and the Victory of God.* London: SPCK, 1996.

———. *The New Testament and the People of God.* London: SPCK, 1992.

Yang, Yong-Eui. "Reading Mark 11:12–25 from a Korean Perspective." In *Reading the Gospels Today*, edited by Stanley E. Porter, 78–99. Grand Rapids: Eerdmans, 2004.

Yarbro Collins, Adela. *Mark: A Commentary.* Hermeneia. Minneapolis: Fortress, 2007.

Yoder, John Howard. *The Politics of Jesus: Vicit Agnus Noster.* 2nd ed. Grand Rapids: Eerdmans, 1994.

Yoder Neufeld, Thomas R. *Killing Enmity: Violence and the New Testament.* Grand Rapids: Baker Academic, 2011.

———. *Recovering Jesus: The Witness of the New Testament.* Grand Rapids: Brazos, 2007.

Zehnder, Markus, and Hallvard Hagelia, editors. *Encountering Violence in the Bible.* The Bible in the Modern World 55. Sheffield: Sheffield Phoenix, 2013.

Author Index

Adams, Edward, 253
Ådna, Jostein, 115n5, 173n69
Aichele, George, 2–3n5
Alexis-Baker, Andy, 162–63n33, 165–70
Allison, Dale C., Jr, 9–10n24, 10, 22, 25–26n18, 38, 44n15, 54–55, 69n30, 85, 88–89n84, 98n7, 143, 184n1, 190n23, 191n27, 208n83, 209–210, 252n69, 257
Arens, E., 35n41
Ashton, John, 131nn53–54
Aslan, Reza, 17n1
Augustine, 203n68
Avalos, Hector, 2n5, 12, 192n29
Bailey, Kenneth E., 64n17
Balabanski, Vicky, 186, 187n11
Bammel, Ernst, 2n4
Barrett, C. K., 180n88
Barton, Stephen C., 28–30, 58n4
Bauckham, Richard, 169, 176n73, 180n90
Beare, Francis Wright, 32, 198
Beasley-Murray, G. R., 23–24n15
Berger, Klaus, 2–3n5, 122n26
Bermejo-Rubio, Fernando, 2n4, 7–8n20, 13n36
Biggar, Nigel, 13
Black, C. Clifton, 43n10, 46n19, 47n24, 119n18, 121n23, 128n44, 142n23
Bock, Darrell L., 50n33, 72n37, 75n47, 79–80n59, 238–39

Borg, Marcus J., and John Dominic Crossan, 120n20
Boring, M. Eugene, 117n10, 120nn19–20, 122n25, 186, 189n20, 190, 198n51, 204
Böttrich, Christfried, 122n26
Bovon, François, 17n1, 64n17, 64n18, 69, 72n39, 74nn44–45, 77n52, 79n58, 79–80n59, 96n4, 99n10, 104–5n16, 106
Brandon, S. G. F., 2n4, 17n1
Bredin, Mark R., 154–55
Brenneman, Laura L., 4, 5n12
Bridge, Steven L., 239n32
Brown, Raymond E., 17n1, 79n56, 79–80n59, 100n13, 111n33, 116, 180n88
Brown, Robert McAfee, 4
Brown, Scott G., 122n26, 126n36
Bryan, Steven M., 179n85
Bultmann, Rudolf, 35n41
Burkett, Delbert, 9n22
Byrne, Brendan, 86–87, 121–22n24
Calvin, John, 167–68
Camara, Helder, 4n8
Campbell, D. Keith, 63n16
Carlson, John D., 5n13
Carroll, John T., 50n33, 64n18, 66, 69n32, 77, 105n18, 130, 241n42, 242n45, 248, 249n65, 250n66
Carroll, Robert P., 67n26
Carter, Warren, 4n9, 35n41, 42n7
Chance, J. Bradley, 63n16

Author Index

Chanikuzhy, Jacob, 116n9, 119n17, 122n26, 130, 173n69, 180–81n91
Charette, Blaine, 224
Clough, David, 13
Collins, John J., 219, 251
Coloe, Mary L., 180–81n91
Combrink, H. J. Bernard, 187n11, 188n18
Conzelmann, Hans, 101n14, 109–10
Cosgrove, Charles H., 10–11, 203n68
Crossan, John Dominic, 6–8, 9–10n24, 11, 94–97, 199n54, 210–14
Croy, N. Clayton, 158, 162–65, 166n45
Culy, Martin M., 122n27
Culy, Martin M., Mikeal C. Parsons, and Joshua J. Stigall, 64n18, 72n37
Davies, W. D., and Dale C. Allison Jr, 26n19, 26n21, 27–28, 38n45, 119n15, 188, 190n21, 190n23, 205n72, 209, 227
Dear, John, 120
Decker, Rodney J., 122–23, 144n28
Denton, Donald L., Jr, 9–10n24
Donahue, John R., 151n49
Donaldson, Terence L., 11, 86–87, 192n28, 215–17
Dowd, Sharon, 122n25
Dowling, Elizabeth V., 49n28, 50n32, 51n37, 53n43, 54n46
Dunn, James D. G., 9–10n24, 195n43
Eck, Ernest van, 50n31, 50n32, 51n37, 151
Edwards, James R., 63, 64n18
Ellens, J. Harold, 155–58
Emerson, Ralph Waldo, 208
Esler, Philip F., 90n88, 122n26, 123n30, 185nn5–6, 192n28, 192n30, 193n34, 194n37, 207n81
Eusebius, 83
Evans, Craig A., 115n5, 136n3, 144n28

Eve, Eric, 9–10n24
Ferguson, Everett, 10n27
Finsterbusch, Karin, 67n26
Fisk, Bruce N., 85–87
Fitzmyer, Joseph A., 64n18, 65n20, 72n37, 73n41, 74, 75n47, 79–80n59
Foster, Paul, 137n6
France, Richard T., 120n19, 149n42, 232–33
Fredriksen, Paula, 7n20, 131
Fretheim, Terence E., 87n77
Freyne, Sean, 198–99
Funk, Robert W., et al., 94, 98, 113n2
Gallagher, Edmon L., 190n22
Garland, David E., 187, 208n84
Garrett, Susan R., 101n14, 104–5n16, 110n31
Gaston, Lloyd, 32n37, 91n91
Gathercole, Simon J., 18n2, 35n41, 36n42, 116n7, 138n9
Geddert, Timothy J., 123n28
Gibbs, Jeffrey A., 231n16, 232n18
Girard, René, 1n2, 155
Glancy, Jennifer, A., 158–61, 228n12
Goodacre, Mark, 18n2, 98n7
Goodman, Martin, 57n2
Gray, Timothy C., 122n26, 127n40
Green, Joel B., 54n46, 64n18, 65, 75nn46–47, 77n50, 130n50
Gundry, Robert H., 122n26, 125n33, 126n35
Gurtner, Daniel M., and Nicholas Perrin, 116n9
Hägerland, Tobias, 9n23
Hagner, Donald A., 118n11, 118n14, 184n3, 188n18, 231n16, 233n21
Hamerton-Kelly, Robert G., 155n10
Hanson, K. C., 205–208
Hatina, Thomas R., 24n16
Hauerwas, Stanley, and John Berkman, 3n6
Hays, Christopher M., 106n20, 107n21
Hays, J. Daniel, 66n22, 72n40, 73n42

Author Index

Hays, Richard B., 13, 84n68, 89n87, 135n1, 180–81n91, 200–204, 220n2
Henten, Jan Willem van, 4n9
Herzog, William R., 55
Hood, Jason, 186–88, 204–205, 207–208
Hooker, Morna D., 24, 118n12, 125nn32–33, 144n28
Horsley, Richard A., 4n8
Hoskins, Paul M., 180–81n91
Irenaeus, 203
Jenkins, Philip, 1n1, 6n14
Jeremias, Joachim, 52n40
Johnson, Luke Timothy, 50, 135n1, 192–98, 201
Jones, Kenneth R., 90n88
Joseph, Simon J., 6n16, 208n82
Josephus, 50n31, 58n4, 59n7, 65n20, 83, 90, 95
Juel, Donald, 90n89, 122n25
Juza, Ryan, P., 241–42n44, 245n56
Kattathara, Thomas, 99n10
Keck, Leander E., 9–10n24
Keith, Chris, 9–10n24
Kerr, Alan R., 180–81n91
Kinman, Brent, 49n29, 71n35, 129
Kirk, J. R. Daniel, 123n30
Kitchen, Merrill, 53
Kloppenborg, John S., 3n6, 58n6, 87n78, 138–51, 190–91
Koch, Klaus, 87n76
Kruger, H. A. J., 112n36
Lampe, G. W. H., 107–8n22, 110n29
Lang, T. J., 239–48
Lanier, Gregory R., 61n12, 67n25, 89n87, 138n7
Leander, Hans, 123n28
Leaney, A. R. C., 245n56
Le Donne, Anthony, 9–10n24
Levine, Amy-Jill, 196–97n49, 200n58
Longenecker, Bruce W., 82n61, 90n88
Luther, Martin, 168
Luz, Ulrich, 28nn25–26, 31n34, 41n3, 43n10, 48n27, 53n44, 117, 184, 188, 190, 197

Macquarrie, John, 4–5
Malina, Bruce J., 4n8
Malina, Bruce J., and Richard L. Rohrbaugh, 51n37, 190n25, 205n75, 207n81
Mann, C. S., 122n26
Manson, T. W., 37
Marcus, Joel, 120n20, 143n27, 149n43, 154n7
Marshall, Christopher D., 42, 54n46, 85, 87n78
Marshall, I. Howard, 238–39
Martin, Dale B., 2n4
Mason, Steve, 83, 90n88
Matera, Frank J., 62n13, 129n46
Matson, David Lertis, 108–9, 110n31
Matson, Mark A., 128, 131n53
Mauser, Ulrich, 25n17, 34n40, 38, 118n11
McConville, J. Gordon, 87n78
McHugh, John F., 180n88
McKnight, Scot, 9–10n24
McNicol, Allan J., 83
McWhirter, Jocelyn, 66n22, 70n34, 84n69, 90n89
Meier, John P., 1–2n3, 40n1, 49–50n30, 122n26, 128n44, 138n9, 146–47n37
Metzger, Bruce M., 162, 188n15
Meyer, Ben F., 9–10n24, 22, 91n90, 136n2, 252n68
Minear, Paul S., 107n21, 110
Miquel, Esther, 127n37
Neville, David J., 12–15, 53n42, 57, 75n48, 82n62, 83n67, 89n87, 98n9, 127n41, 150n44, 150n47, 176n73, 180, 210, 214n102, 219, 234n25, 239n33
Neyrey, Jerome H., 207n81
Nolland, John, 217n108
Origen, 82–83
Painter, John, 191n27
Pao, David W., and Eckhard J. Schnabel, 77nn50–51
Parsons, Mikeal C., 58n3, 63n15

Pate, C. Marvin, and Douglas W. Kennard, 22n14
Pattison, Stephen, 2n4
Perrin, Nicholas, 173n69
Pilch, John J., 51n37
Pitre, Brant, 22–24, 78–79n55
Puskas, Charles B., and David Crump, 84–85
Reid, Barbara E., 4n9, 43n9, 148n40
Reiser, Marius, 9–10n24, 41n5, 42n6
Rensberger, David, 177–79
Rhoads, David, 11–12
Rodríguez, Rafael, 10
Sabin, Marie Noonan, 129n45, 142n23
Sanders, E. P., 113
Schertz, Mary H., 99n10, 100n12, 112n36
Schmidt, Daryl D., 83, 105n17
Schnackenburg, Rudolf, 180
Schnelle, Udo, 9–10n24, 229n14
Schultz, Brian, 50n31
Schweitzer, Albert, 6
Scobie, Charles H. H., 63
Scornaienchi, Lorenzo, 196–97
Seccombe, David, 53
Seeley, David, 113n2
Selby, Rosalind M., 9–10n24, 12n31
Shirock, Robert J., 65n19, 66n22
Shively, Elizabeth E., 123–24n31, 140n15
Smith, Stephen H., 120n20
Snodgrass, Klyne R., 42, 43n10, 50n34, 52n41, 115n5, 136n3, 137n6, 138, 141, 142–43n25, 146–47n37, 173n69, 225n6, 228
Snyder Belousek, Darrin W., 85–86n73
Stanton, Graham N., 146n36, 187n10, 187n12, 190n23, 234n25
Stein, Robert H., 122n26
Stone, Michael E., and Matthias Henze, 90n88
Strauss, Mark L., 12n32, 122n26

Swartley, Willard M., 5n12, 13n34, 46–47, 54n46, 87–89, 98n9, 112n36, 180, 199–201
Talbert, Charles H., 64n17
Tannehill, Robert C., 19–22, 71, 80n60, 86–87, 238
Telford, William R., 118n13, 119n17, 122–23, 127n40
Theissen, Gerd, 220–21n3
Theissen, Gerd, and Dagmar Winter, 9–10n24
Thiselton, Anthony C., 172n67
Tiede, David L., 63n16, 90n89
Travis, Stephen H., 42n8, 231n17
Trocmé, André, 112n36
Tuckett, Christopher M., 105n17, 208n84
Turner, David L., 87n78, 146n35, 185n5, 186n7, 188–89n19, 196–97n49, 200n58
Watt, Jan van der, and Jacobus Kok, 153n1
Verhey, Allen, 13n35
Via, Dan O., 87n76
Villiers, Pieter G. R. de, 1n2, 4n9
Wahlen, Clinton, 122n26, 127n37
Walker, Peter W. L., 63n16
Waltner Goossen, Rachel, 111n34
Wasserman, Tommy, 162n32, 165n40
Watson, Francis, 9–10n24, 10, 97n6, 125n33
Weaver, Dorothy Jean, 26n20, 27–34
Wedderburn, Alexander J. M., 9–10n24
Weinfeld, Moshe, 208n84
Wells, Samuel, 30n31, 31n34
Wink, Walter, 233
Wong, Solomon Hon-fai, 122n26
Wright, N. T., 9–10n24, 50, 249
Yang, Yong-Eui, 122n26
Yarbro Collins, Adela, 121–22n24, 122n26, 149n43, 150
Yoder, John Howard, 111–12
Yoder Neufeld, Thomas R., 4n8, 4n10, 43–48, 52n38, 114, 170–77, 199

Index of Ancient Sources

OLD TESTAMENT

Genesis
1:1–2:3	175–76

Exodus
20:12	20

Leviticus
19:18	1–2n3
19:33–34	1–2n3

Numbers
12:3	117
25	179

Deuteronomy
5:16	20
6:4–5	1–2n3
11:1	1–2n3
16:1–20	68
24:10–22	68
29:22–28	67

2 Samuel
5:8	118n12

1 Kings
4:25	128n44
19:1–18	65n20

2 Kings
18:31	128n44
21–25	59
21:16	65n20
24:4	65n20

2 Chronicles
24:17–22	65n20

Job
41:6	154n7

Psalms
34:14	vii, 4
37	228
37:11	117
69:9	154, 172, 179
106:28–31	179
118:19–29	69
118:26	69

Proverbs
31:24	154n7

Isaiah
5:1–7	137–38, 142–43
6:9–10	24
11:6	28
28:3–4	128n44
29:3	71
36:16	128n44

Isaiah (continued)

52:13–53:12	105
53:12	105
55:6–11	175–76
56:7	129
65:25	28

Jeremiah

2–3	68
2:1–2	68
2:4	68
2:30	65n20, 68
4:5–6:30	73
5:14	74
5:19	74
6:1–8	73
6:9–15	73
6:15	73
7:1–7	68
7:1–15	66
7:11	69, 129
7:13	74
7:32	79
8:13	128n44
9:1	72
10:15	73
12:7	66
12:7–13	59, 66
13:17	72
13:20–27	59
14:17	72
16:11	74
16:14	79
21:1–24:10	67, 68
21:10	67
21:13–14	68
22:1–4	66
22:3–5	67–68
22:5	66–69
22:8–9	67
22:10–30	66n24
22:20–23	68
23:1–8	68
23:5–6	69
25:1–14	59
26–52	68
26:1–24	66
26:20–24	65n20
31:15	223
31:31	79
32:29–30	190n22
38	65n20
51:6	77

Lamentations

1:1	72n40
2	59

Ezekiel

4:2	71
8–11	64n18
14:12–15:8	59
17:4	154n7
18	190n22
38:12	61n12

Hosea

2:12	128n44
6:6	118n14
9–10	85
9:7–9	77
10:8	79
10:14	71
12:7	154n7

Joel

1:7	128n44
1:12	128n44
2:22	128n44

Amos

2:4	79n56
3:6	32
8:1–3	128n44

Micah

4:4	128n44
7:1	128n44
7:6	20, 22, 29, 38

Habakkuk

2:11	72n38

Index of Ancient Sources 283

Zephaniah
1:11 154n7

Haggai
2:19 128n44

Zechariah
1:1 65n20
3:10 128n44
9:9 117
11:7 154n7
11:11 154n7
12–14 154
12:3 77
12:10 154n7, 155
14:21 154n7

Malachi
3:1 154
3:19 79n56
4:1 79n56

NEW TESTAMENT

Matthew
1:1–17 117
1:18–25 197
1:21–23 221
2:18 220, 223
3:1–6 221
3:2 137n5, 221
3:7 221
3:7–12 221
3:10 221
3:12 221
3:13–17 221
4:1–11 61
4:17 35, 137n5, 206, 221
4:23 206, 216
4:23–11:1 25–26, 33–35, 37
5–7 199
5:1 204
5:1–12 204, 205
5:2–8:1 25
5:2–9:34 25, 118n14
5:3–10 205–206
5:3–12 187, 199, 206
5:5 117
5:8 191
5:9 vii, 33, 38, 88, 88n81
5:9–11 35
5:11–12 205n74
5:14–16 191
5:17 35–36
5:21–22 191, 211, 213
5:21–48 36, 199
5:22 209, 212, 221
5:29–30 44, 183
5:33–48 191
5:34–35 58n4
5:35 58
5:38–48 13
5:43–48 43
6:1–18 205n72, 212
6:7–8 191
6:12 42
7:1–12 191
7:15–20 257
7:15–23 187n11
7:19 221
7:21–23 222, 228
7:21–27 204
7:24–27 222, 228
7:29 204, 216
8:6 223
8:10–12 200n56, 223
8:11–12 213, 223
8:12 146n34
8:16 169
8:22 183
8:24 117
8:28–34 114n3
9:13 35–36, 118n14
9:35 216
9:35–11:1 25–36
10:9–10 95
10:11–15 222

Matthew (continued)

Reference	Pages
10:12	222
10:13	88n81
10:17	216
10:23	230, 231
10:34	2, 13–14, 87, 88n81, 199, 255
10:34–36	17–38
10:35–36	20
10:37	183
10:39	237
11:20–24	222
11:29	117
12:7	118n14
12:9	216
12:28	169n58
12:33–37	191
12:34	221
12:36–37	222
12:36–45	200n56
12:38–42	222
12:43–45	140
13:1–2	225
13:1–53	186, 224
13:10–17	224
13:11	225
13:24–30	230
13:34	225
13:34–35	224
13:36	186, 225
13:36–43	230
13:37–43	221, 225
13:40	221, 225
13:42	146n34, 213, 221, 223–24, 225
13:43	225
13:47–50	225, 230
13:49	225
13:50	146n34, 213, 221, 223–24, 225
13:52	25n18, 216, 224
13:54	216
15:1–9	183
15:26	183
16:4	200
16:18	216
16:24–28	29
16:27–28	230, 231–32, 234
18:1	40
18:1–4	40
18:5	44
18:5–10	40
18:6–8	44
18:8–9	44, 183, 221
18:12–35	40
18:17	216
18:21–35	40
18:23–35	14, 39, 40–48, 55–56, 226
18:35	256
19:1–2	116
19:30	137n6
20:16	137n6
20:17–19	116
20:28	35–36
20:29	116
20:29–21:17	118
21:1	116
21:1–9	117
21:1–16	185
21:1–17	117
21:4–5	117, 124
21:9	118
21:10	116–17, 129
21:12	169
21:12–13	119
21:12–17	113, 115, 116–19
21:12–23	118
21:15	118
21:17	118, 119n16
21:18–22	114n3, 118
21:21	119
21:21–22	119
21:23	185–86
21:23–27	136, 185
21:28–32	136–37
21:28–22:14	145
21:33–43	39, 135–51
21:33–22:14	146, 147
21:40	149
21:40–41	143
21:41	58, 146, 149,

	151	23:37	188
21:42	146–47n37	23:37–39	58, 69, 188
21:43	135n1, 137, 146, 200n56	23:38	64n18, 188–89n19
21:44	138, 146, 146–47n37	23:39	190n23
		23–25	186–88
21:45	136	24:1	119, 188–89n19
21:45–46	185–86	24:1–2	115, 119
22:1–14	58, 224n5	24:1–3	186
22:7	58, 145–46, 149	24:1–36	75
22:11–14	146n34	24:2	230
22:13	146, 213, 223–24	24:3	119, 186, 204, 226, 230
22:15	185–86	24:5	187n11
22:23–33	185–86	24:7	117
22:34–45	185–86	24:7–8	249–50
23	15, 183–217, 256–57	24:11	187n11
		24:17–18	237
23:1	185–86, 187, 188, 206	24:23	237
		24:24	187n11
23:1–12	188	24:26–28	239, 247
23:1–36	216	24:27	226, 230, 232–33, 237
23:8–11	195		
23:8–12	207n81	24:27–28	232–33
23:13	188n15, 208	24:27–31	252
23:13–31	206	24:28	237
23:13–33	188, 204	24:29	233
23:13–36	2, 187, 188, 199, 205, 206, 212	24:29–31	232
		24:30	230, 232–33
23:13	212	24:30–31	230, 233
23:14	188n15	24:31	233–34
23:15	208, 212, 213	24:32–34	232
23:16	212	24:36	226–27, 229, 232
23:17	209, 212		
23:19	212	24:36–25:13	226–27
23:23	208, 212	24:37	226–27, 230
23:24	212	24:37–39	227, 237
23:25	208, 212	24:39	226, 230
23:26	212	24:40–41	237
23:27	208, 212, 213	24:42	226–27, 229, 230–31
23:29	208, 212		
23:29–36	58, 222	24:43–51	236–37
23:31	188, 213	24:44	226–27, 229, 230, 233n22
23:32–36	190		
23:33	188, 213, 221	24:45–51	228
23:34–36	188n18	24:45–25:13	226–27
23:35	65n20	24:45–25:46	226
23:36	188, 190n22	24:48	51n36, 228

Matthew (continued)

24:48–51	224
24:51	146n34, 213, 223–24, 228
24–25	186
25:1–13	228–29
25:5	51n36
25:11	204
25:13	226–27, 229
25:14	229
25:14–30	49, 55
25:19	51n36, 229
25:26	52n39
25:30	146n34, 213, 223–24, 229
25:31–46	226n7, 229–30
25:41	121n22, 212, 230
25:46	230
26:1–16	93
26:6–13	93
26:36–46	111
26:51–54	96, 111
26:60–61	115
26:64	230, 234
27:24–25	213
27:25	58–59
27:26	162
27:39–40	115
27:50–54	117
27:51	58, 117
27:54	117
28:2	117
28:2–4	117
28:4	117
28:11–15	216
28:18–20	198
28:19–20	25n18

Mark

2:10	245
2:20	125
2:28	245
3:33	156n12
4:11–12	24
4:35–41	125n33
5:1–20	114n3, 140n15
5:34	87, 88n81
5:40	169
6:8	95, 96
6:35–52	125n33
7:1–13	183
7:26	169
7:27	183
8:1–10	125n33
8:22–10:52	119–20, 124
8:27–33	156n12
8:31	124, 125, 150, 245
8:32–33	124
8:34–9:1	29, 124
8:38	245
8:38–9:1	231
9:9–13	125
9:21–22	140n15
9:25–29	169
9:30–31	124, 125
9:31	125, 150, 245
9:32–34	124
9:35–50	124
9:43–48	183
9:50	88, 88n81
10:31	137n6
10:32	124
10:32–34	124
10:33	124
10:33–34	125, 150, 245
10:35–41	124
10:38–39	21n9
10:42–45	124
10:45	125, 127n38, 128, 245
11:1	119n16, 126
11:1–11	119
11:1–25	123–24n31
11:1–16:8	120n20
11:2	125n33
11:7	125n33
11:9–10	124
11:11	120, 121, 126, 129
11:11–22	128

Index of Ancient Sources   287

11:11–25	113, 119–29	13:28–29	127
11:12	125n34, 126	14:1	126n36
11:12–14	114n3	14:1–11	93, 126
11:12–21	127	14:2	126n36
11:12–25	126, 128	14:3–9	93
11:13	120, 125	14:8	126
11:13–14	121	14:32–42	111
11:14	120, 125n34, 126	14:47	96
11:15	129, 169	14:57–58	115, 174
11:15–16	169	14:62	150, 245
11:15–17	125n32	15:1–16:8	125
11:15–19	115	15:15	162
11:16	132–33	15:28	109n26
11:17	126	15:29–30	115
11:18	126	15:33–34	125n34
11:18–19	121	15:38	58
11:19	126	15:40	125
11:20	121, 126		
11:20–21	122, 128	**Luke**	
11:20–22	114n3	1:5–23	60, 75
11:21	121	1:20	74
11:22	127	1:32	84
11:22–25	122, 127	1:35	84
11:23	121, 122	1:67–79	89
11:23–25	127	1:68–79	75
11:27	126	1:79	87–88n80, 88
11:27–33	136	2:11	84
12:1–8	141	2:14	87–88n80, 88
12:1–9	144	2:22–30	60
12:1–12	39, 127, 135–51	2:22–52	75
		2:26	84
12:9	58, 141–45, 149–50, 151	2:29	87–88n80, 88
		2:35	99
12:10	144	2:41–52	59–60
12:10–11	128, 144, 149–50, 151	2:49	61n10
		3:7	77
12:11	146–47n37	3:7–18	234
12:12	126n36, 136, 144, 150	3:22	84
		4:1–13	61, 110
12:41–44	120n19	4:2	101
13:1	58n4	4:5–7	112
13:1–2	115, 120n19	4:5–8	101
13:1–37	75	4:13	61, 101, 103
13:8	249–50	4:14–9:50	102
13:9–13	27	4:43	61n10
13:26	245	6:20–26	199
13:28	127–28	6:27–36	52, 88

Index of Ancient Sources

Luke (*continued*)

6:27–42	88–89n84
6:43–45	257
7:11–17	89
7:16	75, 84
7:36–50	93
7:41–42	45
7:41–43	40
7:50	87–88n80
8:12	110n31
8:26–39	114n3
8:48	87–88n80
9:1–6	96, 106n20
9:3	95, 98, 104
9:10	96
9:10–45	102
9:18–27	239, 245n57
9:20	60n9, 84, 104
9:21–22	104
9:22	61n10, 243, 245n57
9:23	104
9:23–26	104, 246
9:23–27	29
9:26–27	231, 242n47
9:27	245n57
9:30–31	62
9:31	71
9:35	84, 104
9:40	169
9:44	104, 243
9:44–45	240, 243n51, 247
9:44–46	102
9:45	102
9:46	102
9:46–48	51
9:47–48	102, 104
9:51	49, 62, 67n27, 71
9:51–53	62n13, 64
9:51–55	235
9:51–19:46	49, 56, 62, 129
9:56–57	62n13
9:60	183
10:1	62n13
10:1–11	106n20
10:4	95, 96, 98, 104
10:5–6	87–88n80, 88
10:10–12	235
10:13–16	235
10:17–20	110n31
10:21–22	84
10:25–37	52
10:38	62n13
11:4	42
11:14–26	110n31
11:20	169n58
11:21	87–88n80
11:24–26	140n15
11:29–32	235
11:37–52	183–84, 214
11:45–52	63n16
11:47–51	58
12:2–3	74
12:13–34	52
12:35–40	237, 241, 242–43n48, 246, 250
12:35–48	235, 236–37
12:37	236
12:39	236
12:39–46	236–37
12:40	241
12:41–46	228
12:43	236
12:47–48	236
12:49	235
12:49–50	18
12:49–51	35n41, 36n42
12:49–53	20–21, 37
12:50	104, 243n51
12:51	13–14, 17, 18, 19, 32n37, 37, 87–88n80
12:51–52	18
12:51–53	18
13:6–9	128
13:16	110n31
13:18–21	56
13:22	62n13, 64
13:22–30	223
13:28–29	213
13:30	137n6, 223

Index of Ancient Sources

13:31–33	62n13	19:37	70–71
13:31–35	57, 63, 64–69, 81–82, 83, 85–86	19:37–38	69, 129
		19:38	87–88n80, 88
		19:39	129
13:32–33	104, 243n51	19:39–40	70, 71–72
13:33	61n10, 66	19:40	71, 72
13:34	78	19:41	70–71, 78–79, 86
13:34–35	58, 66, 72, 77, 85	19:41–44	49, 57, 63, 70–75, 77, 81–82, 83, 85–86, 91, 129
13:35	64n18		
14:16–24	145		
14:26	183		
14:32	87–88n80	19:42	87–88n80, 88, 89
16:1–15	52		
16:19–31	52, 234–35	19:43	79
17:7–10	236	19:43–44	66, 71, 72, 76
17:11	62n13		
17:20–37	235, 237–48	19:44	68n29, 71, 78, 84, 89, 91, 130
17:22–37	15, 239–48		
17:25	61n10, 104	19:45	49, 70, 129, 169
17:28–30	235	19:45–46	113, 115, 129–30
18:1–8	235n27, 241		
18:10	130n49	19:45–48	49
18:15	70	19:45–21:38	60–61, 75
18:18–30	52	19:46	129–30
18:31	62n13, 105	19:47	130
18:31–34	240, 243, 247	20:1	130
		20:1–8	136
18:32–33	104	20:9–18	39, 135–51
18:35	62n13	20:15	149
18:35–19:46	70	20:15–16	143
19:1	62n13	20:16	58, 143–44, 146–47n37
19:1–10	52, 70		
19:5	61n10	20:18	138, 146–47n37, 149, 151
19:9	52		
19:10	75, 245	20:19	136
19:11	49, 50–51, 52, 62n13, 70	20:45	76
		21:5	58n4
19:11–27	55, 147	21:5–6	72, 76, 81–82, 115
19:11–28	14, 39, 49–56, 70, 235n27		
		21:5–36	75, 235, 237, 241–42, 248–50
19:13	52		
19:28	49, 70	21:6	68n29, 79, 242
19:28–45	62n13	21:10–11	249–50
19:28–46	61n11, 70, 129	21:12–19	27
		21:20–24	57, 63, 66, 75–78, 81–82, 83, 86, 250
19:29	70, 119n16		
19:29–40	49		

290 Index of Ancient Sources

Luke (*continued*)

Reference	Pages
21:22	241–42n44
21:23	78
21:24	99–100
21:25–27	241
21:25–28	84
21:25–36	242, 250
21:27	241, 242
21:27–28	241
21:34–36	241
21:37–38	130
22:1–6	93
22:3	101, 102
22:3–6	101
22:7–53	93
22:14	96, 100, 107, 110
22:14–16	105
22:14–53	100
22:15	103, 104
22:16	106
22:18	106
22:19	240
22:21–22	101, 104
22:21–30	93
22:23	101
22:24	102
22:24–26	51
22:24–27	101
22:25	103, 112
22:25–27	102
22:26	103
22:27	105, 236
22:28	101, 103, 104, 110
22:28–30	102–3
22:29–30	103
22:30	103
22:31	101, 103
22:31–32	93–94
22:31–62	100n12
22:34	104, 106
22:35	96, 98, 104
22:35–38	2, 17, 93–112
22:35–53	105–112
22:36	94–112, 255
22:36–38	199
22:37	61n10, 106–9
22:38	99, 106–7
22:39–46	94
22:40	110–11
22:40–46	112
22:41–42	110–11
22:42	101, 110–11
22:43–44	94
22:46	110–11
22:47	106–7
22:47–53	100, 101, 107–9
22:49	94, 99, 107, 108
22:49–50	111–12
22:49–51	96
22:50	107
22:51	94, 108
22:52	99, 107
22:53	100, 101, 107, 110
23:26	76n49
23:26–31	57, 63, 78–82, 83
23:27	78n54
23:27–31	78n55, 86
23:28	78n54
23:28–31	66
23:31	128
23:32–43	107
23:32–49	109n26
23:33–49	80
23:44–45	60n8
23:45	58
23:48	78n54
23:49	246n59
23:52	240
23:55	240
24:3	240
24:7	61n10, 243
24:13–35	61, 240
24:21	246n59
24:23	240
24:26	61n10, 243–44
24:33	61
24:36	61, 87–88n80, 88
24:44	61n10

24:47–49	61	12:12–36	128–29
24:50–53	61n11	12:20–36	176
		14:1	127n39
John		14:27	88n81
1:1–18	23, 37, 175–76	16:33	88n81
1:3–5	23, 37	18:10	153n1
1:9–11	37	18:10–11	96
1:9–13	23	19:1	160
1:14–18	75	20:19	88n81
1:19–51	130–31	20:21	88n81
1:29	154	20:26	88n81
1:36	154	20:30	160
2:1–11	115, 130–31, 160		
		Acts	
2:3–4	156n12	1:4–8	62
2:13–22	113, 115, 130–32, 133, 153–81	1:6	246n59
		1:11	84
		2:1–4	235
2:14	164, 165n38, 168	2:22–23	83
2:14–15	171	2:23	109
2:14–16	132, 153, 162–65, 167–70	2:28	62n13
		2:33	246
2:15	159, 162–64, 168, 171, 178–79, 180	2:36	83
		3:12–13	83
2:16	163, 165–66	4:10	83
2:17	132, 154, 172, 179	5:30	83
		6:8–14	115
2:18	131n52, 132, 160	7:26	88n83
2:18–19	158	7:55–56	246
2:18–22	128	8:1	63
2:19	161, 165–66	8:14–17	63
2:20	58n4	9:2	62n13
2:21	132	9:31	88n83
2:21–22	128	10:36	3, 88, 88n83
2:22	132	10:38	110n31
2:23	131n52, 160	10:39	83
3:2	160	11:1–18	63
3:19–21	23	12:2	99
4:46–54	160	12:20	88n83
5:1–9	160	12:23	74
6:1–21	160	13:27–28	83
8:30–31	184n2	15:1–33	63
8:44	184	15:33	88n83
9:1–9	160	16:17	62n13
9:1–34	156n12	16:27	99
11:1–44	160	16:36	88n83
11:45–53	159	18:25–26	62n13

Acts (continued)

19:9	62n13
19:21	63
19:23	62n13
20:16–23:31	63
21:17–26	63
22:4	62n13
24:2	88n83
24:14	62n13
24:22	62n13

Galatians

3:13	125n34

Ephesians

4:15	257

James

3	191, 257
3:1	191n27

Revelation

1:16	99n11
2:12	99n11
2:16	99n11
6:8	99n11
6:12–17	79n57
19:15	99n11
19:21	99n11

☙

APOCRYPHA AND OT PSEUDEPIGRAPHA

Sirach

45:23–25	179

1 Maccabees

2:19–28	179

1 Enoch

26:1	61n12
96:8	245

2 Baruch

	90
10:5–19	59
35:1–5	59

4 Ezra

	90
10:21–23	59

Jubilees

8:19	61n12

Lives of the Prophets

	65n20

☙

GOSPEL OF THOMAS

16	18
49	18
65	141, 142
65–66	138
71	115–16
75	18

www.ingramcontent.com/pod-product-compliance
Lightning Source LLC
Chambersburg PA
CBHW032051220426
43664CB00008B/955